More Than Man

More Than Man

A Study in Christology

by

Russell F. Aldwinckle

William B. Eerdmans Publishing Company

Copyright © 1976 by William B. Eerdmans Publishing Company
255 Jefferson Ave. S.E., Grand Rapids, Michigan 49502

Library of Congress Cataloging in Publication Data

Aldwinckle, Russell Foster.
    More than man.
    Bibliography: p. 294.
    Includes index.
    1. Jesus Christ—Person and offices. 2. Christian-
ity and other religions. I. Title.
BT202.A56   232   76-876
ISBN 0-8028-3456-6

Preface

It is one of the astonishing facts of history that men and women are still debating today the question, Who was Jesus of Nazareth? This is so despite the radical changes which have taken place in our study of history and in our scientific view of the world, not to mention the secular temper of our time. Even the most radical views of God do not seem to escape from Jesus. It is hardly an exaggeration to say, however, that in the last few years it is Jesus the man who is at the center of the modern interest. On the other hand, any suggestion that he was "more than man" or even unique in the sense affirmed by most traditional expressions of the Christian faith is often strongly, if not violently, repudiated. The title "More than Man" will doubtless be provocative to many. Some will interpret it as a denial of the humanity which modern biblical scholarship has so painfully recovered for us. The reader is asked to judge the title after reading the book. Certainly the present author believes that the title is not inconsistent with the true manhood of Jesus. Yet he is also convinced that there must have been something different about Jesus which led people both in New Testament times and ever since to talk "divinity" language.

This work is not a detailed and systematic study of all the relevant New Testament material relating to Christology. I have been concerned not so much with taking sides in the vigorous debates continuing today among New Testament scholars, but with trying to clarify the kind and extent of the historical knowledge required as a basis for the historic Christian affirmations of the divinity. If I am hopelessly wrong on this issue, then further scholarly debate about literary and historical details will no longer be of theological interest, since the possibility of a real Incarnation will have been answered in the negative. No doubt scholars would continue to grapple with the New Testament and its mysteries, but this would be carried on without any complications from the side of the Christian faith. My intention has not been, even if I were capable, to do over again the sort of study so ably done in recent years by New Testament scholars. Rather, I have tried to wrestle with

5

the question whether these modern studies yield any results which could provide a reasonable basis for the historic affirmation of the divinity of Jesus.

It is with this issue that the present work is concerned. The modern challenge to the divinity of Jesus Christ does not come only from atheists, agnostics, rationalists, and sceptics, long regarded as the most serious opponents of the faith. The Christian-Jewish dialogue, which is now well under way, is presenting thoughtful Christians with a theological challenge from the very Judaism out of which Jesus came. Moreover, the increasing awareness in the West of the great non-Christian religions of Hinduism, Buddhism, and Islam is challenging the Christian claim for Jesus from a new perspective, one which is unfamiliar and perplexing to many. In an age when these religions are no longer geographically remote or simply a matter of academic concern, the Christian claim may indeed seem extreme to the point of absurdity. For this reason, I have ventured into the difficult field, not simply of the history of religions and the phenomenology of religious experience, but of value judgments and comparisons. The danger here is daunting, both because of the impossibility of being expert in the history and life of all the great religions, and because of the difficulty of escaping from unacknowledged prejudice. Nevertheless, it seemed right to make the attempt, even at the risk of revealing one's own folly. To consider the divinity of Jesus as if the only two religions in the world were Judaism and Christianity seemed an irresponsible bit of parochialism. I am only too conscious that what I have written about Jesus and Gotama is no more than one man's halting step in a worldwide wrestling for truth which Christians will have to undertake in the days ahead.

However, our concentration upon the ''divinity'' of Jesus accounts for, and we hope excuses, the omission of many aspects of the subject which would otherwise demand attention. I am also conscious of the inadequacy of the incidental references to process theology in the body of the work. The problem here was twofold. First, I wanted to develop a particular view of the Person of Christ without getting too involved in technical discussions which would confuse the main direction of the argument. Secondly, as I did not wish to employ the concepts or vocabulary of process theology, it seemed unwise to emphasize process theology in the text without a much fuller treatment of its concepts than seemed desirable. I have tried in an appendix to indicate a few of the reasons which influenced my decision not to tackle the Christological question in the context of process thought.

Acknowledging my intellectual and spiritual indebtedness to others is an almost impossible task. The Christian theologian above all will not strain after a forced originality as if he is presenting the truth for the first time. He is not the originator of the Christian faith. Jesus Christ is not his invention, nor does his understanding of Jesus' person depend only on his own insight divorced from the continuing experience and testimony of the community of faith through the ages. The book itself will reveal my large indebtedness to Christian thinkers of all ages and all forms of the Christian tradition. If I had to single out one person who has been an abiding influence transcending the realm of scholarship only, it would be the late Austin Farrer, whose lectures on Aquinas I attended at Trinity College, Oxford, many years ago. His life and work have powerfully influenced and shaped my own thinking and Christian life. His full stature has not yet been measured in our generation, but I believe his influence will grow.

I would like to add some personal thanks to my colleagues on the Faculty of McMaster Divinity College, and to generations of students whose incisive questions effectively prevent any teacher from assuming that he has answered every question and said the last word on any subject. I am particularly grateful to Dr. M. R. Hillmer, Professor of New Testament, who read my chapter on the New Testament Basis of Christology, and to Dr. T. R. Hobbs in Biblical Studies, who, in addition to proofreading, called my attention to relevant material which I would never have discovered on my own. Of course, they cannot be held responsible for my errors both of knowledge and judgment, but at least they are many fewer than they would have been without their help. My colleagues Dr. Murray Ford and Dr. G. G. Harrop and Emeritus Professor H. W. Lang also gave generous assistance in reading the proofs.

It would be dishonest to pretend that such a book as this is written only as an academic exercise. One hopes and prays that hard and honest thinking about Jesus Christ may lead others to share one's own faith. Time and the illuminating activity of the Spirit of God will presumably sift the wheat from the chaff.

Russell F. Aldwinckle

McMaster Divinity College,
Hamilton, Ontario, Canada.

Acknowledgments

The publisher gratefully acknowledges permission to quote from the following sources:

Bartsch, H. W., *Kerygma and Myth* (trans. by Reginald H. Fuller), published by S.P.C.K., London, 1953.

From *The Structure of Human Existence,* by John B. Cobb, Jr. Copyright © MCMLXVII, The Westminster Press. Used by permission.

Conze, Edward, *Buddhism: Its Essence and Development,* published by Bruno Cassirer Ltd., 1954, and Harper & Row, New York, 1959.

Dodd, C. H., *The Founder of Christianity,* published by Collins Publishers, London, 1971, and Macmillan, New York, 1970.

Fuller, Reginald H., *The Foundations of New Testament Christology,* published by Lutterworth Press, London, 1965, and Charles Scribner's Sons, New York, 1965.

Harvey, Van A., *The Historian and the Believer,* published by SCM Press Ltd., London, and Macmillan Publishing Co., New York, 1966.

Käsemann, Ernst, *Essays in New Testament Themes,* published by SCM Press Ltd., London, 1964.

Knox, John, *The Humanity and Divinity of Christ,* published by Cambridge University Press, London, 1967.

Macquarrie, John, *Principles of Christian Theology,* published by Charles Scribner's Sons, 1966.

The Path of the Buddha, edited by Kenneth W. Morgan. Copyright © 1956 The Ronald Press Company, New York.

Parrinder, Geoffrey, *Avatar and Incarnation,* published by Faber and Faber Ltd., London, 1970.

Quick, Oliver, *Doctrines of the Creed,* published by James Nisbet & Co. Ltd., London, 1938, and Charles Scribner's Sons, New York.

Ramsey, Ian T., *Words About God,* published by SCM Press Ltd., London, 1971, and Harper & Row, New York.

Robinson, H. Wheeler, *The Christian Experience of the Holy Spirit,* published by James Nisbet & Co. Ltd., London, 1928, and Harper & Row Publishers Inc., New York, 1928.

Robinson, H. Wheeler, *Revelation and Redemption,* published by James Nisbet & Co. Ltd., London, 1942, and Harper & Row Publishers, Inc., New York, 1942.

From *The Human Face of God,* by John A. T. Robinson. © SCM Press Ltd. 1973. Published in the U.S.A. by The Westminster Press, 1973. Used by permission.

Smith, John E., *Reason and God,* published by Yale University Press, New Haven, 1961.

Thomas, Edward J., *The Life of Buddha as Legend and History,* published by Routledge & Kegan Paul Ltd., London, 1969.

Wiles, Maurice, "Does Christology Rest on a Mistake?", from *Religious Studies,* Vol. 6, No. 1 (March 1970), published by Cambridge University Press, London, 1970.

Contents

1.
Jesus Without Dogma?

There are many signs at present that we are moving into another period of intense questioning and sometimes complete rejection of the traditional forms of doctrine. A few years ago everyone was debating whether God is dead or not. Now the emphasis has shifted and interest is being directed to Jesus of Nazareth and the church's traditional language about His divinity. This, of course, is not new in the history of Protestantism. Even Roman Catholicism had its eruption of so-called modernism long before Pope John XXIII's call for an updating of aggiornamento of the church's life and witness. Most people today, even outside the Roman allegiance, are aware of the manner in which the more ''advanced'' Roman priests and theologians are seeking to re-express the historic doctrines in fresh language. As far as the theologians are concerned, irrespective of their confessional loyalties, these matters have constantly been discussed ever since the eighteenth century. The active participation of the Greek Orthodox churches in the World Council of Churches has brought the Eastern and Western Christian traditions into dialogue again. The importance of this for our re-thinking the problems of the Person of Christ will be evident in what follows. One could, of course, go back even earlier to the debates over the Person of Christ in the patristic period before the Definition of Chalcedon in A.D. 451. There are, however, indications that the issues of interpretation concerning Jesus have ceased to be the exclusive concern of the professional theologians. Instances could be cited of rather heated recent debates in assemblies, synods, and councils over the ''divinity'' of Christ. The World Council of Churches, in originally formulating its theological basis as a confession of Jesus as God and Savior, found itself exposed to criticism from no less a person than Bultmann for adopting a statement which seems to go beyond any such precise claim made in the New Testament. After pointing out that ''neither in the Synoptic gospels nor in the Pauline epistles is Jesus called God; nor do we find Him so called in the Acts of the Apostles or in the Apocalypse,''[1] he sums up his convictions as follows: ''The formula 'Christ is God' is false in every sense in which God is understood as an entity which can be objectivized, whether it is understood in an Arian or a Nicene, an Orthodox or a liberal sense. It is correct if God is understood here as the event of God's acting.''[2] We shall return later to a discussion as to exactly what Bultmann means by this distinction. By modifying its original declaration to include the phrase ''according to the Scriptures,'' the World Council went some way to meet the objections of some who felt that such a blunt confession of Jesus as God could be interpreted in a way damaging to the real humanity of Jesus. The ''God is Dead'' debate and the attempt by some radical theologians to combine agnosticism about God with loyalty to Jesus has only accentuated the importance of the Christological issue. To this may be added the extraordinary role Jesus has come to occupy in some of the popular music of our day. *Jesus Christ Superstar* may be cited as one instance. Who is the Jesus about whom the young are singing today? Is it really the Jesus of the New Testament? And what is the relation of their Jesus to the Christ of faith confessed by the churches in their inherited creeds and symbols? Nor can we eliminate the profound questioning expressed in the contemporary interest of many in mysticism and the great non-Christian religions. Can one make any claims for Jesus of Nazareth today without taking into account such a striking personality as the Buddha? It seems that any claims made by Christians will have to be defended today not only in a Christian ecumenical context but in a world-religious ecumenical setting. It is impossible in such a short treatment as this to deal adequately with all these questions. We shall, therefore, seek to clarify and understand what is implied in the Christian attitude toward Jesus Christ in the context of Christian history and experience. Yet we shall try to do this in full consciousness of the existence and claims of the other world religions. From time to time, specific reference will be made to these other religions with a view to enabling Christians to see more clearly what is involved in their own faith.

In tackling the Christological question, it is important at the start to distinguish clearly between the way in which the issue presents itself to those who are already confessing Christians and the way it presents itself to those who are not. The nonbeliever's difficulties usually spring from a variety of causes. For example, doubts about God may make it impossible for the nonbeliever even to state in a meaningful way the question of divinity. On the other hand, the believer may be sure on the basis of faith and experience

---

[1]Rudolf Bultmann, *Essays Philosophical and Theological* (London: S.C.M., 1955), p. 275.
[2]*Ibid.*, p. 287.

that he has known the unique presence of the divine, redeeming, holy love of God in the Person of Jesus of Nazareth and yet be troubled with the way in which the church has sought to express the truth of that experience, and in particular with the language which the church of today has inherited from the past.

This chapter will be devoted to the attempt to state what the basic issues are as seen from the Christian perspective. In its simplest form, the problem may be stated in Jesus' own words: "Who do you say that I am?" To this may be added the further question: Is it not enough to be a loyal and devoted follower of Jesus without trying to express my faith in Him in complex dogmatic statements, often couched in technical and abstract language which is beyond the understanding of the average man? Provided I try to live in His spirit and express His kind of love to my neighbor, does it really matter what I believe about Him in terms of doctrine? In technical terms, do we need a "Christology" as a basis for a living faith in Jesus Christ?

It has often been said that the nineteenth and early twentieth centuries emphasized a religion of Jesus rather than a religion about Jesus. One readily recalls, among others, the significant names of Ritschl and Harnack and somewhat later Canon B. H. Streeter. It is probably not fair to these men to say that they reduce Jesus to a mere teacher, if by this is meant a complete indifference to His Person. In much of the liberal work, there appears an attitude of profound reverence, respect, admiration, and indeed devotion to Jesus as such and not simply to His teaching. There is also a deep suspicion of the classical attempts to formulate a doctrine of His Person, whether this be the Chalcedonian Definition of A.D. 451 or later Protestant attempts which build substantially on the same dogmatic foundation. How far is this suspicion justified, and if it is, can we today formulate a more adequate doctrine or can we dispense with the doctrine altogether? William Temple once pointed out the important distinction between what may suffice for the individual believer and what may be necessary for the survival of the church and the fulfilment of its mission. The believer may get away with very little technical knowledge of Christian doctrine. Worshiping in church, reading the Bible devotionally, attempting loyally to follow Jesus day by day in his life and conduct—all these may result in a radiant and effective Christian life and witness. Nevertheless, the believer is more dependent than he often realizes upon the church's faith and witness. He often assumes the validity of a certain understanding of the Person of Jesus Christ without ever having brought it into the full light of consciousness and subjected it to any kind of examination. On the other hand, it is true that he may have rejected for reasons which seem good to him certain doctrines without this damaging the quality of his Christian life. Yet, as Temple argued, while heresy in the individual may be tolerable, if it becomes part of the church's thinking to such a degree that it distorts worship and the church's understanding of its mission, then it becomes much more serious, because it means that the believer is no longer helped or safeguarded by the collective witness of the believing community. The church holds the gospel in trust for generations still to come. What might be tolerated in the individual cannot for that reason be complacently accepted as part of the church's official teaching. But this argument is likely to appeal only to those who still regard the church as the proper custodian of the eternal truth of the gospel.

Indeed, one of the chief reasons for the modern suspicion of doctrine and dogma lies in the reaction against ecclesiastical authority. It is well known that the inspiration behind the liberal Protestantism of the nineteenth century was the conviction that it was possible to penetrate behind the formulations of traditional doctrine and reach the historical Jesus whose teaching and example could now become the norm in the light of which all later developments could be judged and evaluated. It was assumed that modern historical methods, when applied to the gospels, would enable us to arrive at such a knowledge of Jesus, a knowledge at least reliable enough to give us the essential insights into the way He thought of God and the nature of His mission in relation to the coming rule of God among men. Needless to say, if later doctrinal developments are to be tested with reference to the Person and teaching of Jesus, then substantially trustworthy knowledge of the latter is required. If, as some have argued in this present century, the Jesus of history fades into complete obscurity behind the Christ of faith, then such comparison of Jesus and dogma is no longer possible. If we can only become acquainted through historical investigation with the faith of the church and can never reconstruct with any plausibility the historical X which lies behind it, then we cannot appeal to Jesus against later dogma. In such a case, only two options are available: to accept the church's faith and dogmas on authority, even though we can say nothing confidently about the historical events which lie behind the faith and the dogmas; or to reject both the doctrine and the church which proclaimed it and work out a philosophy of life which no longer depends either upon Jesus or upon any form of church authority. Both of these extremes have their contemporary representatives, not to mention mediating positions which lack clarity for the reason that they are compromises.

There is no space here to discuss in detail the question of how much we can know of Jesus of Nazareth. It has often been confidently affirmed in recent years that the "Quest of the Historical Jesus" has failed completely and that there is no point in pursuing any longer this dead end. This, however, would seem to be a premature conclusion. It is well known that some of Bultmann's disciples are taking up this question again. T. W.

Manson had the courage to entitle his Commemoration Day address at Cambridge "The Quest of the Historical Jesus—Continued."[3] A recent book by Professor John McIntyre contains the following significant statement in his discussion of the psychological model: "There is, I should say, a too great readiness, an almost indecent haste, to be done with the detail of historical knowledge."[4] A recent small but penetrating volume called *Vindications* takes up this theme.[5] It is clear that this issue of the historical knowledge of Jesus is not closed. As McIntyre points out, even those who totally reject the idea of any psychological study of Jesus—such as Barth, Bornkamm, Bultmann, and Käsemann—nevertheless speak of the attitudes, motives, ideas, reactions, and even feelings of Jesus.[6] Suffice it to record the writer's agreement with Dr. Manson's dictum that "It is time we began to consider the gospels again as historical source material and not merely a case book of the early church's theology."[7] This judgement is shared by C. H. Dodd's book *The Founder of Christianity,* which gives us the mature reflections of this distinguished New Testament scholar on many of the questions with which we shall be concerned.[8]

All theological students in the last few generations have had it ceaselessly impressed upon them that it is no longer possible to write a "biography" of Jesus. If one is thinking of the two-volume standard works so beloved of Victorians, this is obviously true. One further consequence of this emphasis, plus the emphasis of form-criticism upon oral tradition, has been to undermine any confidence that we can get back to the very words of Jesus in the exact form in which he delivered them in Aramaic. This, however, by no means dispenses with the question as to whether in a deeper sense we can know the "mind" of Jesus. It is difficult to read Professor Dodd's latest work without feeling compelled to accept his judgment, which I quote at some length:

> When all allowance has been made for these limiting factors—the chances of oral transmission, the effect of translation, the interest of teachers in making the sayings "contemporary", and simple human fallibility—it remains that the first three gospels offer a body of sayings on the whole so consistent, so coherent and withal so distinctive in manner, style, content, that no reasonable critic should doubt, whatever reservations he may have about individual sayings, that we have reflected here the thought of a single, unique teacher.[9]

---

[3]T. W. Manson, *Studies in the Gospels and Epistles,* ed. Matthew Black (Manchester: Manchester Univ. Press, 1962), p. 13.

[4]John McIntyre, *The Shape of Christology* (London: S.C.M., 1966), p. 120.

[5]Anthony Hanson, *Vindications* (London: S.C.M., 1966).

[6]McIntyre, *Christology,* p. 127.

[7]Manson, *Studies,* p. 8.

[8]C. H. Dodd, *The Founder of Christianity* (London: Collins, 1971).

[9]Dodd, *Founder,* p. 22.

It is extremely unlikely that sayings which bear to such a remarkable degree the stamp of an individual mind should be the product of collective thinking or "tradition." All our present experience tells against such a supposition. Dodd is not concerned in his book to discuss the degree to which later doctrinal formulations can be shown to be reasonable deductions from what we do know of the "mind" of Jesus, though he makes fascinating hints from time to time. It is evident, however, that any Christology presupposes our ability to know something significant not only about the outwardly observable behavior of Jesus of Nazareth but about the processes of His mind and the characteristic direction of His thought. This does not necessarily mean that we can plumb the "mind" of Jesus to a point where all mystery is dispelled and He becomes completely transparent to our understanding. This is never true even of our relationship to ordinary human beings. How much less can we expect this to be the case in regard to one who at the very least must be regarded as an outstanding personality of great originality and spiritual power. If, of course, He is what Christian faith confesses Him to be, then our capacity fully to understand Him will be to that degree less likely. For the moment, however, we are concerned not with the dogmatic claims but with the striking individuality of the Jesus who emerges from the gospel pages. This is the bare minimum without which any doctrine of the person of Christ cannot get started. It is important to realize that Dodd is contending that when all allowance has been made for the interpretative factor due to faith and the life-situations of a later period to which the teaching of Jesus was applied by the early church, it is still possible to discern the stamp of a highly individual mind and the lineaments of a decisive personality, whatever mystery remains. The question, therefore, of the actual words of Jesus takes its proper place within this dominant impression made by the gospels.

At first sight, Dodd's position seems very similar to that of Paul Tillich in Volume II of his *Systematic Theology*. There Tillich tells us that "Jesus as the Christ is both a historical fact and a subject of believing reception."[10] Tillich stresses the importance of doing justice to both sides of the truth. He also seems to agree that "Christian Theology must insist on the actual fact to which the name of Jesus of Nazareth refers."[11] The believing response of faith presupposes some factual basis.

On closer examination, however, Tillich's position seems to be vitiated by an excessive scepticism about the very possibility of historical certainty of any kind. Dodd would presumably contend that the figure of Jesus emerges clearly from the gospel records when the most rigorous scrutiny is made of these documents by the methods which any professional historian

---

[10]Paul Tillich, *Systematic Theology*, II (Chicago: Univ. of Chicago Press, 1957), p. 98.
[11]*Ibid.*, p. 98.

would recognize. He does not say that faith was not a factor in the way in which the gospel writers used their material. He does seem to imply that faith is not necessary to arrive at a convincing picture of the man Jesus and His "mind" from rigorous study of the gospel records.

We agree that an unbeliever could read Dodd's book and come away highly impressed with the personality there encountered without feeling compelled to go the further step of making his own such momentous assertions as that this Jesus was "truly God and truly man." There is no simple and uncomplicated move from Dodd's historical portrait to the deeper affirmations of faith. Nonetheless, it is difficult to see how faith could arrive at these later declarations if the historical evidence was completely ambiguous and opaque to our understanding.

Tillich, however, insists not only that all historical judgments are only "probable" but that Christian faith must be prepared to face the possibility that historical study may not even be able to "guarantee his name to be Jesus of Nazareth."[12] Tillich, no doubt, might reply that this is of secondary importance. Just as an astronomer may be reasonably confident that another planet is there, pulling the known planets out of orbit, even when he has no other empirical evidence to back up his belief, so the Christian church may be confident that the source of faith is in the reality of the "new being" of Jesus as the Christ, even when we can say little or nothing about such a Jesus in terms which an historian would acknowledge as involving certainty. As we have seen, Tillich leaves the door open to the possibility that the historian may not be able to guarantee the name "Jesus," and therefore, presumably, even the term "Christ"—which, one is compelled to respond, lacks all meaning when divorced from history. Tillich would perhaps be more consistent to say that Christians have experienced a new quality of life in the community of faith and are certain that this has its source in some historical X which now eludes us except in terms of the moral and spiritual consequences produced. This, of course, logically involves a doctrine of the church which would make it impossible to subject the church to any criterion of judgment other than its own experiences. On this basis there could be no appeal to Jesus against the church since we know nothing of Jesus except what the church's faith declares. Not even that most authoritative of churches, the Roman Catholic Church, has ever gone quite this far. If this were in fact the case, it is difficult to see why anyone in the early church should have thought it important to write gospels at all or to preserve anything which purported to be a record of the acts and teaching of Jesus of Nazareth.

That the early church did seek to preserve such a record is highly

---

[12]*Ibid.*, p. 114.

significant, and Dodd's book certainly suggests that it did not entirely fail in preserving for future generations such an account of the authentic Jesus. The fact that the early Christians did not think of history, as we do, as stretching into a limitless future does not affect their deep interest in the founder of their faith. We repeat that it is not being argued that historical knowledge guarantees the emergence of faith in the full Christian sense. It obviously does not. What is being contended is that we are not left without some reliable historical knowledge of Jesus of Nazareth and that this knowledge is more extensive than the simple fact that He was "crucified under Pontius Pilate."

The more difficult problem which now faces us is how and why the Jesus of the gospels made such an impact upon the early disciples, and through them upon later men of faith, that the church was led to use about Him the kind of language which we find in the later creeds and confessions. Was this later doctrinal development a sheer subjective reading into the record of what was not in fact there? Was it a corruption of the simple gospel of Jesus (Harnack), or was it the legitimate drawing out and intellectual articulation of what men actually experienced when they were brought into a certain kind of relationship with this Jesus? Before tackling this issue, we must examine more carefully the reasons for the strong modern reaction in some quarters against the very conception of doctrinal development itself.

One important factor in the reaction against doctrine, while it often includes the reaction against church authority as such, also springs from a certain misunderstanding of the nature of religious experience and the attempt to express its meaning and significance in language. Implicit in all such distinctions between "life" and "doctrine" is the view that all intellectualizing of experience must inevitably be a distortion. Abstract concepts replace the warm immediacy of experience. The academic is contrasted unfavorably with life. Such a view played an important part in Protestant theology before the modern vocabulary of existentialism became part of our theological stock in trade. Schleiermacher, of course, is the great figure in this connection. His influence is traceable in many later thinkers who insist that theology is important but secondary, while religion is all-important and primary. Some indeed would deny that theology is important at all. Often accompanying this emphasis is the view that religion, wherever found, is basically the same. Only theology changes. How religious experiences not expressed linguistically and in concepts can be known to be identical raises an epistemological question incapable of being answered. However, this issue will be ignored for the time being. We shall invoke Schleiermacher simply to illustrate the nature of the objections to doctrine which have frequently been expressed since his day.

Our concern is with the relationship between the believer's living experience of Christ and the doctrinal forms which express the meaning and significance of this. Schleiermacher puts it as follows: "Christian faith-propositions are conceptions of Christian religious soul-states set forth in speech."[13] We can agree that theoretically there is a vast difference between a total commitment to Christ which involves the transformation of a man in thought, word, and deed—every man in Christ is a new creation—and a merely intellectual assent to theological propositions which seems to have little bearing upon how a man lives. Yet is there in actual fact such a thing as merely intellectual assent? If "intellectual" here means a *conviction* about truth, then can one have a conviction which is truly such without it deeply affecting the totality of a man's life? The difficulty with this sharp distinction between faith and its theological expression is that it is impossible to talk meaningfully about faith without assuming some intellectual content, some affirmation of truth, as belonging to the essential nature of faith itself. Schleiermacher, despite his distrust of some of the traditional doctrinal formulations, is himself compelled to make statements about God, man, and the Person of Christ. Such statements, however, imply that we know that God exists and that we know His character and His purpose for men. These claims involve theological statements of a far-reaching kind. Many of our modern philosophers, not to mention the radical theologians, would call these basic premises into question. How can we make meaningful statements about God? What is meant by saying that Jesus is Lord? Does this imply some concept of divinity; if so, where does such a concept come from? Does it mean that Jesus' relation to God is unique in a sense which distinguishes Him from all other men? Does it signify that Jesus can rightly claim the total obedience and commitment of a man; if so, what gives Him this right? The point I am concerned to maintain is simply that with the best will in the world we cannot push this distinction between faith and theology to the limit. On examination, faith always turns out to contain some basic affirmations about God, man, and Jesus Christ which are taken to be true.

But what is this but theology? If the criticism of theology is directed against the inadequacy or the unnecessary intellectual complexity of some forms of doctrine, then most of us would agree that all "theology" is not necessarily good theology and that some of it is definitely misleading, if not downright distortion. To admit this, however, is by no means to concede that faith can be defined as if it were devoid of all theological content, i.e., of all affirmations about God and Christ taken to be true and not merely the expression of subjective states of feeling. Thus, even Schleiermacher did not

---

[13]Friedrich Schleiermacher, *The Christian Faith,* Vol. I, No. 15 (Edinburgh: T. & T. Clark, 1928), p. 76.

believe that experience could be either expressed or communicated or indeed made meaningful at all without being expressed in language, and therefore through the use of mental concepts, symbols, and images of varying degrees of abstraction. His use of such an expression as "God-consciousness" shows that he could not do without some concepts to express the significance of Jesus Christ. We may agree that human language is never totally adequate to the experience it seeks to express. Equally impossible, however, is an experience totally devoid of ideas, of all thought. Even the least sophisticated believer has some ideas, however undeveloped, even if they are no more than simple ideas about God's reality and character and the significance of Jesus Christ in making the Father known to men.

It is vital to be clear in our minds, therefore, that experience and doctrine cannot be played off against each other as if the former can be completely separated from any kind of intellectual expression whatsoever. In actual fact, the attack upon dogma is usually a criticism of certain dogmas which are believed to be inadequate, distorting, or unscriptural. It is rarely an attack upon all doctrine, since the critics always go on to formulate a different set of doctrines. They substitute new language and fresh concepts and symbols.

The basic issue, therefore, is not "pure" experience versus distorting doctrinal expression, but what kind of doctrine is needed to express as adequately as possible the meaning of Christian experience. We cannot dispense with "models" altogether, to quote Ian Ramsey's language, however qualified the models are.[14] This is clearly seen in the more radical attempts at reinterpretation in our own time. Albert Schweitzer may have rejected traditional formulations, but he offers us a new doctrine, in fact a new Christology in which the significance of Jesus is derived from the fact that He is the perfect embodiment of love, or as Schweitzer formulates it, of "reverence for life." Whether or not this is adequate is not for the moment our prime concern. We simply want to point out that it is a doctrine concerning the significance of Jesus expressed in ethical rather than ontological or metaphysical categories, such as the two natures or the hypostatic union of Chalcedon.

Bultmann's program of demythologizing is subject to similar comment. It is not simply that the New Testament "myths" are to be rejected completely in favor of no doctrinal statements at all. Bultmann's claim is rather that they must not be interpreted literally as if they referred to events in this world which a modern historian or scientist could investigate or verify.

---

[14]Ian Ramsey, *Models and Mystery* (London: Oxford Univ. Press, 1964) and *Religious Language* (London: S.C.M., 1957).

Nevertheless, they do express truth about authentic human existence, and this truth can and must be expressed in existentialist categories. Further, whether consistently or not, Bultmann does speak of an "act of God" in Jesus. Unless "God" in this context is only another term for "man," and I am convinced that this is not his intention, then Bultmann is giving us some doctrine about the relationship of Jesus to God, however difficult it may be to understand exactly how Bultmann conceives this. The point is that this is still doctrine, i.e., a linguistic and intellectual expression of the true meaning of human life. It is only a different form of doctrine, a different way of expressing the significance of Christian experience. Bultmann does not appeal to pure experience, but to a certain kind of experience, expressed in fact in very sophisticated intellectual terms. It is unfair, therefore, to condemn Chalcedon simply because its doctrinal form employs concepts and ideas difficult for or alien to the average man of today. It is highly doubtful whether modern man, however we define this elusive concept, will find Heidegger more congenial and easier to grasp than Chalcedon. However, I repeat again, it is not being said here that the Chalcedonian language and concepts are sacrosanct for all time and that Bultmann may not have reminded us of implications of Christian experience to which the traditional formulations do not do full justice. I am only saying that Bultmann has his own doctrines, his own language and intellectual concepts.

The same is even more true, perhaps, of Paul Tillich. No one can read the three volumes of the *Systematic Theology* without being aware that he is being offered a comprehensive, sophisticated, and impressive restatement of the total corpus of Christian belief. This is doctrine we are being given, even if very different from some previous expressions of Christian truth.

A scientist-philosopher such as R.B. Braithwaite, who finds the essence of Christianity to consist of an "agapeistic" way of life, is also offering us a Christology of a kind.[15] Although he insists that the factual truth of the stories about Jesus is irrelevant in the sense that a life of agape-love remains normative and binding upon us whether the stories refer to actual events or not, he admits that in practice the stories have played a decisive role in persuading men to live according to love.

Likewise, the so-called radical theologians, such as Altizer, Hamilton, and Van Buren, while they try to lift the Jesus of pure agape out of any cosmological and theological setting, also offer us a Christology in the sense of holding that Jesus, stripped of all the traditional dogmas, remains the normative, and in that sense final, manifestation of agape-love. This is equally so of Bishop Robinson, who in his recent *Exploration into God* has

---

[15]John Hick, ed., *The Existence of God* (New York: Macmillan, 1964), pp. 228ff.

dissociated himself from the extreme "God-is-Dead" group of thinkers. Although Robinson has severe things to say about the classical dogmas in most of his books, Jesus remains central for him as the embodiment of agape-love which at the same time opens up for us a knowledge of the depth of being. This depth is not merely the psychological depths of the individual believer but points to the nature of ultimate reality itself. Van Buren is not content to leave the figure of Jesus uninterpreted. Because He was the only truly free man, He is able to liberate others into a life of authentic freedom. This, however, is to give Him a unique role which implies a doctrine of some kind, i.e., certain statements about what Jesus was in Himself, without which character He could not have been the creator of freedom in others. And so we could go on.

The conclusion is that there is no such thing as a Christ without Christology, since the word "Christ" itself is charged with interpretative significance. There are only *differing* Christologies. If our dislike of dogma is that intense, we should, of course, drop the designation "Christ," which is a theological interpretation of the significance of Jesus in Jewish Messianic categories. We should stick to the bare name "Jesus."

The fact is, therefore, that once we commit ourselves to any statements about the significance of Jesus, we are, explicitly or implicitly, offering some kind of doctrine, using the term here to indicate an intellectual formulation in language of the nature of that significance, and therefore of the "nature" of Jesus. In order to defend a Jesus without any doctrinal significance, we should have to show that Jesus did not think of His own Person as integral to the gospel he preached. Even if we say that Jesus was only a proclaimer of the Kingdom and not Himself the unique bearer of it among men, we are still offering a Christology in which the basic category is that of Teacher. This may not be an adequate Christology to those who defend Chalcedon, but it is a Christology nonetheless. That such a view might have been adopted by the early Christians is shown by the case of the Buddha. Gotama did apparently distinguish clearly between his teaching and his person. Dr. E. Conze, the noted Buddhist scholar, has reminded us that the historical figure of Gotama has never been essential to Buddhism in the same way that Jesus has been to Christianity. "The existence of Gautama, or Shakyamuni (the sage from the tribe of the Shakyas), as an individual is, in any case, a matter of little importance to Buddhist faith."[16] This, of course, is not the case with Jesus, who says, "Come unto me, all ye that labour and are heavy laden,"[17] and goes on to emphasize the unique role of the Son as

---

[16]Edward Conze, *Buddhism: Its Essence and Development* (Oxford: Bruno Cassirer, 1954), p. 34.
[17]Matt. 11:28.

the Mediator of knowledge of the Father. It could, of course, be argued in the case of Buddhism that although the Buddha did not regard himself as integral to the saving doctrine, yet in fact his followers have often regarded him for all practical purposes as essential. This, however, does not affect the theological point we are making.

It is true, of course, that we do not find in the gospels any sophisticated doctrine of His own Person by Jesus expressed in non-Jewish cultural terms. We shall look in vain for the language of the "two natures," not to mention such debatable terms as the *homoousios* of the Nicene creed. The point, however, is not whether Jesus used a particular kind of language, or a technical vocabulary which belonged to a later age, but what He intended by the language He did use. If He saw Himself as related to God in a special, unique, and decisive sense, then how He expressed this, though important, is not decisively so. It is not the particular words we use but the intent and meaning we wish to express which is crucial. Nevertheless, He did give some linguistic expression to His convictions about His role. Provided we are clear as to what the intent and meaning are, then it may be possible to express these in many different linguistic forms. We are not saying that what Jesus said is unimportant. If Jesus had said nothing at all and if there were no records which gave us some idea of his thinking on certain basic themes, then no Christology of any value could be constructed. We are simply saying that because Jesus did not give us a "doctrine" of His Person expressed in the language of later developments, it does not follow that He said nothing which could be the legitimate basis of this later language.

The Councils of Nicaea and Chalcedon were fully aware that some of the language they used was not that of the Jesus of the gospels or of the New Testament in general. They believed, nonetheless, that they were expressing, however inadequately, the true meaning and intent of the biblical language. This, of course, can be debated. It can be argued that the Fathers completely misunderstood both the intent of Jesus Himself and of what the rest of the New Testament says. But this must be shown and not simply asserted; it is not self-evident that the creeds contradict the essential intent of what Jesus said and did.

The crucial question, then, concerns the manner in which Jesus conceived Himself to be related to God and His saving purpose for men and how important He understood His own role to be in this redemptive process. In the narrow and more technical sense of the term "Christology," a doctrine of Christ is required only if we want to speak of the presence and activity of God in Jesus as unique and indispensable for the fulfilling of God's saving purpose. If we already knew, prior to and independent of Jesus, all that we need to know about God, then Jesus would not be in any fundamental sense necessary to Christian faith. He might be psychologically helpful to us as an illustration of truths we already possessed. In the last analysis, however, we could get on without Him, since we would already have certain and reliable knowledge of God from other sources. If it is objected that biblical "knowing" is not simply a matter of intellectual awareness but of immediate personal experience of the saving activity of God, Jesus would still be unnecessary if we believed that the same kind of help could be obtained just as effectively elsewhere. Our relationship to God would not be absolutely dependent upon knowledge of Jesus in any sense of the word "knowledge." Jesus might help and confirm us to a stronger assurance about spiritual realities we already apprehended and possessed. In this case, we would not even have to claim any originality for the ideas of Jesus. He may very well have only confirmed existing ideas, as He did, for example, in regard to the basic Jewish doctrine of God. As Wheeler Robinson pointed out years ago, the category of actuality needs to be added to the ideas if we are to arrive at an adequate understanding of what constitutes the uniqueness of Jesus. The Person of Christ includes not only what He thought and said, but what He was in Himself and how that reality was expressed in action as well as in words. It is not a case of either-or. If Jesus had acted without giving us any clue at all in language as to why He was acting in this way, we would be in the dark completely. On the other hand, if He had only talked about God's Kingdom and purpose without demonstrating in action what this meant for practice, then He would have been only an interesting purveyor of ideas. He could not have been the proper object of the kind of language used in the New Testament itself and by later Christian thinkers.

This raises again the age-old question of whether the category of Teacher is adequate for a satisfactory Christology. We do have some knowledge of moral and spiritual truths apart from Jesus. To a considerable extent Jesus rejected or confirmed what men already knew in principle about God. This is notably the case in regard to the Old Testament—Jesus did not claim to be inventing afresh but to be recalling the Jews to what God had already made plain to them in the history of their covenant-relationship with Yahweh. This raises the question of whether Jesus conceived His function to be that of revealing new truths about God or of showing God in saving act or both. There is, after all, a vast difference between telling men that God is love and showing that love in action, actually saving and reconciling men. If the latter is the decisive factor, and we believe it is, then an adequate Christology must concern itself not simply with formulating further the truths which Jesus uttered, but with the Person of Jesus. It is the total action of Jesus in His earthly ministry, His death, and His resurrection which becomes of central importance. It is the action, and the teaching as expressive of that action, which reveals God in an existential manner, i.e., in a way which actually touches, transforms, and saves the real lives of men. It is because Christians believe this to be profoundly true that the problem of Christology arises. This is why Bonhoeffer insisted that the proper question to address to Jesus is not "How are you what you are?" but first and foremost "Who are you?"[18] If Jesus in His Person actually does this for men, then who is He? It is not simply a question of adding to the stock of ideas which men already possess about God. Rather, it is a matter of actually meeting, and therefore of knowing, God in the deepest personal sense, in the Person of Jesus Himself and His total action on our behalf. Bonhoeffer was right to remind us on the basis of the Protestant understanding of the Bible and the gospel as expressed by Luther, Calvin, and others, that we must know the "benefits" of Christ before we talk of His Person. It is what Jesus Christ does in and for us which gives us the basis for saying something about Him. If this is what is meant by a functional Christology, then we need not quarrel with it. Nevertheless, what Jesus does affords grounds for at least some statements as to what and who He is. This means that we cannot avoid what Reginald Fuller calls the "necessity of ontology."[19] A functional Christology which speaks only of the effects of Jesus upon men and shrinks from seeking to express what He must have been in Himself in order to produce such effects is rending asunder what God has joined together.

This is a criticism which can justly be made against some of the remarks of Oscar Cullmann. He says about Jesus that it "is his very nature that he can be known only in his work." Agreed, but it should be noted that Cullmann does not say that we know His very nature in such work. In fact, he goes on to say that "speculation about his natures is an absurdity."[20] Yet this is hardly consistent. If Cullmann is simply asserting that the doctrine of the two natures does not adequately express in appropriate language the "nature" of Jesus as known in His work, then this could be accepted as a reasonable thesis and would then have to be discussed on its merits. If, on the other hand, he is saying that the "effects" of His work on men do not permit us to make any statements at all about His nature, then this is equivalent to denying any kind of Christology at all, whether functional or otherwise. In fact, Cullmann shows in his book that many statements can and must be made about the "nature" of Jesus. He accepts the scriptural witness that Jesus Christ is God in His self-revelation.[21] Yet what is this but a statement about who Jesus is, even if such knowledge is of necessity mediated through

---

[18]Dietrich Bonhoeffer, *Christology,* trans. John Bowden (London: Collins, 1966), pp. 30ff.

[19]Reginald H. Fuller, *The Foundations of New Testament Christology* (London: Collins, 1969), p. 249.

[20]Oscar Cullmann, *Christology of the New Testament* (London: S.C.M., 1959), p. 326.

[21]*Ibid.,* p. 325.

the "effects" which He has upon us? Cullmann, like Ritschl before him, cannot really escape from the ontological question.

It is also a fact that the power of Jesus so to act upon us does depend upon our conviction that He is such as to be able to reconcile us and make us anew in accordance with God's saving purpose. Jesus might have been mistaken in His interpretation of the will of God or of His own relationship to God. It is because Christians are deeply convinced in the light of their experience that He was not mistaken that they have been driven in many different ways to develop a doctrine of His Person. They have found themselves compelled irresistibly to exclaim "My Lord and my God" as the only possible deduction to be made from their experience of God's saving power manifest in Him. If we want to affirm the truth of what Jesus revealed in word and act and by being what and who He is, then this involves some estimate of His Person, whatever the language used. It involves the attempt to say in some manner who He was and is "in Himself." The objection often made against talking of God "in Himself" or Jesus "in Himself" often rests on a misunderstanding. If it meant that we could say what God is "in Himself" by bypassing all the media of His self-revelation, then it would be absurd. On the other hand, if it means that what is given through such media is a reliable insight into the true nature and character of God, then the Christian can surely say no less. In the same way, if it is implied that we could talk of the "nature" or "natures" of Jesus in complete detachment from the total activity of Jesus in saving and transforming men, then again it would be mere speculation in the bad sense. If, on the other hand, we truly know Jesus in such activity, then we are in a position to speak of what Jesus was "in Himself," however much mystery still attaches to His Person which the human intellect can never completely plumb.

Whether we say "God was in Christ reconciling the world to Himself"; or "The Word was made flesh"; or that Jesus was "truly man and truly God"; or that "He was the embodiment through obedience of the beyond in our midst, of the transcendence of love" (J.A.T. Robinson); or that in Him the "ground of our being" was made transparent to us in the "new being" in Jesus as the Christ (Tillich); or that, as Schleiermacher had earlier maintained, Jesus was "the unique man in whom the perfect God-consciousness was actualized"—in every instance we are in fact offering some kind of doctrine. All these varied expressions indicate that men are not content to speak of Jesus Christ simply as a human person. They want to say that God, or the ground of being, or ultimate reality, or the "depth" of reality, or the search for authentic existence, is somehow disclosed in the life, death, and resurrection of this man. In other words, Jesus opens up for us a knowledge of the supreme Reality, however that is characterized, upon which we all in the last analysis depend. In other words, when we speak of Jesus, we are compelled to speak of the power which produced the world, ourselves, and finally Jesus Christ. The only alternative is to say that the Person of Jesus has no significance at all for our knowledge of God or the nature and character of whatever cosmic power or process produced us. This means that He tells us something about human existence but nothing about divine existence. Some today would want to say precisely this, but if so, we should all have the courage to draw the logical consequences.

For example, the agapeistic way of life may attract us and exert a strange fascination over us. We may nobly opt for agape in a godless world. We would, however, have no right to speak of the necessary or ultimate triumph of agape. We have no logical right to argue that agape is sovereign over all the endless changes of the cosmic process, still less over death itself. In short, agape is not obviously of the nature of God apart from convictions about the victory of Jesus over sin and death. Even the heroic life and death of Jesus might very well be a "sport," a "freak," a "surd," a mysterious accident in a process otherwise without rime or meaning. If this seems an impossible position to take (and it would be difficult to show that it has any biblical foundation), then we are driven to formulate some doctrine of the Person of Christ which both expresses and safeguards what Christians believe they have found in Him about the reality and presence of God.

If the latter is what we "want" to say, then the question can be legitimately raised as to what is the most appropriate language in which to express these convictions. For example, it could with perfect propriety be argued that the historic language of the two natures is conceptually inadequate and that we must search for a more adequate way of expressing the same truth. I assume that this is what is intended by H.R. Mackintosh in his classic book on *The Person of Christ* when he says: "With the religion of the creed [i.e., Chalcedon] we have no quarrel."[22] He is not, in other words, questioning the faith which inspired the creed, only the once-for-all conceptualization of the faith in this particular form. He is not disagreeing with the intent behind Chalcedon, but only its intellectual and theological expression. The same comment could be made concerning William Temple's declaration that "The formula of Chalcedon is, in fact, a confession of the bankruptcy of Greek patristic theology. The Fathers had done the best that could be done with the intellectual apparatus at their disposal."[23] Whether we agree with these comments or not, or even whether both men would have wanted to stand by this exact criticism in their later years is not of itself

---

[22]Hugh R. Mackintosh, *The Person of Christ* (Edinburgh: T. & T. Clark, 1937), p. 213.
[23]B. H. Streeter, *Foundations* (London: Macmillan, 1929), p. 230.

important. The point is that they did not disagree with what the Fathers wanted to say, only with the way in which they said it.

Even Bultmann wants to talk about an "act of God" in Jesus or should this not be demythologized or dekerygmatized, as Fritz Buri has suggested? How does he know that "God" is active in Jesus except on the assumption that Jesus reveals more than simply a further dimension of human nature? He may be inconsistent, but Bultmann's heart is sound on this point, or perhaps one should say his Christian instinct. There cannot be a religious experience without any intellectual content at all, unless one is thinking of something like the practice of yoga. Some element of belief, in the sense of affirmation of truth, must be present. Even if we stick rigidly to the biblical language, this is so. We have to relate such truth to the cultural situation in which we find ourselves, and to the way in which men understand truth in any particular period. In this sense, there may be, indeed must be, an evolution of dogma and doctrine and many changes of language. The basic point is, however, that we are still trying to talk meaningfully of God's activity in Jesus of Nazareth, an activity manifested in Him in a manner decisive for the reconciliation of man with God and man with man, whether in time or eternity.

A Jesus without Christology not only ignores elements integral to Jesus' understanding of His mission and calling. It turns its back upon a good deal of the New Testament experience and witness and it lacks an adequate appreciation of the real inspiration behind the long labor of Christian thought to give some kind of answer to Jesus' own question, Who do you say that I am? We can, therefore, proceed to discuss doctrine on its merits. R.H. Fuller declares: "It is sheer biblicism to maintain that the church should merely repeat 'what the Bible says' about Christology as about everything else. The church has to proclaim the gospel into the contemporary situation. And that is precisely what the Nicene and the Chalcedonian formulas were trying to do."[24]

The basic issue is now clearly defined. It is not a question of whether we should go beyond the biblical language to express the significance of Jesus of Nazareth. We can and we must. The question thus becomes, How effective and adequate a job are we doing in this regard? This challenge can also properly be put to the Fathers as it has to be put to modern attempts at restating Christology. It is important, however, to recognize that these attempts cannot be criticized for what they are attempting to do, however limited their success in doing it. Christians will never be exempt from grappling with this task as long as history continues. At least, it should be

---

[24]Fuller, p. 250.

acknowledged that a Jesus without "Christology" can never be an effective foundation for a living and dynamic faith in the present.

We have left until last a consideration of the issue discussed by Professor Maurice Wiles in his article entitled "Does Christology Rest on a Mistake?"[25] The question raised in this article is much more fundamental than any we have previously considered. It is not simply whether we can produce a more adequate linguistic formulation of the significance of Jesus than that bequeathed to us in the creeds and confessions of the church. Rather is it being asked whether the entire theological effort in the past to frame a doctrine of the divinity of Christ was in fact mistaken. Obviously this is a crucial question, and if it is answered in the sense indicated by Wiles, then there is no need of this book or of any other books with similar intent.

Let us try to summarize the main points of Wiles' thesis. He notes the problem of the intelligibility of traditional Christology as a result of modern historical thought. He does not question that there is some New Testament evidence which made it reasonable for the church to develop its later Christological doctrines. Nevertheless, there are elements of the New Testament evidence which are not easy to reconcile with the traditional dogmas. Wiles' conclusion is that the New Testament evidence taken as a basis for the later Christology is ambiguous and inconclusive.[26]

If this starting-point is valid, then Wiles is correct in asserting that the basic assumptions which governed the doctrinal development become all-important. What were these assumptions? The life of Jesus took place not in a vacuum but in a specific historical and cultural context. Beliefs about Him were developed in a context where certain views about creation, fall, and redemption naturally determined the way in which men would assess the significance of Jesus and talk about Him. Modern science and historical knowledge, however, have compelled us to modify considerably our thinking about these themes. Now if the earlier doctrines of creation, fall, and redemption must be pronounced to rest on a mistake, then a fortiori any doctrine of incarnation and divinity based on those assumptions must likewise be pronounced a mistake. This is, in fact, Professor Wiles' basic thesis.

But it is at this point that his ideas do not seem as clear as might be desired. In what sense do the ideas of creation, fall, and redemption represent a mistake? This is not simply a matter of a literalistic, fundamentalistic handling of the Genesis narratives. The basic point of Wiles' criticism seems

---

[25]Maurice Wiles, "Does Christology Rest on a Mistake?" *Religious Studies,* ed. H.D. Lewis, VI, No. 1 (March 1970).
[26]*Ibid.,* p. 69.

to be that the biblical ideas about creation and the fall of man, and the doctrines developed therefrom, tried to bind such doctrines logically and historically to particular events, in the one case a divine act of creation "at the beginning" and at the transition from animal to man, and in the other case, a "fall" of man as a definite historical event in the past. Such views, we are led to believe, have been rendered impossible by the theory of evolution and modern historical studies of the past of the human race. To that degree, the classical doctrines of creation and the fall rest on a mistake. This is not to say that the Christian thinkers of the past were stupid or that their way of understanding their doctrines was not perhaps the only way in which they could be expressed, given their historical situation and their cultural context. The fact remains that from our modern point of view they were mistaken.

How does this affect the way in which past Christians interpreted the significance of Jesus? Naturally they saw it as the "crowning of God's creative work and the reversal of the fall."[27] Since the fall was a single act with universal consequences, therefore the work of Jesus must have been an equally decisive and single divine act which reversed those consequences. From this it was a quick and easy step to the view that Jesus and His activity were unique and without parallel and that God must have acted in Him in a way which clearly separates Him from all other human acts and human lives. If, however, the doctrine of creation does not require the "postulation of any specific divine act within the process as a whole,"[28] then no specific act, such as the classical doctrine of the Incarnation implies, is required. The same is true of the fall and the unique saving death. "If the doctrine of the fall 'relates not to some datable aboriginal calamity in the historic past but to a dimension of human experience', may not the same both negatively and positively be said of the doctrine of redemption?"[29] Professor Wiles notes that early Christian thinkers felt that the fully divine character of redemption in Christ could be maintained only if the "redeemer was divine in a direct and special sense." Because they felt this, they tied the significance of Jesus to a "mythological story of God's total self-giving, God's compassionate acceptance of pain and evil whereby that overcoming [i.e., of the separation of man and God of which the fall speaks] is made possible and effective."[30] Such a tying of a supposedly unique event to a divine, mythological story was a mistake. "The theological conviction of the reality of divine redemption was felt to require the underpinning of a distinct divine presence in

---

[27]Ibid., p. 72.
[28]Ibid.
[29]Ibid.
[30]Ibid., p. 73.

Jesus; but in the light of the comparison with other related doctrines, it seems reasonable to suggest that that very natural feeling rests on a mistake."[31] The feeling is understandable but a mistake nonetheless.

If all this is true, then why hold on to Jesus' significance at all? Why not make a clean break with history altogether, and talk of divine redemption actively mediated in countless and diverse ways without linking it with any special historical figure, as indeed was the case in some forms of Hinduism and Buddhism? Professor Wiles evidently does not wish to go so far. Even if we do not succumb to the category-mistake of "confusing the human historical story with the divine mythological story,"[32] a case can perhaps still be made out that the "story of Jesus is not an arbitrarily chosen story."[33] There may indeed be grounds for seeing the life and death of Jesus as a part of the human story which is of "unique significance."[34] This is not only because the life of Jesus created a new and effective realization of divine redemption in a continuing historical community, the church. It also, according to Wiles, affords a clue to interpreting the nature of the divine redemptive activity in and through the whole of the human story, by which is apparently meant the total historical process. And there, presumably, we must stop. To attempt to go further and develop a Christology, a doctrine of the unique divine presence and activity in this one figure, Jesus of Nazareth, is on Wiles' view basically a mistaken enterprise. This would be to tie the significance of Jesus to a divine mythological story, and this we are forbidden to do both by modern science and the modern understanding of history.

It is not altogether clear what precise weight should be given to the word "mythological" in this discussion. Does it mean obsolete science, legend or fiction, sheer subjective imagination, or any use of metaphorical, symbolical, and analogical language for the expression and communication of Christian truth? It is notorious that these different meanings are not clearly defined and distinguished in Bultmann's writings. Professor Wiles does not even give us a hint as to where he stands on this issue. We shall not attempt to reply to all these points in this chapter, since the rest of the book will be devoted to the elucidation of some of them. However, since Wiles himself suggests that the Christological mistake depends on a previous mistake in regard to the doctrines of creation and the fall, this would seem to be the proper place to begin making a reply.

To respond adequately to Wiles' comments on the doctrine of creation

---

[31]*Ibid.*, p. 74.
[32]*Ibid.*, p. 75.
[33]*Ibid.*, p. 74.
[34]*Ibid.*, p. 75.

would require a more thorough discussion than would seem to be proper at this stage of our investigation. It is also made more difficult by the fact that Professor Wiles does not develop his ideas in detail. It may be, therefore, that I shall attribute or seem to attribute to him ideas which he does not in fact hold. Our endeavor, therefore, will be simply to make some comments on the relation of the doctrine of the creation to the doctrine of the Incarnation in general terms and try to clarify what the real issues are.

It is not clear what are the implications of the charge that the doctrine of creation is tied to a specific event. If the issue is whether the world began at a point of time in the past which could be dated if our knowledge were more adequate, then such a criticism would not seem to be particularly cogent against the doctrine as it was historically developed. If it is implied that the doctrine of creation means that God created the world and then stood aside to let it run on its own steam, as it were, then we have fallen into a deistic view of the Creator-creation relationship which has not been the view of the mainstream of Christian thinking on this subject. If Wiles is wanting to assert the eternity of the world, he has Aquinas' philosophical, if not theological, permission. But the problem of God and such a sequence of finite beings is still up for discussion. If Wiles is a process theologian, so be it, but it is not, to say the least, self-evident that this is either philosophically intelligible or religiously adequate. In view of the critical remarks of Austin Farrer and H.P. Owen upon process theology,[35] a second look at that modern substitute for theism needs to be taken.

The last paragraph is full of ifs and buts because we do not know where Wiles is situated in this contemporary discussion about God. There is nothing inherently absurd in the idea that the world had a beginning in time, i.e., that there was a "time" when such a process was not in fact going on. In Wiles' discussion, which leaves so many of these questions in complete obscurity, the issue of evolution is somehow introduced. He does not consider the many different views among biologists of the manner in which this mysterious evolution works. Presumably, if we accept some theory as to the development of more complex organisms from simpler ones, we are not obliged to accept Darwin's natural selection as the final and unquestionable interpretation of that development. Wiles criticizes all those, Catholic and Protestant alike, who drag in God to explain the gap between the inorganic and the organic or between the organic and man as "rational" being. The gaps are undoubtedly there, no matter how we choose to explain or not to explain them. Aubrey Moore's remarks, quoted by Wiles, are surely unacceptable. Moore tells us that "the theory of evolution is infinitely more

---

[35] Austin Farrer, *Faith and Speculation* (London: A. & C. Black, 1967), Chapter X; H.P. Owen, *Concepts of Deity* (London: Macmillan, 1971), pp. 75ff.

Christian than the theory of special creation.''[36] This makes no sense until we know what theory of evolution is involved. Certainly chance variations and natural selection do not constitute a more Christian theory. Wiles does not discuss any of the teleological interpretations of evolution from F.R. Tennant to Teilhard de Chardin. Does he mean that evolution goes on, à la Darwin, with God a distant spectator watching to see how it turns out? If, on the other hand, to use the traditional terminology, God is immanent as well as transcendent, then His presence in the total process does not rule out specific acts within the process which might be more revealing than other acts. That is, if God is the personal God of Christian theism. If He is not or is to be simply identified with the process, then it follows that "He" cannot act in specific ways because one should not call Him "He" at all.[37] Years ago William Temple rightly contended that "if that reality [God] is not personal, there can be no special revelation, but only uniform procedure."[38] Is this what Professor Wiles is saying, that evolution only gives us uniform process in which no characteristic divine acts can be expected? Again Temple rightly stresses that "personal wisdom is not shown in rigid uniformity of behaviour but in constancy of purpose expressed through infinitely various response to different conditions."[39] In the last analysis, it would seem to be our doctrine of God which is crucial, and on this point Wiles is strangely silent. If his thought of God leaves no place for characteristic revealing personal acts in the evolutionary process, then the doctrine of a unique Incarnation is rendered impossible from the start. I am not at all sure that this is where Professor Wiles stands. Perhaps it is sufficient to say that I do not accept that position and that I see nothing in the Christian theistic interpretation of the relation of Creator to His creation which rules out Incarnation in advance. If Christology rests on a mistake, it is not because the doctrine of creation is a mistake. It would, however, be a mistake if Christian theism were a mistake, but this surely needs to be shown, not simply implied.

The traditional doctrine of the fall is also declared to be a mistake. Apart from the question whether there is one version which can be called "traditional," it is not exactly clear why it should be a mistake simply because it is tied to a past event. Is this in itself a sufficient ground for so regarding it? To assert that the Adam and Eve stories are not scientific or anthropological accounts in our meaning of the term "scientific" does not resolve this question of past event. Nor does the rejection of the Augustinian view of original sin as biologically transmitted dispose of the issue. On any view sin began somewhere and began in time. Even Tillich admits this, despite his

[36]Wiles, "Does Christology Rest on a Mistake?" p. 71.
[37]Austin Farrer, *Reflective Faith*, ed. Charles Conti (London: S.P.C.K., 1972), p. 178.
[38]William Temple, *Nature, Man and God* (London: Macmillan, 1935), p. 306.
[39]*Ibid.*, p. 307.

obvious desire to free Christian anthropology from a dependence upon a literalistic interpretation of Scripture.[40] If the origin of sin cannot be pinned down to a single man, described with all the graphic details of Genesis, the fact remains that sin as moral deviation and estrangement from God began with some man or men in the past. There was a time when there was no sin and a time when it was present, whether it began with one man or with several men simultaneously. It must have been a datable event in the sense that it began at some point in the sequence of events which we call the evolutionary process. There was a transition from a nonmoral animal to a free and responsible man for whom sin became both a possibility and a reality. Thus, if one asks questions about the origin of sin, and such questions are permissible, then the entry of sin into the world process cannot be detemporalized. It is no answer to this problem to assert that sin is a present dimension of human experience and that Adam is a symbol of Everyman. This kind of language is legitimate, and indeed helpful, if one is wanting to make the point that sin for us is not simply a past event but a present reality with overwhelming existential implications for our life today. But this in no way renders void the claim that sin began in the past. There is something primordial, temporal, historical about it, whatever the difficulties of describing that event in detail. It is difficult to see why the early fathers of the church should be faulted on these grounds. Their pictures of the past event may have been naive and dressed in mythical garb as far as sophisticated modern men are concerned, but their basic point may well have been valid.

That God should have acted in history in a specific event or person to reverse the consequences of sin's entry into the world does not on the face of it seem absurd. If God exists, as Christians believe, then the notion is conceivable and would make sense. Whether God has in fact so acted is, of course, a different question and places us back with all the questions of biblical history and interpretation, plus the history of the church and Christian experience in the widest sense. We simply wish to point out at this stage of our argument that Professor Wiles has not made out his case that Christology is a mistake because it rests upon a mistaken understanding of creation, the fall, and redemption. It is true that Wiles contends that we could still speak of the unique "significance" of Jesus even if we have no doctrine of the unique divine presence and activity of God in Him, and indeed reject such a doctrine as illegitimate and mistaken. But this calls for more examination than has yet been given to it in Professor Wiles' provocative article. For the moment, we make bold to ignore the "No Road Ahead" sign and push on with our theological investigation.

---

[40]Tillich, *Systematic Theology,* II, p. 29.

2.
How Definitive Was Chalcedon?

We have already seen that any attempt to assess the significance of Jesus involves some sort of Christology, whether this latter turns out to be what is called orthodox or not. Furthermore, we have shown that whatever Jesus affirmed about His own Person, or however Christians later expressed His significance for them, Jesus was firmly anchored in the faith in Israel's God. The reality of the living God of Israel, active in history, was not for Jesus an open question but a basic premise from which He started. This, however, does not solve for us all the problems. If one looks at these issues with detachment, and not from the perspective of faith which already commits us to a certain kind of confession, he might argue that Israel was mistaken in its understanding of God and that Jesus was mistaken in taking this for granted. It could be argued too that modern biblical study shows that Jesus made very few claims for Himself and that the later church misinterpreted what it thought He said. Or that the church might have attributed to Him a significance which cannot reasonably be claimed for Him. It is true that Christian faith will not be able to take this detached view of the matter. Yet even a believer can recognize that these are real questions and that the church has to try to give some kind of answer to them if we are to give a reason for the faith that is in us, as Scripture tells us to do (I Peter 3:15).

We shall in this chapter be concerned with the classic definition of the faith given at Chalcedon in A.D. 451. This famous ''symbol'' of the faith has played a decisive role in the theological articulation of the Christian faith for succeeding generations. Its importance is obvious for the Roman Catholic, Eastern Orthodox, and Anglican churches. And the Protestant Reformers, despite their attack upon the church as they knew it, did not repudiate the fundamental affirmations of this ancient creed. It is also worth remembering that modern ''conservative evangelicals'' such as Carl Henry have defended Chalcedon with considerable vigor.[1] It is unfortunate, no doubt, that even in World Council circles the habit has grown of attaching

---

[1]Carl Henry, *The Protestant Dilemma* (Grand Rapids: Eerdmans, 1949).

the label "conservative evangelical" to certain Protestant groups exclusively. Obviously, other churches and groups might want to claim the adjectives for themselves in a very significant sense. However, we are concerned here only to emphasize the continuing appeal of the Chalcedonian Definition of the Faith to a very wide range of Christians—Catholic, Eastern Orthodox, and Protestant.

Our first task will be to try to understand what was affirmed at Chalcedon and what was the religious intent behind the language used. The following points need to be made at the start:

(a) The Chalcedonian formula was a protective device against certain heretical ways of thinking which the church saw as endangering a true understanding of the gospel, and therefore of the redemption of men through the grace of God in Jesus Christ. This negative aspect of credal definition has often been the occasion of bitter criticism. Nonetheless, unless one wishes to divorce faith from any intelligible expression of its meaning in language, this can hardly be avoided. Even Bonhoeffer, who is often cited as sympathetic to the more radical attacks on tradition, expressed himself thus: "If critical Christology is thus concerned with marking out limits, that means that it is concerned with the concept of heresy. We have lost the concept of heresy today because there is no longer a teaching authority. This is a tremendous catastrophe."[2] The contemporary church is being compelled to face again the question as to whether any or all philosophical or theological positions are compatible with the Christian faith. So extreme has become the attack upon all forms of authority in some quarters that even the use of the word "heresy" has become identified in many minds with intolerance and narrow-minded dogmatism. Yet a complete repudiation of the concept of heresy logically implies the denial of any normative truth which is authoritative for the Christian. In as far as heresy is linked with the idea of religious intolerance and the use of torture and other physical and mental bullying to compel men to accept certain beliefs, it must be repudiated. If, however, heresy is taken to indicate deviations which upset the balance of Christian truth, with serious consequences for worship, behavior, and the Christian experience of salvation, then it still points to something significant and the notion cannot be eliminated. Chalcedon, therefore, must be judged on its merits. A defence of the substance of the Definition does not mean a defence of the ways in which the church attempted to secure its acceptance or to secure theological uniformity. One could defend Chalcedon's theological validity and usefulness while having grave reservations about the manner in which its acceptance became mixed up with ecclesiastical politics and bitter personal rivalries.

---

[2]Bonhoeffer, *Christology,* p. 78.

(b) Chalcedon was, of course, an attempt to express the significance of Jesus Christ for the Christian community within a particular cultural context. Few would argue with the proposition that the language of Chalcedon was inevitably that of the ancient classical culture, even when that language was stamped with Christian meanings which it obviously did not have in a purely pagan and classical context. We have, therefore, to ask about the basic intent which underlay this use of the language. We have already noted that H.R. Mackintosh wrote some years ago, after a critical appraisal of the language: "With the religion of the creed, accordingly, we have no quarrel."[3] How far we can separate the religious intent from the language used to express it is a matter to be considered more fully later. That such a distinction must be made is as true of Chalcedon as of all the other creeds and forms of religious language, unless we are prepared to argue that one kind of theological language has validity and unchangeable authority for every age and place. This, indeed, would be a difficult thesis to sustain. The practical question still remains. If Christians can accept the religious intent of the Chalcedonian language, what new forms of language would express the same intent equally well?

(c) Chalcedon is not an attempt to express the "how" of the Incarnation. That is to say, it does not try to give a coherent philosophical and theological system of thought in the light of which we can understand, with more or less adequate images and concepts, just how God became man. If this is what is wanted, we must turn to individual Christian thinkers—to Origen, Athanasius, Apollinaris, Nestorius, Augustine in the patristic period, or to Schleiermacher, Thomasius, Tillich, or Barth in more recent times, to name only a few. Chalcedon is concerned rather to set up theological guideposts which aim at preventing a mutilation or distortion of the wholeness of Christian truth. Though its function appears in this light as mainly negative, there is a positive element at stake in the negation or denials of certain heresies.

(d) Last, but not least, the Council of 451 believed itself to be expressing the intent of Scripture. That it had to use nonbiblical language should not blind us to this fact. The men who framed the Definition were not ignorant of the Scriptures. Again this does not mean that this claim must be accepted uncritically at its face value, as if the Council was infallibly protected against a misreading of the scriptural witness. Nevertheless, their intent to do justice to Scripture should be taken seriously and not dismissed out of hand. If their drawing out of the implications of Scripture was inadequate, we must try to show where and at what points this was so by an

---

[3]Mackintosh, *The Person of Christ*, p. 213.

appeal to the same Scripture which the men of Chalcedon were trying to interpret.

Despite its historical importance, however, it must also be remembered that Chalcedon was never understood or accepted without question by all Christian thinkers, particularly in Eastern Christendom. It is said that when Nestorius heard of it he thought that it had confirmed the main points of his own position. After 451, others moved in a Monophysite direction, which was a departure from the spirit of Chalcedon and which seemed to many to involve the swallowing up of the humanity into the divinity.

Yet even Tillich, who is by no means an uncritical supporter of the Definition, affirms that "The doctrine of Chalcedon, whatever we think of the use of Greek terms in Christian theology, saved the human side of the picture of Jesus for our Western theology, and even for the East."[4] The use of nonbiblical philosophical language is defended by Professor John McIntyre on the grounds that openness to so-called secular concepts has always been an inevitable mark of Christian thought:

> In the light of the evidence, it is historically inaccurate to claim that theology has, in the past, been open only to the Word of God and closed in every other direction; and intellectually impossible that it ever should be so. Theology always has been and always will be open towards logical, epistemological, ethical, psychological, cultural, scientific and technological concepts, principles and methods.[5]

If this is a correct assessment of theological method, as I believe it is, then it follows that any criticism of Chalcedon cannot be directed merely at its use of philosophical concepts and language. It must be directed rather to the adequacy or inadequacy of those concepts; and if we think we can do a better job than Chalcedon on the theological level, then we are obliged to go beyond a simple repetition of the biblical language and use categories from some other philosophical tradition and culture.

What, then, was the religious and theological intent behind the Chalcedonian formula? Despite criticism to the contrary, which we shall consider in a moment, the intention was not to disrupt the unity of the Person of Christ. "In an almost literal sense, its first and last words about Jesus Christ are that He is one."[6] The doctrine of the two natures was not intended to deny the basic truth of the "one and the same Son and Only-begotten God the Word, Lord Jesus Christ." We may contend, as many have done, that the

---

[4]Paul Tillich, *A History of Christian Thought* (London: S.C.M., 1968), I, 89.

[5]John McIntyre, "The Openness of Theology," *New College Bulletin*, IV, No. 3 (Autumn 1968).

[6]McIntyre, *The Shape of Christology*, p. 93.

use of the language of two natures makes it impossible to give an intelligible theological account of the unity of the one Person. This must be debated on its merits. But we are not free to assume that the Fathers wanted to destroy the unity, or would have been satisfied with the doctrine if they had thought that this would be its chief result.

There seems little reason to doubt that they wanted to defend the full humanity of Jesus. The "truly man" is qualified by the further phrase "consisting also of a reasonable soul (ἐκ ψυχῆς λογικῆς) and body." Furthermore, adopting the well-known nonbiblical word employed at Nicaea to affirm the divinity, Chalcedon applies it directly to the humanity—of one substance (*homoousios*) with us as regards his manhood. Here again it is possible to argue that language is no final protection and that despite its formal pronouncements, the church continued to be basically Apollinarian in its emphasis. This thesis, as is well known, was very forcefully argued some years ago by Canon C.E. Raven.[7] The Monophysite developments which followed Chalcedon might seem to confirm this. John Knox has recently repeated the same point: "Those who formally and explicitly affirm the humanity can define it in ways which, in effect, deny its existential reality."[8] But again, the intent of Chalcedon was to protect the humanity. Our conclusion, then, is that the Definition of 451 intended to be loyal to Scripture and to secure both the full humanity and the true divinity of Jesus, however limited its success in safeguarding the true humanity in the later developments.

Our task now is to pursue the further question as to whether the Fathers, in spite of their intention, failed in their undertaking because they lacked adequate concepts and language to express what they wanted to say. Or did they make certain philosophical assumptions too uncritically, so that the end result of their thinking was far less satisfactory than they hoped or even involved downright distortions?

Let us consider again the obvious emphasis of Chalcedon upon the unity of the one Person Jesus Christ. E.L. Mascall has argued very strongly that the two-nature model is not intended by the users of it to be a literal description of the psychology of Jesus.[9] If it were so intended, it might be difficult to rebut the criticism that Chalcedon gives us a monstrous hybrid, an example of dual personality like that of Robert Louis Stevenson's Dr. Jekyll and Mr. Hyde, rather than the one Person who impresses us so clearly

---

[7]Charles E. Raven, *Appollinarianism* (London: Cambridge Univ. Press, 1923).

[8]John Knox, *The Humanity and Divinity of Christ* (London: Cambridge Univ. Press, 1967), p. 71.

[9]E.L. Mascall, *Christ, the Christian and the Church* (London: Longmans Green, 1946), p. 38.

from the pages of the New Testament. In Mascall's view, the two-nature formula is an ontological statement—i.e., it purports to say something about the reality of the God-Man, not to give us an insight into His psychology as this would be understood by a contemporary psychologist. Indeed, if Jesus is what Christians have claimed Him to be, it is very unlikely that sinful men like ourselves will ever be able to give a complete account of the inner consciousness of Jesus, who was tempted in all points like as we are, yet without sin. This is not, however, to say that we can know nothing at all about Jesus' self-understanding.

However, even if we accept this point of Mascall's, the question remains whether the two-nature model does not still pose insuperable difficulties for the reality of the humanity if to be a real person involves a psychological unity. The debates in the early centuries about whether the God-Man had two wills or only one shows that the difficulty was a genuine one, even then. It has to be remembered, too, that the Council of Chalcedon did also give its blessing to the Tome of Leo in which the dualistic implications of the two-nature formula are spelled out in a more specific way than in the credal statement itself. Further, both the Creed and the Tome take for granted the impassibility of God (i.e., God's inability, by the very fact that He is God, to experience suffering, or in more general terms, to be subject to *apathe* or feeling). Can we, then, say that religiously the Chalcedonian formula is adequate and definitive, while the linguistic and conceptual articulation of this demands to be replaced in later generations by a vocabulary and a set of concepts which do not imply the dubious metaphysical assumptions which underlay the ancient language?

What does it mean to say that Chalcedon is religiously adequate? And adequate to what or to whom? The very question implies the substantial reliability of the New Testament in its witness both to the historical actuality of Jesus of Nazareth and the Christian confession of Him as Savior and Lord. Further, it involves some kind of genuine continuity and even identity between Jesus of Nazareth and the risen Jesus of the kerygma, the proclamation by the church of the risen Lord as experienced by the first apostles and disciples. To say that Chalcedon is religiously adequate and definitive in this sense is to say that this is so for Christian men. It is adequate both to historic reality and faith's experience of certain events as "saving," i.e., as the means whereby God delivers us from sin, guilt, and death and enables us to be reconciled to Him in faith, love and hope.

It may be argued that to talk like this is precisely to employ a vocabulary which is strange and meaningless to modern secular men. But such glib generalizations must not be accepted as if they were self-evident. In fact, not all modern men are secular in this sense, even in the Western world. Millions of Christians all over the world still use this kind of language. It presumably means something to them, unless Christians are assumed to have less than average intelligence and to use language which is completely meaningless to them. This, of course, does not solve our problem. It merely reminds us that it is equally ridiculous to set up an average, generalized "secular" man as the final judge of all truth, religious or otherwise. Of course, Chalcedon will not be adequate religiously or intellectually, still less authoritative, for the atheist, the agnostic, the scientific or literary humanist, the non-Christian existentialist, etc. How could it be since its intention is to express the significance of Jesus of Nazareth in His unique relationship both to God and to the men God seeks to redeem and restore to Himself? If for any reason this evaluation of Jesus Christ by faith is doubted, then obviously Chalcedon will not be either true or authoritative since its rootage in Christian experience will be lacking. One might add that the same problem arises for the orthodox Jew, the Muslim, the Hindu, and the Buddhist.

But, many will say, so much the worse for Chalcedon. What it does is only to give a certain doctrinal articulation to what is essentially a subjective faith-principle of the Christian believer. A collective expression of many individual subjectivities does not guarantee the truth of what is being affirmed, particularly when this involves such stupendous assertions as that the Christian God is real and that Jesus Christ is the unique God-Man.

Christians may as well concede this point with as much grace as they can muster at the start. Until the unbeliever can be led to know in experience what the believer thinks he knows about the reality of God and the significance of Jesus, the unbeliever simply cannot get started on the process of doctrinal development which led to Chalcedon.

The question now becomes evangelistic, pastoral, and apologetic. The unbeliever must be led to faith in God and in Jesus in the Christian sense. What, then, is faith? It cannot be identified with intellectual assent to a series of theological propositions, even Chalcedonian, divorced from the only experience which could make them meaningful. Brunner, I believe, is perfectly correct in protesting against this view of faith and against the way in which the church, at one time or another, has tried to impose the correct formulae upon unwilling men by invoking the authority of the institutional church, sometimes aided by the coercive powers of the civil law of the day.[10] Pannenberg is also correct in stating that for many today who do not share the Jewish inheritance and for whom the reality of God is not a basic starting-point but the greatest of all question marks, a Christology "from above"

---

[10]Emil Brunner, *Dogmatics*, III, trans. David Cairns and T.H.L. Parker (London: Lutterworth, 1962).

cannot be the premise from which a man must be required to start.[11] By a Christology "from above" he means one which simply assumes God and such notions as the preexistent Word or Son, and then discusses how God, thus defined, can have become the man Jesus of Nazareth. On the contrary, we must start with Jesus and lead men from there to the God whose agent He believed Himself to be. The language of the Christology "from above" may then appear to be meaningful and religiously adequate, but this will be at a later stage of an experiential process initiated by faith, not the starting-point which all men must blindly accept at the beginning. After all, this was the way in which the early disciples grew in the faith. No doubt Peter, James, and John would have been as baffled as so-called secular man today with the language of Chalcedon, even if for different reasons.

The conclusion drawn from this, however, is not what it is sometimes taken to be. It is not enough to say that the whole process of doctrinal development to Chalcedon was simply a Hellenizing corruption of the simple gospel (Harnack).[12] This oversimplification can no longer be held in the light of the patristic researches of men like G.F. Prestige and H.E.W. Turner.[13] Nor can we say that the language, images, concepts of a Peter or a Paul must never be developed, changed, transformed, or replaced as a result of the church's ongoing experience of the power and presence of God in Jesus Christ. This would be to fixate Christian thought to a limited segment of first-century Palestine or even of the Graeco-Roman world. We are not asking for another Jesus *than* the one whom Peter and Paul loved and served. We are saying that all that Christ means demands the total experience of the whole people of God both in time and place. Jesus without the "people of God" is in one important sense an abstraction.

To return, then, to Chalcedon! How far was its formulation influenced by concepts of God which are neither strictly biblical nor obviously rooted in the thought and practice of Jesus Himself? How far has its way of putting things proved to be a hindrance, so that men have been unable to start with Jesus as the disciples did, and consequently have ended up with disgust at a language so far removed, it would seem, from experience? Is Chalcedon really open to the charge levelled against the whole of the classic theological tradition by Charles Hartshorne, namely that it is in bondage to a metaphysics or a set of philosophical concepts which are invalid as philoso-

---

[11]Wolfhart Pannenberg, *Jesus: God and Man,* trans. Lewis L. Wilkins and Duane A. Priebe (London: S.C.M., 1968).

[12]Adolf Harnack, *History of Dogma,* trans. Neil Buchanan (New York: Dover, 1961).

[13]George L. Prestige, *God in Patristic Thought* (London: S.P.C.K., 1952); Henry E.W. Turner, *The Pattern of Christian Truth* (London: Mowbray, 1954).

phy and which have really nothing to do with the distinctive Christian notion, central for Jesus, that God is love?

My own view is that the religious intention behind Chalcedon is not given adequate conceptual expression in that formula, adequate in the sense of enabling us to make sense of Jesus Christ and His significance for men of faith. It does have negative value in warning us against unbalanced emphasis upon certain aspects of Christian truth to the exclusion or distortion of other aspects. And it does have positive value in reminding us of the unity of the Person of Christ and of the impossibility of reconciling both the scriptural witness and the Christian experience with a Christology which reduces Jesus Christ to the limitations of "mere manhood." Having said this, it remains true that Chalcedon's finality is not the end but also the starting point of further reflection. Christian thought has still to wrestle with the problem of the "how" of the Incarnation and to search for a more adequate language, even while recognizing that human language will never be totally adequate and that "mystery" will remain. We can never remain content, however, with a premature appeal to "mystery" which involves a disregard for some degree of intelligibility. The post-Chalcedonian experience of the church confirms this demand. We shall see evidence of this in our later discussion of the concept of divinity.

3.
The New Testament Basis of Christology

The present chapter will be concerned with the problems of exegeting the New Testament documents and interpreting that material as a basis for a doctrine of the Person of Christ. It has been customary in the past to describe this attempt as "Christology," but the use of this term is itself misleading. It suggests that the basic question is whether Jesus was the Christ or not, and if so, in what sense. Yet this leaves out of account a good many other issues. The term "Christ" or "Messiah" is strictly a Jewish category, and in Judaism it never meant divinity in the sense in which this latter term was applied to Jesus in the later doctrinal developments. No orthodox Jew would have said that the Messiah was "God," however exalted the status which he might give to this figure. One could, therefore, believe Jesus to have been the Messiah without this necessarily signifying divinity or deity. It is this issue with which we are chiefly concerned. It would be more accurate, therefore, to talk of the New Testament basis for the *divinity* of Jesus. In deference to traditional language, we shall continue to talk about Christology, but it is important for the reader to remember that the question at issue is that of divinity and not simply of the ascription to Jesus of a Jewish category of thought.

Let us then formulate the issue more precisely. Does the New Testament clearly center on the divinity or deity of Jesus? The word is absent. So is the two-nature doctrine in that linguistic form. The two-nature formula may be a legitimate deduction from the implications of what the New Testament says. The point is that the New Testament does not develop the issue in this kind of language. Jesus nowhere says, "I am God," a point to which further attention will be given later in this chapter. The question whether Jesus is God, therefore, is not simply a matter of language, important as this is, but rather of the basic meanings which underlie the New Testament itself. When these have been clarified, it is then possible to ask further questions about the kind of language it is legitimate to use, whether that language be biblical or nonbiblical.

It can be argued that the absence of the word "divinity" is not important since the New Testament clearly implies it in the language used about Jesus. Others hold that the problem of language is nonetheless vital and in particular as this involves the titles given to Jesus in the New Testament. If, for example, it can be shown that Jesus claimed Messiahship or Lordship or some other title, such as the Son of Man interpreted in a certain way, then this decides the issue. The question of divinity thus rests upon our ability to show beyond any reasonable doubt that Jesus spoke of Himself in certain ways which clearly imply divinity. Can this in fact be done? Yet others would maintain that although Jesus cannot absolutely be known to have used certain language about Himself, yet nevertheless His actions and words were such as to convey the reality of God through His life and ministry in such a way as to compel the disciples and later men of faith to talk of Him in terms of divinity. This would leave a good deal of freedom as to what we can claim about the language Jesus used, while leaving enough knowledge of His Person and activity to enable us to move a further stage to the confession of divinity. The latter claim would then depend, not upon any specific claim which the earthly Jesus made, but upon the total impact which He made upon men of faith and what they felt to be the inevitable implications of the divine reality they had experienced in Jesus.

We shall now try to clarify in more detail the problems raised by these positions. Since the question as to whether the New Testament concentrates upon the "divinity" demands at least some study of the actual content of the New Testament documents, we shall proceed first to this second point. This concerns the actual language of the New Testament itself and divides into two separate questions: (a) Are we in a position to talk about Jesus' self-understanding, and how did He express this and communicate it? (b) What language is used about Him by those who responded to His call? Where they employ language not used by Jesus, why did they feel it imperative to go beyond the language He used, and what did they intend to say and to mean by this new language?

Let us deal first of all with the self-understanding of Jesus. This obviously implies that at least some historical knowledge is available to enable us to give some answer to this question. How did Jesus conceive of His mission as one to which God had called him? How did He think of His own relationship to the God and Father of Israel whose agent He felt Himself to be? Did He conceive His role to be not only necessary but unique? Could He have believed both these things without claiming in any sense to be "God"? Is there any reason to believe that Jesus thought of Himself as not only a divine agent but as in some sense God present among men? And if He thought thus of Himself, how did He relate this stupendous claim to the fact that He prayed to the Father as Lord of Heaven and Earth and worshipped Him, as Jewish tradition required, as the transcendent Creator? These at least are the basic questions, even if it is discovered that Jesus never attempted to answer some of them.

As we have already indicated, it is now generally agreed that there is no evidence in the Synoptics that Jesus said "I am God" in so many words. Since Jesus spoke Aramaic, He would not in any case have used the word *Theos,* but rather the Jewish Yahweh or its Aramaic equivalent. In fact, Jesus calls Himself neither *Kyrios* nor *Theos* in the present Synoptic versions which we have in the Greek, with the possible exception of Mark 11:3. There are reasons which we shall mention later why Jesus would probably not have used such language about Himself. However, this does not resolve our question about the divinity in the negative, though it does emphasize the importance of being clear about the meaning of the language used. In the New Testament writings other than the Synoptics, there is evidence of a tendency to exalt Jesus to a status in relation to God which transcends the usual categories of Messiah or prophet. The Fourth Gospel seems to identify the Logos with God ($\theta\epsilon\grave{o}\varsigma$ $\mathring{\eta}\nu$ $\acute{o}$ $\lambda\acute{o}\gamma o\varsigma$, John 1:1). John 1:18 describes Jesus as the only God ($\mu o\nu o\gamma\epsilon\nu\mathring{\eta}\varsigma$ $\theta\epsilon\grave{o}\varsigma$) and in some ancient manuscripts as the only Son. In John 20:28 Thomas calls Jesus "My Lord and My God" ($\acute{o}$ $\kappa\acute{u}\rho\iota o\varsigma$ $\mu o\upsilon$ $\kappa\alpha\grave{\iota}$ $\acute{o}$ $\theta\acute{e}o\varsigma$ $\mu o\upsilon$). In Paul we have several striking phrases. Romans 9:5 is under debate, though some scholars think that Paul could have called Jesus "God" in this passage.[1] Philippians 2:6 refers to Jesus as being "in the form of God" ($\grave{\epsilon}\nu$ $\mu o\rho\phi\mathring{\eta}$ $\theta\epsilon o\hat{\upsilon}$). Colossians 2:9 speaks of the whole fullness of deity dwelling bodily in him ($\grave{\epsilon}\nu$ $\alpha\mathring{\upsilon}\tau\mathring{\omega}$ $\kappa\alpha\tau o\iota\kappa\epsilon\hat{\iota}$ $\pi\hat{\alpha}\nu$ $\tau\grave{o}$ $\pi\lambda\mathring{\eta}\rho\omega\mu\alpha$ $\tau\mathring{\eta}\varsigma$ $\theta\epsilon\acute{o}\tau\eta\tau o\varsigma$ $\sigma\omega\mu\alpha\tau\iota\kappa\hat{\omega}\varsigma$). Paul appears to pray to Christ in 2 Corinthians 12:8 ($\mathring{\upsilon}\pi\grave{\epsilon}\rho$ $\tauo\acute{u}\tau o\upsilon$ $\tau\rho\grave{\iota}\varsigma$ $\tau\grave{o}\nu$ $\kappa\acute{u}\rho\iota o\nu$ $\pi\alpha\rho\epsilon\kappa\acute{\alpha}\lambda\epsilon\sigma\alpha$). Titus 2:13 and 2 Peter 1:1 refer to Jesus as God and Savior. Hebrews 1:8ff. says "Thy throne, O God," apparently referring to the Son. In Revelation 1:13ff. the Ancient of Days of Daniel 10:5–7 becomes the Son of Man. Whatever precise meaning such language had for the writers who used it, it seems clear that the New Testament documents other than the Synoptics have moved beyond any language which Jesus used about Himself and that they are giving to Him a status in relation to God which transcends that of Messiahship as this was traditionally understood.[2]

The attempt to prove the divinity of Jesus by arguing from the significance of certain terms is illustrated again by the debate concerning the

[1]D.E.H. Whiteley, *The Theology of Saint Paul* (Oxford: Blackwell, 1964).

[2]Rudolf Bultmann, *Theology of the New Testament* (New York: Scribners, 1970), I, 3. For a clear discussion of the previously quoted texts, cf. Raymond E. Brown, *Jesus: God and Man* (Milwaukee: Bruce, 1967).

meaning of "Lord" (*Kyrios*). It is no longer possible to maintain in a simplistic way that since the Septuagint renders *Yahweh* by κύριος, and the latter term was used by the New Testament of Jesus, therefore the early Christians identified Jesus with Yahweh and consequently thought of Him as divine. Even if this argument were sound from a purely linguistic point of view, it would only demonstrate an interesting fact about the language used by the early Christians. It would not of itself clinch the matter as far as the theological issues are concerned.

In fact, the linguistic basis of the argument seems far from conclusive. As Conzelmann points out, "It is possible that even the primitive community called upon Jesus as Lord."[3] After all, the Aramaic *maranatha* has been preserved. In Hellenistic Christianity, however, the cry is now κύριος 'Ιησοῦς, the worship of the present reigning Lord, not the Coming One awaited at the end-time. Yet "the historical derivation of the title is an unsolved problem."[4] The fact that *kyrios* occurs only in Christian manuscripts of the Septuagint and not in Jewish ones, and that outside the LXX *kyrios* is unusual in Judaism as a designation for God makes it impossible to argue from the term to specific theological assertions of divinity.[5] This does not mean that the term *kyrios* is without significance in this connection. The fact that of the "lords many and the gods many" of the Graeco-Roman world, Jesus was believed to be the Lord in a unique sense is highly significant for the theological question as to His divinity. The question as to the precise implication of the term remains.

An identification of Jesus with God (*Yahweh*) on the basis of language, even if valid, would still leave unsolved the fundamental question of the exact meaning of the word "God" in this context. The problems raised in later chapters of this book under the question "Was all of God in Jesus?", i.e., the question of the principle of divine self-limitation in relation to the real limitations of power and knowledge in the historical figure of Jesus of Nazareth, show that the theological issues cannot be resolved by a simple appeal to linguistic usage, whether in the Septuagint or the New Testament. This is the basic reason why the church was compelled, as time went on, to grapple with the question of divinity as a theological issue and not simply repeat the biblical language without further comment as if this solved the problem.

The basic question is whether the attribution of divinity to Jesus which seems to be present in the New Testament writings other than the Synoptics

---

[3]Hans Conzelmann, *An Outline of the Theology of the New Testament*, trans. John Bowden (London: S.C.M., 1969), p. 82.
[4]*Ibid.*, p. 83.
[5]*Ibid.*

can justify itself in the light of anything which Jesus said about Himself, and even if it cannot appeal to any words of Jesus, whether the impact of His total life and ministry can be invoked as a reasonable basis for this "higher Christology." A further question is whether this language of the higher Christology meant "divinity" or "deity" in precisely the same sense as was implied by Nicaea and the later doctrinal developments up to Chalcedon. The rest of this chapter will be devoted to grappling with this issue.

We shall begin by trying to indicate the position taken by Rudolf Bultmann, not because we regard him as the only New Testament scholar worthy of consideration, but because his results are such as to raise these questions about Jesus' self-understanding in the most acute form. It is not the details of Bultmann's exegesis which concern us most at the moment or how far that exegesis would command the agreement of New Testament scholars in general. Rather our aim is to show what results would follow for Christology if certain historical conclusions are reached.

One of Bultmann's opening statements in *The Theology of the New Testament* deserves more than a passing reference: "But Christian faith did not exist until there was a Christian kerygma."[6] By this is presumably meant that in as far as Christian faith means the recognition of Jesus Christ crucified and risen as God's eschatological act of salvation, there would be no Christian faith until there had been such recognition. In one sense this is obviously so. In fact, the remark is trite unless there is more in it than meets the eye. If, however, the implication is that what faith confessed Him to be was in no sense what Jesus believed Himself to be, then this is a far-reaching theological proposition which is by no means self-evident and one which Bultmann should hardly make as if it were so obvious that no discussion of it were needed.

Bultmann tells us that the theology of the New Testament begins with the kerygma and not before. This at first might seem odd to the simple-minded. One would have thought that theology would have taken note of the message of Jesus or of His self-understanding or of certain events such as the resurrection. That, in Bultmann's view, it cannot do so can only mean either that we know so little about Jesus' mind as to make this starting point impossible, or that the real faith of the church is based upon ideas and interpretations which have no basis in Jesus' own understanding. Perhaps for Bultmann it is a bit of both. Yet neither assumption is self-evident. Bultmann himself goes on to say that the kerygma nevertheless presupposes the fact that Jesus had appeared and had proclaimed a message. What, then, can we

---

[6]Bultmann, *Theology of the New Testament*, I, 3.

know about the appearance of Jesus and His message according to Bultmann? Let us list the basic points:

(a) The dominant concept of Jesus' message was the Reign of God conceived as a miraculous event which will bring an end to the present evil age and usher in the final rule of righteousness, peace, and love. This God will bring about "without the help of man." This latter phrase is ambiguous. Why call for repentance at all if God can act so independently of human response? Jesus' basic presuppositions are apocalyptic and involve a cosmic catastrophe before the new age of the reign of God is established. Jesus, however, according to Bultmann, is very reticent about using the apocalyptic images or "painting in the details of the judgment, the resurrection and the glory to come."[7]

(b) The new age is very near and Jesus calls on men to make a decision. God's reign is dawning, even if it is not already here.

(c) Jesus is a "sign of the times," i.e., of the near approach of the Kingdom. Yet the Jesus of the Synoptics does not summon men to acknowledge or "believe" in His Person.[8]

(d) He does not proclaim Himself as Messiah. His life and work were not traditionally Messianic. There is no evidence that He reinterpreted or spiritualized the Messianic concept by fusing it with the Suffering Servant idea or in some other way.

(e) Jesus points ahead to the Son of Man as other than Himself.

(f) He did not found an order or a sect, still less a "church."

(g) There is no trace of a consciousness on His part of being the servant of God of Isaiah 53.

(h) He protests against Jewish legalism.

(i) All cultic and ritual regulations are excluded from the demands of God.

(j) He promises rewards and threatens hell-fire.

(k) He did not contest the authority of the Old Testament but He did make "critical distinctions among the demands of the Old Testament."[9]

(l) He indulges in no polemic against the temple cult.

(m) He refrains from making the love-commandment "concrete in specific prescriptions."[10]

(n) His preaching is directed, not to the nation as with the great prophets, but only to individuals. This shows that He is not interested in

---

[7]*Ibid.*, p. 5.
[8]*Ibid*, p. 15.
[9]*Ibid.*
[10]*Ibid.*, p. 19.

world reform in the sense of transforming institutions. He "de-historicizes" God and man, i.e., releases the relationship of God and man from its previous ties with history conceived as the affair of nations. The individual is now lifted out of history in the sense of a member of a national entity or collectivity and is confronted in splendid aloneness by the call of God for radical decision for or against the coming Kingdom which is now very near.

This in brief is what Bultmann thinks we can reconstruct of the historical Jesus and His message when stripped of later myth, legend, and theological interpretation. The Virgin Birth and the empty tomb are not historical facts. If the tomb was indeed found empty, it was not because Jesus had risen "corporeally" from the dead, for this is plainly impossible.[11] The atonement and the Parousia are "myths" and cannot be grounded in anything Jesus said, still less believed to be literal historical or eschatological "events." That Jesus "is the victim whose blood atones for our sins"; that "he bears vicariously the sins of the world, and by enduring the punishment for sin on our behalf, he delivers us from death"—"this mythological interpretation is a hotch-potch of sacrificial and juridical analogies, which have ceased to be tenable for us today."[12] Further, "an historical fact which involves a resurrection from the dead is utterly inconceivable."[13]

Professional New Testament scholars, not to mention the ordinary reader, will have no difficulty in recognizing how controversial or debatable many of the above statements are. For the present, however, we will provisionally accept Bultmann's reconstruction and ask what kind of a Christology could be built on this foundation. Since, on Bultmann's view, Jesus did not think of Himself as the Messiah, presumably the term "Christology" is itself a misnomer. We would have to rephrase our language and ask whether this account of Jesus could become the basis for any doctrine of divinity or whether the Chalcedonian "truly God and truly man" could possibly be applied to such a figure. The answer to this would seem to be no. Since Jesus was not at the center of His own message, according to Bultmann, it would seem illegitimate in principle to develop a theology in which He did occupy that central position.

Bultmann's position, however, is apparently a little more subtle than this. Let us start with the summary given by André Malet, something which we can do with some confidence since Bultmann has given his blessing to this exposition of his thought.[14]

---

[11]*Ibid.*, p. 25.

[12]Hans W. Bartsch, *Kerygma and Myth,* trans. R.H. Fuller (London: S.P.C.K., 1953), p. 35.

[13]*Ibid.*, p. 39.

[14]André Malet, *The Thought of Rudolf Bultmann,* trans. Richard Strachan (Shannon, Ireland: Irish Univ. Press, 1969).

Bultmann acknowledges that the early church was not content simply to repeat what Jesus said. Paul and John do in fact preach His Person. And Jesus Himself, says Bultmann, though He taught no doctrine about His Person, put forward the "fact of His Person" as decisive since He is the bearer of the message of the Word which calls for man's radical decision. Therefore, to decide for or against Him is to decide for or against God and His rule (Luke 12:8–9). A man's fate in the kingdom to come does, therefore, depend upon his attitude to Jesus and His message (Matthew 12:30). Bultmann then draws a subtle distinction between the "person" and the "personality" of Jesus. "Personality is the biological, psychological, sociological datum. Contrariwise, the person is the man insofar as he is ec-sistence and deed."[15] Jesus represented Himself to be God's saving deed, but His personality "has no importance at all in regard to this claim." The early Christians were aware that Jesus' personality could not offer a guarantee that He was God's saving deed for man. In any case, we cannot now write a biography of Jesus in which we penetrate into the mind or piety of Jesus in the psychological sense implied in a study of His personality.

The first obvious comment is to ask how "person" and "personality" can be distinguished in this sense without reducing "person" to a quite mysterious cipher. Malet argues that Bultmann's thesis involves a Christology but a Christology very different from the traditional one. Bultmann does apparently want to speak of an "act of God" in Jesus, though he realizes that he is open to the charge of using "mythological" language in thus speaking of God. Perhaps in as far as he sticks to his language about an act of God, he is logically compelled to admit that at this point there is a nonmythological element in the fact of Jesus and His death. It is important to realize what Bultmann includes in "personality," for this is expendable, not necessary as a basis for what we say about His "person." Personality includes the facts connected with Jesus' Jewishness. To call Him teacher, prophet, Messiah, Son of Man, Lord, or to speak of His expectations of the end of the world or of His Parousia, is simply to give us information about a personality conditioned by Jewish nurture and tradition. Even if it could be proved that Jesus had a Messianic consciousness or claimed to be the Son of Man, this would in no way guarantee or lead to the confession of faith that in this Jesus we meet God's final appeal to men and God's eschatological act which summons men to decision for the Kingdom which is about to come. "Messianic consciousness is only a psychical phenomenon. It has no bearing on whether the man with it is the man in whom God encounters us and the deed by which He saves us."[16] There have been other claimants to Messiahship, and the

---

[15]*Ibid.*, p. 153.
[16]*Ibid.*

Jewish community did not feel compelled to make their claim the basis for a doctrine of their "persons" comparable to the claim later made by Christians for Jesus.

It is clear, however, that Bultmann does not go the whole way in his distinction between "person" and "personality." What Jesus has to say about the imminent Kingdom is presumably not expendable, nor is it simply an interesting sociological fact rooted in His Jewish nurture and experience. It represents a new summons to a new relationship to God who is really acting through Jesus to bring men into the Kingdom when it comes. Yet if this can be said about Jesus' teaching of the Kingdom, by what criteria does Bultmann judge that other elements in His "personality" are to be excluded from consideration?

Moreover, even if we give him the benefit of the doubt on this question, it seems that Bultmann could not consistently develop a Christology in the later sense. Jesus, on Bultmann's view, is the divinely appointed messenger of the Kingdom; He is not God in the sense of Nicaea or Chalcedon. If one says, "So much the worse for the creeds," the problem remains. Jesus' claim to uniqueness, according to Bultmann, rests solely on His function as messenger, and man's salvation in no way depends upon a relation to Him but only to Him as the proclaimer of the Kingdom. Bultmann does not satisfactorily answer the question why Paul, John, and others are led to make Jesus Himself part of the message, instead of keeping strictly to what he considers to be Jesus' own message. One could always argue that it is a natural tendency for men to exalt outstanding religious personalities. Just as the Buddha's role in later Buddhism, particularly the Mahayana, is significantly different from the way in which Gotama thought of his own relationship to his teaching, so the early followers of Jesus gave Jesus a role which was alien to His own thinking about Himself. This, of course, is possible. But is this the explanation to which one is inevitably led by a rigorous historical analysis of the New Testament itself?

John, Paul, and the writer to the Hebrews all bear witness to the idea of a cosmic Christ. It seems certain, however, that the Jesus of the Synoptics did not speak of Himself in these cosmic terms, unless we accept some of the language of the Fourth Gospel as the actual words of Jesus. Even a fairly conservative exegesis of that gospel would hesitate to take such a stand. On the other hand, no Jew would have called the Messiah "God," though he might have given him the highest role among the "sons of God." If Jesus had said, "I am Yahweh," there can be little doubt that it would have thrown the disciples into complete mental and spiritual confusion. It would have been equivalent to saying, "I am the transcendent Creator of the Heavens and the Earth and the one through whom all that is has been made." We shall leave on one side for the moment the question of whether such ideas as preexistence were legitimate theological developments. What we need to give full weight to is the fact that they were later developments and not the actual language of Jesus Himself.

Granted this, the issue can now be formulated as follows. Do we know enough about Jesus of Nazareth to be able to affirm that He Himself is at the center of His proclamation and not merely His message about the near approach of the Kingdom? If we can show that in any sense His Person as well as His teaching is involved, did His own understanding of His role imply some concept of divinity? Furthermore, was there a sufficient basis for the later New Testament developments and for the credal statements which appeared in the post-apostolic era and found their authoritative formulation in the great ecumenical creeds?

Before trying to answer these questions, we shall take a brief look at the theological developments in the New Testament, with special reference to R. H. Fuller's analysis. Fuller distinguishes three basic Christological patterns:

(a) The earthly ministry, followed by the Resurrection and Ascension, then a period of inactive waiting until the Parousia when Jesus would return to consummate and vindicate his word and work. He becomes Messiah-designate at the Resurrection, but will enter the full expression of that role only at the Parousia. The continuing work of Jesus, according to this pattern, was thought of as an extension of the earthly work or an anticipation of the Parousia.

(b) A major shift of emphasis takes place in the Jewish Hellenistic stratum to an "exaltation" Christology. Jesus is no longer only Messiah-designate. He is already enthroned as Messiah and reigns as Christ and Lord over the continuing historical development of the church. The Parousia is still in the future. A more positive assessment is now given of the earthly life, and the Messianic titles are read back into the earthly ministry.

(c) Later Hellenistic Gentile developments. In order to meet the Gentile search for redemption and deliverance from the powers which hold men in servitude, the Christian missionaries took the further step of affirming the Redeemer's preexistence and incarnation. Here appears the language of descent from above, the idea of victory over the cosmic evil powers, and the re-ascension. When the pattern first appears in Philippians 2: 6–11, nothing is said about any *activity* of the preexistent One. Probably this was not a Pauline innovation but a common feature of the Gentile mission. Though at first conceived as a kenosis or self-emptying, the conception of the incarnate life soon became that of epiphany, that is, the full manifestation of God in the flesh. "Pre-existence, agency of creation, atoning death, resurrection and

exaltation, victory over the powers, continued reign in heaven until the
parousia, final consummation at the parousia—this represents the full pattern of the Christology in the gentile mission, though it never appears in
toto.''[17] It is this pattern, says Fuller, which lies behind the process which
culminates at Chalcedon.[18]

However, Fuller rejects Cullmann's view that the Christology of the
New Testament is purely functional. He does admit nonetheless that in the
earliest Palestinian stage and the earlier Jewish Hellenistic stratum, it is
predominantly functional, i.e., it is concerned with affirming what God has
done, is doing, and will do through Jesus. It is not concerned with ontic
statements, i.e., the attempt to make statements or develop a doctrine about
the ''nature'' or ''being'' of Jesus. It is only in the later Gentile mission
statements that we have the attempt to do this, e.g., in Philippians 2:6, where
it is asserted that the preexistent Son had the mode of existence of God. At
this stage ''encounter with Jesus is encounter not only with God in revelatory
and redemptive action, but encounter with His being.''[19]

Yet it must be confessed that this kind of language about function and
being is highly ambiguous. After all, what precisely is the difference
between encountering God in Jesus in redemptive activity and encountering
God in His being? One suspects that ambiguous and ill-defined notions of
''being'' are the cause of the confusion. If it is really the activity of God
which meets us in Jesus, then in some sense we are encountering the reality
of the presence of God, i.e., His being. Again one suspects that by the
''being'' of God is often meant God the transcendent in isolation from the
world which He has created. But neither the Bible nor Christians generally
have ever believed that God as Infinite Spirit can be directly perceived and
met. If we were confronted with naked, unmediated deity in this sense, we
would be overwhelmed. Indeed, Scripture assures us that no man has ever
''seen'' God. A modern philosopher of religion puts it in this way: ''For if
God were to disclose Himself to us in the coercive manner in which our
physical environment obtrudes itself, we should be dwarfed to nothingness
by His infinite power thus irresistibly breaking open the power of our
souls.''[20] For this reason and because God wishes to establish a relationship
of love and trust with his human creatures, ''God does not force an awareness
of himself upon them.''[21] God, therefore, never comes into a relationship

[17]R.H. Fuller, *The Foundations of New Testament Christology* (London: Collins, 1964),
p. 246.
[18]*Ibid.*
[19]*Ibid.*, p. 248.
[20]John Hick, *Arguments for the Existence of God* (London: Macmillan, 1970), p. 105.
[21]*Ibid.*

with men except in a mediated way. It would be alien to the Bible's way of thinking to speak of an unmediated manifestation of the divine being. Even in the case of Jesus, this would hold true, so that it is possible to "see" Jesus and not "see" His divinity as one sees an object with the compellingness which belongs to sense experience. Therefore, when the New Testament uses the language of divine activity rather than of nature or being, it does not follow that God is not really present and active, not only by proxy, as it were, but with what the late John Baillie called "mediated immediacy."

What Cullmann and Fuller call functional Christology, then, does not really evade the question of the nature of the reality involved. What or who is functioning? The answer can only be: God is functioning in this activity manifested through Jesus of Nazareth. The real question is therefore not "functional" versus "ontic," but whether the activity of God in Jesus is such as to justify faith in giving to Jesus an absolutely unique role in the locus of the divine activity without parallel elsewhere. Fuller's threefold pattern seems to show that the church was led irresistibly to this conclusion. Was it merely wishful thinking or was it authentic discernment? Was it only human reflection or response to a divine self-disclosure? The answer to these questions will determine the meaning we give to the term "divinity" as applied to Jesus. The New Testament expressed its positive convictions on these points in the later theological developments of the mission to the Gentiles by using the language of descent and ascent, preexistence, etc. These were no doubt the "models"[22] which came naturally to them in their particular religious and cultural context, even though these models were not used by Jesus Himself, or by the early Palestinian Christology (see Fuller's first stage). The crucial question for modern Christianity is whether these models have enduring value for us today or whether we can find other models which will do for us what descent and ascent, preexistence, etc. did for those earlier generations of Christians.

First, however, we must try to fill in the details of the most primitive Christology if we are to see whether these later models were justified, even in the New Testament period itself. Fuller's first stage seems comparable to what John Knox has called the "adoptionist" Christology of the earliest stage of the tradition. The word "adoptionist" is reminiscent of the later debates in the patristic period. Here, however, it means no more than the

---

[22]Perhaps I should add that I am using the word "model" here in the sense in which it has been used by I.T. Ramsey. He explains his preference for model over image because the latter has too strong psychological ancestry and tends to by-pass too many epistemological and ontological questions. 'Model is more neutral and leaves open the ontological issues for proper consideration.' Cf. Ian T. Ramsey, *Religious Language* (London: S.C.M., 1957), *Models and Mystery* (London: Oxford Univ. Press, 1964), and (ed.) *Words About God* (London: S.C.M., 1971), pp. 202ff.

view that Jesus' earthly career is presented without any advanced theological reflection except for the belief that through His death, resurrection, and ascension He was designated and appointed the Christ who would come again at the Parousia. Knox contends that it is not a question of whether the author of Luke-Acts himself held such an adoptionist Christology, since other elements are present in these books, but whether he affords evidence for the existence of such a Christology in the very earliest stages of the Christian tradition. Knox believes that Luke does afford such evidence and cites Acts 2:36: "God has made this man Jesus, whom you crucified, both Lord and Messiah." Knox admits that the notion of preexistence appeared very early and was already implicit in the idea of God's foreknowledge of Jesus.[23]

However, the point is that the adoptionist Christology is nearest in time to the earliest stages of the developing Christian tradition and presumably nearest to the way in which Jesus thought of His present and future role. Knox also raises the question of whether this early adoptionist Christology might not have been an adequate and continuing basis for the life, faith, and mission of the church. He seems to feel that it could have been sufficient, and this interpretation of Knox is strengthened when he implies later that "belief in the pre-existence of Jesus is incompatible with a belief in his genuine normal humanity."[24] We shall have to return later to this problem of the theological value or validity, if any, of the later models. For the moment, our concern is with what we have if we keep to the adoptionist model of Knox or Fuller's stage one. It is necessary to add that both these men begin with what Pannenberg calls a Christology "from below," i.e., they start with the career of Jesus of Nazareth in the simplest sense, stripped of later theological elaboration. Fuller, on the other hand, seems more convinced of the necessity of the later doctrinal developments and the importance of giving some kind of answer to the ontological questions of the nature and being of the reality disclosed in the life, death, and resurrection of Jesus.

To anyone, of course, who starts from Chalcedon and later doctrine, this so-called primitive Christology must inevitably seem so minimal as to be hardly worthy of the name at all. Indeed, to many still today, it seems a plain denial of His divinity. The kind of diagram given by Fuller in his book[25] appears to leave us with only a man later exalted to some kind of divine role, while the "orthodox" (in later credal terms) Christian wants to talk about God becoming man. If we do not go beyond this primitive pattern, then whom did the first Christians encounter when they met Jesus? They encountered God's

---

[23]Knox, *Humanity and Divinity*.
[24]*Ibid.*, p. 73.
[25]Fuller, *Foundations of New Testament Christology*, p. 243.

eschatological agent, making the call for the final and radical decision of men, a prophet of fearless courage who lived His obedience to the call of God to the bitter end in the Cross, a man through whom God's loving concern for men was manifest with a power and purity never seen before. In the strict sense, however, the first Christians were not confronting God in Jesus except in the sense that this was so with all the great prophets of the past and, some would say, is still so in the contemporary activity of God in modern men who are likewise obedient and faithful to His summons. Jesus may be the most significant and important of all the messengers of God. He is not, and could not be, so some would contend, God literally become man in the sense of Paul and John and the later creeds.

Yet, even on this view, we would be left with a remarkable person. Karl Barth once said that Jesus may have appeared as a normal Jewish rabbi to most people and not at all as an extraordinary personality. This seems a strange judgment since it seems unlikely that any momentous historical movement could be inaugurated by a very ordinary person. A reading of C.H. Dodd's chapter on Jesus the Teacher hardly leaves the impression of an average personality.[26] Those of us who lived through the period of Mahatma Gandhi's activity know what it is to be aware at the very least of the presence in the world of a very remarkable personality. Could Jesus have been any less remarkable? But however remarkable He was, it is still the case that this does not of itself add up to the later claim of divinity for this man Jesus.

The question, then, still needs to be asked, Were there any elements in the most primitive account of Jesus and His ministry which point beyond the adoptionist view of Knox and Fuller in his stage one? Both these men agree that the early church moved rapidly beyond this first stage. Was the church justified, and if so, on what basis? Professor Dodd has an interesting comment in his discussion of the incident in which the Roman centurion approaches Jesus on behalf of a sick member of his family (Matthew 8: 5–10; Luke 7:2–9). The soldier cites the kind of authority he exercises in his profession with the implication that Jesus too can command the authority of His superior. Dodd's comments: "But still more remarkable is it that Jesus seems to have endorsed it [i.e., the centurion's argument] and this could be only in the sense that the authority he exercises is that of Almighty God."[27] But a man who is already exercising the authority of God is beyond the category of prophet or teacher as normally understood. Certainly the Fourth Gospel thought so (John 8:28–29; 14:24), but we will not invoke that gospel for the moment. Dodd is also surely right in his contention that the famous

---

[26]Dodd, *Founder of Christianity*, Chapter IV.
[27]*Ibid.*, p. 50.

saying in Matthew 11:27 (Luke 20:22) implies a whole theology: "No man knows the Son but the Father, and no one knows the Father but the Son." On the lips of Jesus, this may be a spontaneous personal statement and not theological doctrine in the technical sense. On the other hand, can it be disregarded for that reason? At the very least, Jesus seems to be making some kind of special claim on the basis of his unique intimacy with the Father. This is confirmed by Jeremias, who insists that Matthew 11:27 by language, style, and structure "must be clearly assigned to a Semitic-speaking milieu."[28] In his view it is highly unlikely that a Johannine logion has found its way into the Synoptic corpus at this point in Matthew. What, then, does this saying mean? To quote Jeremias again: "Matthew 11:27 is a central statement about the mission of Jesus. His Father has granted Him the revelation of Himself as completely as only a father can disclose himself to his son. Therefore, only Jesus can pass on to others the real knowledge of God."[29] If this is so, then we must surely reject the categorical form of Bultmann's statement, previously quoted, that the Jesus of the Synoptics did not summon men to acknowledge or believe in His Person. Bultmann tries to justify this statement on the basis of the rather obscure distinction between person and personality. Yet this is still not convincing. Jesus does appear to be calling men to a special relationship to Himself as an indispensable means of their relationship to God. And this surely has enormously important consequences for any Christology or any doctrine of His Person or of His activity.

Did Jesus claim to forgive sins? As F.W. Dillistone has written: "If there is one pattern of His earthly activity which can be regarded as supported by a remarkable cluster of converging evidences, it is his going forth to seek and to save the lost."[30] This seems to have been accompanied by the promise of the gracious forgiveness and acceptance of the repentant sinner by God issued by Jesus on His authority. We are so used to this as Christians that we have forgotten how strange and offensive it would be both to the Jews and to others. If, of course, Jesus had said no more than "If you repent, God will accept you," then presumably no one would have been offended. The ground of offence seems to have been the linking of the promise and the effectiveness of the forgiveness with the words and actions of Jesus Himself. This point is brought out clearly and forcibly by Jeremias in his analysis of the meaning of the "poor" to whom the good news is preached. This term

---

[28]Joachim Jeremias, *New Testament Theology Part One–The Proclamation of Jesus,* trans. John Bowden (London: S.C.M., 1971), p. 57.

[29]*Ibid.,* p. 61.

[30]F.W. Dillistone, *The Christian Understanding of the Atonement* (London: Nisbet, 1968), p. 270.

covers not only the economically poor or only sinners in a very restricted moral sense, but also those who occupied despised trades, such as tax-collectors, publicans, and money-changers. In fact, it means all who bear public contempt and in addition are excluded by their self-righteous neighbors from all hope of God's salvation.[31] These poor are offered God's forgiveness by Jesus not only in word but in action to the scandal of many of His contemporaries when He invites them to share table-fellowship with Him. There is nothing comparable in contemporary Judaism, says Jeremias, and this is confirmed by the Qumran documents: "his table-fellowship with sinners was the pre-Easter scandal."[32] Here, says Jeremias, we certainly have the *ipsissima vox* of Jesus, an expression of an authentic attitude shown by the pre-Easter Jesus in his historical activity.

It is worth dwelling for a moment upon Jeremias' distinction between the *ipsissima verba* and the *ipsissima vox* of Jesus. The former has often been interpreted as if the absence of a tape-recorded collection of Jesus' sayings means that we can never discover the mind or the attitude of the pre-Easter Jesus. This, however, is not so. It is meanings, not words, which count, and by this criterion we can speak of knowing the mind of Jesus in His pre-Easter activity, as Jeremias does in the impressive number of occasions when he speaks of an element in the tradition which must be taken to reflect the *ipsissima vox* of Jesus. Dodd has also pointed out that the charge of blasphemy at the trial has a special significance. "The term is a heavily loaded one, and the charge suggests an affront to powerful sentiments of religious reverence and awe, evoking both hatred and fear."[33] Jesus must have done or said something which could provoke such a revulsion of feeling against Him. Let us recall again the purpose of this discussion. We are asking whether in the very primitive strata of the tradition there are elements which already point to an at least implicit doctrine of His Person. Our conclusion is that already at this stage Jesus is part of His message, even if this is not spelled out in terms of later doctrine. If this is so, then it would at least explain intelligibly why Paul and John go beyond the message of Jesus to include Jesus Himself in their proclamation of the kerygma. The question, however, still remains as to whether the "models" they employed to express this were simply distorting or of limited value, confined to a particular historical and cultural stage in the church's development. This problem we shall defer until other wider issues have been considered.

To return for a moment to Bultmann's list given earlier, it must be emphasized that his judgments are by no means universally shared. We

---

[31]Jeremias, *New Testament Theology*, p. 113.
[32]*Ibid.*, p. 121.
[33]Dodd, *Founder of Christianity*, p. 78.

may cite, for example, Cullmann's discussion of such basic ideas as Messiahship and the Son of Man. It is true that to show conclusively that Jesus applied these to Himself in some sense would not settle once and for all the question of divinity. On the other hand, it might throw very important light on the way in which Jesus conceived His role in the pre-Easter period, and this could be very significant for any doctrine of His Person. Bultmann, as we have seen, rejects the idea that Jesus applied the title Son of Man to Himself in any sense. Cullmann insists that we must distinguish between Jesus' sayings about the Son of Man which refer to the eschatological work He must fulfil in the future and those sayings in which He applies the title to His earthly task.[34] The former sayings, at the very least, represent a pronounced statement of majesty. Says Cullmann, "Anyone who accepts these sayings as genuine [i.e., the eschatological ones] but tries to explain them by the theory that Jesus designates someone other than himself as the coming Son of Man, raises more problems than he solves."[35] This leaves us with the question whether Jesus could have ascribed the function of the Son of Man to Himself within the framework of His earthly life's work. Cullmann answers this in the affirmative on the basis of Jesus' fusion of the suffering ebed Yahweh with the Son of Man concept. This involves in turn the view that the Son of Man becomes incarnate in man in the ordinary human framework, a radically new idea both in respect to Philo and Jewish Christians as well as in respect to Daniel and Enoch.[36] Cullmann's conclusion, therefore, is that Jesus used the title Son of Man:

(a) to express His consciousness of having to fulfil the mission of the Heavenly Man in glory at the end of time.

(b) in the humiliation of the Incarnation among sinful men.[37]

Cullmann admits that the Synoptic writers do not develop a Son of Man Christology but rather see Him as the Messiah, i.e., the Christ. However, if the pre-Easter Jesus did think of His role in this way, it is significant for any further theological elaboration of the answer to the question, Who do you say that I am?

To sum up this complex discussion, our conclusion is that Jesus Himself is integral to His proclamation of the Kingdom. In this case, it is not

---

[34]Oscar Cullmann, *The Christology of the New Testament*, trans. Shirley G. Guthrie and Charles A.M. Hall (London: S.C.M., 1959), p. 155.

[35]*Ibid.*, p. 156.

[36]*Ibid.*, p. 159.

[37]*Ibid.*, p. 164.

adequate to detach the message from the messenger, the teaching from the teacher, the proclamation of the Kingdom from the bearer of the Kingdom. This means that the significance of Jesus demands an interpretation of His Person as central to all He said and did. In short, it demands a Christology which requires some attention to His being and nature. That the language of being and nature in a non-Christian philosophical context sometimes suggests a "static" concept of God by no means requires the abandonment of this kind of language altogether. However, it is not the language as such which matters but the reality to which the symbolic linguistic activity of men refers. In other words, faith felt compelled to say something about what Jesus intrinsically is in Himself. These are questions about being and nature, even though we wish to interpret this ontological language in those dynamic terms demanded by the biblical understanding of a living and creative God in contrast to certain philosophical concepts of deity which are supposed to imply a "static" God.

Before we continue to draw out the implications for later Christian experience and reflection of what has been said, we must pay attention to certain basic issues concerning the way in which the historian arrives at historical judgments and the importance which historical statements have for the man of faith. It is in this area where the most acute difficulties lie for many thoughtful contemporary Christians. The first thing which needs to be said is that a historical judgment to the effect that certain events and certain human actions took place at some time in the past does not of itself resolve the questions which one can ask about God. One might, for example, arrive at a high degree of certainty about what Jesus said or did but we could still raise the question as to whether His claims about God were well founded. A purely historical judgment would not solve this problem. An affirmation to the effect that God is real involves certain value judgments as well as statements about what happened historically. In other words, there is no automatic and logically inevitable progression from historical judgments to the assertion that God "is" or "acts" in a certain way.

The conclusion to be drawn from this, however, is not that we should seek refuge in a mysticism which dispenses with historical media altogether. Some historical basis may be necessary for the statement that God acts in history. For example, it would hardly make sense to say that God was active and present in Jesus if we had absolutely no historical confidence that Jesus of Nazareth was truly a human figure who had actually lived and died. Christian faith, therefore, is profoundly concerned with our ability to arrive at some reliable knowledge of the historical reality, even if the latter does not make faith's interpretation of that reality a logically inevitable consequence.

Van A. Harvey, who has written one of the most penetrating of recent books
on the subject, correctly writes:

> The criteria for deciding whether believing in the trustworthiness of God is a
> morally responsible act or not are quite different from the criteria for judging
> whether a belief that a given event happened in such a way or not is justifiable,
> just as both sets of criteria will differ from that brought forward to assess some
> historical standpoint.[38]

We shall not attempt to go over again the ground so ably covered by
Harvey but to consider his conclusions as they bear upon our question of the
possibility of a Christology. In our judgment, he rightly refuses to be forced
into a position where the alternatives are either a "presuppositionless history" or the claim that "every historian has his presuppositions."[39] These
claims, he says, are not so much false as crude. There is no such thing as a
bare uninterpreted fact. On the other hand, the historian is not a romantic
novelist who can weave any story he likes. Furthermore, when one talks of
presuppositions, one has to remember that there are different kinds of
presuppositions which determine the writing of different kinds of history.
"We see that historians do not carry around monolithic sets of warrants that
apply in the same way in every field."[40] Thus, says Harvey, "the real
issue . . . is not whether faith is independent of all historical criticism but
whether Christian faith requires certain specific historical assertions that, in
the nature of the case, are dubious or not fully justified."[41]

This is indeed the crucial issue, and we propose to make certain
comments upon it. It is important at the outset to be clear about the meaning
of the word "history." Do we mean by it what actually happened as this
might be known or interpreted by an omniscient observer, or do we mean the
knowledge of the past which men can reasonably arrive at from a reconstruction of the past based on whatever sources or records are available? Clearly
the latter is the only alternative open to us. In the case of Jesus, when we ask
what the phrase "Jesus of Nazareth" refers to, the following components
seem to be involved, according to Harvey: (1) the actual Jesus; (2) the
historical Jesus; (3) the perspectival image or memory impression of Jesus;
(4) the biblical Christ.

The actual Jesus, according to this classification, would be Jesus as He
really was—the actual historical person with all the determinate relation-

---

[38]Van A. Harvey, *The Historian and the Believer* (Toronto: Collier-Macmillan, 1969),
p. xvii.
[39]*Ibid.*, p. 248.
[40]*Ibid.*, p. 249.
[41]*Ibid.*

ships He had to God, nature, other persons, and the particular society and culture of which He was a part. In this sense, we do not have, and by the nature of the case cannot have, an absolutely complete knowledge of any person living or dead. Only God, if such there be, could have this total knowledge. This, however, does not entail complete historical agnosticism. The fact that we do not have this kind of complete knowledge about any person does not mean that we have no knowledge at all about any actual person. The "actual person" may mysteriously transcend our knowledge of him. Yet the knowledge we have may be both significant and illuminating.

The historical Jesus, to adopt Harvey's use of this phrase, will be the Jesus we can know on the basis of inferences from our present sources—written, archeological, institutional, etc. Since historians differ as to what may be inferred from the sources, we have to distinguish between what most historians agree upon and those elements about which there is a diversity of historical judgment.

The perspectival or memory image of Jesus presupposes some of the facts arrived at in the search for the historical Jesus but differs in the sense that here we have the record of how the person in question affected those with whom he came into contact. At some point, there must have been memory impressions of Jesus which go back to some eye-witnesses, i.e., people who were in actual contact with Him. However, as we know from our present experience, memory is both selective and fallible. We remember some things more vividly than others, and this remembrance is determined not only by the vividness of the sense-impressions but by what at the time seemed to us to have special significance and value. We are apt to forget or overlook features which at the time seemed to us unimportant or which did not evoke our interest. Some people see or hear more than others not because they have better seeing or hearing in the physical sense, but because they are sympathetically and imaginatively sensitive to aspects of a human personality to which others may be completely blind. The memory-impression is intrinsically bound up, therefore, with value judgments, and in this realm of value, spiritual things are spiritually discerned.

This perspectival image or memory impression raises very complex problems for our subject of Christology. The earliest Christian community remembered some things about Jesus more vividly than other things. It made its own selection of sayings, parables, teachings, and actions because these seemed to be especially significant and characteristic of Jesus. The Crucifixion obviously left a profound and permanent memory impression upon the original disciples, and this was communicated to succeeding generations of Christians. The Resurrection appearances, whatever they were, were indelibly stamped upon the memories of certain persons, and their witness to their experience shaped, as we know, their interpretation of the events and the documents of the New Testament which record them. Harvey reminds us that such a perspectival or memory impression need not be arrived at through the methods associated with modern historical research, nor is it less true for that reason. The problem still remains, however, as to whether this perspectival image is reconcilable with the kind of inferential knowledge of a human personality arrived at by a scientific analysis and study of the available sources. If the contrast between them is so great as to result in a complete disparity, then one would be faced with accepting the perspectival image on the authority of the image alone and abandoning all effort to relate it to historical knowledge arrived at by modern methods of investigation. On the other hand, as Harvey insists, modern historical research may discover that the image represents a reliable memory impression and that this latter impression has "some real correlation with the historical Jesus and the actual Jesus."[42]

The fourth heading of Harvey's, the biblical Christ, raises a further series of complicating factors. One could, for example, have a number of perspectival images and memory-impressions, reconcilable with knowledge arrived at by historical methods. Pontius Pilate, Annas and Caiaphas, Judas, the Roman centurion could all have transmitted memory impressions of Jesus which would not necessarily contradict the historical reconstruction but which would give us a very different moral and spiritual assessment of Jesus than the one we have. In actual fact, we have only the memory impressions preserved in the living tradition of the Christian community. This, of course, raises other problems, for how do we know whether the selection of important elements involved in the perspectival image was not quite arbitrary and subjective? How do we know that the early disciples' selection of significant detail was not an arbitrary imposition on the authentic reality? Why should not Pilate's assessment of Jesus be just as valid as that of the believing disciples?

We shall have to return to this issue again. For the moment, it is important to clarify the meaning of the phrase "the biblical Christ." Here we are not only dealing with a perspectival image rooted in memory impressions and involving the selection of some elements as more significant than others. We are also dealing with an interpretation or a series of interpretations of those selected elements. For example, the perspectival image includes the Cross as a fundamentally significant fact in the career of Jesus. When, however, the death is intepreted in relation to the foreordaining will of God or as a sacrifice or a vicarious and substitutionary punishment on the ground

---

[42]*Ibid.*, p. 267.

of which man receives divine forgiveness, we have obviously moved far beyond a generalized assertion that the Crucifixion was a highly significant element to very specific statements to the effect that this or that way of looking at the Cross is the "true" meaning or significance of the event.

In addition, we are confronted by the fact that there is not in any simple sense one unified view of the "biblical Christ." As we have already seen in the study of the biblical material, there is a remarkable variety of standpoints and attitudes. Once again, however, we must not prejudge the question of whether the varied interpretations could not be applied without contradiction to the "one reality."[43] Yet, as Harvey again insists, unless the historian is a merely passive transmitter of traditions, "his task compels him to interpret the interpretations."[44] He must decide whether the different interpretations are reconcilable with the actual Jesus, the historical Jesus, and the perspectival image based on memory impressions. He must decide whether this further interpretation is a legitimate development or merely wishful thinking.

But how could an historian simply as historian go about answering this kind of question? Let us try to answer this by an oversimplified attention to one fact. Remembering the precise meanings given by Harvey to the phrases "the actual Jesus" and "the historical Jesus," we could say the following. If the inferential knowledge from the available records and sources made it overwhelmingly probable that there was no historical figure who was crucified under Pontius Pilate, then we would have to say that there was no actual Jesus and no historical Jesus. In this case, we would have to concern ourselves with the psychology and genesis of myth and not bother further about historical statements about what happened. If we were driven to this position, then a doctrine of the Person of Christ would no longer be a meaningful possibility. We might still want to argue that a certain kind of truth about God or man was being mediated through these myths. But it would no longer make sense to make the truth of these myths depend upon historical assertions. This is an attractive solution to many, yet the result is so different from any form of Christianity known to us that we are no longer talking about the same thing. For the moment, however, let us assume that the "historical Jesus," in the sense above defined, is known at least in part,

[43]C.H. Dodd, "The Portrait of Jesus in John and in the Synoptics" in *Christian History and Interpretation: Studies Presented to John Knox,* eds. W.R. Farmer, C.F.D. Moule, and R.R. Niebuhr (London: Cambridge Univ. Press, 1967), pp. 183ff. "He [i.e., John] will have had, through memories or tradition available to him, access to the sitter, and the similarities we have noted will go far to assure us that behind the two renderings of the portrait there stands a real historical person" (*Christian History and Interpretation,* p. 195).
[44]Harvey, *Historian and Believer,* p. 277.

and that the historical picture reconstructed from all the sources is not hopelessly in conflict with the perspectival image rooted in memory impressions. Then we might say that there is no reasonable doubt that Jesus was crucified under Pontius Pilate and that He went to His death in the belief that He was doing the will of the Father and that His death would be a decisive factor in establishing a new relationship of forgiveness and reconciliation between God and man. Historical certainty about these things does not logically compel the theological certainty of faith. How would an historian as such go about deciding whether Jesus was justified in interpreting the significance of His death in this way? Obviously, more is involved here than simply the reconstruction of an historical account of a certain sequence of events. As Harvey says, the historian must interpret the interpretations. But what sort of criteria now become relevant to this question?

Before making our final comments on Harvey's discussion of the biblical Christ and his claim that the historian must now become an interpreter of interpretations, we shall digress briefly to consider Ernst Käsemann's thesis.[45] The name of Käsemann is associated with recent tendencies in New Testament scholarship to seek a more positive answer to the question of the historical Jesus than Bultmann was apparently prepared to allow. This, however, in no wise means that Käsemann is associating himself with the liberal quest in its nineteenth-century form. If it is possible to claim authentic knowledge of the historical Jesus in terms of criteria which would be acceptable to the professional historian, this is simply because the primitive Christian community was concerned to maintain the identity of Jesus of Nazareth and the risen Christ whom it worshipped as its present Lord. On the other hand, the New Testament does not permit us to arrive at a mere history of the man Jesus which can be separated from the interpretation of faith. "For this purpose," observes Käsemann, "primitive Christianity allows mere history no vehicle of expression other than the kerygma."[46] Or again: "For Cross and Resurrection are no longer regarded from the standpoint of the historian but are expounded in their saving significance."[47] This means that it is no longer possible to write a history of Jesus as a detached historical figure. In Harvey's terminology, the actual Jesus, the historical Jesus, the perspectival or memory Jesus, and the biblical Christ are so inextricably combined that they can no longer be separated. "Our only access to Jesus is through the medium of the primitive Christian gospel."[48] "The historical

[45]Ernst Käsemann, *Essays on New Testament Themes,* Studies in Biblical Theology No. 4, trans. W.J. Montague (London: S.C.M., 1960), pp. 15ff.

[46]*Ibid.,* p. 21.

[47]*Ibid.,* p. 23.

[48]*Ibid.*

Jesus meets us in the New Testament, our only real and original documentation of Him, not as he was in himself, not as an isolated individual, but as the Lord of the community which believes in him.''[49]

The ambiguity of this language about God in Himself or Jesus in Himself raises issues with which we shall have to deal again and again in this study. If all it means is that our sources only permit us to see Jesus from the perspective of faith, this has already been conceded. The crucial problem is whether we could talk of Jesus in Himself as essentially not what faith discerned Him to be. This recalls the well-known criticism levelled against the liberal quest for the historical Jesus by Martin Kähler at the end of the nineteenth century.[50] Kähler made the oft-quoted remark that ''I regard the entire Life-of-Jesus movement as a blind alley.''[51] This sweeping statement came from his conviction that the Christian is saved by his belief in the exalted and risen Christ. A reconstruction of the historical Jesus in a manner which fails to show the essential connection with this faith not only involves an illegitimate handling of the sources, i.e., the New Testament documents, but is also motivated by the desire to get behind the Christ of dogma to a Jesus who could then be invoked as a norm for the criticism of dogma. For Kähler, this is not only historically but also theologically illegitimate. It simply canot be done. This point has been emphasized many times since both by New Testament scholars and by systematic theologians. One need only mention Bultmann, Käsemann, and Tillich, and among non-German scholars, John Knox,[52] Denis Nineham,[53] Gerald F. Downing,[54] and the late C.H. Dodd.

There seems, therefore, widespread agreement that what we know of Jesus can come only through sources which already have a faith-perspective. Thus, says Käsemann again, the very formula ''the historical Jesus'' should perhaps be dismissed as inappropriate if it suggests, as it does to most people, the hope of a life story of Jesus completely free from the faith-interpretation of the community which acknowledged Him as Lord. ''We only make contact with the life history of Jesus through the kerygma of the community.''[55]

---

[49]*Ibid.*

[50]Martin Kähler, *The So-Called Historical Jesus and the Historic Biblical Christ,* trans., ed., and with an introduction by Carl E. Braaten (Philadelphia: Fortress, 1964).

[51]*Ibid.,* p. 46.

[52]John Knox, *The Church and the Reality of Christ* (New York: Harper & Row, 1962).

[53]Denis Nineham, *Saint Mark,* Pelican Gospel Commentaries (Harmondsworth: Penguin, 1963).

[54]Gerald F. Downing, *The Church and Jesus,* Studies in Biblical Theology, Second Series, No. 10 (London: S.C.M., 1968).

[55]Käsemann, *Essays,* p. 24.

Yet this must be taken at its full weight. We do, after all, know something of the life history of Jesus through the kerygma, and its importance must not be underrated. Although primitive Christianity took the view that the earthly significance of Jesus can be understood only from the far side of Easter, yet "the event of Easter cannot be adequately comprehended if it is looked at apart from the earthly Jesus."[56] The eschatological event, the coming of the Kingdom into the present aeon, is bound to this man from Nazareth. The Gospel of John, so concerned to stress the abiding presence of the exalted Lord, makes its point by placing this "within the framework of a history of the earthly Jesus."[57] "The story of the exalted Lord and that of the humiliated Lord . . . [is] one and the same story."[58]

The conclusion to which this leads is, for Käsemann, paradoxical in the extreme. If we start with the New Testament faith in the risen and exalted Lord, we have to postulate a historical Jesus because the earthly and the exalted Lord are one for that faith. On the other hand, modern biblical study has failed to provide us with any foolproof criteria by which we can identify the authentic Jesus material. The nearest we get to the *ipsissima vox,* if not the *ipsissima verba,* of the historical Jesus is in the parables. Even here, however, form-criticism presents many problems about assigning the material to Jesus, even though it may feel that it can speak with a high degree of probability about the gospels, and in particular the parables and certain sayings. Further, we lack a conspectus of the very early stage of primitive Christian history.[59] Certainly Jesus was a Jew and made the assumptions of Jewish piety; yet He also shatters the Jewish framework by His astonishing claims. For example, the ancient worldview antithesis of sacred and profane and its demonology can no longer stand in the face of Jesus' challenge. Käsemann, like Bultmann, is quite sceptical about ascribing to Jesus' own usage such titles as Messiah and Son of Man. Certainly he still insists that there are pieces of the Synoptic tradition which the historian must accept if he is to remain a historian, but they are only pieces. On the other hand, the earthly Jesus has been so swallowed up in the exalted Lord, yet the early Christian community still insists on the distinct identity of the two. The historian establishes the riddle but cannot solve it. Only as we share the community's faith do we come at the same time to share their confidence that the earthly and the exalted Lord is one and the same. There is, however, no way by which we can reach the earthly Jesus by purely historical research, and so this kind of confidence can be attained only by sharing now the

---

[56]*Ibid.,* p. 25.
[57]*Ibid.,* p. 31.
[58]*Ibid.,* p. 32.
[59]*Ibid.,* p. 36.

community's faith. We have to go by way of the primitive community's faith to gain their confidence about who the historical Jesus really was and what His significance for men might be.

Despite the cogency and persuasiveness with which this thesis is presented, it can hardly be taken as the final word. If the early Christian community was so deeply convinced of the identity of the humiliated and the exalted Lord, then its interest in the historical reality of the humiliated Jesus must have been more than nominal. The very fact that it produced the gospels at all suggests that it was not content only to proclaim the power of the exalted Lord in the present but wished to establish His continuity and identity with the life and ministry of the earthly Jesus. The fact that the community was controlled in its activity by faith does not mean that it had no interest in historical reality, even though they did not work consciously with the criteria determined according to the canons of historical research developed from the eighteenth century onwards. That the authors of the gospels were not historians in the modern sense does not dispose of their claims to be giving us history, even as this would be defined today. Käsemann, indeed, would not deny this, though one could wish that he had more fully considered the possibility that faith might discern reality as well as interpret it. This way of speaking may strike us as odd, but this is because faith today is often defined primarily in terms of its psychology to the exclusion of the possibility that faith may be an insight into reality, and that it is therefore cognitive as well as merely psychological. This would seem to be implied in Bornkamm's remark that "our task is to seek the history in the kerygma and in this history to seek the kerygma."[60]

Another problem which emerges from Käsemann's thesis concerns the nature of the primitive Christian community, which, it now seems, must support the whole weight of the faith. As F. Gerald Downing points out, this only renders more urgent the "quest for the historical primitive church" which must now replace the quest of the historical Jesus in the nineteenth-century sense. If one says, for example, with John Knox that to deny the actual existence of the church would be to deny more than the possibility of our knowing God's act in Christ, it would be to deny the very existence of the act itself[61]—then it becomes imperative to have a clear idea of the church for which such great claims are being made. Yet this may prove to be an even more exacting task than the old "quest." A further consideration which Knox's position raises springs from the imperfection and sinfulness of the church, however we define it and at whatever period of history we study it.

---

[60]Günther Bornkamm, *Jesus of Nazareth,* trans. Irene and Fraser McLuskey with James M. Robinson (London: Hodder & Stoughton, 1960).
[61]Downing, *Church and Jesus.*

Norman Pittenger is certainly correct in affirming that "it is impossible to talk as if there were a precise identity between him [i.e., Jesus] and the Church."[62]

Since the "problem of the historian's own historicity has become a fundamental problem,"[63] the interpretative element in the historian's work and the relativity of his judgments will be just as real for the study of the primitive church as it was for the old "quest." Could one achieve any more "objectivity" in the study of the early church than in the case of Jesus? The same sceptical conclusions about this quest for the primitive church could be reached as in the old quest for the historical Jesus. Faith will interpret the significance of the development of the early church in a way strikingly different from the way an historian who is far removed from all theological presuppositions would interpret it. An historian might seek for a sociological phenomenon called the "church" or "the church in itself," apart from the way in which faith interprets the sequence of events. Yet it is as impossible from the records to penetrate to a church in terms of sociology alone as it is to get to a Jesus stripped entirely of the significance which faith found in Him.

Downing has seen very clearly that there is no way out of this impasse unless historians are willing to embark upon a thorough philosophical analysis of what it means to talk of a fact, whether historical or otherwise. On the other hand, Downing points out that the historian is no worse off than any other kind of investigator.[64] Downing is obviously not happy with Alan Richardson's claim that "history is from first to last interpretation."[65] There is, of course, an interpretative factor, but this is not peculiar to history. It belongs to all the sciences, including physics. "There is no perfectly 'objective' relation of statements to facts by comparison with which the relation of the historian's statements to facts must appear *uniquely* subjective."[66] Nevertheless, as we have emphasized, the historian is not a romantic novelist. True, he may have to be an interpreter of interpretations, but "the interpretation must refer to evidence, in detail and in large, that can be shown to be as nearly factual as circumstances allow."[67]

Certainly one could assert that the Resurrection is indispensable to a reasonable explanation of certain events and human actions, or at least that in

[62]Norman Pittenger, *Christology Reconsidered* (London: S.C.M., 1970), p. 98.
[63]James M. Robinson, *A New Quest of the Historical Jesus*, Studies in Biblical Theology, No. 25 (London: S.C.M., 1968), p. 30.
[64]Downing, *Church and Jesus*, p. 137.
[65]Alan Richardson, *History Sacred and Profane* (London: S.C.M., 1964), pp. 161, 190ff.
[66]Downing, p. 143.
[67]*Ibid.*, p. 146.

all probability a certain sequence of events makes little sense, even on strictly historical grounds, apart from the conviction that Jesus was raised. But the meaning of the fact and the nature of the fact itself in the Christian sense requires a response of faith and certain value judgments which faith spontaneously makes. In this case, as Tillich once remarked in other connections, the circle of our reasoning may not be vicious. Faith's interpretation of the evidence may be wishful thinking or it may a true discernment of the fact, but this question is obviously not going to be settled by further historical research. Certainly, the response of faith in the Christian sense could not arise if the factuality of the Resurrection was denied in any and every sense. The crucial question is whether faith is interpreting some given reality, whatever that is, or creating the reality out of its own psychological resources. Thus the historian cannot be merely an interpreter of interpretations. Otherwise, he would never be dealing with reality in any sense other than the psychological.

Another facet of this same problem emerges from J.M. Robinson's discussion of the "procedure of the new quest." If the relation of the earthly Jesus to the kerygma cannot be solved by simply assuming that Jesus proclaimed the later kerygma in full detail in his earthly ministry, it is still legitimate to ask whether through faith and historical study we can have an "encounter" with Jesus as significant as that had, according to some, by the primitive church. Robinson believes that we can. There is enough material, historically assured, both in quality and quantity, to make such an encounter possible. Jesus' "action, the intention latent in it, the understanding of existence it implies, and thus his selfhood, can be encountered historically."[68]

The difference between this view and the earlier quest must be stressed again. The nineteenth-century search for the Jesus of history was prompted by the hope that it would be possible to discover a Jesus who, stripped of dogma and the kerygma's interpretation of His significance, could then be used as an independent norm to judge the church's faith and its later doctrinal expressions.[69] It hoped to dispense with faith as an existential commitment involving risk and to substitute an historical figure who would turn faith into sheer historical actuality, which could be accepted without such a risk. But this, we have asserted, can never be the case.

The conclusion would appear to be that there is no understanding of Jesus of Nazareth in His earthly existence or of the faith of the church concerning Him unless my own present existence is somehow challenged

---

[68]Robinson, *New Quest*, p. 105.
[69]Kähler, *Historical Jesus*, pp. 42ff.

and my personal response evoked in a manner which transforms my present existence. In a sense, this should have been obvious all along. If we had the most detailed and reliable historical knowledge of Jesus, plus all that the modern media could provide, this would not and could not compel the faith which transforms my existence now. This did not happen in the days of His flesh; it could not happen later or now. Understanding Jesus means understanding His "transcendent selfhood."

It becomes ever clearer, then, that the crucial question is the reality and present activity of God. To talk of encountering Jesus' essential selfhood or His transcendent selfhood involves a faith which cannot simply be read off from the historical evidence alone. One of the enduring marks of the impression which Jesus made was His power to awaken in men faith in God. This involves more than a historical judgment about certain evidence. Obviously Jesus could not awaken faith if He was not an actual historical person. But Jesus' historicity does not guarantee that faith will be aroused. Of course, it is possible to argue that faith in God could be aroused by a myth which was in no way dependent upon historical fact of any kind. The response to this must be that such is no longer Christian faith, since, as Käsemann emphasized, the primitive church insisted on identifying the exalted and the humiliated Lord. This identification is at the heart of Christian belief, even if our knowledge of the earthly Jesus, in terms which would satisfy a modern historian, is very limited. We are back to our fundamental issue, namely whether it is possible to find enough history in the kerygma and the gospels to sustain and make sense of the faith which was aroused by the proclamation.

To return now to Harvey, certainly the criteria for the validity of faith's interpretation of the interpretations will be much more complex than those involved in making an historical judgment about a past event or events. Whether the kind of God Jesus talks about and discloses in His actions is more than a psychological projection based upon the peculiar individual experience of Jesus can be resolved only in the context of a whole series of assertions about the nature of the "ultimately real."

Once faith is self-conscious enough to begin to ask about the proper understanding of itself, then its decision about the ground of faith will involve many elements. One could, of course, believe in God on the basis of authority alone, whether of book or institution or both. It is safe to say that for many Christians the role of such authority is very great and often decisive. Nor does any Christian turn his back entirely upon Scripture and the continuing experience of the "people of God" in history. Yet, once faith seeks understanding, the basis of that authority becomes more complex. It is no longer sheer authority of an external kind. The authority itself becomes internal to the degree that the believer's acceptance of that authority now includes rational, moral, and perhaps logical factors, and a series of value judgments which he finds it proper to make on the basis of his total experience. In other words, he is constrained by the authority of the truth as he sees it, and the truth as he now sees it includes all the varied factors above mentioned. It follows that the historian ceases to be merely an historian if he allows himself to make statements about God's presence or God's action in history. He is not denying historical truth, but he is going beyond a purely historical judgment to an "interpretation of the interpretations." In as far as Harvey is right in claiming that this is indeed the role of the historian, he is implying that historical study leads inevitably to more than historical judgments.

Let us assume for the moment that the historian is not a positivist or a secularist or an agnostic, and that he is open to the possibility that the word "God" can be meaningfully applied to action in history. He is still confronted with the problem of the degree to which statements about God's activity demand specific historical assertions. It is at this point that Harvey has obvious difficulties making up his mind. Indeed, he even suggests that if we are clear as to the nature of faith, then we could say that "faith has no clear relation to any particular set of historical beliefs at all."[70] Faith, he tells us, has to do with confidence in God and the trusting acceptance of life as a gift and a responsibility. "This awareness, to be sure, may be linked in the minds of some people with certain historical beliefs, but it is by no means clear that it must necessarily be so linked."[71] Now this is a very sweeping statement, and it is not easy to see how far Harvey intends us to take it. He seems to be saying more than that God can speak through myth or through historically false stories of a certain kind. On the other hand, he appears to be saying more than that the "biblical Christ," which we have previously considered, goes beyond the portrait of an historical figure which a pure historian might give. In fact, he seems to be implying that faith might detach itself from all and every kind of specific historical assertion and still remain the kind of faith which a Christian would wish to talk about. If this is what Harvey really means, then it is doubtful whether Christian faith could survive such a limitation. A certain kind of mysticism might survive. When Tillich defines faith as "ultimate concern" or when he says that the serious sceptic "is not without faith, even though it [i.e., faith] has no concrete content,"[72] he seems to be expressing more definitely what is implied in Harvey's statement. Neither position has been found satisfactory by most

---

[70]Harvey, *Historian and Believer*, p. 280.
[71]*Ibid.*
[72]Paul Tillich, *Dynamics of Faith* (New York: Harper & Row, 1957), p. 20.

Christians. If, as Harvey contends, the basic questions are, Is God gracious? Is my life significant in some sense that transcends the world? Can the last power be trusted?[73]—then most Christians have, rightly or wrongly, regarded the confident answer to this question as depending upon the action of God in history and a specific kind of action in Jesus of Nazareth. Some set of historical beliefs would, therefore, appear to be an integral element of Christian faith, even if that faith in its fullness is more than a set of historical judgments. It is agreed that such a claim raises momentous difficulties for Hindus, Buddhists, and many kinds of philosophers and mystics, as we shall see in our later discussions. The Christian, however, cannot retreat at this point, however formidable the opposition. Faith and some historical beliefs are inextricably combined and he has to live with this tension.

Having said this, however, we must acknowledge that the Christian still has to wrestle with the question as to which historical beliefs are indispensable if his faith is to stand. This involves the issue of our knowledge of Jesus of Nazareth and the so-called problem of miracles. The main point to be emphasized here is that Christian faith, and a meaningful Christology, cannot sever their roots in history. While it is true that faith is more than a series of historical judgments, as these are understood by the professional historian today, it is also true that faith demands some historical judgments to make sense of its own experience. If these cannot be made with any confidence at all, then Christianity will have to be superseded by another kind of faith. Some believe this to be the case. The rest of this book will argue the contrary position.

Let us now try and sum up the basic implications of our rather complex discussion. Granted that the sources compel us to seek the history in the kerygma, the question still arises whether we can find any reliable historical fact in the kerygma. At the very least, we must say with Heinz Zahrnt that "it began with Jesus of Nazareth."[74] Even if we doubt whether Jesus uses any of the titles ascribed to Him by the documents, the judgment of Ernst Fuchs seems compelling: "This attitude [of Jesus] is neither that of a prophet nor that of a sage; it is rather that of a man who dares to act in God's place, by drawing to Himself sinners who without Him would have to flee before God."[75] Certainly we have to face the fact that the debate will continue as to exactly how much history can be reached in the kerygma and through the faith-controlled documents. This may prove to be far from negligible, as

---

[73]Harvey, p. 281.

[74]Heinz Zahrnt, *The Historical Jesus,* trans. J.S. Bowden (London: Collins, 1963), Chapter 8.

[75]Ernst Fuchs, *Die Frage nach dem historischen Jesus,* Zeitschrift für Theologie und Kirche, 53 (1956), pp. 219 and 229, as quoted in Zahrnt, pp. 115–116.

will be seen if we select only such names as T.W. Manson, Joachim Jeremias, C.H. Dodd, and Ernst Käsemann, to mention four men with rather different approaches to this question.

The fact remains, however, that theologians and biblical scholars must, to quote Austin Farrer, stop "hunting for a pure datum of revelation prior to the necessary evils of reflection and communication."[76] Faith is obviously more than a series of historical judgments. We never draw a hard and fast line between the purely revealed and the human interpretative reaction to such revelation. The Christian knows through the present experience of faith that the imperfections of the media of revelation have not defeated the divine purpose. This does not mean that the Christian places himself completely beyond questions of historical fact. It does mean that a "fact" in history is a complex notion and that we must not import limited positivistic notions of fact into our scheme of thought at this point. "History differs from natural science, for its object is in part constituted by meaning and value, while the objects of natural science are not."[77] History may be value-free in the specialized functional sense that it aims at historical truth, as far as this is possible, and is not directly concerned with social and cultural goals.[78] On the other hand the historian cannot avoid value judgments, and hence he must, as we have admitted, be an interpreter of interpretations.

Yet such interpretation cannot be carried on in a vacuum. There must be something to interpret which is not merely the act of interpretation itself. If the Christian came to the conclusion that there was no history at all in the kerygma, then this would constitute a crisis of the first magnitude for him, whatever some scholars today may say. He would be faced with the prospect of substituting sheer myth for the faith which he now holds. We believe that this is not yet the position at which we have arrived. Nineham, replying to the strictures of A.T. Hanson on his commentary on Mark, remarks that "when we bear in mind the wonderfully retentive memory of the Oriental, who being unable to read and write, had perforce to cultivate accuracy of memory, it will not seem surprising that we can often be virtually sure that what the tradition is offering us are the authentic deeds, and especially the authentic words of the historic Jesus."[79] By the side of this, we can put Jeremias' contention, quoted earlier, that if we are not always certain of the *ipsissima verba* of Jesus, we can be virtually certain that we are hearing His *ipsissima vox.*

---

[76]Austin Farrer, *Faith and Speculation,* p. 101.

[77]Bernard Lonergan, *Method in Theology* (London: Darton, Longman & Todd, 1972), p. 219.

[78]*Ibid.,* p. 232.

[79]Denis Nineham in *Christian History and Interpretation,* p. 202.

Our final judgment, therefore, is that, despite the strictures upon the old quest, Manson was right in claiming that the "quest of the historical Jesus must be continued." We must continue to seek the history in the kerygma. This attempt cannot yet be pronounced a failure. Whether we are justified in going further and saying that the early church's confession from the post-Easter perspective that Jesus is Lord was a reading *into* rather than a correct reading *of* the evidence, this is more than a historical judgment as this is normally understood. Faith and its value judgments depend also upon some experience of the power and presence of God now, mediated through the life and worship of the church and of the living fellowship.

Thus we have to live with the tension between the kerygma and the history in which it is rooted, even though faith may be confident that historical criticism will never be able to overturn the conviction of the early Christian community that the humiliated Jesus of Nazareth is indeed the same as the risen Lord known in this present faith. The reader now knows our basic presuppositions. We shall proceed to wrestle with those problems of Christology which inevitably arise even if the above understanding of the Christian faith and its relation to history is accepted.

4.
Is All of God in Jesus?

Our review of the New Testament material seems to confirm the judgment of Donald Baillie—no more docetism.[1] Biblical scholarship, with rare exceptions, is agreed in holding that whatever else Jesus was, He was a *man* and lived a genuine human existence. The problem for modern men centers upon the divinity and not upon the humanity. Few today take the divinity for granted and then ask how Jesus could have been truly man. There are exceptions, of course, and it could be argued that whatever their declared intentions some modern Christian thinkers are doing precisely this. For example, this criticism has been levelled at Karl Barth. Yet, it is generally true that in the present climate of theological and biblical thought, the humanity is taken for granted and is not a subject for serious debate. The real issue is how much more we can say than that Jesus was a man.

We shall turn later to a more detailed study of what is "humanity" or "human nature" or what it means to be a "man." But in order to set the stage for a consideration of Jesus' divinity, we must take a preliminary look at the doctrine of the Trinity. To ask in the abstract, Was Jesus divine?, raises so many intricate problems that until these have been clarified, the question itself is liable to lead to complete confusion of mind. This is illustrated not only in the doctrinal debates of the early church but also in the popular language of the Christian layman today who believes that the statement "Jesus is God" is a fair statement of the Christian belief.

The title of this chapter may seem crude and naive, but it emphasizes a difficulty which troubles many theological students and indeed any Christian who thinks about the Christian faith. Anyone who has tried to expound the doctrine of the Trinity to students is made keenly aware both of the inherent difficulties of the subject and of the pitfalls which await an uncritical use of metaphors and images. Our old friend the problem of religious language here confronts us in its most acute form. We are fond of saying, and this has been

---

[1]Donald Baillie, *God was in Christ* (London: Faber, 1956).

much accentuated by certain theological trends in this century, that the
Christian understanding of God has its beginning and end in Jesus Christ. In
one sense, this is obviously true; in another sense it is dangerously misleading. Contrary to what is commonly believed, the Christian faith does not
simply say that Jesus is God and leave it at that. At least, not if we accept the
ancient creeds, including the Chalcedonian definition, as a statement of
"orthodox" belief. Jesus is "truly God and truly man, of a rational soul and
body"; or if we speak in terms of later doctrine, He is the second Person of
the Trinity. But, it is sometimes impatiently asked, what can this kind of
language possibly mean and why did Christians ever come to speak in this
way? It is this issue which we shall try to tackle in this chapter. We have
already seen how the question of Jesus' divinity has become involved in
controversy because of ambiguities in the term "divinity" itself. The doctrine of the Trinity was in part an attempt to meet some of these difficulties.
We shall try to assess how successful this attempt was.

We return, therefore, to the strange question which heads this chapter:
Is all of God in Jesus? The phrase "all of God" contains, of course, a spatial
metaphor and we must frankly recognize this. We must clear our minds of all
quasi-physical ideas which would think of God as literally a kind of ether
pervading space or water filling a sponge. The operative word is "literally,"
and we must remind the reader again of what has been said about religious
language in the preceding chapters. If God is an infinite, transcendent Spirit,
He cannot fill His creation in this literal sense. The question, then, becomes,
What could such language possibly mean if it is interpreted symbolically or
analogically?

Let us try to rephrase our naive question in more sophisticated language. Is the idea of God to be defined exclusively in terms of our knowledge
of God mediated through the Person of Jesus Christ? The answer to this
cannot be a simple Yes. It can be affirmative only if we recognize that Jesus
assumed the Old Testament understanding of God. Jesus nowhere suggests
that the Jewish people knew nothing of God prior to His coming. They
obviously knew a good deal about Him, and we have no reason to believe
that Jesus questioned this. Let us formulate the problem in another way.
Would it be possible to arrive at the idea of a transcendent God, Creator of
Heaven and of Earth, simply by concentrating upon the fact of the man
Jesus? The answer to this is No, unless in the phrase "man Jesus" we
include Jesus' idea of God derived from the Hebrew and Jewish experience.
There is a wide range of God's creative activity in the natural order which
could only be manifested in and through that order. Insofar as Jesus was truly
man, He could not by the nature of the case express the totality of God's
creative and sustaining activity. This requires the whole of the natural or

created order for its medium. In other words, if the Old Testament understanding of God is called radically into question, it is extremely doubtful whether Jesus Himself can provide sufficient foundation for the classical affirmation that God is the Creator of Heaven and Earth, Maker of all things visible and invisible. On the other hand, it is surely not permissible to abstract Jesus from the Jewish tradition and therefore from the idea of God presupposed in that tradition.

This brings us to the heart of the contemporary debate. Much of our confusion springs from the fact that the idea of God, which was a datum for Jesus, is being called in question. It is challenged and for a variety of reasons: a narrow empiricism which defines verification solely in relation to sense-data, philosophical and linguistic analysis, science, the influence of Kant, the real difficulty of verifying a "reality" beyond the process of events in this world. Clearly, if transcendence is called into question in the theistic sense, then the divinity of Jesus would have to be defined in terms which exclude the idea of God in the Jewish experience recorded in the Bible.

The implication of all this is that neither the "divinity" of Jesus Christ nor the doctrine of the Trinity can be expected to be intelligible until we have answered a prior question. What grounds have we for accepting the essential features of the Hebrew and Jewish understanding of God as true? To this could be added yet another question: How did the Jews arrive at such an idea of God? To deal with this latter question first, it seems evident that they did not reach this position by inferential reasoning characteristic of the famous proofs of natural theology. This does not mean that the cosmological and teleological arguments have nothing of value to say to us. It does mean that taken by themselves as arguments from the contingency of all finite creatures, they would not inevitably lead to the Jewish understanding of God. As Alfred North Whitehead once wrote, "Any proof which commences with the character of the actual world cannot rise above the actuality of this world. . . . It may discover an immanent God, but not a God wholly transcendent."[2] Some might react to this by saying that it only shows that one can never in fact arrive at a transcendent God at all. The historical fact, however, is that the Jews did so arrive at such a conception. How did this come about? In general terms, one could say that in a manner mysterious to us, this idea of God somehow arose in the Jewish mind. Somehow the idea of a transcendent God, on whose creative will the whole world depends for its existence, became implanted as a dominant spiritual intuition in the Jewish

[2]Alfred North Whitehead, *Religion in the Making* (Cambridge: Cambridge Univ. Press, 1930), p. 71.

mind. That the idea persisted and endured, despite the pressure of alien idolatries and national disasters, can only be because many Jews found it confirmed in their personal and corporate existence. Karl Barth once said that the strongest natural argument for the reality of God is the existence of the Jewish people.

The modern critic, however, is likely to respond in a different way. All this proves, he might argue, is that many Jews believe and still believe in a transcendent God. It does not prove the validity of that belief. This, then, is the crucial question to be answered before one can proceed with a useful discussion of either Christology or the doctrine of the Trinity. If the Jews were fundamentally mistaken in this most basic of all their beliefs, then not only is Judaism rendered invalid, but the basic presupposition of the distinctive Christian beliefs is also rendered questionable. It will be noted that up to this point, much of the traditional theological language has not been used, and this has been deliberate. Now, however, this must be considered. Before we do this, it should nonetheless be noted that it is not only Jewish man who has arrived at a reality transcendent to the spatio-temporal world we experience here below. The Hindu has arrived at Brahman-Atman, Plotinus at the One, and the Muslim at Allah, though it could be argued that this is only a variation of the basic Jewish theme. While a certain type of contemporary "secular" man might think that the Jewish idea of God is very peculiar indeed, and repeat the old adage "How odd of God to choose the Jews," in the long perspective of history the Jewish peculiarity is not the fact of his belief in some kind of transcendent reality but the special character of that reality.

Contrary, therefore, to what is often assumed, the fundamental question which has first to be answered concerns not the Incarnation but the validity of the Jewish intuition or apprehension of the nature and character of God. Without that apprehension of God, the doctrine of the Incarnation cannot even be stated in an intelligible form. One might add that this is true even for the so-called primitive or adoptionist Christology discussed in a previous chapter and defended by John Knox. Take away from this Christological pattern the Jewish understanding of God, and Jesus' teaching of the near advent of the Kingdom makes no sense. Without the Incarnation, on the other hand, there is no point in raising questions about the Trinity in the specific Christian sense. Some have doubted whether the early Christology requires a doctrine of the Trinity at all. Yet this Christology would seem to demand at least some ontological assertion about the Person of Jesus, i.e., some affirmation about the "nature" of Jesus as implied in the role or function which He believed He was called by God to perform. One might, of course, develop some kind of philosophical Trinity in the sense of a Stoic or

Plotinus or Hegel or some oriental theories of emanation. This, however, is not to be confused with the Christian doctrine which presupposes the biblical nature of God and His unique activity in the Person of Jesus Christ.

What, then, of the validity of the Jewish intuition of the reality and nature of God? There are only a limited number of options here:

(a) The Bible is authoritative per se and, therefore, what it says about God must be accepted because it says so.

(b) The Bible is authoritative but it needs interpreting. Since the canon of Scripture came into being as the result of a selective judgment on the part of the synagogue and the church, the synagogue or the church can alone interpret it correctly because it alone possesses the active presence of the Spirit of God to enable it so to interpret.

(c) It is not possible to regard the Bible, or the synagogue or the church, without asking questions about the basis and nature of that authority. The Jewish apprehension of God, and Christian developments therefrom, must meet certain criteria before their validity can be accepted by a thoughtful man.

(d) The validity of the Jewish or Christian claim depends upon the conformity of that claim to certain criteria, and these criteria can be provided only by reason in the broadest sense. Otherwise, we must remain agnostic about the validity of that experience in as far as it makes ontological claims, i.e., insofar as it not only affirms a certain character of God but insists that such a God "is." This means that God is an extra-mental objective reality and can never be reduced simply to the functioning of man's psychological states or activities, even if the knowledge of God must be mediated by those states and activities. This subjection of the biblical understanding of God to rational criteria could be affirmed in two different senses. One view would maintain that the Jewish understanding of God can be accepted as valid only if it can be shown to be "rational" by natural theology; i.e., it must be given independent philosophical justification. If this were truly the case, then the idea of God could be arrived at without any necessary reference to the Jewish experience. Few, if any, significant Christian thinkers have taken up this position. A second view would be to accept the Jewish understanding of God as disclosed in special experiences of the men of the Old Testament and then to argue that it is "reasonable" in the sense that when thus accepted it can be shown to be consistent with the rest of our knowledge and able to throw light upon our total interpretation of all human experience. This would a case of faith seeking understanding. Whether successful or not, this is the kind of approach adopted by the overwhelming majority of Christian thinkers.

(e) If this second approach is adopted, further conclusions follow. Since the Jewish apprehension of God was not reached by a process of logical inference in the first place, but emerged as a spiritual perception or intuition, it follows that it cannot be proved by discursive reasoning in the usual sense. A certain kind of spiritual sensitivity is required if the nature of the Holy God is to be apprehended. This means that no logical knock-down argument can ever be advanced in defence of the biblical faith in God. This, however, does not mean that such faith is blind. It is possible to maintain that once the biblical idea of God had arisen in the mind of Hebrew and Jewish man, such a view of God meets the demands of reason for an intelligible interpretation of the world, the reality of other minds, and those moral and spiritual values which alone give meaning to human existence. We believe this to be the case.[3] Professor John Hick has recently given us an interesting defence of the reasonableness of accepting a theistic view of God without proof.[4]

Assuming, therefore, the validity of the biblical intuition of the reality and nature of God and of the doctrine of the Incarnation as previously discussed, what does this involve for any attempt to articulate a Christian doctrine of God in theological propositions? Or the question might be expressed in another form: Why Trinitarian rather than Unitarian? Or more concretely, why cannot we remain Jews, not racially, of course, but in our sharing of the Jewish intuition of the one God? In this context, we could simply give a special status to Jesus without fundamentally modifying our theological doctrine of God. The more liberal types of theology since the eighteenth century have done precisely this without always frankly confessing it. And why not? Would not such a position be simpler and theologically more intelligible and give the follower of Jesus all that he basically needs? What is inadequate about a Christian Unitarianism?

It is important in attempting an answer to this question to maintain some consistency in our use of language. If Unitarian is defined as the affirmation of one God, then it can be argued that the Christian doctrine of the Trinity is Unitarian. It does not intend to deny the "unity" of God, still less to give sanction to any kind of tritheism or polytheism. There have been many subtle debates about the nature of that unity and the precise shade of meaning to be attached to *hypostasis* or *persona* in the later formulations of the doctrine. Some writers on the subject, both ancient and modern, have used social analogies about the Trinity which in the view of others have come very near to tritheism. Nevertheless, the church has never formally accepted the view that there are three "gods." God is one in all the forms or modes of His activity, and in this sense all Christians are Unitarians, believers in one God.

---

[3]H.P. Owen, *The Christian Knowledge of God* (London: Univ. of London, Athlone Press, 1969).
[4]John Hick, *Arguments for the Existence of God.*

Why, then, did the church find it necessary to modify its inherited Jewish monotheism by the use of Trinitarian language? The simple answer to this, of course, as we have seen, is the fact of Jesus Christ and what believers have experienced of God in relation to Him. The doctrine of the Trinity is, therefore, directly related to the doctrine of the Incarnation. This is why, theologically and experientially, one cannot move from the Trinitarian formula by logical deduction to the Incarnation but rather vice-versa. Only if the Incarnation represents an authentic insight on the part of Christian believers do we have any basis in experience for a doctrine of the Trinity. Put in the simplest terms, the early disciples, followed by later generations of believers, found it impossible to explain the effect of Jesus upon their lives in terms of such categories as prophet or religious genius. If, for example, we could be content only to see Jesus as the bringer of a message from God or as a man of exceptional spiritual insight or as the highest manifestation of the Hebrew prophetic consciousness, then the problem we are concerned about would not arise as a matter of theological principle. It is because Christians have discovered in Jesus not only an ambassador from God but God Himself in redeeming activity that the above interpretation of His Person has been found inadequate. Faith in the Christian sense has found God in Jesus, not by proxy but in some sense directly present in a manner without parallel at any other time or place. This is the basis of the doctrine of the Incarnation, and there can be no going back upon this central affirmation. If Christians have been mistaken on this vital point, then we might as well frankly recognize that Christianity, as historically known, cannot be regarded as a valid apprehension of the way things are. We are then delivered from the theological problems with both the Incarnation and the doctrine of the Trinity. We must restate the issue in quite different terms.

Since, however, in the writer's opinion, this is a path which does not force itself upon us, we must still face the issues involved in the historic faith and the language used by it. Christians must still affirm the validity of the Jewish intuition and apprehension of God. They must still affirm the unique presence and activity of God in Jesus of Nazareth. They must still bear witness to the presence of that same God here and now in the believer through the inner witness of the Holy Spirit. In what language can we most appropriately express these convictions and do full justice to all the historical problems connected with the life and ministry of Jesus as well as to the continuing Christian experience in succeeding generations?

Assuming, therefore, that the Christian apprehension of God in Christ is a valid one, how can one state the Christian belief in a manner which secures this fact without at the same time losing the basic biblical convictions of both Testaments that God is one? As in all the questions we have discussed so far, the problem of language is fundamental. We know before we begin that human language is not going to be totally adequate to the reality we are seeking to indicate. Augustine's well-known admission must be borne in mind that we use Trinitarian language not because it says perfectly what we want to say but in order that we may not be reduced to utter silence in the presence of the divine mysteries. The introduction by the church of nonbiblical language to articulate the nature of the Christian apprehension is not in itself an objection. It is, however, a legitimate question whether this nonbiblical language seriously distorts the apprehension.

In the history of the evolution of the doctrine of the Trinity, both in the ancient church and since, we can discern two main emphases. There are those who believe that the unity of the one living and personal God must be preserved at all costs and that any tendency to move in a tritheistic direction must be sternly resisted. On the other hand are those who think that the notion of unity itself calls for searching examination. A bare unity, conceived of mistakenly after the analogy of the mathematical symbol of oneness, makes it impossible to do justice to the rich complexity of the Christian experience of God. Such thinkers, therefore, tend to stress the complex nature of the divine unity and to emphasize the differentiation of functions within that divine unity, even if this involves the use of language which appears to have dangerously misleading tritheistic suggestions. It is only fair to emphasize that this group would vigorously repudiate the charge that they are endangering the unity of God when this is properly understood.

It is not necessary to go over again the ground which has been covered so many times before. The student may be referred to the technical discussion of language in the books listed below.[5] Rather, we shall try to bring out as clearly as possible the issues which seem to be at stake in the debates between the two groups of thinkers mentioned above and cite some contemporary illustrations. Among those who stress the importance of the unity of God are two thinkers of rather different theological attitudes who yet agree on this particular point. As far back as 1928, H. Wheeler Robinson asserted that whatever other problems theism may involve, it is straightforward in the sense that it ascribes to God a personal nature analogous to human personality. "The philosophic strength of theism lies in this principle of unity—the unity of a single divine consciousness and will."[6] Since personality in its human form is the strictest unity of which we have any experience, it also is

---

[5]George L. Prestige, *God in Patristic Thought;* Henry E.W. Turner, *The Pattern of Christian Truth;* and Robert V. Sellers, *The Council of Chalcedon* (London: S.P.C.K., 1971).

[6]H. Wheeler Robinson, *The Christian Experience of the Holy Spirit* (London: Nisbet; New York: Harper & Row, 1928), p. 268.

the source of the postulate of unity which philosophy must employ to give an intelligible account either of God or of the world. Furthermore, he maintained, we know nothing of human personality possessing three centers of consciousness. If, then, the Christian experience compelled us to speak in these terms, "it seems doubtful whether we ought to speak of Christian monotheism at all."[7]

From the perspective of a different theological tradition, Karl Barth made similar statements: "Three-in-oneness in God does not mean a threefold deity, either in the sense of a plurality of deities or in the sense of a plurality of individuals or parts within the one deity."[8] Barth goes on to say that "person" in the doctrine of the Trinity has nothing to do with personality, that the meaning of the doctrine cannot, therefore, mean that there are three personalities in God: "We can as little speak of a tripersonality of God as of a triessentiality."[9] It is well known that Barth would have liked to substitute "mode" for "person" in order to avoid misunderstanding, while insisting that "mode" is not to be interpreted in the sense of the ancient Sabellian heresy which was condemned by the church. Let us, then, start with the position taken by these two men and see where it leads us. If the term "personality" is interpreted in the modern sense as the activity of one will which expresses a unified consciousness and is then applied analogously to God, then how do we arrive at the reality of individuals on the human level, and how does the "personality" of Jesus Christ fit into this context?

If God is one in the sense indicated above, it is also a fact that the creative will of such a God has brought into existence a created order characterized by what appear to be real distinctions between individual objects and persons. If it is asserted in the manner of some forms of Hindu philosophy that such distinctions are in appearance only (*maya*), then to affirm the unity of God is at the same time to deny the reality of persons. From our limited human perspective, it may seem that there are many individual persons. If, however, we escape from the ignorance due to such perspective (*avidya*), we shall arrive at the conviction that there is only One Eternal and abiding Self (Brahman-Atman). On this view, all persons, including Jesus Christ Himself, may manifest for a limited time the activity of the ultimate Self but they cannot be regarded as possessing any permanent and enduring actuality in themselves.

It is clear that there is no way of combining this view with the biblical

[7]*Ibid.*, p. 269.

[8]Karl Barth, *Church Dogmatics* I, 1, eds. Geoffrey W. Bromiley and Thomas F. Torrance; trans. G.T. Thomson and H. Knight (Edinburgh: T. & T. Clark, 1935 and 1956), p. 402.

[9]*Ibid.*, p. 411.

doctrine of creation. According to the biblical doctrine, the one transcendent and living Creator has brought into existence persons who now possess a reality distinct from God and are endowed with a measure of real, though limited, independence and freedom. It is not part of Jewish and Christian belief to assert that such persons could continue to exist apart from the continuous creative and sustaining activity of the one God. It does, however, affirm that once the divine purpose has brought such persons into existence, they do exercise their initiative over against God in genuine independence. They can opt for independence in the form of rebellion or they can accept a freely-willed relationship of trust, obedience, and love. It has been held by the Christian tradition that it is incompatible with the love of God to have brought such persons into actual existence only to let them be absorbed again with a complete loss of their individuality and personal identity.

It is obvious that a choice has to be made between the Christian view and such other accounts of the nature of human personality as characterize some forms of Hinduism and Buddhism and certain types of philosophical pantheism which have appeared in both ancient and modern times. The doctrine of the Trinity in the Christian sense, therefore, arises from a special set of assumptions, namely that God is one but that He is also related to a created order, including persons, who stand over against Him with an independence permitted by Him. In as far as Jesus Christ is truly man, He must stand on the human side of the Creator-creature relationship. Like all other men, He owes His existence and actuality to the creative and sustaining activity of God. Like them, He is conscious of His dependence which finds expression in His praying to the Father, in His recognition that all goodness comes from God ("Why call me good? There is none good save God only"), in His frank acknowledgement that the Father has knowledge (e.g., concerning the end of the age) which is denied to the Son. That Jesus prayed to the Father seems as certain as anything in the New Testament. This in itself often raises questions often put by students. If Jesus is God or divine, how can God pray to Himself, and if the claim that God prayed to Himself makes any sense at all, does it not destroy at the same time the reality and significance of Jesus' prayer life and of His real dependence upon the Father. Or put in another way, how can God manifest Himself in the created order, which by His creative act is distinguishable from Him, without destroying the relative freedom and independence which He Himself has given? It is worth remembering that the problem is a real one for any relationship between God and the human person. Putting aside for the moment the special issue of the Incarnation, how can a person be related to God or experience what is sometimes described as the "presence of God" in him without finding his human individuality and freedom completely overwhelmed, if not destroyed? The very existence of a world at all, which contains persons capable of initiative and freedom, demands some self-limitation on the part of God if it is to be made intelligible. If the presence of God to and in a human being is to be possible without destroying that humanity, there must also be, as Wheeler Robinson insisted, a "kenosis of the Spirit." Here too, God has to conform the nature of His presence to the inherent limitations involved in any form of finite personality,[10] limitations, it may be added, put there by God Himself in the first place.

In the case of the Incarnation, the same principle must be operative. If the direct and immediate activity and presence of God is asserted to be in Jesus in a manner absolutely unique and without parallel, it is still difficult to see how this could be without some kind of kenosis or self-limitation on the part of God. It is interesting to notice another facet of this same question in regard to the nature of all human knowledge of God. In his *Faith and Knowledge,* John Hick has argued persuasively that the knowledge of God is not given to us "as a compulsory perception but is achieved as a voluntary act of interpretation."[11] If the knowledge of God was as coercive and compelling as, for example, our apprehension of the world through the physical senses, then once again freedom would be imperilled. If our perception of God's reality and nature was necessary in this sense, then faith as a truly personal act with moral and spiritual significance would be impossible. If God is to receive a response which is not compelled, then He has to limit Himself in relation to us in such a way as to permit us "cognitive" freedom, the freedom to interpret His activity and presence even to the point of a negative interpretation which might deny His reality at all.

The implications of this for the doctrine of the Trinity are important. Insofar as Jesus is truly man, he stands over against God by virtue of His creaturely nature and existence with the independence and freedom which belong to such creatures. Insofar as He is truly God, we are wanting to assert that the relationship between Jesus and God is more than an instance of the general relationship which exists between God and all His creatures. In this special instance, the relationship is of such an intimacy and depth that it can be described as God's first-hand activity in and through this historical person. First-hand means that in and through this finite creature Jesus, God is wholly and personally present in a redeeming and saving activity. Yet "wholly" here must not be taken in a spatial sense. The fullness of God dwelt bodily in Jesus intensively, and not by spatial extension. There is, as we have seen, a presence and an activity of God in the whole of the created

---

[10]H. Wheeler Robinson, *Revelation and Redemption* (London: Nisbet, 1942; New York: Harper & Row, 1942), pp. 290ff.

[11]John Hick, *Faith and Knowledge* (London: Macmillan, 1967), pp. 121ff.

world which cannot be telescoped into the figure of Jesus. There is also a presence and activity of God in the koinonia of the mystical body of Christ which likewise cannot be reduced to the one historical figure. Provided we understand what we are saying, it is legitimate to affirm that the "fullness" of God in Jesus requires the existence of the redeemed community, the church, or the mystical body before this fullness can be complete. This is an important point to which John Knox has given notable attention. In this sense "all" of God or the "fullness" of God is not in Jesus, if Jesus here means the actuality of the historical person who lived some thirty odd years on this planet and was crucified under Pontius Pilate. To say that the fullness of God is in Jesus Christ can only mean the complete indwelling of God as far as this is possible within the limits of a finite human existence.

If we speak in this way, are we in fact denying the reality of the Incarnation or simply reducing Jesus to the best man among many? I think not. Whatever the logical and semantic problems involved in the various doctrines of kenosis elaborated from Thomasius in the nineteenth century to Mackintosh, Quick, and at the radical extreme, Altizer, in the twentieth century, we must frankly confess that some self-limitation of God in His act of incarnation in Jesus Christ seems to be required both by Scripture and reason. The difficulties of ascribing omnipotence, omniscience, and omnipresence to Jesus of Nazareth are so enormous that no satisfactory doctrine of the Incarnation can be built on this basis. Fortunately, Scripture itself does not lend it any convincing support. But the doctrine of the Trinity does allow us to do justice to all these factors. In distinguishing between the "presence" or "modes" or *hypostases* in the Barthian sense, we are delivered from the perils of a spatial interpretation of the language. We are able to speak of the reality of God's presence and activity in and to His creation, in Jesus Christ, and in the community of faith without having to telescope all this into the historical figure of Jesus. We are able to assert that it is the one and the same God who is active in these various ways and to do justice to the genuine manhood of Jesus without seeing Him only in humanist terms. It also means that the language of the Trinity is not a literal description of the Godhead but a useful formula which helps us to preserve the rich diversity of God's self-revealing to men. It is, in Ramsey's sense, a "model" which preserves all the essential elements in the threefold activity of God in creation, redemption, and sanctification. Needless to say, unless these three terms stand for real divine self-disclosures apprehended by men in experience, then there is no experiential, or empirical, foundation for the Trinitarian doctrine. It is hardly necessary to say that the word "empirical" must have a broader meaning here than that associated with some forms of logical positivism and verification by exclusive appeal to sense-data. Obviously, on this latter view, there is no place for God and consequently no basis for a doctrine of the Trinity.

We have deliberately omitted from our treatment of the Trinity in this chapter the further question as to whether our experience of God in salvation-history entitles us to frame a doctrine of the "immanent-Trinity," i.e., to give some account of the "inner life" of the Godhead in terms of the mutual indwelling of the three "personae" of later Trinitarian doctrine. It would seem better to postpone this aspect of the question until the model of preexistence has been more fully considered.

To return to the title of this chapter, if all of God is not in Jesus, then there is a need to clarify two basic questions. The first concerns the reality of the manhood of Jesus; the second relates to the kind of presence of God and of divine activity manifested in and through the ministry, death, and resurrection of Jesus of Nazareth.

5.
God and Divinity

In Chapter Four we considered the doctrine of the Trinity and what it does not mean. Now we shall turn to the word "divinity" and see how this is related to the Christian understanding of God on the one side and of Jesus on the other. It might have seemed more logical to treat the manhood of Jesus first. Since, however, an inadequate concept of divinity will influence profoundly what is said about that humanity, it seems preferable to clarify our understanding of divinity first.

Our earlier discussion of Chalcedon maintained that the religious intention behind the formulation was a sound expression of that which Christian faith desires to affirm, namely the active, redeeming presence of God in Jesus of Nazareth in a manner which led to the claim for Him of uniqueness, later expressed in terms of "divinity." It will be necessary to examine what is involved in this very notion of uniqueness. It presumably means at least one of its kind, i.e., not exactly paralleled anywhere else. On the other hand, the very notion of uniqueness implies our ability to make some kind of comparison between the "unique" and other phenomena. Otherwise, how could we distinguish it in any significant sense from the general run of instances? In concrete terms, Jesus is different, it is said, from any other man who has ever lived or walked on this earth. Yet does this mean that He has absolutely nothing in common with all other men? If this were so, it is difficult to see how the doctrine of the Incarnation in its classical sense could ever have been formulated. "God becoming man" would be such an isolated and mysterious fact that we would have nothing in our general experience to enable us even to gain a partial understanding of the mystery. If the conclusion of our last chapter is sound, namely that all of God is not in Jesus, then it obviously becomes necessary to define more carefully what the term "divinity" implies before we can answer the question whether and in what sense Christian faith can apply it to Jesus. We have already had occasion to reject the notion of uniqueness as involving complete isolation from all other men. If "truly man" means anything at all, then it must be possible to find some genuine resemblances between His existence and ours. The question thus resolves itself into the fact that Jesus is man "plus," but what exactly is the nature of the "plus" or "more" which Christian faith wishes to assert is the fundamental issue at stake.

It may be noted in passing that for the reasons given briefly above Norman Pittenger prefers to abandon the description of Jesus as unique and substitute the term "decisive." He would feel equally unhappy with our phrase "more than man." He evidently feels that "unique" not only may endanger the true manhood of Jesus but also implies an arrogance and a false judgment about the possibility of salvation for those who have never heard the gospel and encountered the Word Incarnate. [1] But this latter would be true only if physical death was the point of final judgment and if the eschatology adopted closed the door to any possibility of knowing the Incarnate Lord after this life. I have argued in another book that the New Testament does not require us to accept that kind of eschatology. [2] If this is the case, then to be born ignorant of the gospel, when the individual is in no way responsible for his ignorance, would not mean automatic condemnation and eternal separation from God in Christ. Christ would still be the one mediator of our salvation, but the opportunity to come to saving belief in Him would not be confined to this life. This solution has its own problems, but it is preferable to the rather artificial and forced attempts to pretend that Christianity and Buddhism, for example, are saying the same thing. Christians have wanted to say that Jesus Christ is Lord and Savior in a manner which cannot be in the same sense true of Gotama the Buddha, or of other great religious personalities of the race. "It has been a terrible mistake," says Pittenger, "as so much propaganda for the Christian mission has seemed to do, that apart from this proclamation [i.e., of the Christ-deed of God] no possibility of salvation is open to man." [3] This, as we have argued, is true only on the basis of a certain eschatology which some Christians may indeed have accepted but which in our view is not a necessary implication of the New Testament. If uniqueness is arrogance, the charge must be risked by the Christian. "Arrogance," however, is an emotive word and the reader is asked to defer judgment on this issue until he has read the chapter in this book on Jesus and Gotama.

To claim that Jesus is unique, in relation to the saving knowledge of God and reconciliation with Him in the fullest sense, is not to say that there is no God-given truth anywhere else or in any other religion. It does mean,

---

[1]Pittenger, *Christology*, p. 105.
[2]Russell F. Aldwinckle, *Death in the Secular City* (London: Allen & Unwin, 1973; Grand Rapids: Eerdmans, 1974).
[3]Pittenger, *Christology*, p. 105.

however, that such truth falls short in one or more respects of the saving truth embodied in Jesus Christ. Decisiveness is not an adequate substitute for unique in this latter sense. Pittenger is very hard on Father Thornton in *The Incarnate Lord* for abandoning Whiteheadian process philosophy at the crucial point and making Jesus transcendent, i.e., not simply an emergent from the continuous process. By applying such question-begging words as "intrusion" and "intervention" to Thornton's position, he evades the real issue. If there is creative novelty in the process at all, then either something new emerges or it does not. If the former, there is in one important sense a breach of continuity, and the careless use of spatial images such as intrusion does not alter the fact that something new has appeared. It may be that Thornton's Christology does not preserve the authentic manhood of Jesus, as Pittenger understands it. But Thornton ought not to be faulted for asserting that Jesus was really different in significant respects from other men. To talk of God as working in the process rather than intruding into it from outside is to take this spatial language literally without asking about its meaning. If God is at work in the process, then there is no reason why He should not vary His working in a distinctive and perhaps unique form of personal action. This, of course, could be true only if God is the living, transcendent God of Christian theism and is not simply identified with the process. Yet it is clear that God was not this for Whitehead, and it seems doubtful whether God is thus defined for Pittenger. In other words, Pittenger's fear of uniqueness as a real breach of continuity in the process depends upon his view that process philosophy is an adequate conceptuality for expressing the Christian idea of God. If it is not, then his arguments are no longer conclusive. In this connection, Temple bears a careful rereading,[4] as well as H.P. Owen's recent critique of the process theology.[5]

Nor should we forget the acute and penetrating essay of the late Austin Farrer on "The Prior Actuality of God."[6] To go back a few generations, however, there is no doubt that the language of Martin Kähler is nearer to that which spontaneously comes to the lips of Christian believers. The Christ of faith of the New Testament witness is not simply an extraordinary human being.[7] He is more "than a mere man in his essence, his mission and his present function."[8] "The distinction between Jesus Christ and ourselves is not one of degree but of kind."[9] Again, "The inner development of a sinless

---

4Temple, *Nature, Man and God.*
5Owen, *Concepts of Deity.*
6Farrer, *Reflective Faith*, pp. 178ff.
7Kähler, *Historical Jesus*, p. 77.
8*Ibid.*, p. 47.
9*Ibid.*, p. 53.

person is as inconceivable to us as life in the Sandwich islands is to a Laplander."[10] Pittenger dislikes this kind of language, which he thinks is fatal to Christ's true humanity. Nevertheless, most Christians, however naive it seems, have wanted to say "more than man," believing that they could say this without destroying his genuine humanity or turning Christ into a monstrous hybrid neither God nor man. Can this "plus" or "more" still be defended, and in what language can it be most appropriately expressed? In short, is there any sense in which Jesus can be said to be different without this making nonsense of the authentic humanity? Certainly Christians have wanted to say that Jesus is both one of us and different. Nor is this difference only the "decisiveness" of any historical figure who has exercised a great influence upon humanity. It is a decisiveness in regard to God's saving activity through Jesus crucified and risen which cannot be applied to any other historical figure. Pittenger might agree with this, but the question is still legitimate as to whether "decisiveness" is an adequate category to describe this difference between Jesus and other men.

It is clear, then, that when questions of this divine "plus" are raised, some idea of God is presupposed. If this were not so, divinity would not be a reference to a relationship between God and man, but simply a description of some unusual features of his manhood. We would merely be saying that Jesus is an odd, strange, peculiar, unusual, extraordinary instance of manhood. It may be that in fact this is all that some of the more radical forms of Christology are saying. But this is not what Chalcedon intended to say, nor, generally speaking, what Christians have intended to say either in the past or now. One might argue that Christians ought to have been content to say no more than that Jesus was an extraordinary man. It is difficult to sustain the thesis that this has in fact been their position.

Others, however, would contend that this is not the only alternative. The real problem, it is contended, arises from the fact that "divinity" has been used with a notion of God which is wholly alien to the way in which Jesus thought about God. The unsatisfactoriness of previous definitions of "divinity" springs, so it is asserted, from the inadequacy of the concept of God employed. If, of course, the idea and the reality of God were entirely problematic, i.e., open to question and incapable of solution, then the question of divinity would not arise at all. We would be forced to seek explanations of Jesus in terms of some unusual aspect of his humanity. Let us, then, return to the first issue raised above. As we have seen, it could be asserted that a certain metaphysical form of theism dominated the discussion of divinity with dire consequences. Or it could be maintained that even if

---

[10]*Ibid.*

Jesus' understanding of His Person and mission were rooted in faith in Israel's God, this does not resolve the question since both the Jews and Jesus Himself may have been mistaken on this point.

We have already contended that Jesus cannot be understood when He is uprooted from faith in Israel's God. This is a vital factor when the issue of divinity is raised. An idea of God is presupposed in raising the question. If it is argued that the idea of God often assumed philosophical ideas alien to the Bible, it would still be true that the God of Israel would have to be assumed if the idea of divinity is to be raised in any meaningful sense. If the God of philosophical theism and the Bible are both rejected for whatever reason, the idea of divinity in the classical Christian sense could not arise. Whether the God of the philosophers and the God of the Bible can be reconciled is not a question we have to answer now. Suffice it to say that the question of the divinity of Jesus cannot be properly understood in isolation from Jesus' own relationship to the God of Israel and His saving acts among men. If the biblical idea of God is rejected, then divinity would have to be defined in terms of some other scheme of thought about the nature of the transcendent. If transcendence in any sense is repudiated, then the question of divinity could hardly arise.

Professor Trevor Ling, however, insists that Hebrew and Jewish ideas of God were dominated by the model of the absolute and all-powerful monarch.[11] Jesus modified this to such a radical extent that He can no longer be considered a Jew at this decisive point. This thesis involves a radical discontinuity between the Hebrew idea of God and the one which Jesus had, presumably springing from His own distinctive personal experience. All one can say about this is that it makes a point but in an altogether exaggerated way. It does not ring true to Jesus' attitude toward His own Jewish past. Furthermore, is it really a fair summary of the Jewish understanding of God to give such a dominant and one-sided emphasis to the ancient and monarchical concept of power? Not many Old Testament scholars would be content with this characterization. It is not our concern here to enter into the debate about the precise role of the monarchy in Jewish history.[12] The king was never deified in the strict sense. Elsewhere, the king was a god, but in Israel it was God who was King. The fact that this distinction between Yahweh and the king was never lost sight of suggests that Yahweh's character was never simply the projection of an image which originated in an earthly monarchy. This is not to say that Hebrew and Jewish thought of God was not expressed analogically by way of concepts of varying degrees of

---

[11]Trevor Ling, *A History of Religion East and West* (London: Macmillan, 1968), p. 74.

[12]Edmond Jacob, *Theology of the Old Testament,* trans. Arthur W. Heathcote and Philip J. Allcock (London: Hodder & Stoughton, 1958), pp. 234ff.

concreteness or abstraction taken from their experience of this world, including monarchy. It is readily admitted today that all theological language is talk about the "other world" or the "transcendent" world in terms of this world. It is misleading, as Bultmann does, to call this myth, since this would stretch the word myth to include all metaphor, analogy, and symbol. To do this illuminates nothing and solves no theological problem. If it is a fact, to adopt Bishop Ian Ramsey's terminology, that the monarchy "model" was applied to Yahweh, it is also true that holiness, righteousness, compassion, and fatherly pity were also applied to Yahweh in the Old Testament. Divine power was never unqualified, arbitrary, and exercised in the manner of a Near Eastern potentate.

There seems to be in the minds of some writers on religion these days a kind of mental block when the concept of power is mentioned. The modern distrust of the establishment, the radical dissatisfaction with the current exercise of power in political and social institutions—all this has led to a powerful inhibition against ascribing any kind of power to God, unless it be the paradoxical power of "weakness" or of "love." Now it is obvious that the power of "love" must play a central role in any Christian understanding of God. Yet this cannot exclude other kinds of power too. If God is the Creator, then He is the source of all natural power from Niagara Falls to nuclear fission. Hebrew thought never failed to recognize this fact, nor did Jesus. "I thank Thee, Father, Lord of Heaven and Earth," He says in Matthew 2:25. Any attempt, therefore, to discuss divinity in a way which implies that God has no power except that of love is to depart from both Jewish and Christian presuppositions. Prof. G.A.F. Knight lists the divine attributes which the Old Testament understanding of God assumes. The list includes eternal, transcendent, omniscient, omnipotent Creator. "God," he says, "is described in the Old Testament . . . as Sovereign Lord of all, as King and Creator of the ends of the earth."[13] Paul Tillich has likewise warned us against an analysis which results in the untenable antithesis of "powerless love" or "loveless power."[14] It is true that God created the world and continues to sustain it because His purpose for it is a loving one. On the other hand, His power to produce such a world, and to keep it in being, or even to fulfil His purpose for it, cannot be simply identified with love. In other words, the notion of power or of omnipotence in some sense cannot be eliminated from our idea of God if we are to think biblically, and that is true not only for the Old Testament but for the attitude and teaching of Jesus Himself. The Genesis creation narratives "set forth the personal

---

[13]G.A.F. Knight, *A Christian Theology of the Old Testament* (London: S.C.M., 1964), pp. 94–95.

[14]Paul Tillich, *Love, Power and Justice* (New York: Oxford Univ. Press, 1960), p. 11.

activity of a Person who is above Nature, a Person who will control it through all the successive generations of men until His purpose is accomplished and His will is fully done. For this, He must be its Master, and nothing could so forcefully express this mastery as to show Him as the Creator of Nature.''[15]

If these judgments are accepted at all, it follows that we need to be particularly cautious about the cavalier disregard of the metaphysical attributes of God in the biblical sense. As we all know, the word ''metaphysical'' has become in some quarters a word of abuse. Nothing can be more damning than the use of the adjective ''metaphysical,'' whether this be applied to some form of philosophical theism or to the biblical understanding of God. Certainly the view of God in the Bible is metaphysical if by that is meant that nature and history point beyond themselves to the reality of the transcendent, living, and personal God on whose creative activity both nature and history depend. Even if all forms of natural theology are rejected, it is still a fact, as Gollwitzer maintains,[16] that biblical faith requires the affirmation that God in the above sense ''is.'' The fact that the Bible does not use the vocabulary of the philosophical schools does not change this.

This preliminary discussion has been a necessary introduction to our consideration of divinity in relation to Jesus. The question has to be posed against the background of the biblical view of God. From one point of view, this only augments our difficulties. Christian theology might find it a lot easier if the notion of God could be eliminated. A neater and less complex account could then be given of the fact of Jesus, but this would have been achieved at the expense of coming to grips with the real issue. The basic question concerns the significance of Jesus for our understanding of the reality, nature, and activity of God. It is the merit of Chalcedon, whatever its defects, that it never lost sight of this issue. The question of Jesus' divinity can, therefore, be formulated again as follows: How could the God of Israel's faith become man without ceasing to be the living and transcendent God, Maker of Heaven and Earth and of all things visible and invisible? It is not our concern at the moment, granted the above possibility, to explain how this could be without falling into tritheism or destroying the sovereignty of God. This involves the doctrine of the Trinity, which we have already considered. Our concern now is whether, in addition to faith's affirmation that Jesus is both divine and human, the Incarnation can be made intelligible in part to the human understanding or whether it is a sheer paradox which, in

---

[15]H. Wheeler Robinson, *Inspiration and Revelation in the Old Testament* (Oxford: Clarendon Press, 1946), p. 21.

[16]Helmut Gollwitzer, *The Existence of God as Confessed by Faith* (London: S.C.M., 1965).

Kierkegaard's words, makes the reason sweat blood. Let us first of all state the various aspects of the problem before we proceed to a discussion.

(a) If it is asserted that the so-called metaphysical attributes do in fact characterize the God of Israel, then how can a transcendent Being or "Person," omnipotent, omniscient, and omnipresent, become a specific and particular man at a definite point in history? It seems as if there can be only one answer to this: Either the human Jesus was omnipotent, omniscient, and omnipresent (and if so, what becomes of any resemblance to the kind of humanity we know) or God's indwelling of the man Jesus, or if preferred, His union with Jesus of Nazareth, involved some restriction, limitation, or latency of these attributes as far as the being and activities of Jesus were concerned. Whatever we may think of the various theories of divine self-emptying or kenosis and the subtle arguments pro and con, it is difficult to resist the idea that some kind of divine self-limitation is involved in the very fact of God's becoming man. It is, perhaps, worth pointing out again that this problem also arises in regard to human freedom and responsibility in general. How can any of us possess any measure of freedom, initiative, and responsibility in a world-order maintained by a sovereign God? Some voluntary self-limitation on the part of God would seem to be required in order to make this possible.[17]

It is worth observing in passing that the refusal to consider this principle of divine self-limitation seems to be at the root of Paul Tillich's strictures upon "Incarnational" language.[18] He contends that such a statement as "God became man" is not only a paradox but a "nonsensical statement."[19] If God connotes ultimate reality, how could ultimate reality conceivably cease to be ultimate reality? Are we talking any kind of sense, logical or otherwise? We have already considered this issue in our chapter "Is All of God in Jesus?"Whatever its defects, the doctrine of the Trinity was an attempt to defend a doctrine of the Incarnation without the absurdity of concluding that God could ever cease to be God. If God's reality was to be found nowhere else but in the man Jesus, then we would have the absurdity of a total kenosis, an act of God by which He ceases to be God. This is the impasse into which the radical theologians such as Altizer seem to have fallen.[20]

Tillich seems to think that it is impossible to protect the concept of Incarnation from superstitious connotations and that it is therefore better to

---

[17]Oliver Quick, *Doctrines of the Creed* (London: Nisbet, 1938), pp. 132ff.
[18]Tillich, *Systematic Theology*, II, 94ff.
[19]*Ibid.*, p. 94.
[20]Thomas J.J. Altizer, *The Gospel of Christian Atheism* (Philadelphia: Westminster, 1966), pp. 102ff.

drop it. This seems a desperate expedient in view of the long and widespread use of the term "Incarnation" in Christian thought and doctrine. But why should not the infinite and transcendent Creator be able to establish a special relationship to one of His creatures through whom the fullness of His holy love can be manifest without the destruction of the human reality of the creature? Indeed, Tillich admits this in terms of his particular philosophy and its terminology. Jesus is the "new being," the man in whom essence and existence are one because Jesus is not alienated from the Ground of Being. It seems fair to take this as Tillich's affirmation of transcendence, and not as a statement only about the human psychology of Jesus. God has become man even for Tillich in the sense that "God is manifest in a personal life-process as a saving participant in the human predicament."[21] This does not necessarily mean that Tillich is saying all that the historic faith has wanted to say. After all, God might be manifest as saving participant in many personal centers, though Tillich seems to give to Jesus the absolute preeminence as far as the human race is concerned. Nevertheless, he does speculate about the possibility of divine manifestations in "other areas or periods of being." It is not altogether clear what he has in mind here, but probably he was thinking of the possibility of rational creatures in other planets than the earth, or of another cosmos or series of "worlds" either preceding or following the one we now inhabit. We shall defer comment on this kind of issue until the end of the book.

(b) It is also clear, however, that the metaphysical attributes, taken by themselves and as abstract concepts, tell us little of what we really want to know. It is the character, nature, or essence of Godhead in terms of our highest moral and spiritual values which is of practical importance to men. Can God in any sense share my suffering as I seek to bear it with courage and fortitude, and wrest spiritual victory from it? If it is said that God is wholly and totally impassible, i.e., unable to feel with, or have any empathy for, human suffering, what can we make of the Cross? We could, of course, limit the suffering to the humanity only of Jesus. In doing so, however, God's involvement in the sufferings of men is eliminated and the result is a violent contrast between a compassionate Jesus and an aloof and distant deity untouched by the sufferings of men. This is destructive of the Christian understanding of God and of His oneness with the Son. Jesus becomes a nobler figure than the Father, if indeed the term "Father" can be significantly applied to One who is indifferent and untouched by the weakness, infirmity, suffering, and sin of men. It is at this point that Chalcedon is open to the most serious objections. By assuming from the philosophical tradition

---

[21]Tillich, *Systematic Theology*, II, p. 95.

the dogma of divine impassibility, it made the reconciling of humanity and divinity in Jesus an impossible task. "And it expels from the company of the priests those who dare to say that the Godhead of the Only-begotten is passible."[22] So also the Tome of Leo tells us that "the impassible God did not disdain to be passible man"; "as the Godhead is not changed by the compassion, so the manhood is not absorbed by the dignity."[23]

H. Wheeler Robinson stated some years ago that modern theology has largely returned to the assertion of divine passibility, though he recognizes that the earlier view was intended to safeguard a biblical view of God against serious philosophical objections. It was intended to safeguard Christian thinking against the ascription to God of all-too-human feelings and imperfections. Furthermore, if God is entangled in the time process so that He becomes wholly subject to its frustrations, what becomes of His sovereignty or of the Christian confidence that God will ultimately triumph over weakness, sin, and death, which are the marks of our estranged situation or the characteristics of all finite existence? The issue then becomes whether one can state the reality of God's active and redeeming participation in human suffering without leaving us with an impotent God who is as subject to frustration as we are. Robinson believed that it could be so stated. He firmly maintained that the meaning of God's love is destroyed if it is not costly to Him as well as to Jesus. Again, self-limitation in God or His submission to suffering is not damaging to His sovereignty over the time process provided such self-limitation is not conceived of as due to frustration imposed upon Him by factors over which He has no ultimate control. I believe this line of argument to be sound, and if accepted, it releases us from some of the great difficulties implied in the Chalcedonian attempt to reconcile an impassible divinity with a passible humanity in the one Person Jesus Christ.[24]

Assuming, therefore, that God can voluntarily accept some self-limitation in His revealing activity and presence in Jesus Christ, how could He do this without ceasing to be God and in such a way that men could accept the words attributed to Jesus in the Fourth Gospel: "He that hath seen me hath seen the Father"? It is not enough to say that God's power is revealed in the suffering, weak, and humiliated Christ, or, to vary the language, that the power of His love is most clearly manifested where the love is shown at its most impotent. ("God is weak and powerless in the world, and that is exactly the way, the only way, in which He can be with us and help us. . . .

---

[22]Thomas H. Bindley, *The Oecumenical Documents of the Faith,* rev. by F.W. Green (London: Methuen, 1950), p. 234.

[23]*Ibid.,* p. 227.

[24]For a sensitive and penetrating discussion of the problem of suffering, see H. Wheeler Robinson, *Suffering Human and Divine* (London: S.C.M., 1940).

The Bible . . . directs . . . [us] to the powerlessness and suffering of God; only a suffering God can help.'')[25] The faith of the church originated not only from the suffering but from the suffering and the *risen* Christ, together with the giving of the Spirit. If the Resurrection and the Spirit are not dismissed as merely the "subjective" experiences of the early disciples, then is it accurate to talk only of the "powerlessness" of God?

Obviously important truths are being asserted when this kind of language is used, but it is not the whole truth. It is not enough to affirm that Jesus was moved by agape love, even suffering love, and say no more. We need to know whether this is "powerless love," to quote Tillich, or whether love reigns from the eternal throne of God (if Professor Ling will permit a monarchical image again). Nor is it adequate to say that love can triumph or ought to triumph only by its intrinsic appeal as such. If we are speaking of the human heart, this is true. God can never transform the rebellious human heart by the sheer display of naked power. The final word for Christians cannot be the voice from the whirlwind of the book of Job. Nevertheless, the power of love as the "ultimate" power cannot be taken as self-evident. Did the agape love of Jesus perish with His death? If one is still enough of a traditional Christian to assert the Resurrection as more than a reinterpretation of the meaning of the Cross and more than merely subjective visions, as we have maintained, then one has to say, as the New Testament does, that God raised Jesus from the dead by His power. The word "love" cannot be substituted for power in this connection. True, God raised Jesus because He is the Son of His love, but such a victory over death was not possible unless God has a power which includes but is not exhausted by what we call love, even the special agape love of the Cross.

We are back with God's sovereignty over His creation, requisite for love's victory over death. What was true for Jesus at this point is also true for the rest of us. I may be moved to penitence and inspired to new life by the divine love in Jesus at its point of greatest weakness and humiliation in the face of death and the evil of men. But if death is the last word on my life, then love has not triumphed. It has gleamed, perhaps rather fitfully, in the Christian believer only to be swallowed up again in eternal night. There is no way out of this dilemma by appealing to utopian ideas of a millennial or any other earthly society. Love, to be victorious, requires power stronger than death, man's last enemy. This means stronger not only in that it leaves an indelible impression on the minds and hearts of succeeding generations of believers but stronger than the whole human race, past, present, and future, which lives in this age under the reign of mortality. Nor does talk of eternal

---

[25]Dietrich Bonhoeffer, *Letters and Papers from Prison* (London: Collins, 1959), p. 122.

life as a present possession, or of realized eschatology, meet this point, important as these truths are in their proper place.

This digression, if it be such, has been necessary before the question of Christology can be properly treated. No Christology which uses the concept of love to destroy the power of God as Creator and Sustainer of this world can be satisfactory. Not only does such a procedure call into question the eternal reality of this love itself. It ignores undoubted elements in the New Testament witness and leaves the believer with a basic uncertainty about the triumph of the very Lord who has brought him the message of God's love and secured his reconciliation. Chalcedon is not open to the previous objections in that it never obscures the sovereignty of God over His creation, even if its concept of power is unnecessarily linked with the doctrine of impassibility. What shall we say of later attempts to grapple with the Christological problem?

Professor Pannenberg has drawn our attention to the distinction we have already used between a Christology "from above" and a Christology "from below":

> For Christology that begins 'from above', from the divinity of Jesus, the conception of the Incarnation stands in the centre. A Christology 'from below', rising from the historical man Jesus to the recognition of His divinity is concerned first of all with Jesus' message and fate and arrives only at the end at the concept of the Incarnation.[26]

This difference in starting-point is of vital importance for any attempt to commend some doctrine of the divinity of Christ. This is not always made sufficiently clear when theological discussion is involved. If the person to whom our arguments are directed is already a believer who accepts the Trinitarian dogma and some version of the preexistence of the Word or the Eternal Son, much of the argument may seem unnecessary since the divinity is assumed. It then becomes simply a question of intellectually clarifying, as far as possible, the mystery of the Incarnation of the preexistent Word or Son which is already accepted on faith, and already interpreted in terms of descent and ascent. In other words, the aim is to confirm the believer in his basic conviction and help him to a deeper understanding of the faith he already holds. This is faith seeking understanding.

However, as Pannenberg points out, a Christology "from above" is not the self-evident starting-point for modern man, not even when he is a believer. There is a vast difference between our contemporary intellectual climate of opinion and that of the early church, when a Logos philosophy and some concept of divinity could often be taken for granted, even among

---

[26]Pannenberg, *Jesus: God and Man,* p. 38.

pagans. For good or ill, this is no longer the case. Neither the Logos nor notions of preexistence nor for that matter the Jewish concept of God can be assumed. This is often as true for theological students as it is for modern "secular" man, assuming again that such students can be distinguished from "secular" man, a view some at least would passionately repudiate. The theological teacher today has to begin with the man Jesus of Nazareth and show, if he can, what evidence justifies the further application of such categories as uniqueness, divinity, the descending and ascending Redeemer, and preexistence. These categories are no longer accepted as in themselves validating the "divinity" of Jesus Christ. Rather they themselves have to find their justification in what is revealed of God's activity and presence in the career and fate of Jesus of Nazareth. In other words, our Christology must start from below and lead, if it can, to the point where these other categories can be seen to be reasonable and illuminating.

Some will object very strongly to this method of approach on the ground that by starting with the career and fate of Jesus of Nazareth one has already begged the question of divinity. That this has sometimes been true of this kind of Christological approach can hardly be doubted. However, it need not necessarily be so. We have already noted Kähler's criticism that an important motive at work in those who undertook the quest of the historical Jesus was to get behind dogma, including presumably that of the divinity as formulated in the later developments of the doctrine. However, this need not be so. To begin Christology "from below" does not mean that the New Testament permits us to construct a Jesus completely divorced from the interpretation of faith. It does mean, however, that there is a history of the interpretations of faith. Many models are used both in Scripture and later doctrinal history. Some rightly contend that in the earliest strands of the New Testament witness and tradition such concepts as preexistence and divine descent were already employed. This is true, as can be seen from the Pauline letters, the letter to the Hebrews, and the Fourth Gospel. On the other hand, it is not easy to read the gospels and the Acts of the Apostles and arrive at the conclusion that the early apostles and disciples always spontaneously expressed their faith in Jesus in these terms. Furthermore, there have always been Christians in the post-apostolic experience of the church who seem to have been able to sustain a faith and a confession of divinity without employing the concept of preexistence. One could argue that if they had been fully aware of the logical implications of their faith, they would inevitably have arrived at the use of such a category. This may be so, but some evidently did not feel this to be so. Among contemporary Christians, particularly the young, there are many who not only feel that such categories are not logically implied in their confession of faith but strongly repudiate the suggestion. As a matter of method, therefore, especially if our purpose is to present Jesus Christ to men and women outside the church, a Christology "from below" would seem to be the necessary starting-point. We may end with affirmations not very different from those of the classical Christology "from above." We cannot start with the latter as a self-evident datum. It is, however, important to realize that this is precisely a matter of method. Pannenberg's thesis seems to be that if modern man is to be led to a confession of divinity, then he must retrace in his own experience the stages through which the New Testament and later theological reflection passed. He must begin where they began with Jesus of Nazareth and seek to experience what they experienced in relationship to Him before they can understand why the early disciples and the post-apostolic church were led to formulate a doctrine of divinity in the manner now familiar to us in the creeds.

There are, however, important implications in starting at this point. It implies that it is now possible to distinguish in some measure at least between fact and interpretation in the New Testament. If we cannot speak of the "faith of Jesus," or if we actually know next to nothing about Jesus' own thinking concerning His mission and His vocation, then a Christology "from below" is hardly possible. If all that we can be certain of is the faith of the church expressed in the documents of the New Testament, then a Christology "from above" can make out a very strong case for itself. The New Testament already contains, in important sections, the use of interpretive categories (preexistence, divine descent and ascent, etc.). Unless at least some distinctions can be made between the use of these categories and that which they purport to interpret, then a Christology "from below," in Pannenberg's sense, is not possible.

I believe that such a distinction can be made between Jesus of Nazareth and the interpretation of His Person, though it has to be admitted that this is still one of the most hotly debated of all New Testament problems. If such a distinction can be made, then it means, in T.W. Manson's words, that the quest of the historical Jesus must continue.[27] How, then, shall we go about constructing a Christology "from below" if the above considerations are valid? Just as God can be known experientially only in a unique spiritual intuition, so the divinity of Christ can be known only on the basis of a spiritual discernment given to faith. "We are reminded that Christological doctrine only arises because a worshipful situation arises around the ac-

---

[27]Manson, *Studies in the Gospels and Epistles,* p. 3; see also Anthony Hanson, *Vindications;* C.F.D. Moule, *The Phenomenon of the New Testament,* Studies in Biblical Theology, Second Series, No. 1 (London: S.C.M., 1967).

knowledged humanity of Jesus.''[28] This obviously cannot be proved by any appeal to logic or history. ''But the impulse to believe itself must come, if it comes at all, from the direct perception that a particular kind of life is the life most worth living. For those who have it, the perception is a supernatural call which, according as they will, they may follow or they may refuse.''[29] Thus, in the last resort there is no ''proof'' of the divinity of Christ to anyone who completely lacks this perception.

Paul Tillich makes the same point when he asserts that ''every understanding of spiritual things is circular''[30] and that in this case the circle is not vicious. Before a man can speak of divinity in the deepest sense of Jesus of Nazareth, he ''must have an immediate experience of something ultimate in value and being of which one can become intuitively aware.''[31] If it is objected that this is to erect bias into a principle, it can be replied that this is equally true of all the spiritual intuitions which lie at the heart of all the great religions which have ever swayed large numbers of men.

It can also be pointed out, with Dorothy Emmet, that at the root of all philosophies is a judgment of importance, rooted in such a spiritual intuition which determines the perspective from which the philosopher views the whole of his experience of reality.[32] The religious man is not, therefore, committing some heinous intellectual sin peculiar to men of faith. He is only doing what all men do when they think about the world, themselves, and what lies beyond the world. And even if the philosopher denies the supernatural, his purely this-worldly philosophy conceals a basic judgment of value about our present existence which lies at the root of all his work.

Thus, even a Christology ''from below'' has to acknowledge that an encounter with Jesus of Nazareth, however achieved, does not of itself guarantee or inevitably produce the Christian confession of the divinity. Not all who met Jesus in the days of His flesh recognized who He was. It is not likely that modern man, confronted with Jesus by historical knowledge of Him, will of necessity be led to faith. Yet the fact remains that such knowledge of Jesus remains an indispensable basis for faith, even if it does not inevitably generate faith. Even if modern man is led to faith in the full Christian sense, the question still arises whether that response of faith gives us a genuine discernment of who Jesus was or whether it is only a projection of subjective aspirations or interpretations. In other words, how does faith

---

[28]Ian Ramsey, ed., *Words About God* (London: S.C.M., 1971), p. 221.

[29]Edwyn Bevan, *Christianity* (London: Home University Library, 1932), p. 254.

[30]Paul Tillich, *Systematic Theology,* I (London: Nisbet, 1953), p. 12.

[31]*Ibid.*

[32]Dorothy Emmet, *The Nature of Metaphysical Thinking* (London: Macmillan, 1935), pp. 194ff.

become certain of the reality and character of the object of faith, namely the unique redeeming presence of God in Christ?

The conclusion to be drawn from this, however, is not that we all have what R.M. Hare calls our particular "blik," that all spiritual intuitions are equally valid, and that there is no disputing about tastes, in this case spiritual tastes. Before a spiritual intuition can claim to be a true discernment of reality, certain criteria need to be satisfied. In regard to the matter we are now considering, the fact that a man believes himself to have in the presence of Jesus Christ "an immediate experience of something ultimate in value and being" does not of itself resolve the question of the validity of that experience in as far as it is supposed also to involve a true discernment of the nature of Jesus and thereby of God. There is no question that it is valid for him. The question is whether he can affirm its validity for others unless he can show that his experience meets certain criteria. In relation to Jesus, the following criteria would seem to be involved.

(a) Is this spiritual intuition of faith congruous with what we know about Jesus of Nazareth in the light of the most rigorous historical investigation?

(b) Does it find support in the way others have responded to the same fact?

(c) Does what the man of faith says about Jesus on the basis of his experience conflict with logic (i.e., is it free from self-contradiction), with science (i.e., well-ascertained knowledge about the nature of the world in which we live), and with history?

(d) Does the intuition of faith run into insuperable difficulties from the point of view of philosophy? This raises special problems since there is not one philosophy, and Christian faith is obviously not compatible with each and every philosophy. The matter, therefore, might be put in another way: Does the affirmation of Jesus' divinity increase the intelligibility of our total experience in a manner which would be lacking if this particular kind of affirmation were not made?

I believe that it is possible to give an affirmative answer to these questions without a *sacrificium intellectus,* while remembering that the spiritual intuition which is involved in faith's confession of Jesus as Lord is not a simple logical deduction from nonreligious premises. This, in the nature of the case, it could never be. It must be remembered again that there can be no proof of the divinity of Jesus to a man who completely lacks the experience of the power of Jesus to produce certain transforming effects in his life. Nevertheless, the intuition of God's reality and presence given in Jesus and thus experienced can be shown to be "reasonable" in the sense that it illuminates the whole of human experience and history. It can be shown to cohere with the rest of our knowledge of the world and of man. Beyond that we cannot go in proving the validity of the Christian experience of God in Jesus Christ. This, however, is not surprising and should not be disturbing. If it were possible to prove the divinity of Jesus Christ to the unbeliever by a knockdown series of logical arguments, then the spiritual value and significance of the Christian confession would be nil. Acceptance of Jesus' divinity would be no different from accepting the existence of other persons or of the natural world around us. It would be a neutral statement without moral and spiritual import. Such a proof would give us a postulate of some reality, but not a reality with which or with whom we are involved at the deepest level of moral and spiritual apprehension.

Thus, it is legitimate to start with a Christology "from below" as a matter of evangelistic and pastoral concern. We may start with the man Jesus of Nazareth but we cannot stop there. There is no transition from such a Jesus to the Lord of Christian faith unless we can come to see Him and His significance from the post-Easter perspective, which is that of all the New Testament documents. Thus Christology may start "from below," but faith will demand that it arrive at a Christology from above, i.e., from the affirmation that in this Jesus, including his death and resurrection, God in His saving power is truly encountered. From the Christian point of view, therefore, the starting-point is a matter of strategy rather than of principle. To start with the man Jesus does not imply that faith only reads into the historical actuality a truth and reality which are not there. It may be that the Christ of faith is a truer discernment of the full historical actuality than a Jesus of history stripped of all interpretation. This must be considered on its merits. The point we are making here is that there are good reasons in the present climate of opinion for starting from the man Jesus. A Christian can never be content simply to remain there.

6.
How Much of a Man Was Jesus?

The popular title of this chapter is in itself open to severe criticism. This way of phrasing the question seems to suggest that Jesus might have been part man and part something else, and therefore to involve the very difficulties for which Chalcedon has been so criticized. There is, however, some merit occasionally in stating a problem in the inexact language of the ordinary person. The latter is often troubled and perplexed about this issue. Was Jesus really a man? If so, can the Christian claim possibly be true? If not, how can His mysterious otherness ever be relevant to my all-too-human existence? The problem is real, even though the title's way of putting it leaves much to be desired.

Our previous discussion now calls for a more concentrated study of the humanity of Jesus, particularly if we are to justify, as a matter of theological method, the working out of a Christology "from below." It should be repeated that the question of the reality of the humanity arises only in the context of some claim to divinity as well. If the claim to divinity has been dismissed or is not even under consideration, then presumably no one will raise questions about the humanity. If Jesus is classified as only the greatest of the prophets, or as the finest flowering of the religious genius of the race, it is clear that no question concerning the humanity will arise. We may have difficulty in explaining the why and the how of the emergence of such a genius, but this is no different in principle from asking why Mahatma Gandhi appeared in India when he did. Jesus might still be mysterious in the sense in which all human genius has something elusive and inexplicable about it, but this would be a matter of degree. The appearance of genius might compel us to modify our opinion about the potentialities of human nature. It would not raise any basic question about the humanity of the genius himself. On this assumption, Jesus would by definition not be basically different from his fellow men, however great the difference of degree in regard to his genius. It is only when the Christian asserts the true humanity of

Jesus in the context of a similar assertion about His divinity that a theological problem arises in the sense intended in this discussion.

Canon Charles Raven, in the preface to his book on Apollinarianism,[1] tells how he was stimulated to write the book by a teacher's suggestion that Apollinarianism was the prevalent heresy of the day. Raven explains that when he started to work on the book, he accepted the traditional view of the "impersonal" humanity of our Lord. But by the end of the study he had given this up as unsatisfactory and come to share his teacher's view that Apollinarianism was indeed the most widespread modern heresy. This was in 1934. In 1959 there appeared Norman Pittenger's *The Word Incarnate,* the main thesis of which is sympathetic to the point Raven was making nearly forty years ago.[2] Pittenger is obviously convinced too that modern theology does not do justice to the genuine humanity of our Lord. He is greatly annoyed with Karl Barth, and rightly, for asserting that Jesus was probably not a very interesting or significant human personality. Barth's assertion is certainly reacting against liberal theology with a vengeance.

There can be little doubt that what Professor H.E.W. Turner calls "the great church" intended to assert the full and complete humanity of our Lord.[3] It strenuously resisted all gnostic attempts to dissolve the physical body into a phantasma, an unreal appearance. The emphasis on the Virgin Birth no doubt did as much to safeguard the reality of the body as it did the miraculous nature of His entry into the world. Whatever Apollinaris may have intended to say, the church understood him to be denying the complete humanity of Jesus and condemned him accordingly. The long process of Christological debate which culminated in the Definition of Chalcedon affirmed that Jesus Christ was truly God and truly man: "the self-same of a rational soul and body ($\theta\epsilon\grave{o}\nu$ $\dot{\alpha}\lambda\eta\theta\tilde{\omega}\varsigma$ $\kappa\alpha\grave{\iota}$ $\ddot{\alpha}\nu\theta\rho\omega\pi\sigma\nu$ $\dot{\alpha}\lambda\eta\theta\tilde{\omega}\varsigma$) consubstantial with the Father according to the Godhead, the self-same consubstantial with us ($\dot{o}\mu\sigma\sigma\acute{\nu}\sigma\iota\sigma\nu$) according to the manhood." This seems unequivocal and definite enough. What more needs to be said? Has not the Spirit of God led the church to a definitive judgment on this matter and cannot we leave it at that?

To this may be added the following comments. An authoritative conciliar definition does not in itself guarantee preservation of the truth. We have already noticed the misgivings of Raven, Pittenger, Knox, and others as to whether the church and Christian piety have in fact given full weight to the humanity, whatever may be the formal declaration of the creeds. Each generation must, of course, grasp and appreciate Christian truth afresh. It

---

[1]Raven, *Apollinarianism.*
[2]Norman Pittenger, *The Word Incarnate* (London: Nisbet, 1959), p. 10.
[3]Turner, *Pattern of Christian Truth.*

may justifiably be asked whether the church itself fully understood the full implications of what it was saying in A.D. 451. Furthermore, it seems impossible to repress the desire for at least some understanding of the Christian mystery. *Fides quaerens intellectum* is a permanent situation for all thoughtful Christians in every age. Men are not content merely to assert but wish to understand what they assert in terms which are relevant to their current experience of the world.

Before entering into a more technical discussion of the problem we have raised, it may very well be asked what is its practical import and value, particularly for the worship, witness, and devotion of Christians. As St. Paul would say, "Much in every way." Preachers are fond of reminding their people that Jesus was one of us, that He knows and shares our experiences, that He knows what it is to be tested and tried and to struggle against evil, that He has truly lived our life and gained the victory, not in some far-off dream world but in this world of torturing uncertainty and crippling sin. He is our Lord and Savior, but He is also our Elder Brother, bone of our bone, flesh of our flesh. As Irenaeus said long ago, "He became what we are . . . in order that He might make us as He Himself is (*propter suam immensam dilectionem factus est quod sumus nos, uti nos perficeret esse quod et ipse*)."[4]

Those fathers whom we associate most definitely with the orthodoxy of the creeds of the ecumenical church of the first centuries, up to and including Chalcedon, all affirm that the Logos became man ($\dot{\epsilon}\nu\alpha\nu\theta\rho\omega\pi\dot{\eta}\sigma\alpha\nu\tau\alpha$). Athanasius in *De Incarnatione* affirms that "He was made man ($\dot{\epsilon}\nu\eta\nu\theta\rho\dot{\omega}\pi\eta\sigma\epsilon\nu$) that we might be made divine ($\theta\epsilon\sigma\pi\sigma\iota\eta\theta\dot{\omega}\mu\epsilon\nu$)."[5] Many were content to use the familiar Johannine language, but the ambiguity of the term "flesh" in the face of heretical misinterpretation compelled the framers of the Niceno-Constantinopolitan creed of A.D. 381 to add, "and was made man ($\dot{\epsilon}\nu\alpha\nu\theta\rho\omega\pi\dot{\eta}\sigma\alpha\nu\tau\alpha$)." The verbal affirmation that the Logos became not only flesh but man is firmly embedded in the pre-Chalcedonian period. How is this to be interpreted? It is often assumed that "humanity" is an easy term to define and that to assert that the Jesus of the gospels was truly man is to make a simple statement of fact. Yet the history of the debate concerning the person of Christ shows that things are not as simple as they seem and that in fact Christian thinkers are deeply divided as to what "truly man" means in this context. The two positions are roughly as follows.

Some maintain that it is possible to determine what constitutes "humanity" by an empirical study of man. "The proper study of mankind is man," and by taking advantage of all that the various disciplines can reveal

---

[4]Irenaeus, *Adversus Haereses* 5, praef.

[5]Athanasius, *The Incarnation*, trans. A. Robertson (London: David Nutt, 1911), c. LIV.

about the nature of man, we can arrive at a definition. Biology, psychology, sociology, history, philosophy—the cumulative result of all these studies is to enable us to define what it means to be "truly man." Having arrived at our definition of humanity, we can then apply it to the historic Jesus. If we wish to assert that He was truly man, then it must be in the sense that these previous studies have already given to the term. The ordinary man with his lack of specialized knowledge in the exact and social sciences assumes that he knows what "humanity" means on the basis of his own experience of himself as a thinking, willing, purposive being. He knows love, hate, fear, temptation, sin, failure, remorse, the pull of the ideal. If Jesus was truly human, then he must have shared fully the kind of experience with which he, the ordinary man, is familiar. Like the more sophisticated thinker, the layman assumes a prior knowledge of the nature of genuine humanity which he can then bring as a norm by which to define the "truly human" of the Word Incarnate.

Against this is the vigorous protest of those who assert that this is a false and dangerously misleading starting-point. It is true that we may fashion some kind of anthropology by studying man as he is in his empirical historical existence. The trouble is, it is asserted, that we have no means of deciding which of the various doctrines of man is true. According to what norm do we select between Platonic and Aristotelian man, the man of Hobbes or of Rousseau, of Marx or Freud, of Watson or Sartre? We cannot choose until we know man's telos, the goal in which his true nature is realized. This telos cannot be known in the Christian sense until we know what end God has in store for men. To look at man empirically is to see him in bondage to sin and corruption. To look into myself is not to see genuine humanity but to see man estranged from God and divided from his fellow man. Such an empirical study of man, so the argument goes, is a dead end. The only solution is to study the Word made man, to see man not in the characteristics of empirical man in general, but in the perfect manhood assumed by the God-Man, Jesus Christ. To know what true humanity means, we must look at the humanity of our Lord. When we do this, we discover that His humanity is not necessarily an exact duplication of our own. From the point of view of sinful and empirical man, his human nature will be seen as unique, since in the light of the premise from which this argument starts, no actual man displays "true humanity" in the sense that God intended it to be. The "truly man," therefore, cannot be defined in terms of human nature as we know it, but only in terms of the humanity assumed by the Word, and this is by no means the same thing. This is the point of view argued with passion and learning by Karl Barth, and many who are not Barthians will sympathize very much with what he has to say at this point. "I believe," says Leonard Hodgson, "that a great deal of error in christological thinking is due to our taking ourselves as the standard of manhood, and asking how far the Jesus of the gospels conforms to that standard. But if the Christian faith be true, we are poor specimens of manhood, even the best of us, not only imperfect but corrupted by sin."[6]

Are we confronted here with two irreconcilable points of view? If we cannot know what it means to be human by studying empirical man, how can we distinguish the humanity of our Lord from His divinity? Would we not be completely without a norm by which we could decide such a question, except by arbitrarily choosing certain features from the gospel portrait to designate as human? In any case, the gospels are so sparing in the detail they give us about the inner life, the psychology, of Jesus that it would be no easy task to define manhood from the meagre information provided. Of course, the reason for this reticence on the part of the evangelists may be that they assumed that Jesus' human nature was the same as ours, and that readers did not need to be told what it means to be human. There must be something in common between our unregenerate human nature and Christ's sinless human nature. Otherwise, we would have to say that sinful men are no longer human, and this is an assumption that creates too many difficulties.

The conclusion we draw, therefore, is that if the term "truly man" is to be applied to Jesus, then it must be in a sense that is normally given to the term in our own experience. It does not mean that Jesus was an "ordinary" man if by that is meant average and undistinguished, with no outstanding qualities which mark Him off from other men. C.H. Dodd's book has already been cited as giving us an impressive portrait of a real man, whatever else we may feel it necessary to say about Him. If the gospels do not enter into any elaborate discussion of whether He was a real man, the most reasonable assumption is that it was never called in question.

Let is be repeated that we are not suggesting that the gospels are unable to give us any information about the man Jesus of Nazareth. This involves a radical scepticism to which the historical study of the gospels is not driven. However, we are saying that if we approached the gospels without any prior knowledge in our experience of what it means to be a man, then we would find it very difficult indeed to construct a satisfactory account of manhood simply from the records as such. But, then, this would be equally true of Plato or Julius Caesar. There would seem, therefore, to be no option but to start with an analysis of our general experience of what it means to be a man, whatever qualifications we may want to make later in regard to Jesus.

Let us approach the matter, then, from a broadly empirical point of

---

[6]Leonard Hodgson, *Christian Faith and Practice* (Oxford: Blackwell, 1952, p. 67.

view. What kind of definition of human nature do we arrive at if we keep to such information as ordinary observation and introspection would afford? There is no need to trace the history of philosophical, scientific, and psychological thought from Aristotle onwards. The following conclusions appear to emerge with reasonable certainty.

(a) To be truly human implies the possession of a genuine physical body with certain instincts, passions, desires, etc. I am aware that "instinct" is out of fashion among many modern psychologists, but our definition does not demand our adherence to any particular school of psychology. No one disputes that men eat and drink, seek their own preservation, engage in sexual behavior, etc.

(b) Despite the behaviorists, man is also a conscious being. More than that, he experiences a dynamic psychic life, part of which is in the subconscious or the unconscious. If William James, Freud, and Jung are even partially correct, human nature everywhere will possess this wider and deeper psychical life. Dean Matthews has rightly asked what bearing this modern understanding of our human psychology will or should have upon our understanding of our Lord's genuine humanity.[7]

(c) A genuine human life involves gradual growth to maturity in interaction with the human and the nonhuman environment.

(d) A human being possesses rational, moral, and spiritual capacities that distinguish him from the animal world. This is true whether we are thinking of the Australian aborigine or the most refined product of Christian culture. Whether such capacities involve the "objectivity of values" or a theistic worldview or a particular philosophy can be left aside for the moment. Men communicate through intelligible language; they think; they fashion tools; they have a sense of "ought," however explained; they worship, however diverse may be their objects of worship. It is an anthropologist, not a Christian theologian, who tells us, after studying the significance of symbolic language, that there is an "irreducible distinction in kind between the mental functions of man on the one hand, and those of the animal kingdom on the other."[8]

(e) All human knowing involves trial and error and progress from inadequate to more adequate knowledge. There is what Wheeler Robinson has called the "ministry of error"[9] as the means of arriving at fuller truth. Would a genuine human nature permit a harmonious growth in knowledge without the ministry of error entering in?

---

[7]W. R. Matthews, *The Problem of Christ in the Twentieth Century* (London: Oxford Univ. Press, 1950).

[8]David Bidney, *Theoretical Anthropology* (New York: Columbia Univ. Press, 1953), p. 4.

[9]H. W. Robinson, *Revelation and Redemption,* Chapter 11.

(f) Human nature, as we know it, involves being subject to temptation in the sense of being enticed to evil. Empirically, all men seem to have yielded to temptation; this appears to be a fact, apart from any theological explanation of the origin of sin or the way its consequences have been transmitted from one generation to another. Can there be a genuine human nature subject to temptation but not necessarily yielding to it? Meanwhile, we must assert that a genuine human nature at least involves the possibility of being tempted.

(g) Finally, all the existing points have implied the existence of an enduring "ego" as the active center of personal life. A Humeian or Buddhistic dissolution of personal unity into a mere juxtaposition of psychological states would render null and void our previous contentions. The self becomes a string of beads with no string to hold them together. James Ward's defence of the "organizing self" in his *Psychological Principles*[10] still remains to be refuted. The well-known witticism that modern psychology first lost its soul, then its mind, and finally with the behaviorists lost consciousness seems no longer quite so applicable to the present situation. In spite of what E.L. Mascall calls Professor Gilbert Ryle's highly sophisticated behaviorism, there are powerful voices being raised against the absurdity of a psychology without a "self." We may note in the first place Professor A.A. Bowman's remarkable *Studies in the Philosophy of Religion,* which deserves more attention than seems to be given the philosophy of religion these days.[11] Among slightly newer works, Mascall's own treatment of the question in *Christian Theology and Natural Science,* Austin Farrer's *Finite and Infinite,* C.A. Campbell's recent Gifford Lectures, John MacMurray's *Self as Agent,* and the essay on soul by J.R. Lucas in *Faith and Logic* all add up to a formidable case.[12] Still more recently, *Prospect for Metaphysics,* under the editorship of Ian Ramsey, and last but not least, H.D. Lewis' remarkable Gifford Lectures have argued the same case.[13] It seems more and more evident that a human nature without a "self" bears no relation to a person whether viewed from the angle of an adequate psychology or philosophy or from the daily experience of the so-called average man.

---

[10]James Ward, *Psychological Principles,* 2nd ed. (Cambridge: Cambridge Univ. Press, 1920), ch. 15.

[11]A.A. Bowman, *Studies in Philosophy of Religion,* 2 vols. (London: Macmillan, 1938), II, ch. 22.

[12]E.L. Mascall, *Christian Theology and Natural Science* (London: Longmans Green, 1956), ch. 6; Austin Farrer, *Finite and Infinite* (Westminster: Dacre, 1943); Charles A. Campbell, *On Selfhood and Godhood* (London: Allen & Unwin, 1957), pp. 73–94; John MacMurray, *Self as Agent* (New York: Humanities, 1957); J.R. Lucas, "The Soul" in *Faith and Logic,* ed. Basil Mitchell (London: Allen & Unwin, 1957), pp. 132–148.

[13]Ian T. Ramsey, *Prospect for Metaphysics* (London: Allen & Unwin, 1961); H.D. Lewis, *The Elusive Mind* (London: Allen & Unwin, 1969).

Of the seven points we have mentioned, is there any compelling reason either in the records themselves or in theological reflection upon them to lead us not to ascribe them to Jesus of Nazareth? The reality of the human body is hardly a matter of dispute, though in the course of Christian history some have come very near to denying it, and some influenced by Gnosticism did in fact deny it, as Marcion did. It is nowhere suggested in the gospels that Jesus could dispense with food and drink, even if spiritual succour enabled Him to endure long periods of fasting, as in some striking modern instances such as Gandhi. That Jesus did not marry must surely be ascribed to His single-minded concentration on His divine vocation and not to His freedom from sexual instinct or the feelings and desires which determine the relationship between man and woman as an integral part of the marriage relationship.[14] Or are we really prepared for a dualism of a thoroughgoing kind which thinks that Jesus could not possibly have had our instincts? If we are prepared to say that Jesus had in common with all men certain rational, moral, and spiritual capacities, and that His life was a genuine growth in "wisdom and stature," does this not involve limitations of knowledge and power which such a real development would seem to demand? Karl Rahner has some interesting reflections on the significance of "become" in the time-honored phrase "The Word became flesh."[15] Similar questions are also considered by John Macquarrie.[16] Or again are we prepared to say that the baby Jesus controlled the planets from His cradle, that the man Jesus knew the secrets of nuclear fission, that the whole of future history was consciously in His mind, even to the end of the age, a claim which He expressly repudiates in Mark 13?

It may be objected that all this simply means that the Christian must accept what the secular mind has established empirically about human nature and then assert this of Christ, sin excepted. In a sense this is true, though the use of the word "secular" may obscure the fact that the human nature thus studied is the result of God's creative act, if man is really made in the image of God. If limitations in the man Jesus are not accepted at all, then we must find the "divinity" not in a perfected human nature *homoousios* with ours but in the exercise of unlimited power or the possession of unlimited and infinite knowledge. It is difficult to imagine how any man could be "man" in any sense meaningful to us and be completely without any limitations of consciousness, power, and knowledge. The Jesus of the gospels revealed by even the most conservative study would seem to make such a conclusion impossible. Donald Baillie's "no more Docetism" must be accepted, and we must have the courage to mean what we say.

[14]Tom Driver, *Sexuality and Jesus,* New Theology No. 3 (New York: Macmillan, 1966).

[15]Karl Rahner, *Theological Investigations,* Vol. I.

[16]John Macquarrie, *Principles of Christian Theology* (New York: Scribners, 1966).

It has been fashionable in some quarters to go a step further than this and say that the Word assumed our "fallen" human nature. What could this possibly mean? Those who assert this evidently do not wish to say that Jesus was sinful in any precise sense, namely that His will was in contradiction with the will of His Father. This would run counter to the orthodoxy to which they are otherwise committed. They do, however, wish to defend a notion of the fall which has permanently affected human nature as we know it. "Fallen human nature" is defined by Harry Johnson as follows:

> It is a nature that has been affected by the Fall and by the sin and rebellion of previous generations. When we come into the world we are born into a spoilt species in the sense that the power of the will has been weakened and the balances of the instincts upset. We share in all the propensities and drives of human nature as they are now in our present post-Fall human situation, we are born into a rebellious race that by its insurrection has been alienated from God.[17]

Later he says: "He assumed what was imperfect, but he wrought out of it a life that was perfect."[18] In order to maintain this position, it would appear to be necessary to maintain that the fall was historical in a very exact and literal sense, that the result of it was a permanent dislocation of human nature, passed on by heredity from generation to generation, that sin is a kind of substance which can be transmitted, that every newborn baby must of necessity sin. It is not at all certain that Dr. Johnson would want to assert all this; if he does, he would need to answer more convincingly than he has done the formidable criticisms of F.R. Tennant.[19]

Whether we are prepared to go this far and use this kind of language, it at least reinforces our plea that the humanity of our Lord has something in common with the human nature which our empirical study reveals. This means that we cannot summarily dismiss what a so-called secular anthropology reveals as though it were irrelevant to what we mean when we speak about the true humanity of our Lord. It may be asked what in this defence of a genuine humanity is incompatible with what Chalcedon was trying to assert about the human *physis* of our Lord. In principle, perhaps, nothing, though the way in which Chalcedon has sometimes been interpreted could hardly be taken as a full defence of the position here maintained. The Tome of Leo, with its doctrine of the two natures which the Council confirmed, is naive in its distinctions between them. Human nature is identified with hunger,

---

[17]Harry Johnson, *The Humanity of the Saviour* (London: Epworth, 1962), p. 24.
[18]*Ibid.*, p. 27.
[19]Frederick R. Tennant, *Sin and Its Propagation* (Cambridge: Cambridge Univ. Press, 1906).

thirst, weariness, sleep, pity; divinity with the nature miracles. Sheer power is regarded as the manifestation of the divine nature, while weakness and compassion are taken as human. But if God is love, the voluntary acceptance of weakness and compassion may be more divine than any impressive nature miracle.

Nevertheless, we know that Chalcedon could be and was in fact interpreted in a Monophysite direction. This suggests that the Definition does not in itself guarantee the truths which the framers were no doubt seeking to express. Karl Barth has defended the "impersonal humanity" on the grounds that it has been misunderstood. He contends that *impersonalitas* did not mean the absence of individuality in our modern sense of "real human personality" but only the existence of an independent and self-subsistent humanity which could exist apart from its "hypostatic" union with the Word.[20] Yet Barth does not really come to grips with the problem of how the Eternal Word could become "a man" without destroying the reality of that specific and individual man. No doubt he would maintain that it is not our business to give a psychological and philosophical account of the "how" but to accept the fact that it did so happen on the basis of the scriptural witness.

Even when all the above has been admitted, however, it does not alter the fact that orthodox Christology has found it difficult to do justice to a full humanity in the sense we would wish to give to the term. It is extremely puzzling, for example, to find Mascall asserting both limitation of knowledge and omniscience as coexisting in the one divine Person of our Lord.[21] It may be possible to restate and defend the ancient doctrine of *anhypostasia,* i.e., that the human nature retains its identity and integrity only as the agent of the divine Logos, that it has no independent existence apart from the latter. H.M. Relton, in his *Study of Christology,*[22] evidently thinks it is possible to defend the real personality of Jesus in the modern sense while continuing to assert that the center of such divine personality was the divine Logos Himself. Karl Barth, as we have seen, thinks along similar lines. Norman Pittenger, however, correctly observes that it is very difficult to state this doctrine without implying that Jesus must have lacked any "strictly human personal centre."[23] Yet this brings us again to the impasse that the Logos took a special kind of human nature, not quite the same as the nature of those he calls brethren.

---

[20]Karl Barth, *Church Dogmatics,* I, 2, ed. Geoffrey W. Bromiley and Thomas F. Torrance; trans. G.T. Thomson and H. Knight (Edinburgh: T. & T. Clark, 1935 and 1956), p. 164.

[21]Mascall, *Christ, the Christian and the Church.*

[22]Herbert M. Relton, *A Study of Christology* (London: S.P.C.K., 1917).

[23]Pittenger, *The Word Incarnate,* pp. 100ff.

How, then, are we going to escape the impasse of either a dual Nestorian Christ or a Monophysite Christ in which the human nature has been swallowed up to the point of its disappearance in any sense which would meet our previous account of human nature? Whether Nestorius was a Nestorian is a question we do not need to enter into now. There is good reason to think that Nestorius was deeply concerned to maintain the unity of the Person of Christ and that he would have repudiated the charge of duality. However, the Nestorianism which the church condemned, and which is the popular image of Nestorianism, is the view which deeply impressed and influenced the Christological debates of both the early and the later history of the church. It could also be argued that whatever his intention, Nestorius' "conceptual tools made it impossible for him to fulfil his intention adequately."[24] There seems to be no alternative but to restate the problem and pose it in fresh terms. It is not enough to affirm that Chalcedon is giving us an ontology and not a psychology of the God-Man and that this is its strength. We cannot refuse to try and frame a Christology which does reasonable justice to the Jesus Christ who emerges from the pages of the gospels. It would be extremely difficult, as Wheeler Robinson asserts, to see how two wills could ever coexist as such in any genuine personal activity.[25] It is equally difficult to see Jesus of Nazareth as having two wills in the sense asserted by some theologians. The only way out of the difficulty is a more adequate doctrine of human personality. When Relton tries to defend his form of enhypostasia by arguing that human nature apart from the Word (i.e., its relation to God), is not a true human nature, he is saying something extremely important. That man fulfils the potentialities of his human nature only in relation to and dependence upon God is something all Christians must affirm. This, however, does not alter the fact that there is some "human centering which makes him an integrated person" even when this relationship to God is incomplete and inadequate because of sin and rebellion. It would seem preferable, therefore, to start from human personality as we know it in the actuality of our own experience and that of other men. We can then tackle the problem of Christology from the premise that the most important aspect of personality is "its potential relationship to higher forms of its own reality."[26] Instead of trying to dovetail the human into the divine or vice-versa, the problem of Jesus Christ will be solved by a "deeper view of what human nature already is."[27] Human personality will then be seen as a fitting vehicle of the divine under the limiting conditions of a particular

---

[24]A.R. Vine, *An Approach to Christology* (London: Independent Press, 1948); J.N.R. Kelly, *Early Christian Doctrines* (London: A. & C. Black, 1958).
[25]H.W. Robinson, *Revelation and Redemption*, p. 208.
[26]*Ibid.*, p. 209.
[27]*Ibid.*, pp. 210–211.

historical environment. We would still, therefore, want to insist upon the seven points listed earlier as giving us the basic features of any conception of humanity we could recognize as an affirmation of what it means to be "truly man."

To develop this in a way that will enable us to construct an adequate Christology and to do justice to the divinity will demand a reexamination of certain assumptions about God, such as His impassibility, and a reaffirmation of the kinship between human and divine in terms of our modern understanding of personality. Our purpose has been to clarify the minimum requirements of a satisfactory definition of the time-honored phrase "truly man." Obviously, there is more to be said by every Christian, but at least this much must be said if we are to safeguard the true glory of the gospel that God has become truly man for us men and for our salvation. It was only after the writing of this chapter that the author read J.A.T. Robinson's *The Human Face of God*.[28] In it we find an even stronger attack upon the Apollinarianism of so much Christian thinking. Robinson thinks that most Christians are still a long way from accepting with complete seriousness Donald Baillie's dictum about No more docetism! Despite some speculative and provocative statements which are certain to get under the skin of some sensitive Christians, his main point is well taken, namely that a modern Christology must affirm not only that Jesus was the "The Man" but that He was also "a man," with all that this means for His biological and social solidarity with the human race. With this we believe that no thoughtful Christian ought to quarrel. Whether Robinson does equal justice to the concept of divinity is a matter we intend to take up again in a later chapter.

---

[28]J.A.T. Robinson, *The Human Face of God* (London: S.C.M.; Philadelphia: Westminster, 1973).

7.
The Who and
the How of the Incarnation

Having considered what is involved in any attempt to formulate a Christology, i.e., a doctrine of the Person of Jesus in terms of divinity, we turn now to the fact itself and ask whether faith's basic intuition can achieve any understanding of what it affirms. We have already conceded that if a man does not have "an immediate experience of something ultimate in value and being" when confronted with Jesus, no doctrine of divinity can be persuasive. The question that now concerns us, therefore, is not the validity of faith's intuition but whether those who have it can make the reality they claim to know in any way intelligible to themselves and whether they can present it to others without asking them to accept intolerable paradoxes and radical self-contradictions.

The heading of this chapter will evoke in the reader's mind echoes of the way in which Bonhoeffer approached the question in his *Christology*. It is well known that in the notes he left to us on this subject Bonhoeffer insisted that the correct question to ask about Jesus is not how the Incarnation occurred but rather "Who are you?" One ought not to begin with such a theological model as that of the two natures and then ask how these can be combined in the one Person. This, says Bonhoeffer, is to concentrate on the "Alchemy of the Incarnation" and can by the nature of the case lead to no definite answer. We can only ask the practical questions of what, where, and who. The question, What is Jesus Christ? can be answered only in terms of Word, sacrament, and church or community. This is the only context where I can meet Jesus as the One who is both my Judge and Savior and where I can experientially know His power to save and redeem my existence from sin, guilt, and estrangement and restore to me my true being. On the basis of this experience, faith is then led on to affirm that here God is truly and uniquely present to do His saving work in me and for me and on my behalf. Beyond this, I cannot and have no right to go. I know His divinity in what this Jesus actually does for me, and this is the only kind of divinity that really matters. To go beyond this and ask how this could be, to seek for an intellectual formula which would rationally explain HOW God and man can be conjoined in this way—this, according to Bonhoeffer, is intellectual impertinence, if not blasphemy.

There can be no question of the attractiveness of this approach. It seems to rescue divinity from the realm of abstract speculations; it anchors it squarely in an experience of what Jesus actually does in and for me, a point we have already stressed, and which is indeed an important point in the thinking of the early Protestant Reformers. It also appears to free us from the barren debate about the two natures which has burdened Christian theology for many centuries. Nevertheless, there seems to be a deep urge in many Christian believers to continue to ask the "how" question, not simply out of an itch for speculation for its own sake but because the ability to go even as far as Bonhoeffer does is sometimes inhibited by some of the stumbling-blocks which later theological developments have put in the way of faith. We seek not only to fall down and declare in faith, "My Lord and my God," but to articulate that experience in a way that illumines the mind of the believer. Indeed, this very declaration is already a theological articulation of a certain kind of experience evoked by the Person of Jesus. Few have ever maintained that the mystery of the Incarnation can be made fully transparent to the human understanding. For that we would need to be the God-Man ourselves. Nevertheless the question is still a very real one whether the reality encountered in Jesus and His saving work can be articulated in any way and expressed in any kind of language. Are there any theological models at all which help the believer to understand more fully both the nature of his faith and the object of his faith, the One Lord Jesus Christ? Can we really be content with a wholly ineffable God and a wholly ineffable Incarnation? Is the appropriate stance one of reverent, nonverbal silence in the presence of completely indefinable mysteries? If this were so, there would have been no Scriptures at all, no linguistic expression of men's experience of God. It is important to see very clearly what is at stake here. One does not have to insist on the complete adequacy of human language to express whatever reality is being experienced. On the other hand, to deny the role of language altogether is to give up the attempt to discern any meaning in our experience which our minds can grasp. Nor is the problem of the communication of meaning through language evaded by putting the stress on images rather than concepts.[1] Language itself is needed to evoke the image in our minds.

Even Karl Barth, who has maintained as firmly as anyone that man of himself lacks the cognitive capacity to know God and that all our pictures,

---

[1]Austin Farrer, *The Glass of Vision* (Westminster: Dacre, 1948); Leonard Hodgson, *For Faith and Freedom,* Gifford Lectures, Vols. I and II (Oxford: Blackwell, 1956); H.D. Lewis, *Our Experience of God* (London: Allen & Unwin, 1959), pp. 131ff.

thoughts, and words are in themselves unfitted to this object God,[2] nevertheless also insists that this does not mean that "theology and proclamation must be completely silenced."[3] The difference between Barth and some others is that in his view the language we use and the way we use it must be determined by the study of the way in which God has been pleased to communicate truth about Himself through the Scriptures. We can accept the validity of this point without tending to avoid, as Barth does, difficult questions concerning the interpretation of the biblical language and whether we can select some scriptural language rather than other scriptural forms as more adequate to the reality and nature of God.[4]

If it is once conceded that God could not avoid using language to disclose to men the nature of His presence and activity, then it seems no longer possible to eliminate beforehand the use of nonbiblical forms of language to elucidate the nature of God's revealing and saving activity. Even if it is contended that this cannot be done without the guidance of the Spirit, and we agree that this is so, the Spirit Himself, working in and through the community of faith, must also use language as He did when the biblical revelation was first given to men. This has important implications for Christology. That later doctrinal elaboration was compelled to use nonbiblical language is not in itself an objection. The question is whether the later language communicates to some extent the meaning of men's experience of God.

Another implication of this same problem concerns the question whether there can be a genuine development of "dogma." Karl Rahner, the Roman Catholic theologian, has offered a very perceptive treatment of this issue.[5] He raises the pertinent question of whether there can be a development of dogma as well as of theology. These two terms are not for him identical. Theology is a second-order reflection upon the meaning of faith's original apprehension of that which is given in revelation. Since theology is a human activity, all theological reflection shares the inevitable limitations of any attempt by the finite mind to express divine truth in human terms. Theology is not in itself to be identified with faith, even though there cannot be any fruitful theological activity without faith. Rahner, however, is concerned with the problem of the development of faith itself. If we say that revelation in the strict sense closed with the apostles, and this is something

---

[2]Barth, *Church Dogmatics*, I, 1, p. 188.
[3]*Ibid.*, p. 193.
[4]Russell F. Aldwinckle, "Karl Barth and Religious Language," *Canadian Journal of Theology*, Vol. XI, No. 3 (1965).
[5]Karl Rahner, *Theological Investigations*, I (Baltimore: Helicon, 1965), chapter 3, pp. 39ff.

which both Protestants and Catholics have said, the question then arises as to whether the church's later experience of that revelation in faith enables it also to see a genuine development in that apprehension. This is to be distinguished from theological reflection in the ordinary sense. Rather it means that the church, through faith under the guidance of the Spirit, is enabled to grasp ever more profoundly the realities grasped by faith. The church could experience in its own life a deepened apprehension of the basic grasp of truth involved in faith, perhaps long before that deepened apprehension is articulated in theological propositions.

For example, is there evidence in the New Testament that the early church developed under the Spirit's guidance a deeper understanding of the reality of Jesus Christ? Were some of the concepts used to "explain" Jesus Christ only secondary reflection, in Rahner's sense of theology, or were they rooted in a deeper and more adequate apprehension of the Person of Christ? Of course, they could very well have been both, and even the New Testament evidence suggests that they were both. Nevertheless, it is important to distinguish between a growing awareness of the nature of the reality apprehended by faith, and the intellectual activity in seeking adequate "models" and language to express that reality once faith has grasped it.

It is worth observing that this is not a peculiarly Catholic problem. Protestants must take account of this issue too. Insofar as Protestants believe that the Holy Spirit was guiding the early believing community into a fuller knowledge of God in Jesus Christ, then they must admit in principle the possibility of a continued growth in understanding the reality to which faith points. In as far as Protestants also accept later developments of dogma as involving an authentic grasp of the realities given to us in faith through the apostolic witness, they are committed in principle to the same position as that occupied by Rahner on this point. They are also committed to doctrinal development in the sense of secondary theological reflection. The Reformers, especially Luther and Calvin, did not conceive themselves to be rejecting the dogmatic definitions of the early councils. Many contemporary Conservative Evangelicals, despite their suspicion of any attempt to put tradition above Scripture, are often strong defenders of the Chalcedonian Definition of the faith. This is rather curious since it seems to commit them to the importance of tradition in a way they do not want to accept.[6]

We may now state the issue in the following terms. Was the dogmatic development up to Chalcedon an authentic reflection of the church's deepening experience of Christian truth, and therefore, a development of dogma in Rahner's sense? Or was it entirely a secondary phase, a phase of essentially

[6]See Henry, *The Protestant Dilemma*.

human theological reflection which played a useful role in its own day but may now be superseded by a different set of theological formulations? Was it, in Bonhoeffer's sense, an arrogant and illegitimate attempt to explain the "how" of the mystery of the Incarnation or was it the result of a true development of dogma derived from the church's profounder understanding and experience of the nature of its own faith?

There can be no doubt that this is a contemporary question of great importance. It raises the issue of whether faith can give birth to authentic dogmas; and the more radical thinkers pose this question not only of later church tradition but even of the developing tradition within the New Testament itself. If this possibility is denied, we are left with a faith which either cannot or ought not to articulate itself either in dogma as above defined or in theological reflection as this is generally understood. But a faith entirely without dogmatic or theological content seems to evaporate into an ineffable mystical experience. The Bible, however, is not mystical in this sense nor, generally speaking, has the later experience of Christian men been interpreted in this way. As we have already seen, even those in the Christian tradition to whom the term "mystic" has been more specifically applied have not been slow to use language to point to the ineffable.

Thus the question of dogma, formulated in language, remains the basic issue to be faced. Was the doctrinal development of the post-apostolic period a human and secondary theological development and therefore dispensable, or did it contain authentic further apprehensions of the reality to which faith points and which faith grasps, namely Jesus Christ? Here again the answer could be both. But if this is the case, how shall we distinguish between the essential and the nonessential? For example, is the concept of preexistence expressing something essential to faith's proper understanding and grasp of the reality of Jesus Christ, or is it a secondary theological model subject to cultural and philosophical influences, which we can now abandon as no longer required by faith to express whom and what it knows?

Many Protestants fear that this way of thinking opens the door to an uncontrolled proliferation of "dogma" on the basis of church authority alone, even when the dogma can lay no real claim to be either apostolic or catholic in the true sense. A recent example is the papal proclamation of the bodily assumption of the Virgin Mary as *de fide* for Catholics. Protestants are perfectly justified in their fears in regard to this and some other Catholic "dogmas." But does the distortion of a principle destroy its validity *in every sense?* Do Protestants really want to deny the possibility that the community of faith, under the guidance of the Spirit, might be led in the course of history to a fuller knowledge and understanding of the length and breadth, the height and depth of the love of God toward men in Jesus Christ and therefore to a deeper understanding of what they mean when they confess Him to be "truly God"? It is to be hoped that in their fear of a misuse of papal authority for the enunciating of dogma Protestants will not allow themselves to take a stance on this issue which would be almost tantamount to denying the creative presence and activity of the Spirit in the experience of Christian people down the ages.

So we now pass to a consideration of the appropriate theological models to be used to express what men have experienced of the divinity of Christ. We say "experienced" because if our previous discussion is valid, divinity has to be experienced in some way—or in our modern jargon, "existentially known"—before its meaning can be put into language. We shall continue to make use of the distinction already employed and introduced by Ian Ramsey[7] and taken up by John McIntyre.[8] This is the distinction between "picturing" and "disclosing" models. A pictorial model is a replica, a literal representation, a kind of photograph of reality. A disclosure model, on the other hand, arises not as a pictorial replica but with structural echoes.[9] In other words, some reality is being disclosed to us and the model does point to authentic features of the reality being disclosed, though it is not and cannot be a literal representation. It is an important part of Ramsey's thesis that there are no picturing models, in the strictly literal sense, either in the natural or social sciences, or in theology.[10] This is not intended to lead to the conclusion that we are not apprehending a reality other than ourselves. If we are not solipsists, we obviously are. The question then becomes, What is the character of the reality we are apprehending and can we indicate what Ramsey calls its structural features in a manner which illuminates our grasp of the reality? That we spontaneously do this with all our experience is hardly open to doubt. The practical problem is to distinguish between the more or less adequate disclosure models and to eliminate those which on examination prove to be misleading or even distorting of the reality.

Let us examine again the question of divinity with this in mind. If Jesus had lived in our age, we would doubtless have actual photographs of Him and video and sound tapes of His activities in first-century Palestine. Would we thereby have a literal picture model of His divinity? Would the photographs come out with a peculiar halo of glory round His head? This hardly seems probable, since many of his contemporaries saw Him in the body without "seeing" the Word made flesh. On the other hand, this kind of language would never have been used of Jesus unless something was

---

[7]Ramsey, *Models and Mystery.*
[8]John McIntyre, *Models in Christology* (London: S.C.M., 1966).
[9]Ramsey, *Models,* p. 10.
[10]*Ibid.,* chapters 1 and 2.

disclosed to those who met Him which made them consider such language appropriate. The apostles and first disciples evidently perceived the physical body of Jesus just as we perceive the bodies of our friends. They could touch and handle Him as we can other people. Presumably His flesh felt the same as other human flesh, and they never seemed to have doubted the reality of His body. He hungered and thirsted, ate and drank, became weary and slept like the rest of us. Though our perception through sight and touch and the other senses never exhausts our acquaintance with another person, yet through His body and the movements and gestures of His body, and above all, through the verbal symbolizing of language, they became aware of His Person at the deeper level of His thought, His ideas, His motives, His intentions and purposes. In other words, they became aware of the "mind" of this Person, meaning by "mind" not only the functioning of the intellect but that total activity of the person which includes feeling and thought, love and reason. Just as we today cannot directly inspect the mind of another person but have to depend upon bodily and linguistic media, so did they. However puzzling philosophers may find the problem of our knowledge of other minds, there seems little doubt that we do know them, though few of us would claim that we know them so transparently as to dissolve away all mystery from the existence of the other person. The disciples, then, experienced Jesus as they did other men, but something was disclosed in that encounter which defeated their attempts to treat Him as just another man. It is worth pointing out too that what Jesus said to them was important, so important indeed that the post-resurrection church thought it imperative to collect and preserve some of His parables and sayings. To that degree at any rate, they were interested in the "Jesus of history." That Jesus used language to convey to them the significance of the Kingdom and His own relation to it is a fact of great importance. It puts in doubt all attempts to separate event and language. If Jesus had said nothing at all, or if He had taught His disciples techniques of meditation which reduced the need for language almost to the vanishing point, Christianity would have been profoundly different from what it was and is. It is difficult to imagine what meaning could be given either to Jesus' acts or to His death if He had never communicated in language how He conceived God or the nature of the divine purpose. That some of His acts had such profound implications that human language is stretched to the breaking point to express them does not alter the importance of language in whatever disclosure was being made.

What, then, was in fact disclosed which made some claim to divinity seem reasonable to the early disciples and to later men of faith? It has frequently been observed that "divinity" is not a New Testament word, nor is there a doctrine of the two natures expressed in that linguistic form in the

Scripture. Whether the later formula can legitimately be deduced from such New Testament models as Son of Man, Son of God, Messiah, Logos, Kyrios, etc. is another question. The point is that the two-nature formula is not there.

It is worth dwelling on the implications of this for a moment. Unless we argue that since the apostles did not use the later formula they must have denied Jesus' divinity, we must believe that they experienced it and expressed it in other ways. We must surely affirm that they had the reality of the divinity as experienced fact, even if the dogmatic articulation of it was incomplete when judged by later standards. Father Rahner's discussion, earlier referred to, is pertinent here. The enunciating of theological propositions at a later time may have been a necessary stage in the church's continuing experience of the full implications of the divinity and in some sense, therefore, binding upon later generations. It is quite another thing to say that the divinity could not be known or experienced in the absence of the later formula. Nor can one deny that a contemporary man might know the reality of the divinity here and now while being relatively ignorant of doctrinal development or intellectually very puzzled by the later theological formulations. But to admit this would not in turn imply that the church has no responsibility to preserve the ''dogmas'' which safeguard the community of faith from damaging misinterpretations that would make it more difficult to know and experience the ''divine'' Jesus Christ.

The conclusion we have arrived at, therefore, is that it is possible to experience the divinity of Jesus Christ without necessarily articulating that experience in terms of the two-nature doctrine. This, as we have seen, was obviously the case with the apostles and the early disciples. It has also been true of simple believers in every age, who through the reading of the Scriptures and the experience of the living Christ through preaching, sacrament, and the Christian koinonia have known Jesus as the power of God unto salvation but who know little of the Chalcedonian formula and would find it difficult to understand it if they did. Again, however, this does not rule out the value of the two-nature formula and the Definition of A.D. 451 as a whole as setting up valuable signposts for the church's thinking. We are simply maintaining that accepting the formula does not guarantee the experience of the divinity. Rather it is the latter which makes the formula meaningful and articulates this meaning, however inadequately, in human language.

What, then, does it mean to experience the divinity? As we have seen, the disciples knew Jesus as they knew other men, through bodily contact and verbal communication. Yet the Person they discovered through these normal media proved to be an extraordinary Person. The reality of God's presence and activity in Him was such as to compel them to say, More than a prophet. He spoke the word of forgiveness and lo, they knew the peace of sin forgiven and the joy of reconciliation with the Father. They saw the signs of the Kingdom in His healing of the sick body and the distraught mind. Even if we demythologize ancient theories of demon possession, the fact of men healed and restored is difficult to excise from the gospel records, whatever hermeneutical method we adopt. Unless the form-critical method is employed in so radical a way as to eliminate all reliable knowledge of the earthly ministry, the facts of the healing ministry can hardly be disputed. The disciples did witness the exercise of extraordinary power by Jesus. It is customary these days to distinguish between the healing and the nature miracles, treating the former more favorably because modern psychology has shown what amazing things can be done through suggestion, hypnosis, etc. The nature miracles, however, are still a stumbling-block to many, though whether we are justified in making this sharp dichotomy between physical and psychological is itself open to doubt.[11]

We are not contending that the miracles as such were a proof of divinity taken in isolation but that they were an important part of the total impression made upon the disciples by Jesus. They heard Jesus speak of the Kingdom as coming near to them in His activity, and the grace, compassion, and truth which flowed from Him gave credibility to the words. The crisis, of course, came with the Cross. The death, and the particularly brutal manner of it, challenged their faith to the depths and revealed to the disciples their own weakness and tragic lack of loyalty. When the risen Lord appeared to them later, however, the darkness was dispelled. The conviction, slowly growing within them during their companionship with Him in the days of His flesh, now ripened quickly as the result of the Resurrection into the glad and certain confidence that death had really been trampled under foot and that all that He had said about the final triumph of the Kingdom at the end of the age was now gloriously confirmed. This was no mere mental assent to a mysterious miracle. In their own experience, they now found that they could face even death itself in the name of Jesus.

This, then, is how they experienced His divinity. When they sought to draw out its full implications, they found that human language was strained almost to the breaking point, yet they had to speak. They naturally turned to categories of thought with which they were already in part familiar—the Hebrew concept of the Word of God, the Logos, preexistence, the fullness of deity (*Pleroma*), etc. In doing so, they were not concerned with speculation

---

[11]A.E. Taylor, *The Faith of a Moralist*, II (London: Macmillan, 1937), chapter IV.

for its own sake. They were seeking for some appropriate "disclosure models" to point men to the unique reality and presence of God in this man Jesus of Nazareth.

The justification for the past use and the continued use of such models depends upon whether the logic of Christian experience still points in this direction. Wheeler Robinson put the matter very clearly some years ago:

> It is just because we find it impossible to regard Jesus simply as a man among men, just because we give Him a unique place on earth and a unique place after the days of His flesh, that we are compelled to ask whether a similar uniqueness attaches to Him prior to the earthly manifestation.[12]

Robinson admitted that similar questions can be raised about all human personality, and speculations about human preexistence were already prevalent in Jesus' day. What makes the case of Jesus exceptional is the exceptional nature of the disciples' experience of God in the Person of Jesus. If that experience was valid, then obviously their thought of God had to be reshaped in order to do justice to the content of that experience. The basic question was now one concerning God. If God was and is as they had experienced Him to be in Jesus, then could the emergence of Jesus be explained solely in terms of normal psychological and historical development? To put it in a very paradoxical way, when did God begin to be a Christian God? Only at that moment in time when Jesus appeared? And if not, then what we see and experience in Him must in some way reflect what is eternally true of God. "In some sense He belongs to the eternal being of God and that which He became on earth and continues to be in Heaven belongs to the divine order from all eternity."[13] Preexistence, therefore, which is a model taken from temporal experience, becomes a "disclosure model" pointing beyond the activity of God in time to what God is in His eternal nature and reality.

There seems to be a good deal of ambiguous language used today on this matter. It is often dogmatically said that we cannot know what God is in Himself or that the Bible is not interested in such an abstract question. If this means that no man can get inside God and look at things as if he were God, then no theologian in his senses ever made such a monstrous claim. Of course, God can only be known by a finite mind in as far as He has made Himself known, whether through nature, history, conscience, the sense of the holy, or specific events and personalities. What Christian faith is concerned to defend is the view that through these media, God is truly known. There may be mystery still, but it is not sheer mystery. Whatever there may be of God beyond our limited understanding, it cannot contradict His

---

[12]Robinson, *Revelation and Redemption*, p. 202.
[13]*Ibid.*, p. 203.

revelatory activity, and in particular that which He has disclosed about His nature and purpose in Jesus Christ. In this sense, we do know what God is "in Himself"—we know what it is most important to know about the character of God, and this is a valid and reliable knowledge.

In our contemporary intellectual climate, however, the problem of appropriate disclosure models is rendered more acute by the radical questioning of the reality of a transcendent God, transcendent, that is, to both men and the universe. The once fashionable "God is dead" slogan, though a passing phase in the theological enterprise, does nevertheless pose fundamental questions which have an intimate bearing upon any doctrine of divinity. Put in its simplest form, if there is no transcendent God in the classical Jewish and Christian sense, then obviously there can be no disclosure models which point to such a God. What the early disciples experienced in the presence of Jesus could not have been "God" in this sense. It must have been something else. Any doctrine of divinity, therefore, and any models employed to express the reality of that divinity, will have to be radically recast and put in other terms. We have already shown that Jesus started from the Jewish experience of and belief in a transcendent God. To eliminate this is to do violence both to Jesus' understanding of His own role and mission and to what Christian men have believed themselves to experience since His day. Assuming for the moment that God in the classical sense is dead, then what meaning could be attached to divinity?

One could respond to this challenge in one of two ways. It could be urged that the whole concept of divinity should be abandoned as no longer relevant. Jesus might then become the vehicle for communicating certain values, such as agape-love, but it would be illegitimate to go on to say that there is a reality beyond the space-time world which is characterized by such love. This would be to drag in again some concept of God, or at least some notion of a philosophical Absolute or perhaps a Platonic eternal realm of ideas. Our modern radicals are no more sympathetic to these philosophical versions of "God" than they are to what they consider to be the anthropomorphic theology of the Judaeo-Christian tradition with its free use of personal analogies about God. In the light of all this, therefore, it would be better to drop the concept of divinity in any sense and concentrate upon expressing the significance of Jesus Christ as a fuller revelation of the depths of human reality. Disclosure models would only disclose man. We have returned full circle to Feuerbach's contention that all theology is anthropology. This position is logical, granted the starting-point, but the question is whether we can accept the starting-point.

Our contention has been that on the grounds of Scripture, reason, and experience, this does not have to be our starting-point. The continued significance of the God-question presses upon us in one form or another.[14] If what is said by such writers as Austin Farrer, H.D. Lewis, H.P. Owen, and Langdon Gilkey is valid, then the question of divinity in the usual sense remains both a possible and a necessary question. We are still asking legitimate questions, not only about Jesus of Nazareth, but about the reality and character of the transcendent reality disclosed in His life and total ministry, including His death and resurrection. The question, therefore, remains: "What are the most appropriate and valid disclosure models to express our apprehension of God mediated through His presence and activity in the man Jesus of Nazareth?" The debate must concentrate not so much on the question of God's reality but on the nature of the language we use to speak about Him. By this is not meant that the question of God can simply be taken for granted as having received its final answer. Our point is rather a different one, namely that before the issue of the cognitive claims of Christian experience can be dealt with satisfactorily, we need to consider Jesus and men's experience of Him and the "models" they employed in order to express the significance of that experience.

It is this issue of language which is basic in many contemporary thinkers who have often given the impression that they are attacking the existence of God, whereas they are actually concerned with the images, symbols, language, etc. which we use to articulate our experience of God. This latter problem must remain a legitimate and continuing preoccupation of every Christian thinker. Indeed, it could be argued with considerable evidence that this has always been true of the Christian theological tradition. The importance and significance of religious language has never been far removed from the minds of the great theologians of the past. It is true that for various reasons this issue has become sharpened in our day. Christians are being compelled to reexamine religious language with a thoroughness which has not been required in many decades. However, it is good to remember that in grappling with these questions the church is not meeting this kind of situation for the first time. She has met it before in her long history and met it successfully. We may have confidence that she will do so again.

Our conclusion, then, is that Bonhoeffer sharpens too much the distinction between the "who" and the "how." It is true that no finite mind can ever completely plumb the mystery of God's reality or of His becoming man, if the latter is fact, as the Christian faith affirms. Nevertheless, the urge of faith to express in language the meaning of its experience of the divinity of

---

[14]See Farrer, *Finite and Infinite;* Lewis, *Our Experience of God;* Owen, *The Christian Knowledge of God;* and Langdon Gilkey, *Naming the Whirlwind–The Renewal of God-Language* (Indianapolis: Bobbs-Merrill, 1969).

Jesus is still both compelling and legitimate. Further, we believe Rahner to be correct in asserting that the door must be left open to the possibility of a real development of dogma, where dogma indicates not merely an optional secondary theological development but a deeper and growing experience and understanding of Jesus Christ, known through the continued activity of the Spirit within the koinonia of faith. The search for disclosure models, not only in Scripture but in the church's later experience, thus becomes a legitimate enterprise. We shall take up this theme again in our later discussion of what exactly it means to experience the divinity and of how the meaning of that experience can be articulated in language.

8.
Truly God

In this chapter we shall continue our discussion of divinity from a somewhat different angle, and try to make more explicit what was the "extra" or the "plus" in Jesus which led Christian men to talk of divinity. We shall then take up again the question of disclosure models and the value of certain traditional models for contemporary man's expression of his faith. It will also be necessary to ask whether other models can be employed today which will serve the same purpose as well as or better than the classic models.

If Jesus was not in the strictly literal and absolute sense omnipotent, omniscient, and omnipresent in the days of His flesh, if He was a man of His time and of Jewish background with all the cultural and religious nurture which this involved, if He had all the marks of manhood such as we have listed in a previous chapter, then what is there in Him and in our relationship to Him which compels us to go further than "manhood"? If we reject all the notions of "impersonal" manhood, even if it is accepted that this concept has been misunderstood at some important points,[1] then where is the "divinity"? If we reject the doctrine of the "two natures" or two "wills," if this is interpreted in a psychologically dualistic sense, then where is the divinity located? We are aware of the incurably spatial nature of the language we have just used. Nevertheless, it makes the point in the kind of language the ordinary person is apt to use. It will be our task to penetrate to the more subtle meaning which such language conceals.

Two fundamental questions arise at this point: (a) Can we locate the divinity in the special and unique personal relationship which existed between Jesus and God, His Heavenly Father? If so, what kind of relationship was this? Was it such as to justify our saying that whatever similarities there may be between our relationship to God and His, God was present in the relationship to Jesus in a way in which He is not present to Christian

---

[1]For a good discussion of this, cf. Donald Baillie, *God was in Christ*.

believers in general? Can we say that Jesus had a "vision of God" comparable to some forms of the Christian mystical experience perhaps but of such an order that He must be regarded as distinct from all other men, however exalted their religious experience? (b) The second question concerns the nature of the believer's relationship to Jesus Christ. What does the believer experience, or think he experiences, which makes his relationship quite different from what it would be if he had a relationship to the Buddha or Plato or Mahatma Gandhi or a modern guru such as Sri Aurobindo Ghose?[2]

We have already hinted at some possible answers to these questions, but it is necessary now to see if it is possible to be even more specific. The first set of questions raises peculiar difficulties because it presupposes the possibility of knowing something about the "consciousness" of Jesus, at least enough to be able to say something significant about His "inner life." It is well known that this possibility has been roundly denied by some because of the limited information afforded by the gospels. The word "consciousness" is perhaps not the best to use in this connection. We cannot directly inspect the "consciousness" of Jesus any more than we look directly into the consciousness of other persons here and now. H.D. Lewis has in our opinion made a decisive case against this possibility. On the other hand, we believe that Lewis is correct in asserting that this does not mean that our "experience" is so private that it is impossible for one person to communicate with another and to know in part what is going on in the "mind" or the "consciousness" of another.[3] If this is so, then it cannot be asserted as a matter of principle that it was impossible for Jesus to "communicate" to His followers some understanding of His Person, His mind, and His purpose. The question, then, becomes not "Can we penetrate to the consciousness of Jesus?" but do we have enough information to make this possible? If Jesus was truly man, whatever else He was, then such communication between Him and us cannot be ruled out, even if mystery is left. In considering the New Testament foundations of Christology, and in particular C.H. Dodd's latest book, we came to the conclusion that Jesus did in fact so communicate, and that His disciples, and we through them, are able to know His mind, at least to a significant degree. That they were sometimes misled by their obtuseness, spiritual blindness, and perhaps sheer stupidity, as we all are, does not render this point invalid. Some understanding was achieved, and the gospel records of His work, His acts, His teaching, especially the parables, enable us also to enter into that understanding. Is it enough to permit us to speak with any confidence about His unique relation-

---

[2] See R.C. Zaehner, *Evolution in Religion—A Study in Sri Aurobindo and Pierre Teilhard de Chardin* (Oxford: Clarendon Press, 1971).
[3] Lewis, *Elusive Mind*, pp. 250ff.

ship to the Father? It is worth noting in passing that Karl Rahner is
open-minded toward the possibility of constructing a Christology in terms of
Christ's consciousness. "All we want to suggest is that a Christology using
categories appropriate to the description of consciousness need not be false a
priori or impossible."[4]

Let us assume for the moment that we are able to do this to a real, if
limited degree. In what sense, if any, was Jesus' experience of God of a
different order from ours? Since the eighteenth century several notable
attempts have been made to answer this question without having recourse to
the classic language of the two natures. Schleiermacher preferred to speak of
a perfect God-consciousness in Jesus, perfect in the sense that His life
developed in entire dependence and filial trust without the deviations and
imperfections which mark our development because of the triumph of the
senses over the claims of the Spirit and our frequent lapses into sinful
self-centeredness. Ritschl saw Jesus as the ideal ethical man, ethical here
meaning Jesus' unqualified devotion to the universal will of righteousness
and love for all men, which for Ritschl was Jesus' understanding of the will
or rule of God.

In more recent years, Donald Baillie appealed to what he called the
central paradox of grace to illuminate the mystery of the Incarnation. The
paradox of grace is that we can experience our utter dependence upon God
and ascribe all goodness to Him while not losing the reality of our freedom
and responsibility. This may appear to involve logical difficulties but the
believer, according to Baillie, finds them resolved and transcended in the
Christian experience of grace. What appears in us a fragmentary and limited
experience seems in Jesus to have been an unbroken and continuous experience of both dependence and freedom.[5] This seems akin to a suggestion
made earlier by Wheeler Robinson that we must seek the clue to the Person
of Jesus in the relationship of personality to "higher" forms of its own
reality, in this case the personal reality of God. Norman Pittenger seems to
have something similar in mind when he speaks of the Incarnation as the
self-expression of God in Jesus,[6] though this phrase does not in itself throw
any light upon the problem of how God's self-expression is compatible with
a genuine independence and freedom on the part of the creature, in this case
Jesus. We are not suggesting that Pittenger does not try to deal with this latter
question. Indeed, some of his critics think that he is more successful in
defending Jesus' humanity than His divinity. Our point here is simply that the
substitution of the language of self-expression for the traditional language,

---

[4]Rahner, *Theological Investigations* (Baltimore: Helicon, 1961), I, 172.
[5]Baillie, *God was in Christ*, pp. 117ff.
[6]Pittenger, *Word Incarnate*.

whatever its merits for contemporary man, does not solve the theological and historical problem of how the divine activity and the human reality can be combined in one person.

Tillich's "new being" in Jesus as the Christ moves in the same direction. Jesus is the single instance of a human life in which estrangement from the Ground of Being is overcome. In Him essence and existence are not in contradiction as with us. Because of this, His life is transparent to the Ground of Being, the character of which is disclosed in Jesus as holy love.[7] For Paul Van Buren, Jesus is the one who has realized in His own life authentic freedom and has shown Himself able to communicate this to other men. Van Buren's difficulties about God make it impossible to raise the question of Jesus' divinity in any meaningful sense, unless "divinity" is so broadly interpreted as to mean no more than a quality of human existence, in this case the special kind of existence which Jesus realized. "It is in this figurative sense that we can say that Jesus' freedom from himself and freedom to be for others became contagious at Easter. It catches the sense of our 'catching' something from another person, not by our choice, but as something which happens to us."[8]

While Käsemann is more positive on the subject of God than Van Buren, he is near in spirit to what Van Buren says about freedom. "We have called Jesus a 'liberal' because He broke through the piety and theology of His contemporaries, and brought God's promise and love in place of the Mosaic law, His own endowment of the Spirit in place of the Jewish tradition, clarity about God's will in place of casuistry, and grace in place of good works." For Altizer too, the belief in a transcendent God is replaced by a doctrine of kenosis which leaves us with a Jesus embodying agape-love whose spirit continues to live wherever men plunge in the spirit of such love into the dark places of sin, suffering, and death. "The crucified Christ does not ascend to a heavenly realm but rather descends ever more fully into darkness and death."

A more balanced statement of the question of uniqueness is found in the work of John Macquarrie. He accepts the point, made in our earlier discussion, that the question of divinity can hardly arise unless some idea of God or at least the Transcendent can be assumed. He is, however, fully aware that these concepts cannot be simply taken for granted in the contemporary climate of opinion. Nor does modern man take for granted the Old Testament understanding of God nor are there any widely accepted philosophical concepts in the modern world comparable to that of the Logos in the patristic

---

[7]Tillich, *Systematic Theology*, II.
[8]Paul Van Buren, *The Secular Meaning of the Gospel* (New York: Macmillan, 1963), p. 133.

period. For this reason Macquarrie attempts in the early part of his *Principles of Christian Theology* to provide a set of philosophical categories by the aid of which the significance of Jesus can be interpreted and illuminated. Since a rigorous, demonstrative natural theology in the Thomist sense is not now possible, we must look elsewhere for our categories. For this purpose, he finds Heidegger the most useful contemporary philosopher. Hence Macquarrie's use of Being and beings, instead of the usual Creator and creature, in this first part of his study.

Macquarrie's new-style philosophical theology starts with man himself as man knows himself and experiences himself in relation to other men. Macquarrie contends that man ''in his quest for the sense of existence is met by the gift of a sense for existence.''[9] He discovers not only the nature of human existence, but in and through existential situations he ''experiences this initiative from beyond himself in various ways.''[10] Thus the notion of transcendence returns. Man experiences his own being as involving a disclosure of Being. Can Being be characterized in any precise way? Yes, says Macquarrie, Being discloses itself (Himself?) as holy and gracious. Obviously such a contention can be defended only by appealing to special experiences as peculiarly significant disclosures by Being of its nature. This Macquarrie believes he can do.[11]

It would prolong this discussion unduly to consider in detail the cogency of this ''new-style'' philosophical theology and whether or in what sense it is departing from the ''old-style'' natural theology. Let us accept Macquarrie's starting-point and see how it is employed in regard to the Person of Christ and the question of Christology with which we have been grappling. First of all, he insists very strongly that ''creation, reconciliation, and consummation are not separate acts but only distinguishable aspects of one awe-inspiring movement of God—his love or letting be, whereby he confers, sustains, and perfects the being of the creatures.''[12] Being has always been disclosing its nature in and through beings. ''No doubt,'' he says, ''there have been many revelations and these have come through many kinds of vehicles.''[13] In this case, then, can one speak of one normative or final disclosure of Being in a being? Christian faith says Yes; this disclosure is to be found in Jesus of Nazareth. Here we have a historical symbol as contrasted with the ''timeless symbols through which the Logos has made itself known to men.''[14] Macquarrie is careful to point out that the word

---

[9]Macquarrie, *Principles of Christian Theology*, p. 75.
[10]*Ibid.*
[11]*Ibid.*
[12]*Ibid.*, p. 247.
[13]*Ibid.*, p. 248.
[14]*Ibid.*, p. 249.

"symbol" involves no diminution or unreality in Christ's relation to Being.[15] Being is present and manifest in any being that truly symbolizes it. So the ontological and the existential are firmly tied together.

What of "uniqueness," however, in this context of discussion? Macquarrie rejects the more radical and sceptical historical analysis of the life of Jesus and believes that some reliable historical knowledge of Jesus is possible and important for Christian faith. He is far removed from conservative scholarship in his negative attitude toward the miracles and some details of the history, but he is certain that we know enough about Jesus to talk meaningfully about Him. He insists that his view does not mean that Jesus evolves or unfolds out of the natural and historical process by some kind of immanent necessity. Being can express itself in close and intimate union with being only if the initiative comes from Being. The Virgin Birth may stand for this "initiative" but must not be taken as biological or historical fact. Jesus can be taken, therefore, as a disclosure by Being without necessarily being tied up with mythological concepts of preexistence, descent, and ascent. Such a Christology must start "from below" in the sense that the reality of being (i.e., Jesus of Nazareth) must be asserted before any talk of a disclosure of Being can make sense. The real humanity, therefore, is a necessary starting-point. Macquarrie believes that by using this kind of language he can avoid the problems connected with the classical doctrine of the two natures, and particularly a static concept of "nature" which might be applicable to physical objects but is quite inappropriate to the dynamic nature of human existence. Christ's nature is not a fixed and static datum. "He progressively realized His Christhood,"[16] a fact to which the gospels testify. The nature of a unified self can only come into being, it is not there in the being at the start. So with Jesus. "The death of Christ is taken up into his life as its climax and fulfilment, and it is in the moment of death that Christhood fully emerges."[17]

At this point we may well wonder whether Macquarrie has not been unduly influenced by Heidegger. It may be true that the total significance of a human life can be estimated only when that life comes to its earthly end, namely death. It seems dogmatic, however, to assert that a unified self can be realized only at death. On naturalistic assumptions, death is the final end, so the very unity of the self achieved at death is destroyed at precisely the moment it is attained. That the life of Jesus comes to its spiritual completion in an act of total self-giving which meant death may well be granted. Yet if the earthly life of Jesus was lived in harmonious unity with the will of God, then his humanity must in some sense have been a truly unified self under

---

[15]*Ibid.*
[16]*Ibid.*, p. 276.
[17]*Ibid.*, p. 278.

divine direction. That Christhood fully emerged only at death seems, therefore, an unwarranted statement. The crucifixion was a publicly verifiable event in which the total dedication of the will of Jesus to the Father receives dramatic expression. Yet the surrender to death was only the culmination of a life lived in total surrender to the will of God. To identify the emergence of Christhood with the moment of death raises enormous difficulties. According to this view, Jesus fully becomes what He is intended to be only at the moment when He ceases to exist as Jesus of Nazareth. Tillich says something similar in his *Systematic Theology:* "He proves and confirms His character as the Christ in the sacrifice of Himself as Jesus to Himself as the Christ."[18]

Christian faith and experience has always had difficulties with this. If the Word became flesh, as the Fourth Gospel insists, then the earthly life must have meant a real encounter of the disciples with God in Jesus in His historical reality as Jesus. If we refuse to raise the question of the moral perfection of Jesus, or if we assert that from the point of view of "personality" Jesus was to all outward appearance only an ordinary Rabbi, as Barth once suggested, then it is obvious that the quality of the human life has no bearing upon the question of divinity. "This plea," as Oliver Quick observes, "makes it impossible to use the human goodness of Jesus as evidence for His divinity and invalidates altogether the witness of the natural conscience to the truth of the gospel."[19] In our judgment, Quick was right to reject this plea. Whatever significance we give to Jesus' death as the disclosure of the full nature and implication of His Christhood, the latter cannot be arbitrarily sundered from the "goodness" manifest in and through the humanity of Jesus as made known in His earthly ministry. Says H. Wheeler Robinson:

> The place actually taken by Jesus in history and experience [and this means the whole life, the death, and the resurrection, not the death as an isolated episode] shows that He does satisfy the highest moral and spiritual needs of men, so that they have been continually urged to apply to Him the highest categories their thought provided.[20]

To return, however, to Macquarrie's contention: It is doubtful whether the substitution of the language of "Being" and "being" for the language of the two natures really resolves the problems raised by the latter. Macquarrie may be right in saying that the ancient use of "nature" implies a reality too static to do justice to the principle of growth and becoming in the actual

[18]Tillich, *Systematic Theology,* II, 123.
[19]Quick, *Doctrines of the Creed* (London: Nisbet, 1938), p. 171.
[20]Robinson, *Revelation and Redemption,* p. 213.

historical existence of Jesus of Nazareth. On the other hand, the language of Being, whether spelled with a large or a small ''B,'' does not of itself suggest the reality of *becoming* in the sense of Jesus' developing awareness of His vocation. Whatever language we use, it seems that we must qualify it in some sense to do justice to the fact that Jesus increased in wisdom and stature, with all that that must imply for a Christology or a doctrine of His Person.

Once again, unless we are content to see Jesus only as extraordinary man, the problem of ''divinity'' reemerges; nor can it be solved merely by a change of language. Whether the language is ancient or modern, it will have to be stretched and forced to do justice to a unique actuality in Jesus of Nazareth. This is not an argument against the attempt to reexpress this actuality in contemporary language. It means that there is no magical resolution of the theological problem merely in a change of language. Modern men will be as much put off by the unusual use of modern language, as of ancient language, unless they have been led to see in Jesus a distinctiveness, indeed a uniqueness, for which the normal categories of manhood are not wholly adequate. To sum up, if Macquarrie means what he says in declaring that Jesus does not simply ''emerge'' out of the physical and historical process and that Being's disclosure in Him is significantly different from its (His?) disclosure in other beings, then the nature of this difference still remains crucial.

Before further treating this and other classical models used to express it, we must now take a look at J.A.T. Robinson's recent book *The Human Face of God.* By any standards, this is a fine book, perhaps the finest that has yet come from this controversial theologian and biblical scholar. Things only hinted at in his other books in a somewhat tantalizing way are here developed in detail in the context of a thorough biblical and historical study. The book not only deserves to be read, but even more, deserves to be treated in a spirit of constructive criticism.

It is not our intention to consider here in detail the book's defence of the true humanity of Jesus of Nazareth. Whatever divergences of opinion we may have in regard to certain modes of expression which Dr. Robinson uses, the main thrust of his argument about the humanity must, in our view, be accepted. There can be no more Docetism, and this book makes us fully aware of the full implications of this statement. However, we choose to begin our discussion with chapter six of Robinson's book, entitled ''God for us.'' Here the issue is plainly stated in the first sentence: ''How can Christ *be* God for us without ceasing truly to be man?''[21]

---

[21]Robinson, *Human Face of God.* p. 180.

It is interesting to observe in this sentence and in the footnotes quoted on the first page of this chapter in Robinson how easy it is for the language of "being" to appear again where one might not expect it. For example, a quotation from Pittenger affirms of Jesus that "it is the very *being* of God Himself here active in human life."[22] We shall have occasion to return to this kind of language later. Robinson is also quick to point out that we must not say that God is exclusively at work in the man Jesus.[23] One might here ask which theologians have in fact ever said that God is nowhere active at all except in Jesus. The mainstream of Christian thought, Catholic, Orthodox, and Protestant, has always affirmed that God was active in sustaining the physical universe and in a particular way in the history of Israel before He was active in Jesus. Some, like Justin Martyr, have gone further and talked of Christians before Christ.

Robinson, however, also shrinks from talking of a difference in kind between God's universal activity and His activity in Jesus. Everything depends upon the meaning to be attached to the phrase "in kind" and to it we shall again return. To summarize Robinson's view, however, is to say that Jesus as Christ is the clue to God's universal presence everywhere and that God "put Himself into this event in a way that was uniquely or specially revealing."[24] There must be a unique disclosure of divine initiative, Robinson insists, as well as a human response by Jesus to that initiative. This means that the answer to our previous question about what constitutes the difference between Jesus and other men must lie in this "unique" disclosure of the divine initiative. If we give full weight to this kind of language, then it is obviously saying quite a lot. What is happening in Jesus is quite different from what is happening elsewhere, namely a unique disclosure of the divine initiative, however much we stress the human response and what is happening elsewhere. Robinson obviously wishes to say this and to give it full weight. It *was* God addressing Himself to men in Jesus. Or, says our author, if we do not use God-language, then at least we must say that Jesus tells us something, not only about human nature, but about all nature, "about the very grain of the universe itself."[25] It is clear that Robinson still has reservations about God-language which might provoke modern man to disagreement because of the confused and inadequate images of God which he has. Yet Robinson apparently does want to say that in Jesus we meet what is more than man, namely a unique disclosure of divine activity. How, then, shall we express this "uniqueness" or this difference of Jesus from other

---

[22]Pittenger, *Word Incarnate,* pp. 121ff.
[23]Robinson, p. 181.
[24]*Ibid.*
[25]*Ibid.,* p. 182.

men? There is, of course, an ordinary, everyday sense in which Jesus is different from other men, since no two men are exactly alike, but this is not the theological point. It is the difference in relation to God's activity which constitutes the Christological issue.

How shall we express the fact that Jesus tells us something about "the very grain of the universe"? Robinson indicates three possible representations of reality—the mythological, the ontological, and the functional.[26] The mythological affirms the identity of God the Sender and Jesus the Sent and personifies the Christ figure as some aspect of the divine being or will. It is in this sort of milieu that the models of descent and ascent and preexistence naturally take their rise. The ontological representation transposes these images or personifications from poetic to philosophical categories, and we get the language of the *homoousios,* of the "consubstantiality" of the Father and the Son. The functional representation expresses these ideas in a more dynamic way in terms of verbs rather than substances: "The Christ is the One who does what God does, who represents Him. . . . He stands in the place of God, speaking and acting for Him."[27] The issue, then, is whether in seeing Jesus, men see the Father in mercy and judgment, whether Jesus functions as God, whether He *is* God to and for them.

Robinson's preference, it is clear, is for the functional. The mythological is too entangled with obsolete worldviews to be convincing to modern man. The ontological is too abstract and in any case is tied up with philosophical categories which no longer mould the way in which modern men think. Yet we must note, as in the case of Pittenger, how the language of "being" creeps in. Jesus "is" God to and for them. Yet, says Robinson again, we must not think of Christ as a divine being who takes on humanity, but though an ordinary human being, one who is nevertheless the carrier of the divine disclosure.[28]

It seems clear that such a man who bears such a disclosure is not a "common" or "ordinary" man in the usual sense of the word. In using such language, we are obviously asserting a remarkable difference between Jesus and other men. Even if Father-Son language is parabolic, yet we are designating by it, as Robinson says, "Jesus in His *unique* relationship to God."[29] The idea behind John 1:14, he tells us, is that "the incarnate Christ is the exact counterpart or reflection of God, his very spit and image, like an only son of his father."[30] He claims John 10: 34–38 for his functional view.

---

[26]*Ibid.,* pp. 182–183.
[27]*Ibid.,* pp. 183–184.
[28]*Ibid.,* p. 185.
[29]*Ibid.,* p. 186.
[30]*Ibid.,* p. 187.

This passage puts Jesus on the same metaphysical level as any other son of God but attests Him "functionally unique" because He always does what is acceptable to the Father. His most intimate union with God is grounded in His utter faithfulness and obedience.[31] Robinson admits the staggering, paradoxical nature of his language and that it is no matter for surprise that later Christology fell apart "at the seams into a disastrous antithesis between moral unity and metaphysical union."[32] The notion of representation is obviously basic for Robinson's Christology. The mythological model of a preexistent divine being becoming man can no longer be our way of speaking. The language of consubstantiality cannot be ours. We are left with the view that Jesus functions for us as God because He represents God in a way that is not true of any other man before or since. "I believe it is impossible to make sense of the gospels, any of the gospels, without the presupposition that he went about, and was condemned for, acting as though He were God's vice-regent."[33] That is, presumably, He stands in the place of God and functions as if He were God.

Robinson claims, in anticipation of criticisms, that this is not a "low" Christology, and he is surely right in this. Yet he also admits that the church was not content with this primitive, functional conception of Sonship, which it labelled "adoptionism."[34] The church went on to develop the mythological and ontological models into the story of Jesus as the becoming man of a preexistent heavenly being who was with God "before the world began." Robinson objects to this supranaturalistic projection because it locates the most real in another realm beyond this world, impinging on it from without.[35]

This section calls for the most careful examination, for its implications are serious indeed. While it appears to be academic, the language is really very emotive; it expresses Robinson's own feelings and evokes feelings in those who read it. The word "projection" will suggest to many people today Freud's reduction of all experience of God to mere projection of subjective psychological states. The word "supranaturalistic" (what is the reason for this departure from the more familiar "supernatural"?) will also convey to many the crudest ideas of God arbitrarily breaking the known and regular "laws" of nature. It is not a far cry then to imply a God who is distant, remote, uninvolved, and therefore not only religiously inadequate but inca-

---

[31]*Ibid.*, p. 189.
[32]*Ibid.*, p. 190.
[33]*Ibid.*, p. 193.
[34]*Ibid.*, p. 194.
[35]*Ibid.*, p. 195.

pable of being integrated into a "contemporary, secular scientific cosmology."[36]

It is clear, therefore, that what is at stake here is the basic idea of God itself. The supranaturalistic projection is rejected because it locates the most real in another realm beyond this world. Now is this not precisely what God in the Judaeo-Christian tradition does in fact mean? Unless Robinson means that the universe is indeed God, then God must be a reality—indeed, the most real reality, if such a curious expression be permitted—above or beyond this world. We assume that everyone today acknowledges the spatial nature of the language used. God is not "beyond" in the literal sense of so many billion miles away from the planet earth, for this would still leave Him in space. Nevertheless, the spatial language is meant to convey the idea that God is not simply the sum total of the sequence of events in the present cosmos, nor is He any one part or parts of this sequence. He is the transcendent Source and Creator of all that is, and therefore cannot simply be identified with the process as such.

The acute mind of Austin Farrer dealt with this issue forcibly and clearly. Farrer correctly maintains that biblical theism cannot abandon "the prior actuality of God" without ceasing to be biblical and Christian.[37] Even when we have purged away Aristotelian and scholastic absolutism, Christian faith must still affirm the prior actuality of God. It refuses to agree with those who say that "the very notion of a life of God in God and apart from all creatures is nonsense."[38] It is this which sticks in the throat of the truly secular thinker. The reader must be referred to Farrer's essay for his further comments on Whitehead, Hartshorne, and the process theology. The most that process theology could give would be a Creative Mind of the cosmic process and nothing more, a mind in some way analogous to the way in which my consciousness is related to the process of my bodily life.[39] Yet, as Farrer insists, the universe is not in this sense an organism or a "body." There is no world process in this organismic sense. The cosmic "mind" of the process philosophers either operates by nature, being just that sort of mind, or is capable of freely initiating and leading the cosmic process. But this latter requires a truly transcendent God, the prior actuality of God, active in but certainly not only the "mind" of the process considered as some principle of "concretion." One suspects that Robinson has drunk too deeply of the wells of process theology and that as a consequence his view of God

---

[36]*Ibid.*, p. 196.

[37]Farrer, *Reflective Faith*, pp. 180ff.

[38]*Ibid.*, p. 183.

[39]*Ibid.*, pp. 186–187. Cf. also Chapter X, "Anima Mundi" in Farrer, *Faith and Speculation*, pp. 142ff.

has become radically different from that held by Christian faith until now. Robinson may say that this is just too bad for Christian theism in its classical form. He does not say this in so many words and there are passages in which he does not really seem to believe this. Yet he is sufficiently influenced by the process thinkers to use language which would, if taken seriously, mean the "end of theism." Nor is it adequate to dismiss the theistic view of God as dependent upon mythological or ontological or metaphysical concepts which are no longer valid. This needs to be debated and rationally assessed, not simply solved by the pejorative use of such words as "ontological" or "metaphysical."

If God is not identified with the process, then the language which Robinson uses must be reconsidered. His charge against the mythological and ontological representations is that "the source, the origin, the patris of the Christ, is elsewhere."[40] By elsewhere, he means "beyond" this world. Yet this is precisely what most Christians have wanted to say. God's unique initiative in Christ (Robinson's language) is God's, not a normal outcome of natural processes. This point is not affected by Robinson's excessive emphasis upon the "immanence" of God. Certainly, Christians have always believed that God is active in and through natural processes, but it must again be insisted that the idea of immanence implies real transcendence. If God were wholly immanent in the process, He (?) could hardly be distinguished from the process and we are back with sheer naturalism. There is also the further problem of how to account for real "emergents" in the process, whether of life from matter, consciousness from life, rational personality in man, and in this case Jesus Christ from the race of men.[41] A mere description of the chronological sequence in which these "emergents" appear is not a satisfying explanation. It is still a legitimate question to ask how the content of the process arises from a prior set of conditions which lacked the later emergents. The use of spatial language to express this Christian conviction that Christ has His true source "elsewhere" in no way justifies Robinson's apparent preference for the solution offered by the process thinkers. God is God, not the universe, and this theistic conviction needs to be argued on its merits, not simply dismissed because the thinkers who hold it have to use spatial and temporal language to talk about it.

Robinson's unhappiness with any suggestion of God "impinging on the

---

[40]Robinson, *Human Face of God,* p. 195.
[41]William Temple's *Nature, Man and God* is still a powerful handling of this theme, not to be ignored because of the recent influence of positivism, philosophical analysis and process philosophy and theology.

universe from without''[42] seems to be bound up with a literal interpretation
of the spatial language. Certainly the biblical view affirms the activity of
God within the created order, but this does not exclude His genuine transcendence. It is doubtful whether Robinson can really claim the support of
Hebrew thought for his interpretation of functional. The process of history
can be shot through with the meaning of God precisely because God is not
exhaustively expressed in the process. Certainly it is not adequate to biblical
thought to see Jesus as an ''invader'' into the world from which God is
completely absent. It does, however, see the coming of Jesus as a unique
activity of God in a process where He is already at work. The Incarnation is
not an intrusion, an eruption, an intervention in a world cut off from God. On
the other hand, it is God acting in a new and different way. The ambiguity of
Robinson's language is seen in the following quotation: ''The Word is seen,
as in the Johannine prologue, as moulding the process from the beginning,
drawing it onwards and upwards like light, immanent in it, yet constantly
transcending it, rather than something transcendent that became immanent.''[43] How is this to be interpreted? If the Word here means God, then it is
the personal activity of the Creator-God of Hebrew, Jewish, and Christian
thought and distinguishable from the process. If He is constantly transcending the process in which He is also immanent, then He is not simply
identifiable with the process. What is the real difference between the Word
constantly transcending the process and the transcendent becoming immanent? Robinson appears to think that the latter way of speaking implies
God's general absence from the world except when He decides to enter it
from without. This, however, as we have seen, is in no way involved in the
biblical view. To counter this unbiblical view of the separation of God the
Creator from the world of His creation, it is not necessary to deny to God a
real transcendence, as Robinson seems to be saying. If we start with the
assumption that God is always active in the process and never absent from it,
the question can still be raised as to whether in the context of His general
activity, there might not be an act or acts of such special revealing quality as
to result in an emergent which is really new, a creative novelty which has no
parallel before or since. It may be rooted in the process but is not simply the
result of God's general activity. It is a unique personal act on God's part in
this Jesus. This, as we have insisted, is possible only if the personal God is
truly transcendent to the process. Robinson himself seems to want to say this
when he remarks that ''Jesus was not a divine pick up.''[44] God, he says, did

---

[42]Robinson, *Human Face of God,* p. 195.
[43]*Ibid.,* p. 203.
[44]*Ibid.,* p. 198.

not hang around waiting for the right man to appear and then adopt Him as an instrument or agent. This would derogate from the divine initiative and freedom. It may be observed in passing that this was one of the points which the model of preexistence was intended to express, whatever other defects this model is deemed to have. We shall discuss this further in our next chapter.

The root of the difficulty for Robinson seems to be in the assumption that in order to preserve the real initiative of persons, including Jesus, and to fit this into a modern, secular, scientific cosmology, it is necessary to limit seriously the power of God by denying Him a truly transcendent existence, not dependent as such upon the process. That God could limit His activity in the process to preserve the initiative of persons without surrendering His ultimate sovereignty over the process never seems to be considered as another option. It would appear that the reason for this is Robinson's reluctance to affirm "the prior actuality of God" in Farrer's sense, and this in turn seems to spring from the desire to combine a "secular cosmology" with belief in God. Yet this is perhaps an impossible undertaking. If God is both transcendent and Creator in the biblical sense, then there can be no such thing as a secular cosmology, i.e., a world working by its own immanent laws and completely cut off from the divine activity. The whole cosmos must be shot through with the meaning of God, just as Jesus is shot through with such meaning according to Robinson. A purely secular cosmology could be related to God, if God is retained at all, only in a deistic way. God created the constituents of the universe and left them to evolve in their own way. This is certainly not the biblical view of God, and it presents serious difficulties from the philosophical point of view.

Robinson criticizes much traditional Christology from the Fathers to Karl Barth for assuming that Jesus could not be both a genuine product of the process and the Word of God to it. [45] He may be right in his view that Barth's version of the enhypostasia is not satisfactory, but this is not the only alternative to adoptionism, whether in its ancient or modern forms. Granted the initiative of persons, it is still possible to conceive of God responding with His initiative to the initiative of His creatures in a way that resulted in a unique personal act and presence of God in and through a real human agent. Robinson says as much when he declares that Jesus is called from within "to a unique response which is not simply that of the prophet to declare the Word of God, but to *be* the Word of God, to act and speak as God for us." [46] Yet how can this stupendous act of representation come about by a Jesus who is

---

[45]*Ibid.*, p. 201.
[46]*Ibid.*, p. 210.

simply one of the normal cases of emergent humanity? If He is to *be* the Word of God for us, and not simply point beyond Himself to the Word, then representation must be redefined to suggest some real identity of God and the Son, not an identity of two physical substances but a real identity of will and love. Such an identity of will and love admittedly implies an ontological bond between God and man for which a model taken from physical substance would necessarily be inadequate. But who decides that this is the only model which has ontological respectability? The acts of Jesus are for practical purposes at least—this Robinson acknowledges—the acts of God in this man for us men and for our salvation. This is certainly not far from the *homoousios,* whatever difficulties we have with this ontological language which is not entirely free from associations of physical substance. He quotes Van Buren as referring to Jesus as "fully man and in no sense more than man."[47] But can this language really be defended? If, as Van Buren says, Jesus is not to be confused with other men, or in Robinson's language, if Jesus is called to be God's vice-regent and to be God for us, then He is more than man in any normal usage of the term "man." He is both our brother and different from us insofar as He is the vehicle for God's unique initiative. And the difference is that between Redeemer and redeemed. To say, as Robinson quotes Knox as saying, that "the uniqueness of Jesus was the absolute uniqueness of what God did in him"[48] is certainly to assert a difference. There does not seem much value in pursuing the rather fruitless linguistic debate as to whether this difference is one of degree or of kind or whether a sufficient difference of degree may eventually become a difference of kind. Christians are not much interested in this kind of puzzle. The difference is between God redeeming in Christ and man at his highest level redeeming himself. There can be no doubt about where most Christians would stand on this issue. We must say of Jesus "more than man" while yet insisting on the real humanity. This apparently logical paradox cannot be solved on the level of the logical manipulation of concepts. If Jesus proves Himself in experience to be both God and man, then that fact must, for faith at least, be accepted. Many so-called facts in the world are mysteries and not completely transparent to the human understanding. This is not to be taken as the repudiation of all attempts on the part of faith to seek intelligible understanding of Him in whom faith is put. The whole tenor of this book is against "blind faith" which prematurely stops the inevitable questioning of the human mind. There is, however, a great difference between acknowledging a genuine mystery when we have reached the limits of the human

---

[47]*Ibid.*
[48]John Knox, *The Death of Christ* (Nashville: Abingdon, 1958), p. 125.

understanding and using mystery as an excuse for not seeking as far as possible to understand the faith we profess and the object of that faith, namely God in Christ reconciling the world unto Himself.

In all the thinkers we have discussed so far, there is one striking common feature. They all seem to be claiming some kind of uniqueness for Jesus. He is able to do for men and in men what no other historical figure has been able to achieve. The crucial issue is whether the term "divinity" is necessary to express this uniqueness and what the term would mean when used in this connection. Where God in the theistic sense is called in question, then obviously the uniqueness of Jesus cannot be found in His relationship to a God the reality of whom is in doubt. Nevertheless, the majority of these views do not seem to intend to reduce the "divinity" to manhood pure and simple. The manhood is seen as a means of mediation whereby a reality more than human is disclosed. Whether this is referred to as the Ground of Being, or simply the Transcendent, or the Spirit as distinguished from merely psychological functions, or simply God as Creator and Father, the implication seems to be that in and through the manhood of Jesus a "cosmic" disclosure is made, to use Ramsey's language. We are enabled through Jesus to become aware of and to experience that greater reality on which we depend. There may be differences of opinion as to the precise character of this greater reality. Is it personal or impersonal, or as Ramsey suggests, perhaps both?[49] In any case, something is disclosed in Jesus which elicits from us the recognition of absolute authority and value going beyond what could properly be claimed for manhood as we normally know it. Does the articulation of this experience of the transcendent reality manifested in Jesus require us to speak of His "divinity"? If, as Karl Rahner maintains, all human existence is ordered toward the supernatural and inevitably moves in that direction, whether consciously or not, then Jesus' relation to God would seem to be only a strikingly complete development of that which is a potentiality in all men. Have we, then, returned full circle to Schleiermacher and is the difference between Jesus and us one of degree only? It might be argued that this is not fair to Schleiermacher since he applies the language of Redeemer to Jesus and insists that we cannot grow in our God-consciousness without the help of the Redeemer. However, our question remains: If the difference is one of degree only, then do we need the category of divinity except in a broad sense which would make it applicable to all men?

Before we come to grips with this question, we shall return to our first enquiry. Is it possible to say anything about the nature of Jesus' own relationship to God on the basis of what Jesus communicated through

---

[49]Ian Ramsey, *Christian Discourse* (London: Oxford Univ. Press, 1965), p. 84.

language and what the disciples were able to discern in and through His actions? That Jesus had a particularly vivid sense of His dependence upon the Father, that He prayed to Him, that His whole life was devoted to the will of the Father as He understood it—all this seems beyond reasonable doubt. Nor does its truth depend upon particular answers to such debatable questions as whether or in what sense Jesus claimed to be the Messiah or whether He identified Himself with the Son of Man. The basic question is whether this relationship of Jesus to the Father was only such as any pious Jew could hope to have or whether it was of such an order as to require us to say that God's presence in this relationship marked Him off in a decisive and ultimate sense from all other men.

Is any light thrown upon the experience of Jesus by the study of Christian mysticism? No word is more loosely used and more ambiguous than "mysticism." For the present, we shall disregard the searching questions raised by W.T. Stace as to whether there is a "common core" of the mystical experience and which form of mysticism can make the most persuasive claim to be a valid intuition of the transcendent reality.[50] Let us assume for the moment that the Bible is correct in its claim that men can "know" God, however partially and imperfectly. Such knowledge, according to the Bible, is always mediated. "No man has seen God at any time" (I John 4:12). Such knowledge has always been apprehended in and through some form of human consciousness and that means through some form of psychological mediation. The oft-repeated assertion that, for the Bible, God is disclosed through "events" does not alter this fact. The "events" have to be known and interpreted in a certain way before they become revelatory. Yet the fact that any self-disclosure of Himself by God must be a mediated one does not rule out the reality of the presence so mediated. If all men are potentially open to an experience of the presence of God, then we would have to admit that the real presence of God was apprehended by men other than Jesus. It is difficult to read the Old Testament and believe that the prophets, for example, or the psalmists, were only talking of God as transcendent and never of God mysteriously present and immanent in that very experience of the faithful and obedient servant of the Lord. Once again, therefore, we have to be careful in talking of Jesus not to define His uniqueness in such a way as to make Him a spiritual solitary with no spiritual kith and kin among other men. To say that Jesus was the only man to experience God, though mediated through the manhood, is virtually to deny to the whole Jewish experience recorded in the Old Testament, and indeed in later Judaism, any genuine apprehension of the real presence of God in and

---

[50]See W.T. Stace, *Mysticism and Philosophy* (New York: Lippincott, 1960).

to men. Such a verdict would be even more hostile to any claim by men outside the Judaeo-Christian tradition to have experienced the presence of the true God.

We are not, therefore, saying that no Jew had ever known the real presence of God before Jesus, nor are we dogmatically ignoring the question of the reality of God's presence to men nurtured in the great non-Christian religions. The basic question is whether it is intelligible to speak of "degrees of divine presence" and whether it is possible for God's presence to be of such a nature in relation to creation, and in particular to a human being made in His image and endowed with freedom, that we can then go on to say that this man is God or divine in the sense that the fullness of God dwells in such a created being as far as the limitations of historical human existence permit. The reader is reminded again of the points emphasized in our discussion of the question, Is all of God in Jesus? Let us assume for the moment that it is possible for created and dependent personality by its own free choice to be so taken up into the reality of the life of God Himself. It would then be possible to speak of the presence of the redemptive personal action of God manifest in a human being without the former being called into question or the latter being so distorted as to be no longer human.

Those conversant with the long and involved history of Christian doctrine may feel that here are echoes of ancient heresies. Is this not simply another version of adoptionism, namely that Jesus is not God become man but only a man elevated by God as performing a special role, a necessary role if you wish, but not in Himself in any proper sense "truly God"? The answer to this is No. The weakness behind all forms of adoptionism lies in its often unspoken premise that the initiative in becoming aware of the divine presence rests solely on the manward side. This, however, is not true, even of many lesser figures than Jesus. On biblical assumptions, it would not in any case make sense. If any man is able to "know" the presence of God, not in a merely intellectual sense but in an existentialist sense in which the whole of the human person is involved, this can be only because God lets Himself be known and experienced in this sense. God gives Himself to the creature according to the measure in which the latter is able to receive Him. If this is granted, then it is at least possible to conceive in principle that God could give Himself wholly to a man and a man give himself wholly to God in a way which would produce a new and unique actuality, i.e., a human personality which was a transparent medium of the real presence and the saving activity of God Himself. If this were fact, then the categories of prophet, teacher, and genius would no longer be adequate. We would be confronted with One who did not reveal God by proxy, as it were, but in whom we met the active and eternal God Himself, powerful to love, redeem, and make us new. Is the language of "truly man and truly God" so inadequate to this reality after all?

If such a relationship between the human and the divine is in fact possible, then what kind of experience would be involved on the human side? It would show the marks of genuine and authentic creaturehood and of humble and freely chosen dependence upon the Eternal Father. At the same time, the man would speak and act with the sovereign authority and confidence of One who knows that the Father's presence is with Him and in Him and that the Father's will is being truly done in and through Him. This paradoxical combination of human weakness and divine authority is precisely what we find in the gospel records of the life and ministry of Jesus of Nazareth.

Let us now return to our earlier question about the consciousness of Jesus. Granted that if the above is true, there will always remain mystery about the Person of Jesus which we can never completely fathom. Does this mean that no glimpses at all are afforded to us of what it meant to Jesus to be the "Son" of the Father in this sense? Did Jesus not reveal in word and act how He experienced this relationship to the Father, even though His disciples could not follow Him beyond a certain point in their understanding of that mysterious intimacy of the Father-Son relationship?

Our discussion of this question will start from a remarkable passage in the writing of C.H. Dodd. Speaking of the attempt of the Fourth Gospel to deal with this issue, Dodd says, "The knowledge which Christ has of God, therefore, has that quality of direct vision which Hellenistic mystics claimed—falsely in the evangelist's view—and which for Jewish thinkers was reserved for the supernatural life of the age to come."[51] It is not altogether clear from the context whether Dodd is only expounding the Fourth Gospel or whether he is giving his blessing to this way of speaking. On what grounds is such a stupendous claim made and how can it be substantiated? What does Dodd mean by Jesus' direct vision of God? Can a view of the divinity of Jesus be worked out in terms of such a concept of "direct vision" which would constitute the element of uniqueness which firmly sets Him apart from all others? Everything hinges upon the sense given to the word "direct" or "immediate" when talking of the vision of God. We have already maintained that on the basis of the biblical understanding of the Creator-creature relationship, no man can "see" God, certainly not with His physical eyes, since God is infinite and transcendent Spirit. But even on the level of consciousness, "vision" is always mediated through psychological experiences of one kind or another. The Bible does not encourage us to

---

[51]C.H. Dodd, *The Interpretation of the Fourth Gospel* (Cambridge: Cambridge Univ. Press, 1953), p. 167.

believe that any man could gaze upon the transcendent glory and splendor of God in a quite unmediated way, even when we mean by vision not physical but some kind of intellectual and spiritual vision. Such "unmediated" beholding of God would be so overwhelming as to annihilate the freedom and initiative of the creature which God is pledged to preserve. If Jesus was truly man, then He, like other men, could not have had a completely unmediated "vision" of God. This, however, still leaves us with the basic problem. Can a "mediated" experience of God be of such a fullness and intensity as to involve a real, though mediated, presence of God which would warrant the use of the term "divinity"?

There is no need for us to enter now more fully into the debate concerning the language of hearing and of seeing in the Bible. It has sometimes been contended that whereas the language of seeing is typically Greek and Hellenistic, the Bible on the other hand prefers the language of word and of hearing. This sharp antithesis is of doubtful validity. There is in fact the language of "seeing" in the Old Testament and even in the New (Matthew 5:8), though as Raymond George maintains, one could hardly maintain that the language of vision is predominant in the New Testament. Certainly, in the New Testament there is language about seeing the Son of Man, or seeing Jesus after the Resurrection. Yet, as George contends, most of the New Testament language about "seeing" refers to seeing Jesus and not to seeing God the Father, with the striking exception of the Matthew passage.[52] Even if we agree that the language of hearing tends to dominate, the theological problem is not solved. When we talk of God communicating with man, the language of both sight and hearing is metaphorical. No man "sees" God with his physical eye any more than he hears Him with the physical ear. The experiences called by the psychologist "photisms" or "auditions" do not alter this fact. It is hardly questionable that some men and women have had unusual psychological experiences in which they believed they had seen "lights" (e.g., St. Paul) or heard voices (e.g., Joan of Arc). Nevertheless, we cannot take these claims uncritically as validating the fact that these people actually gazed directly and in a totally unmediated way upon the transcendent Godhead. The Bible, at least, is against such an absolute claim. Certainly they believed themselves to have experienced the divine presence with an unusual degree of vividness and intensity. They do not generally deny the scriptural statement that "no man has seen God at any time."

It will be better, therefore, in dealing with problems of Christology not to rest our case upon the claim that Jesus had a direct and unmediated

---

[52]Raymond George, *Communion with God* (London: Epworth, 1953), pp. 93–99.

perception of the transcendent God and Father in this sense. To avoid serious misunderstanding, however, let it be repeated again as strongly as possible that this does not mean that the presence of God to Him and His awareness of and full communion with that presence were not real in the fullest sense. We are not denying the reality of the divine presence, only the human ability to know the eternal God in a totally unmediated way, i.e., in a way that completely circumvents the mediation of physical and psychological forms and patterns. To express this in terms of the classic Christological language, we would have to say that in becoming man, God willed that the man He became should have the limitations of authentic manhood, including the limitation of not being able to see Him (God the Father) except through a mediating process involving all the elements of human experience.

This being said, what shall we say to the Christian claim that the Divine Presence and saving activity were manifested in Jesus in a manner so unique that we must use such language as "God manifest in the flesh" with a meaning and intention which forbids us to apply it to any other man in the same sense? It would seem clear that no such claim could ever be substantiated in the abstract or by logical argument. The only possible evidence to which appeal could be made must be rooted in the experience of Christians. Only if Jesus has made it possible for ordinary people to experience in their relationship to Him the real presence and the absolute claim of the holy love of God can we talk of evidence. This does not mean that our experience makes Jesus what He is. The Christian experience is such as to compel us to speak of a reality other than our own creation which makes the experience possible. Ian Ramsey has again expressed this very well:

> Nevertheless I would claim that it is quite clear that cosmic disclosures are ontologically privileged in so far as they disclose that which confronts us as a basic 'given', that which is set over against ourselves in every situation of this kind, that which individuates the universe.[53]

Some may be uneasy about the language used here. Is God being equated with the universe as such and can Christian faith accept such an identification? Certainly the universe is a reality over against us and we might very well receive "disclosures" from it, though the word "disclosure" is already well on the way to becoming "personality" language. In this case, the traditional problem of theism and pantheism arises. If the reality so disclosed is in any sense "personal," then another word than "universe" may well have to be found. However, Ramsey's basic point is well taken. The disclosure is of a reality which is beyond us and other than ourselves. The

---

[53]Ramsey, *Words About God*, p. 212.

Christian believes that in and through Jesus of Nazareth such a reality is being disclosed. On the other hand, to make such a claim for Jesus cannot obviously be substantiated apart from the experiences in and through which such a disclosure has been made. Thus the reality of Jesus' own relationship to God and our experience of the power of God through our relationship to Jesus cannot be separated. What God has joined together, let no man put asunder. In other words, the experiential evidence for the divinity of Jesus must be found in the transforming effects which Jesus has brought in human experience. Apart from these, any claim to divinity would be merely abstract. On the other hand, let it be repeated as strongly as possible, this does not mean that our experience creates the divinity. Jesus is not merely a function of my psychology. Yet apart from my psychology, in the sense of my total experience, I would have no way of learning who He is.

9.
Three Classic Christological Models

We shall now turn again to three well-known models which have been employed to express the unique role of Jesus of Nazareth in relation to both God and man. These are preexistence, descent and ascent, and kenosis or self-emptying. Can this kind of language still be made meaningful to modern man, and is such language a necessary means of preserving what Christian men think they have experienced of God's personal redemptive presence and activity in the Person of Jesus Christ?

Let us start with preexistence. It has already been noted that this model, based on temporal categories, was used to express the Christian conviction that God has always been such as He has disclosed Himself to be in Jesus. There never was a "time" when God was not what we know Him to be in Jesus. Since God is a being who is transcendent, creative, immanent, and personal,[1] and if Jesus is the medium of God's self-disclosure, then there must be in Jesus signs of the presence and activity of God who is not bound by space and time in the same sense as we are. The finite, temporal, human life of Jesus is the means whereby we meet and know the Eternal God. It has already been admitted that this could be true of all devout men in some measure. It is the Christian conviction that the difference between Jesus and us is such that such a difference of degree has become a difference in kind. He is our elder brother and fellow sufferer, true, but He is not only sinful man striving for fleeting and partial experience of the Eternal God. He is the Eternal God living within the limits of human finiteness with a mediated directness and fullness which is absolutely unique. In other words, Christians believe they are saved not by Jesus of Nazareth but by God become man in Him. As we have already maintained, this does not mean that "all of God" is in Jesus, but it does mean that in Jesus we encounter a unique initiative of God as well as a human response, and that in Him we meet God, not by proxy or by a messenger telling us about God, but God's loving and

---

[1] See H.P. Owen, *The Christian Knowledge of God,* p. 1.

saving activity impinging directly upon human lives, even though this is mediated through the manhood of Jesus. The question is, How can this truth be expressed and preserved? Is the language of preexistence still a meaningful and viable way of doing this?

John Knox has argued with considerable force that although it is quite understandable that in the context of Greek and Jewish ideas of Logos and Wisdom some doctrine of preexistence should develop, we do not have to regard this development as either inevitable or permanently valid.[2] Indeed, he sums up his penetrating discussion of this matter as follows: "If it is true that belief in the pre-existence of Jesus is incompatible with a belief in his genuine normal humanity, then it is clear that an affirmative answer to our questions about humanity will require some reassessment of that belief."[3] In short, his conviction is that with the development of theories of preexistence, the reality of the humanity was put under intolerable pressure and that the church has never really succeeded in reconciling the two things in a satisfactory way.

The first question to be asked is whether the church ever intended to speak of the preexistence of Jesus of Nazareth, the historical man of first-century Palestine. What could such a statement mean? We are at once involved in some very difficult questions about what constitutes a person. If it is insisted that the body or the physical flesh is an integral element in the reality of any truly human person, then we would have to say that Jesus, before the world came into being, was "in God" in some bodily form. The preexistence of Jesus or of any man in this sense is admittedly very difficult to conceive. If, on the other hand, we argue that the real self, which is the core of personhood, is not intrinsically dependent upon the physical body as we now have it and know it, then we could argue for the preexistence of nonbodily selves or souls before the present universe came into being. It is well known that this was the thesis advanced by Origen in the second century. Before the world began, according to him, other finite, dependent, spiritual creatures had come into existence through the creative activity of God. The whole realm of angelic beings was there before man emerged. The doctrine of the preexistence of souls in this sense appears to be present in ancient Orphism, in Plato, and in various forms of Hinduism and Buddhism. Starting from this premise, one could then argue, as Origen did, that the Logos became flesh by uniting with a preexistent sinless but finite soul and then became united with the physical body of the man Jesus in Palestine. This had the advantage of allowing Origen to combine the view that Jesus

[2]Knox, *The Humanity and Divinity of Jesus*, p. 60.
[3]*Ibid.*, p. 73.

had a genuine, finite self or soul together with a doctrine of preexistence. This also enabled him to avoid the apparent absurdity of speaking of the preexistent ''body'' or flesh of Jesus.

Whatever may be thought of such ideas, it does seem rather academic to expect that modern men will continue to think in these terms, or that we should insist that they think in this way if they are to be considered Christian. Even if the existence of God is accepted without question, what evidence is there that finite spiritual beings existed before the world began? Let it be said at once that there is no inherent absurdity in the idea if an infinite and creative God is accepted. The contemporary problem is one of evidence. It is comparable to the question about men on Mars or the other planets. Here again he would be a bold man these days who would dogmatically deny the possibility. Yet it must be admitted that the evidence for angelic beings of the Origenist kind or of rational creatures on Mars is virtually nil. We can only wait and see. Meanwhile, it would be theological foolhardiness to attempt to frame a doctrine of the Person of Christ on the basis of what at the moment must be deemed a highly speculative hypothesis.

Against such difficulties, it might be urged that this is not what the church was trying to express in using the model of preexistence. It was simply trying to preserve the uniqueness of Jesus as affording a self-disclosure of God without parallel elsewhere. This, it felt, could be done only by making a deduction from our present spiritual experience of God in Christ. What He was in the specific historical actuality of His life in Palestine was rooted in the Eternal God. Human spiritual discovery was not enough. An initiative from the Godward side was required. This meant that what appeared in Jesus as the self-disclosure of God must have been permanently an element in the eternal character and reality of God. This carries us beyond space and time but can be expressed only in suitably qualified models taken from the temporal. Hence preexistence. There must have been in God ''from the beginning'' all that was later disclosed in the man Jesus.

There can be no doubt that this way of speaking is making an important point for the Christian. That we are in difficulties with our models on this issue is hardly a matter for surprise. Any attempt by finite minds to bring the Eternal God into relationship with created realities in space and time runs into the same difficulties. Yet we cannot be content with utter silence, and neither could the early church. Since it was not prepared to follow Origen's speculations about preexistent souls, the church ended up with a doctrine of the Eternal Son, the second ''persona'' of the Trinity, who assumed our human nature and thereby became man. The Eternal Son was not a preexistent bodily Jesus of Nazareth but one of the eternal hypostases of the one God. This way of speaking enabled the church to affirm the Incarnation without this involving such a complete self-emptying on the part of God as to be equivalent to God's self-annihilation as the Eternal Creator and sustainer of the universe. This latter idea has been revived in our own day by Thomas Altizer, to whom we shall turn later. The distinctions between the "personae" and the "hypostases" of God also enabled the church to avoid the absurdity of saying that God literally died when Jesus died. God could be fully manifest in the flesh as a man without ceasing to be the Eternal Creator and continuing His ever present activity through the Spirit in the experiences of men.

So far so good, but the difficulties in getting over these ideas to modern men are still immense. Outside the church the very concept of an infinite "personal" God is obviously not taken for granted, and some would say is unintelligible. The Logos as the outgoing of such a God in creative activity is not a presupposition of modern thought, though it has valiant defenders from William Temple[4] to Paul Tillich.[5] Let us, however, assume the classic Trinitarian doctrine as a useful and reliable model, though recognizing that it is not what Ian Ramsey calls a "picturing model," a literal description of the inner life of the Godhead. Let us also assume that it makes some sense to speak of the Eternal Son going forth from the Father and eventually producing the universe we know, including ourselves. This would require us to say that the Eternal Son, the Son of God, or the preexistent Son of Man, or the Logos or some other divine hypostasis was an "actuality in God" before He became an actual man the church remembered.[6] Even if we assume all these complex ideas, it is still incredible, says Knox, that a "divine person should have become a fully and normally human person—that is, if he was also to continue to be, in his essential identity, the same person."[7] It will readily be seen that for Knox the crucial problem is one of identity. How could the Eternal Son become Jesus of Nazareth while remaining at the same time an "hypostasis" of God and without destroying the genuine humanity of the man? How can the mind possibly hold together two such ideas without getting into intolerable paradox and contradiction?

One way out, of course, is by what we may call Kierkegaardian defiance. Who says that we must be able to see how such ideas could be combined? If the Christian faith and experience require us to assert such paradoxes, we must live with them and to hell with logic. It is interesting to note that W.T. Stace, in his analysis of mysticism, also argues that the principle of noncontradiction may not be ultimate and that the mystical

---

[4]Temple, *Nature, Man and God.*
[5]Tillich, *Systematic Theology,* Vols. 1–3.
[6]Knox, *Humanity and Divinity,* p. 95.
[7]*Ibid.,* p. 98.

experience requires us to utter paradoxes which the human mind can never reconcile on the basis of logical coherence. Yet this would seem to be a desperate expedient. If logical sense can be flouted in this way, what protection do we have against the proliferation of myth in its most luxuriant and uncontrolled sense? We can say anything and get away with anything in the name of religious paradox. Says Knox again: "Some identity must exist between the Eternal Son of God and the man Jesus. Otherwise, the story falls apart and the pre-existence of Jesus in any sense is again denied."[8] In which case we might as well drop the whole model of preexistence and start again.

Nevertheless, the issues raised are far from merely academic. They cut deep into the faith and confidence of the believer. How can the Christian express the conviction that in his relationship to Jesus he is in touch not only with a man of first-century Palestine but with the Eternal God? Can he still base his life on the truth that "he that hath seen me hath seen the Father," where Father stands for the infinite, transcendent Creator and Lord of Jewish and Christian experience? If we accept with Pittenger that "Jesus as a man did not pre-exist his conception and birth,"[9] yet we must go on to say, as Pittenger also states, that "something did pre-exist."[10] What was it that preexisted? The simple answer would be "God," but this statement alone does not say all that Christians want to say until its implications are spelled out more fully. God preexists all men in the general sense that He was real before the present created order came into existence.[11] This might be denied by some exponents of the process philosophy, but we shall assume for the moment the classic theistic view of God. My own existence and all my intellectual, moral, and spiritual capacities presuppose the reality of the God who brought me into being before I became actualized as a human being in this twentieth century. God in this sense preexists both nature and man. The problem of Jesus, taking this truth for granted, goes on to ask: Since Jesus mediates to men the reality of God in a way not found elsewhere either in nature or history, then what must there have been in God to make this particular disclosure of Himself possible in first-century Palestine?

One presumably can only answer this question by saying that "something did pre-exist" and that this something is not only God as the creative source of nature and history in general but as the source of this particular unique actuality which is Jesus of Nazareth. Pittenger at this point falls back upon the classic language of the faith: "It was the Eternal Word of God who

---

[8]*Ibid.*

[9]Pittenger, *The Word Incarnate,* p. 216.

[10]*Ibid.,* p. 219.

[11]Farrer, "The Prior Actuality of God," *Reflective Faith,* ed. Charles Conti (Grand Rapids: Eerdmans, 1974).

is incarnate in Jesus,''[12] while insisting that the Eternal Word is not a human consciousness and that in becoming Jesus, the Word does not supplant the human consciousness of Jesus or the full reality of his human self. God, through the creative Word, brings all things into existence, including Jesus of Nazareth. In the case of Jesus, however, God is the eternal source, the expression, and the response from the perfectly trusting and obedient manhood of Jesus.[13] Divine initiative and self-expression are operative through the perfectly surrendered manhood in such a way as to produce the historical actuality of a unique reality—God in man—a unique fact which sets Jesus apart from all other men without denying His kinship with all other men. Beyond this it is doubtful whether human language can go.

Furthermore, it is difficult to see how these truths could be expressed without the use of temporal categories such as "preexistence" to indicate what was real and actual in God before it became real and actual in Jesus. Jesus as physical body did not preexist, but the divine source of creative and redemptive love did preexist in the fullness with which it was manifest in Jesus Christ in history. In this case, provided we know what we are saying and interpret it correctly, it would be legitimate to speak, as Karl Barth did, of "The Humanity of God." All the potentialities for full manhood must have been actual in God, since nothing can come from nothing and the lesser presupposes the greater. This does not mean that human personalities or individual men existed in God as actualized individuals before their appearance on the stage of history as men. By the nature of the case this could not be. There is, after all, a great difference between an idea in the mind of God and the actualization of that idea in the concrete reality of a human existence in the created world. We are saying, however, that rational and spiritual persons, including the unique Person of Jesus, could not have come into being unless God is in Himself the actuality or the actual source of all those qualities which characterize His creatures, men.

Our conclusion, therefore, is that when certain qualifications have been made, the language of preexistence is still needed to point to a vital truth experienced by Christian believers in their relationship to Jesus. In the case of Jesus, Christian thought appears to have taken one further daring step. Christian faith appears to have drawn the conclusion that the unique Father-Son relationship, actualized in the perfect obedience and dependence of Jesus upon God, is somehow reflected in the eternal nature of God. What was possible as historic fact in the relationship of Jesus to the Father has its eternal counterpart in the eternal reality of God. This means that we are

---

[12]Pittenger, *Word Incarnate*, p. 219.
[13]*Ibid.*, p. 221.

saying more than that God is the source of all we find in Jesus. This could be true of all of us without implying our preexistence. In this special case of Jesus, Christian faith is saying that in the eternal nature of God there is a real Father-Son relationship of which the earthly Jesus Christ is the true reflection. This means that Christian monotheism must mean more than the affirmation that God is a single, undifferentiated, bare, mathematical kind of unity. God's reality contains within itself the perfect Father-Son relationship, which is the archetype, as it were, of what appears in the historical actuality.

The criticism, of course, has often been made that this destroys the unity of the Godhead. But Christian men have on the whole rejected this criticism as invalid. Because our finite minds cannot conceive (i.e., have a full imaginative and intellectual grasp) of how God can be one and yet contain the reality of a truly personal relationship within Himself prior to and apart from His relationship to men, this does not mean that it must be repudiated as impossible. Indeed, such an assumption has to be made if we are to explain the Father-Son relationship in Jesus as more than the dependence of a good man upon God. If the total event of Jesus Christ is truly a reflection of what God eternally is, then we must have the courage to carry this Father-Son relationship back into the very heart of God. It is this logic of faith which led to the use of the category of preexistence which we have already discussed.

It may still be argued that it is one thing to say that God preexists the created world and that God is the source of all that is, but quite another thing to say that in God there is another reality, a supernatural being or Logos or Son who is distinguishable from the Father, yet in some mysterious way one with Him. J.A.T. Robinson has recently gone on record as saying that he does not believe in a preexistent supernatural divine being who became man in Jesus.[14] The most he allows himself, as we have seen, is to say that the man Jesus functions as God for us. What He does He does as God's vice-regent, and He so acts because of a unique divine initiative in and through this man. This frees Robinson of the need to use mythological language about preexistence or to talk of distinct realities in God which it is difficult to do without falling into ditheism or tritheism. If it is replied that the doctrine of the Trinity was framed to meet precisely these difficulties, Robinson would doubtless reply that this may be so, but that the doctrine fails to achieve its aim, since it itself leans heavily upon mythical ways of thought which we can no longer accept. Yet, while it is admittedly easy for the orthodox Christian to say that the doctrine of the Trinity is inadequate to

---

[14]J.A.T. Robinson, *The Human Face of God.*

the mystery, it is better to use imperfect language than be reduced to the complete silence of which Augustine spoke. This, however, will probably not satisfy Dr. Robinson and those who sympathize with his way of thinking.

The debate really centers on what are considered to be the necessary implications of Christian faith and experience. Somehow that faith and experience have felt it inadequate to solve this issue by talking only of the preexistence in the thought and purpose of God. H. Wheeler Robinson cites Duhm's contention that Jeremiah was a divine thought in the mind of God before he was born.[15] Jewish speculations about a preexistent Messiah could be suggested as another parallel. Preexistence alone, in the mind of God as an idea, does not meet the requirements of the special case of Jesus. It is the unique relation of Jesus to the Father, the fact that Jesus functions as God for us (to use again J.A.T. Robinson's language), which determines the special kind of preexistence in this case. It is this particular Father-Son relationship which is asserted to be preexistent. Nor must we leave out of account the post-existence of Jesus Christ. Again, Christian faith has never been happy to talk as if Jesus after His death was simply swallowed up once more in the undifferentiated unity of the divine being. Somehow the bond established between man and God in the Incarnation is henceforth a permanent reality in God. It is this which leads Wheeler Robinson to affirm that ''In some sense He [i.e., Jesus Christ] belongs to the eternal being of God and that which He became on earth and continues to be in heaven belongs to the divine order from all eternity.''[16]

But does this not leave us with an impossibly difficult conception of God? Have we not destroyed the precious heritage of the Jewish faith, bequeathed to Christianity, that God is truly one and that no qualification of the sovereignty of the one God can really be permitted? To say this is to ask Christians to become Jews or Muslims or at least sophisticated Unitarians. What, then, becomes of the conviction of Christian faith that Jesus Christ, both in time and eternity, is the one who functions as God for us and the everlasting mediator of our salvation and the divinely appointed agent of our reconciliation with Him?

It is pertinent to raise the question at this point as to the real nature of the theological difference between Jews and Christians in regard to the doctrine of God. The Jewish concept of God as one is generally set in sharp antithesis to the Christian ''three-in-one.'' But A. W. Wainwright seems to have made a strong case for the claim that the notion of a God who contained plurality within His unity was not entirely alien to later Judaism.[17] He has no

---

[15]H.W. Robinson, *Revelation and Redemption*, p. 203.
[16]*Ibid.*
[17]A.W. Wainwright, *The Trinity in the New Testament* (London: S.P.C.K., 1962), p. 23.

difficulty showing that both in the Old Testament and in post-exilic Judaism the Jew had no problem conceiving an "extension of personality" in relation to Yahweh. The easy transition for the Hebrew from the one to the many,[18] the notion of corporate personality, the way in which the Spirit, Wisdom, and Word were seen as extensions of Yahweh's personal activity in the world—all these factors show the ability of the Hebrew and Jewish mind to entertain the notion of plurality in relation to Yahweh's distinctive activities. Even notions of preexistence played an important role here, especially in regard to the Word and Wisdom.

The important point to notice, however, according to Wainwright, was that the Jew never intended this way of speaking to qualify in any fundamental way the unity of the one God. There was no intention to depart from the basic monotheism of the Jewish faith. Whether we use such terms as "personification" to indicate this feature of Jewish thought, or "hypostasizing" to express that the Word or Wisdom have a quasi-independent reality from Yahweh, the fact seems to be that the Jew never accepted the idea of real interaction in the Godhead between "persons" in the Christian sense. Wisdom, Spirit, and Word may have been thought of as self-conscious emanations of God, and preexistence models could be used to express the distinctness of these special activities, as with the Word and Wisdom.

If Christians had been content to see Jesus only in terms of the extension of divine personality through a special divine activity in Him, no basic conflict with Judaism would have arisen in regard to the doctrine of God. Jesus could have been linked with notions of the Word and Wisdom without the problem becoming acute. The real problem for the Jew was and is the Christian claim that Jesus is not simply a personified attribute of the one God. He is a real person, a man of flesh and blood who actually appeared in history and in that earthly life prayed to the Father as to one different from Himself on the level of personal being. When this Father-Son relationship was transferred, through the use of the preexistence model, to the inner life of the Godhead, then the Son or Word or Wisdom became a real "person," a real but distinct center of consciousness and activity within the divine life. This had never been the case in Judaism. "For the orthodox Jew, the trouble about Christ was not that he was regarded as an extension of the divine personality but that he was believed to have been incarnate."[19] The Jew could easily have accepted Him as a concept or a personified attribute of Yahweh. When the church tried to incorporate Christ into the very existence of God as a distinct personal reality and worked out the later doctrine of the

---

[18]A.R. Johnson, *The One and the Many in the Israelite Conception of God* (Cardiff, Wales: Univ. of Wales, 1961).

[19]Wainwright, p. 39.

Trinity, it was moving significantly beyond both Jewish and Hellenistic thought. "The idea of interaction within the extended personality [of God] is neither Hebraic nor Hellenistic but Christian."[20]

It is true, of course, that the Father-Son language is itself a model taken analogically from human relationships. It is not, as Ramsey would say, a literal, picture model of God. To put it bluntly, God does not produce the Eternal Son by a process analogous to sexual intercourse or biological procreation, even though the church has used the language of begetting and Origen coined the famous phrase about the "eternal generation of the Son." Since neither God nor the Logos-Son have physical bodies, their relationship cannot be a bodily one. It is not true, however, that once we qualify the model, the Father-Son relationship becomes a useless model. Even in human experience, there is more to the Father-Son relationship than the mere fact that the Son was born by virtue of the Father's act. There is the communion of mind and love, transcending the bodily relationship, which gives us a deeper experience of what that relationship means. The curious modern mind is apt to ask where the mother fits into the picture! The Women's Liberation Movement might well insist that this theological model is a typical illustration of the way in which Christianity has been dominated by the masculine mind. Why should we not speak of a Mother-Son relationship? Would not mother love at its best be a richer symbol or model than the Father-Son image? Provided we know exactly what we are saying and why, this point need not be denied. God is neither father nor mother in the literal sense, but both. The parent-child relationship as applied to God includes the fullness of parental experience at its highest on the side of both father and mother. God transcends the sexual differentiation completely, and this has to be frankly said. When we speak of God as Father, we are not limiting the fullness of His parental concern to only one side of the human relationship. God in the strictly literal sense, we must repeat, is neither father nor mother but the perfect parent where the term "parent" is itself a qualified model stripped of the merely human features connected with the difference between man and woman. Nevertheless, this does not deprive the parent model of any significance. If the above considerations are borne in mind, then we do not need to emphasize the role of the Virgin Mary in order to do justice to the feminine experience of parenthood. Carl Jung has commended the Catholic church for its psychological wisdom in stressing the role of Mary, not because he shares the Catholic dogmas about her, but because he thinks they afford a necessary corrective to the exclusively masculine aspects of traditional Christian thinking and language. This, however, would no longer be necessary if the

---

[20]*Ibid.*, p. 40.

full implications of the parental analogy as applied to God were properly understood. Christian theology is carrying back into the heart of the Godhead all the fullness of the parental relationship, stripped of those features which depend solely on the possession of a physical body and its sexual functions and differences. It seems necessary to say these things at the present time when women's liberation and modern psychology are both pleading for a more adequate recognition of woman as a person in her own right, and not merely as a subordinate and passive figure in a basically sexual relationship.

If it is granted that the Father-Son model may be stripped of biological and sexual characteristics in its application to the Godhead, the question still arises whether the development in the church's doctrine of God was not a return to mythology, even if a somewhat refined and more intellectualized kind of mythology. J.A.T. Robinson evidently thinks so. We cannot today, he implies, see Jesus as the becoming man of a preexistent, real personal being somehow within the unity of the Godhead but yet distinct from the Father as a separate center of activity and will. There is no way such a conceptualizing of the idea of the one God can be defended against the charge of tritheism or at least ditheism. Even if we try to ease the problem, as some have done, by admitting that the Spirit is not a "person" in the same sense as the Son, the difficulty is in no way removed. A binitarian view of God is as fatal to the essential oneness of God as a trinitarian view or a frankly polytheistic view.

If this is truly the case, then the conclusion must surely be drawn, as perhaps J.A.T. Robinson and John Knox admit, that the doctrine of the Trinity in its developed form was a misguided effort which must be repudiated. It may be understandable from a devotional point of view, but as an adequate conceptualizing of the idea of God, it cannot be defended. We should frankly espouse an adoptionist or even Arian position which would leave the oneness of God intact and free from any compromising modifications. The word "Arian" is here used rather loosely to indicate an estimate of Christ as the highest of the creatures, in whom perhaps God is uniquely active but who cannot in any sense be described as truly God. In no proper sense can the *homoousios* be applied to Jesus and the Father. In this broad sense, some modern Christologies might not improperly be called Arian. Historically, of course, there are many features of the original Arianism which, because of the special historical and cultural situation of Arius and certain philosophical assumptions he took for granted, could not properly be attributed to these modern Christologies. The basic view of Christ as the highest of the creatures remains the basic point. The moderns would insist, even more strongly than the historical Arius, upon the full and authentic humanity of Jesus. In either case, the "truly God" is suspect except when interpreted in functional terms, and it is not permitted to advance to a Trinitarian view of God in which the Eternal Son is not only a personified attribute of God, but a distinct and real "person" within the one divine life.

This discussion now brings us to the parting of the ways, theologically speaking. Should the church have remained with unmodified Jewish monotheism and a functional Jesus only, or was it justified in trying to frame a doctrine of God in whom there would be interaction between real "persons" or "modes" or "centers of personal will and activity"? Put in another way, if there were no created order and no finite creatures, would God be without an object of love, shut up forever in the isolation of His eternal loneliness? It is only fair to admit that there is no theological unanimity on this vital point in the Christian tradition. We find thinkers dividing into two main groups: those who are concerned to defend the unity of the Godhead at all costs, as that which is of vital concern both to Jews and Christians; and those who wish to defend real distinctions in God, even at the risk of using language which seems to verge on tritheism. God, say these latter, is more like a society than a mere mathematical unity, though obviously a society which has no exact parallel in the sociological groups and the group dynamics of earthly societies of men.

There is no need to go over the detailed handling of these issues in recent theological debate.[21] The problem is how to discuss the matter without appearing to end up with abstractions and a barren dispute about words. Yet, as Wainwright insists, it was far from being a speculative matter even in the early days of the faith when Christian thought was not yet, as some maintain, so theologically sophisticated as to have lost all contact with reality. "Because they [the early Christians] loved both the Father and the Son, they wanted to know how they were related to each other."[22] The late Austin Farrer left a devotional classic in which he comments: "The Trinity cannot be explored except from the centre. And what is the Centre? It is the love of God."[23] One hesitates to use a devotional meditation of this kind as a basis for theological argument, for this was not in Farrer's mind at the time of writing, yet it is so full of wisdom and Christian understanding that one is tempted to quote again and again. "It is only because divine love has a

---

[21]See Barth, *Church Dogmatics,* I, 1; H.W. Robinson, *The Christian Experience of the Holy Spirit;* Claude Welch, *In This Name* (New York: Scribners, 1952); Leonard Hodgson, *The Doctrine of the Trinity* (London: Nisbet, 1943); Karl Rahner, *The Trinity* (New York: Herder & Herder, 1969); Wainwright, *The Trinity in the New Testament;* and Pittenger, *The Word Incarnate.*
[22]Wainwright, p. 6.
[23]Austin Farrer, *Lord, I Believe* (London: S.P.C.K., 1962).

natural object that it overflows to embrace an adopted object. We are the children of God by adoption, the Eternal Son is Son by nature.''[24] Farrer takes his stand with those who do not hesitate to say that the oneness of God is essentially a society of love. We know this not by drawing precarious analogies from human fathers and sons but by experiencing our own adopted sonship into God through our access to Him who is the actualizing in history of the Eternal Son. Jesus differs infinitely from us precisely because He is the bodying forth of an eternal relationship which constitutes the nature of God from all eternity. Not only does Jesus function as God or represent God, to use J.A.T. Robinson's language. He is the manifestation in time and history of the very nature and being of God. Such an understanding of God is essentially rooted in the Christian experience of God in Christ through the indwelling of the Spirit. It in no way depends upon Aristotelian or any other purely philosophical conception of the unity of God. Robert Jensen expresses a similar idea in his discussion of Leslie Dewart's *The Future of Belief* and the view of Karl Barth: ''Only a doctrine which insists that God would be, for example, love, even though He did not love *us*, i.e. only a seriously trinitarian doctrine, can sustain the polemic against hellenism.''[25]

It is hardly a sufficient objection to this view to pin on it the label ''mythological'' in a pejorative sense. Even Robinson's functional view seems to want to say what this doctrine of the Trinity is trying to express. For all practical purposes, Jesus is God for Robinson, and through Him we discover and receive our own true sonship. It seems that the root of the difficulty in Robinson's case is the fear of carrying back the full content of the Christian experience of God into the eternal life of God and modifying the doctrine of God accordingly. It must be conceded to him that the dangers are great and that some of the more barren episodes in theological history are connected with discussions of the Trinity. Yet it also seems to be true that when the Christian heart and head are given full play, as they should be, Christian devotion, by the logic of its own experience, will inevitably push back beyond the functional Jesus of historical actuality to the Eternal Son of the Eternal Father whereby we dare to approach the awful mystery of the Godhead with the cry ''Abba, Father'' on our lips. The reader will, we hope, forgive what some may consider a regrettable lapse from scholarly objectivity into the language of devotion. This is inevitable. Obviously, no one is going to be persuaded of the meaningfulness of any doctrine of the Trinity on the basis of the careful analysis of concepts alone. For the Christian, the doctrine may illumine his own experience without removing

---

[24]*Ibid.*, p. 19.
[25]Robert Jensen, *God After God* (Indianapolis: Bobbs-Merrill, 1969), p. 142.

all mystery. For the non-Christian, it can only appear a hazardous step into the unknown.

Yet can this language about the Eternal Son of the Eternal Father be made intelligible within a strictly monotheistic emphasis? Are we not committed by this language to at least two consciousnesses and two activities within the divine life? Have we not, thereby, disrupted any meaningful conception of divine unity? Barth has insisted with the utmost force that we cannot speak of a tri-essentiality in God nor can we speak of a tri-personality, if we are using the word "personality" in the modern sense?[26] Karl Rahner from the Catholic side has warned us against the danger of a popular, unverbalized, quite massive tritheism: "There can be no doubt about it: speaking of three persons in God entails almost inevitably the danger of believing that there exist in God three distinct consciousnesses, spiritual vitalities, centres of activity and so on."[27] If this is so, and if we must not think in this way, how can we speak, as Farrer does, of the Eternal Son as Son by nature, whereas we are only sons by adoption. How can God have a Son by nature within the unity of the one divine consciousness? It must be remembered that we are dealing here with the eternal nature of God as He is in Himself, even prior to creation and the appearance of man on this planet. It is true that we would lack any impulse to talk of God in this way unless we had known Him as the God and Father of our Lord Jesus Christ in the historical actualities of salvation history. On the basis of this, however, we are talking of the essential nature of God in a way which transcends the historical process as such. In other words, we proceed, to use Rahner's language, from the economic Trinity to the immanent Trinity, from God as He acts in history to God as He is in Himself by virtue of being God. Nor can we know anything of God in Himself apart from the ways, modes, or personae in which He has revealed Himself to us. Granted this, however, our problem is still to find the language which is not wholly misleading about the immanent Trinity, i.e., God in Himself.

How do we do this without ending up with a static God who remains aloof from the dynamic and revealing process which we know in His historical self-manifestation? Macquarrie reminds us that we cannot think of primordial Being (his language for the infinite, transcendent, creative source of all things) as an "uncarved block."[28] This would result in a view of the divine nature belied by the dynamic way in which He has made Himself known. There must be movement in God, even before creation. To quote Macquarrie again, God is not only primordial Being but expressive Being,

[26]Barth, *Church Dogmatics*, I, 1, pp. 402, 403, 411.

[27]Rahner, *The Trinity*, p. 43.

[28]Macquarrie, *Principles of Christian Theology*, p. 182.

and it is this which is designated by the traditional language of the Eternal Word or Son. This second "person" of the Trinity must be coeternal with the Father since God is always moving to self-expression. There never was a time when God was not dynamic, moving to self-utterance and self-expression. We cannot think of God the Father dwelling in isolation, however splendid, since the term "Father" would be meaningless apart from an object of His eternal love.[29]

There are two options open to us at this point. On the one hand, we can say that before the creation, including man, there was no object of God's love except Himself, and self-love can hardly be granted the highest state of existence from a Christian perspective. On this view, God would be isolated and alone until man came on the scene to give Him the fellowship He craves. On the other hand, we can contend for the Eternal Son as the eternal object of the divine love and see the creation as the showing of an expressing and responsive love already "actual" within the one God. This brings us back to Farrer's position. We are fully conscious of the anthropomorphic nature of the language we have been using, yet how else can the basic point be put in human language at all? The Holy Spirit, in this context of discussion, becomes "unitive being" since the function of the Spirit proceeds from the Father as primordial Being and as expressive Being to bring all beings into the unity of the divine love.[30]

If, then, we are going to talk of the Father-Son relationship and the love which unites them, as constituting the essential and eternal nature of God, what can we possibly mean by this if we still insist on one consciousness? Even such strong defenders of the oneness of the triune God as Karl Barth sometimes speak in the manner we might normally associate with those who hold the "social" view of the Trinity. This oneness, says Barth, is neither singleness nor aloneness.[31] God's relation to man is not necessary for God to know what it is to be personally related, since this is already constitutive of the divine existence as such. As Robert Jensen summarizes Barth's view: "He [God] is one not as a solitary monad, but as a person living of Himself."[32] Jensen asks if these neat Barthian formulations really mean anything. Only, he says, if we remember that for Barth God is not a substance but a deed, a series of activities.[33] Yet even if we substitute a more dynamic concept of God than the traditional language of substance would seem to suggest, our basic problem remains. How can God within His own

---

[29]*Ibid.*, p. 183.
[30]*Ibid.*, p. 185.
[31]Barth, *Church Dogmatics,* I, 1, p. 373.
[32]Jensen, p. 110.
[33]*Ibid.*

existence, apart from creation, experience the active communion of a real personal relationship between Himself and the other posited as the Son, while still remaining in a meaningful sense one God?

Problems of theological language here reach their most acute and difficult expression. Here we are compelled to qualify our models in the most radical way. Obviously God is not a human consciousness limited to a body located in space. God's single consciousness is not that of a merely magnified human being. In venturing to say anything about God in Himself, it is almost impossible to free ourselves from spatial models. We think of the Father over there and the Son over here with an intervening space such as separates human bodies. Or if we try to think of a single consciousness with two centers of activity, or maybe three, we inevitably tend to use a psychological model, and then God becomes a multiple personality, in this case a dual one. But this is a model taken from a highly abnormal human situation. Michael Schmaus expresses the matter by saying that we must not think of God as a supra-consciousness of which the Father's and the Son's consciousnesses constitute partial forms. There is only a "single divine consciousness of self and a single self-comprehension which is effected in the mode of consciousness as Father and Son."[34] Schmaus seems to be saying that while for men knowledge of ourselves as persons develops only in our encounter with other persons, both being also bodies spatially located, in the case of God this kind of relationship exists in the one divine consciousness. "God encounters himself in self-knowledge in a manner similar to the way a man does"[35] except that in the case of God the personal other is not distinguishable, as in the case of interpersonal human relationships. "God as knowing subject stands in relation to himself as the one known."[36] There is a self-antithesis in God which involves God as subject and a truly personal other which is a perfect reflection of the subject, both involved in a mutual relationship of perfect love, expressed by the concept of the Holy Spirit. And all this is within a genuinely single consciousness.

It is clear that by the time we reach this kind of speculation, we have travelled a long way from the normal significance of such models as person, subject, and consciousness. Nor does the problem get any easier by insisting that the models are qualified, or in terms of an earlier scholasticism that we are talking analogically. The fact remains that as men, we have absolutely no real knowledge of what it would be like to be an infinite consciousness, still less of a single such consciousness which is constituted by a real inner

---

[34]Michael Schmaus, *Dogma 3: God and His Christ*, trans. Ann Laeuchli and William McKenna (New York: Sheed & Ward, 1972), p. 160.
[35]*Ibid.*, p. 159.
[36]*Ibid.*

personal relationship without the distinctness of bodily location and separate consciousness which we know on the human level. In other words, we have been led to an absolute mystery which must be forever beyond our comprehension. But then why try to talk about it at all? Why not frankly take refuge in mystical ineffability or Augustine's silence or be content with a functional Christology which makes no attempt to develop the doctrine of God any further?

The simple answer to this in Christian terms is that God has made Himself known to us through three modes of His single activity—creation, redemption, and sanctification. We know Him as the Creator and source of all that is, including, of course, ourselves. We know Him as the God and Father of our Lord Jesus Christ, and we know the Son as Jesus of Nazareth who lived His life and died His death in a unique and unbroken Father-Son relationship. We know God as present power and love, and in knowing Him thus, we know Him to be one with the risen Christ as well as our Creator. Because this is so, we want to say that God is eternally what He does, and does in all these three modes (personae). In other words, whatever perplexities we have when we seek to talk of the ultimate mystery of God, we know by faith that God cannot ever be less than the fullness of all that He has disclosed.

It is when we subject these insights of faith to careful philosophical analysis that we get into difficulties. It cannot be too strongly insisted, however, that the language we have used about the triune God is not a philosophical speculation in the usual sense. No philosopher outside the faith could possibly speak or want to speak in the way we have done. What we have been doing is to articulate the implications of Christian faith and experience and we should never pretend otherwise. This is why any doctrine of the Trinity stands or falls with what a man is led to believe about Jesus Christ.

The problem, then, becomes, What kind of language is the least misleading? Perhaps we should say that God is personal but not a person. Perhaps with Ian Ramsey we should substitute the language of activity for the dominant model and admit that "neither a personal nor a non-personal model will ever with complete adequacy replace the word 'God' in a sentence."[37] Yet, as Ramsey has himself admitted, the highest priority must be given to the personal model, whatever its limitations. Austin Farrer has less hesitation in saying that "It remains that if we talk theology at all, we are committed to 'personality' language."[38] This confidence does not spring

---

[37]Ramsey, *Christian Discourse*, p. 83.
[38]Farrer, "A Starting Point for the Philosophical Examination of Theological Belief," *Faith and Logic*, ed. Basil Mitchell (London: Allen and Unwin, 1957), p. 96.

from a rather vague philosophical claim that God bears some remote analogy to human personality. "But while we are immobilized by logical mist, God sends us His Logos."[39] And that means, in the context of Farrer's discussion, Jesus Christ and all that that means.

To return to J.A.T. Robinson in the light of this discussion, we ask again, Why not stay with a functional Christology and be content to say that Jesus functions "as God" for us? The answer again is not to be found in logic but in Christian faith, experience, and devotion. The latter wants the assurance that in the Son—i.e., the life, death, and resurrection of Jesus Christ—we know the eternal, loving, and redeeming God, not by proxy, but in real encounter. "He that hath seen me hath seen the Father."

This admission that we know God truly in the modes of His threefold activity and yet that He remains a "mystery" beyond our full comprehension, is, of course, nothing new in Christian theology. Ian Ramsey has gathered some selected passages of great interest.[40] We will content ourselves with three. The first is from Clement of Alexandria: "It is a difficult task to discover the Father and Maker of this universe; and when we have found Him, it is impossible to declare Him to all; since expression such as we use in other instruction is here impossible."[41] The other is from Hilary: "What presumption to suppose that words can adequately describe His nature, when thought is often too deep for words, and His nature transcends even the conception of thought."[42] The third is a less well known admission of Thomas Aquinas: "This is what is ultimate in the human knowledge of God; to know that we do not know God" (*Quaestiones Disputatae de Potentia Dei*, 7, 5 add. 14).[43] From the perspective of a man who looks at Christian faith from the outside, these statements appear to be sheer agnosticism. But obviously such statements were not made by the ancient equivalents of Bertrand Russell, A.J. Ayer, etc. As Ramsey rightly comments, the above language is not the expression of intellectual agnosticism but of religious awe and is more akin to reverential abstinence from the use of God's name, as in Judaism, than to any sympathy with a philosophical exaggeration of the divine transcendence.[44]

Thus Christian faith has never found a basic contradiction between the admission of God's incomprehensibility and the equally strong conviction that we know enough of Him through His threefold activity for our salvation.

---

[39]*Ibid.*, p. 98.
[40]Ramsey, *Words About God.*
[41]*Ibid.*, p. 15.
[42]*Ibid.*, p. 17.
[43]*Ibid.*, p. 1.
[44]*Ibid.*, p. 18.

Mystery and saving knowledge are not opposites but complementary aspects of the Christian experience of God. It is against this background that we must set the long and arduous intellectual endeavor of the early church to frame a doctrine of the Trinity. Any modern attempt to reexpress it must be placed in the same context of combined intellectual modesty and religious confidence.

Such an attempt to carry back the Father-Son relationship from the historical actuality of Jesus into the eternal existence of the Godhead has provoked, as we have seen, the strong reactions of John Knox and others. By doing this, so it is contended, the church has made it impossible to preserve a real humanity in the historical Jesus. Some continuity there must be, on this view, between the Eternal Son and Jesus of Nazareth. Yet unless we are going to argue for Jesus' own consciousness of preexistence, which seems impossible to do from the Synoptics, we can only appeal to certain reflections of the Fourth Gospel which few scholars today would defend as the actual words of Jesus of Nazareth. On the other hand, if Jesus was not conscious of being in some significant sense the Eternal Son, what is the point of the preexistence model at all? If He was conscious of this, how could He really be considered to have a normal human consciousness or a human mind or center of personal activity? These arguments add up for many to a conclusive reductio ad absurdum of any use of the preexistence model.

I think it has to be conceded that the Synoptic Jesus never claims such conscious awareness of His identity with the Eternal Son as this latter concept is developed in later Trinitarian doctrine. There is, however, in our view, no question of His awareness of a unique Father-Son relationship. The theological issue is whether the church was justified in developing from this implications for the nature of God which were not consciously in the mind of Jesus. The answer to this must be in the logic of Christian devotion. For some this is a contradiction of terms and at best wishful thinking. However, there is little doubt that Jesus believed Himself to be showing forth the will of the Eternal God, rooted in this special Father-Son relationship. The full implications of this could hardly be developed in the earthly ministry alone. The death and resurrection and the post-existence of Jesus the Christ were required before one could intelligibly ask about the source of this total Christ-event within the divine life itself. The main difficulty again, for Knox and others, is that if we say that the life, death, resurrection, and ascension of Jesus were the actualizing in history of a Father-Son relationship which is constitutive of the eternal nature of God, then this seems to involve a kind of divine determinism or predestinationism which would make a mockery of the growth of Jesus in wisdom and stature, indeed of the whole process of becoming in which Jesus exercises a real human initiative and freedom of choice. Does it not make the temptation and suffering unreal if Jesus is only unfolding in historical terms a character which He already is as the Eternal Son? His "goodness" is not the result of the blood, toil, tears, and sweat of real moral and spiritual struggle, but the inevitable and necessary expression of an already achieved goodness, namely the character of the Eternal Son as the perfect reflection of the character of the Father. Furthermore, this goodness preexists any of the actual moral struggles of the historical Jesus.

It is this consideration more than any other which often leads the ordinary believer, as distinct from the sophisticated theologian, to opt for a human Jesus engaged in real struggle in which He might possibly have been defeated rather than to hold to this drama of a preexistent divine Son becoming human. Better a Jesus who is a real fellow sufferer than a disguised deity who is not really one of us and does not know what it is to have to battle against real sin and weakness and never know beforehand whether victory will be obtained. Whether Jesus was aware of His divinity or not has become a subject of debate again in modern Roman Catholic theology. Galtier opts for a far-reaching autonomy of the human "I" and argues that the divine "I" remains outside the sphere of Jesus' human consciousness. Pascal Parente, on the other hand, maintains that the human consciousness of Jesus does have a direct experience of its hypostatic union with the Logos, and of the "I" of the Logos as its own "I."[45]

On any view of God, however, unitarian, binitarian, or trinitarian, the problem of divine sovereignty and human freedom is a real one. This can be solved only by postulating a voluntary self-limitation on the part of God whereby independent human centers of initiative are permitted, even to the point of open rebellion and disobedience. If there are built-in limitations to God, then this could be ruled out completely. It is hardly possible for a theist in the classical Christian sense to say that God could not possibly limit Himself in this way. This would be to deny the infinite and sovereign freedom of God. This, however, it will be urged, is only a small part of the difficulty. The real difficulty concerns the actual freedom to choose of Jesus of Nazareth. Could Jesus really have chosen not to do the will of the Father, and if this was a real possibility, then did not our salvation hang upon the slender thread of this man's human will at a crucial moment of history? Those who are familiar with the history of the patristic debates will realize at once that these are no new questions in Christian theology. Yet, to return to the present, can even Robinson's functional Christology really be content to rest everything upon the human will of Jesus, and if so, how is this related to

---

[45]Schmaus, *Dogma 3*, pp. 246–247.

his language about a unique divine initiative in Jesus, or that Jesus functions as, is indeed, God for us?

Is there then any intelligible sense in which we can speak of a real moral and spiritual struggle in Jesus and yet maintain that He could not sin? Some speak, indeed, as if Jesus could not be a true Savior of men unless He really shared and participated in every dimension of human experience. But are we really prepared to carry this to its logical conclusion? Must we say that Jesus must literally do and experience what all men do and experience if He is to be their deliverer? Must He sin in order to free us from sin? Must He literally be all things for all men—a murderer for the murderer, an adulterer for the adulterer, a homosexual for the homosexual, a robber for the thief, a victim of ambition to help those in the power struggle, a drug addict to help the deviants, etc., etc.? Must He be, literally, all these things in His own experience before He can diagnose our ills and cure us? It makes nonsense to argue that to be truly human Jesus must actually have tasted every facet of human experience, good, bad, and indifferent. Certainly, no one rooted, as Jesus was, in the Jewish conviction of the righteousness of God could possibly have argued in this way. As far as literal participation in certain kinds of experience, Jesus remains forever not one of us. If He were, He could never lift us out of ourselves. Modern man's difficulty at this point may not be primarily intellectual or even moral. It may spring from a pride which objects to the idea that a man could be good by nature and therefore different from us at this vital point of sin.

If, however, He did not literally share, perhaps He was able to understand, sympathize, and bear our bitter experiences. This is to say something very different. Temptation and testing is not the same for this view as actual consent to evil inclination and its subsequent expression in evil acts. A thought of evil is not necessarily an evil thought.

Our problem, however, concerns Jesus Himself. What prevented Jesus from yielding to evil, from saying with Satan in *Paradise Lost,* "Evil, be thou my good," and becoming the supreme embodiment of evil rather than of good, of disobedience rather than of loving and trustful obedience? It is hardly adequate to the depth of this problem to say simply, Well, He chose the one course rather than the other—fortunately for us! The problem is, Why this choice? It seems to be generally agreed that all other men in varying degrees have made an imperfect choice, to put it mildly. All have sinned and fallen short of the glory of God. Only this man apparently stands out by virtue of His solitary choice of consistent, trustful submission to the will of the Father.

The root of the difficulty seems to lie in inadequate conceptions of person, will, and freedom. The will is the whole person in activity, not an isolated faculty. The practical question, therefore, is how the will becomes the expressive activity of a perfectly integrated character, to use our modern psychological jargon. Freedom is not an abstract choice between good and evil. Freedom is to act in accordance with true character. Sometimes, even on the human level, we say, He could not possibly have done that. I know him too well and I am sure he was incapable of acting thus. We have all met some people who by virtue of their character are incapable of mean, malicious, and brutal behavior. Are we going to say they are not free because of this? Would their freedom be more "real" or more convincing if they chose to do things completely out of character? Generally, we would regard this as a lapse, not a higher manifestation of true freedom. The more a man is constrained by the good, so that he becomes progressively more unable to act in certain evil ways, the more truly is he free, at least according to the Christian understanding.

So be it, it may be objected, but even in the case of the so-called saints, such character has been achieved only through an arduous struggle in which at some points evil could have been chosen. Furthermore, no man is that completely good, and even men who appear incapable of evil may surprise and shock us by what they can do under the pressure of certain situations and circumstances. This is true; no man is free in the perfect sense, i.e., incapable of choosing evil because his character has been so thoroughly moulded by the good that he is now a perfectly good man, literally incapable of the evil choice. Even on the limited human level, however, some men and women are incapable of certain kinds of evil action, yet this "inability to sin" does not exempt them from feeling the full force of temptation and the agony of enduring the powerful solicitations of evil.

These considerations give us some clues in regard to Jesus. What can it mean to say that Jesus could not sin, whether we assert this on the grounds of the real continuity between the Eternal Son and Jesus of Nazareth, or simply want to assert His sinlessness on the grounds of the gospel witness and the conviction of the New Testament writers on this point? If Jesus' inability to sin is rooted in unbroken trust in the Father and the unity of their willing, it is not a mechanical or deterministic "inability" that we are talking about. It is because He has a "character" derived from the God on whom He is completely dependent. But how can a man grow into the character which He already has by virtue of His unity with the divine will, and can such a man in any meaningful sense be said to be free? Some would say, Impossible, like squaring the circle! How could Jesus know that He could not sin, and yet at the same time feel the reality of evil and its testing? How can a man know the agony of real moral and spiritual struggle and yet at the same time live in the confidence that the battle has been won because the Eternal Goodness rules in his own character? True, we are up against another ultimate mystery, but our difficulty is not intellectual but moral. None of us knows what it is to be good in this sense, just as H.R. Mackintosh says that we cannot understand the atonement because we have never loved as God has loved.

Put in the simplest terms, therefore, the question comes to this. Could Jesus have been aware of the Father-Son relationship, which He expressed in His total life, as rooted in the Eternal God, even though He did not in His earthly existence conceptualize this in terms of the model of preexistence? Could He experience the full impact of evil and know the agony of the moral and spiritual struggle against it while remaining confident that the integration of the divine and human wills in Him would prevent Him from a disobedience and a moral failure which would destroy the effectiveness of the divine purpose being actualized in His earthly existence?

It is obvious that such questions cannot be answered in the abstract. If the Christian is able to answer Yes to these questions, it is because of a variety of factors at work in his present Christian experience. These factors are the New Testament witness to God's activity in creation, redemption, and sanctification, his present faith in a God who acts now to deliver him from the bondage of sin, guilt, and fear into the glorious freedom of the children of God, his confidence that Jesus came from God and returned to God in a triumph which will have its full consummation at the end of the age, when the rule of God is established in the communion of just men made perfect. When faith in this full sense is present, despite our admission of mystery, the truths stumblingly expressed by the doctrine of the Trinity and the model of preexistence will not present insuperable difficulties. Starting with the functional Christ who acts as if He were God, he will be led irresistibly from the functional Christ to the Eternal Son. Jesus Christ, as the express image of the Father, will be seen as actualizing in the realities of historical existence and genuine manhood the mystery of a perfect Father-Son relationship, expressed through love in the Holy Spirit, which constitutes the eternal nature of God Himself. God for all eternity contains within the mystery of His own life all that we have learned from His activity in Jesus of Nazareth and in the transforming presence of the Spirit in our own lives.

Helmut Gollwitzer rightly observes that we must not shrink from talking of God in and for Himself for fear of getting lost in speculative propositions about a God who does not really concern us. ''Those who hold with Schleiermacher [in the *Dialektik*] that to think of God apart from and before the world, is an 'empty fantasy' will have to pay the price of no longer being able to understand creation and redemption as triumphant acts of His free condescension."[46] In short, Christian faith can never be content to live as if God were so, any more than it can be content with a Jesus Christ who functions *as if* He were divine. Faith depends upon the confidence that it truly knows the Eternal God in the earthly Jesus, not by proxy, not as a speculative hypothesis, but as the deepest reality personally experienced.

It is true that certain individuals may get along reasonably well with a functional Christ. It is doubtful whether the church could survive on this limited basis, if past history is anything by which to judge. Even a functional Christology tends to live by a confidence which transcends the strict implications of its own Christology, even when it refuses to rethink its doctrine of God in the manner to which Christian history bears witness. It is true that men are not saved by concepts, even that of preexistence, but by the present experience of the power and presence of the Eternal God. But a concept need not remain a mere concept. Preexistence and Eternal Son models have been and still remain powerful in Christian thought and devotion because they express the conviction that Jesus bodies forth what God has forever been, the Eternal Father of the Eternal Son, through whose threefold activities knowledge of Him has been disclosed to us men for our salvation. Mystery in the proper sense, of course, remains, but it is not sheer mystery for those who have seen the glory of God in the face of Jesus Christ.

We now turn from this use of a temporal category to the use of a spatial one, namely the image of descent and ascent, of coming down from the Father and returning again or going up to the Father. The temporal and spatial images are often closely connected in the language of the New Testament. This is easily understandable. Since the category of preexistence implies something about the nature of the transcendent God, who is "beyond" time and space, it follows that if the transcendent is to enter time and space and become man, then the language of "coming down" becomes natural and indeed inevitable. "The New Testament language about Incarnation is irretrievably 'katabatic'. That is to say, it speaks in terms of a descent into the world. This is, of course, mythological language."[47] There is no need to repeat the discussion that has taken place since Bishop J.A.T. Robinson challenged our traditional images. It is widely agreed that the spatial imagery of descent and ascent cannot be taken literally in a simple sense. God is not located so many billion miles above the earth, so that in principle He could be reached by a powerful rocket. For the same reason, the Eternal Son could not come down in the sense of traveling to this earth as

---

[46]Gollwitzer, *Existence of God*, p. 218.
[47]R.H. Fuller, *Foundations of New Testament Christology*, p. 255.

if from a distant star or planet, like Dr. Ransom in C. S. Lewis' space-fiction trilogy or the characters of Isaac Asimov's science fiction.

However, this is not by any means the end of the matter. What is at stake here is the whole concept of God as Christian theism conceives Him. Can we speak, as Austin Farrer did, of the "prior actuality of God"?[48] Can God be said to be real apart from His relationship to the world which He brought into being? Classical Christian theism answered Yes to this question. Some modern reinterpretations of this, such as Charles Hartshorne's panentheism, are ambiguous on this point.[49] Admitting, however, that the images of descent and ascent are not to be taken literally in the sense defined above, the problem still remains. What kind of language are we going to use to express the Christian conviction that the coming of Jesus Christ into the world was not simply the natural outcome of an evolutionary development guided by forces and powers solely immanent in the process?

We must be clear on what the question involves. Christian theism has no difficulty in talking of God active and in some sense immanent within the processes of nature and history. Christians are not deists, nor does the emphasis upon transcendence mean that God has no continuously creative and sustaining relationship to the world He has made. It does mean, however, that neither nature nor the whole spatio-temporal process is self-explanatory or self-sustaining. This means again that immanence implies transcendence, and this again is true for all men to some degree. Man's existence requires for its explanation the working of a creative power not exhaustively expressed in natural process alone. If this is true of all human beings, how much more must it be the case in regard to Jesus? The difference here, as we have already argued, is that we have in the case of Jesus a unique historical actuality in which divine presence and human obedience become fused in a once-for-all event which we call Jesus Christ.

Once again it is difficult to see what other language we can use than that of the temporal and spatial models, in this case the language of descent and ascent. That some Christians have interpreted this language in the most naive sense does not mean that we are forbidden its use altogether. Nor does it seem to help to call this language "mythical." There are passages in Bultmann which suggest that he considers all language of a metaphorical or symbolical kind to be mythical. This, however, is to stretch the meaning of myth to a point where it ceases to have any precise meaning. Since by the nature of the case all talk of God must involve metaphor, symbol, analogy, models, etc., then all language about God must be mythical.

---

[48]Farrer, "The Prior Actuality of God" in *Reflective Faith*, ed. Charles C. Conti.

[49]For a penetrating critique of this aspect of modern process philosophy when adapted to Christian purposes, see H.P. Owen, *Concepts of Deity*.

This, however, is bound to cause complete semantic confusion. Whatever the experts say, for most people myth is so closely linked with unexamined notions of the primitive in the sense of superstition, with legend, with obsolete science, etc. that to apply the word to all symbolic and analogical language is only to make confusion more confounded. The language of descent and ascent is not mythical in the technical sense. "If the truth of the case requires something like personal categories to express it, no light is shed on the issue by calling personal language mythical."[50] For the Christian at least, it is the inevitable symbolic form in which the conviction is expressed that Jesus' coming into the world and His departure from it was the result of a prior initiative of the transcendent God, and a divine activity in and through the human.

The language of ascent raises a rather different set of problems from that of descent. One might understand why we use the language of "coming down," but what religious interest do we have in the language of "going up"? First, the Christian faith wishes to assert that the unique actuality Jesus Christ, the union of divine presence and obedient human creature, did not cease to be at the moment of death. Jesus Christ is alive now after death in the fullness of His divine-human reality. It is not simply a case of the Logos or the Eternal Son reverting to the creative functions He performed before this unique relationship was established with Jesus of Nazareth. This new relationship which the Logos/Son has assumed is permanent. From henceforth the Son is forever the Son who became man in the Person of Jesus. The human reality of Jesus is now also an eternal aspect of the being of the Logos/Son.

This again is true in both the general and the specific sense. If human persons in any sense survive death, then God no longer exists only in Himself as Father, Son, and Spirit, but together with those persons whom He created and redeemed in Christ. If one may use what some would call grossly anthropomorphic language, God now has a family which He did not have before. There is a vast difference between God thinking about having a family and actually having a family which is now the object of His everlasting love and concern. For Christians, however, their confidence as to this possibility rests upon the conviction that in the special and unique case of Jesus this bond between God and man has been manifested in a way which neither life nor death can break. Nothing can now break the bond which unites man to God except the final refusal to accept the covenant which He made with man in the Person of Jesus. It is, therefore, implicit in the logic of faith that somehow Jesus Christ, the God-man, lives forever as the mediator

[50]Farrer, *Faith and Speculation,* p. 39.

of the Father's love and grace to man and thereby guarantees our eternal destiny as reconciled men, not merely as vague beings or spirits unrecognizable as man. We live forever as redeemed persons because He lives forever as the one who was man, and who remains man, without ceasing to be the perfect manifestation of God in our manhood. Once again it is difficult to avoid the spatial language of ascent. Certainly one can express the same idea by somewhat cumbrous and roundabout language, as we have just tried to do. Perhaps it is better to have the courage of our faith and continue to use the language of descent and ascent and hope that an informed Christian education will be able to liberate us from a literal interpretation of the language which would inevitably raise intolerable difficulties. The language is still saying something significant for Christian faith, and if we do not use it, we must find some other way of uttering the same truth, not a different truth.

10.
Kenosis or Divine Self-Limitation

Another image which has played a notable role in Christian theology is that of kenosis or self-emptying. The idea, as is well known, is taken from the passage in Philippians 2:5–11. There is no reason to believe that Paul in this passage is trying to develop a theology which would want to answer all the questions we would ask today. Any discussion of the idea of kenosis must begin by defining our attitude toward the critical questions involved in the exegesis of the passage.

The first thing to be said is that the historical source of an idea does not settle the truth or the validity which it possesses. Because a concept or an image (Ramsey's model) has its roots in Gnosticism, it does not follow that it is thereby condemned out of hand. This would seem to be self-evident, but it is not so. Often we read church history under the influence of strong presuppositions. Because the church fought Gnosticism so bitterly in the early centuries, we can easily assume that every idea associated with it must be proscribed. The same issue arises in connection with the influence of Jewish apocalyptic upon the New Testament documents. The historical source of ideas, however, still leaves unresolved the question of both truth and usefulness. Christians have often used images, models, concepts, and language generally which do not derive directly from what we would consider to be the mainstream of Jewish and Christian life and thought. Yet even here the problem is very complex. Judaism was never able to insulate itself completely against alien cultural influences, though it fought hard to defend its Jewish integrity and distinctiveness. In like manner, Christianity has at all periods of history been involved in constant interaction with its cultural environment. Thus in discussing the truth and adequacy of theological concepts, several factors have to be kept in mind. What is the abiding significance and meaning of Jesus of Nazareth for Christian faith and experience? What implications follow for our doctrine of God? What images and concepts express most adequately in human language what Christians want to say on both these subjects?

These considerations are of great importance in regard to the language of kenosis. The problems connected with the Pauline authorship of the Philippian passage are not theologically decisive. If with many New Testament scholars we accept the view that Philippians 2:6–11 is a Christological hymn taken over and adapted by Paul, we may still ask whether it expresses an important Christian truth in a reasonably adequate way. If such ideas of incarnation and preexistence were quite foreign to the Christology of the earliest strata of the New Testament tradition,[1] this does not mean that the ideas are necessarily invalid as attempts to express the church's developing understanding of the full implications of its faith. These matters have to be considered on their merits. If, for example, it is possible to reconstruct an Aramaic Christology completely uninfluenced as far as ideas and language are concerned by Hellenistic patterns of thought, it cannot thereby be assumed that this Christology is normative or contains the only model for Christian thinking. The unexamined assumption here is that the historically earliest attempts to express the significance of a personality are necessarily most adequate. This is by no means self-evident. Nor does it follow that a man is understood better by his contemporaries than by those who come after him. This might sometimes be true, but there is no inevitability about it. In any event, it is rarely, if ever, the case that contemporaries see the whole truth about the remarkable men and women in their midst. With Jesus Christ this is even more likely to be the case. Since He came to inaugurate a new humanity, it is not probable that the full measure of grace and truth in Him can be understood apart from the community of which He is the founder and the redeemer.

We shall begin our discussion of kenosis with a series of statements to which many, if not all, New Testament scholars would subscribe.[2] In leaning heavily on the account of R.H. Fuller, we are not implying that all his judgments can be accepted without question or even that the majority of scholars would always back him up on particular points. It will be useful, however, to see what kind of Christology could be constructed on the basis of a fairly radical handling of the biblical material. The following statements seem to emerge from Fuller's treatment:

(a) Philippians 2:1–11 is non-Pauline in origin and belongs to the common stock of the Gentile mission. Its *Sitz im Leben* must be sought in Hellenistic Jewish Christianity.

(b) The question of its Aramaic origin is unresolved, and it is not possible confidently to assert that Paul used it and interpreted it in terms of

---

[1]Fuller, *Foundations of New Testament Christology,* p. 205.
[2]*Ibid.,* pp. 204ff.

the preexistent apocalyptic Son of Man who became incarnate as the ebed Yahweh, the servant of the Lord. The idea of incarnation is, of course, a Christian fusion of these ideas and not itself a part of apocalyptic.

(c) The basic presupposition of the hymn is the Hellenistic worldview, with its three-storied universe—heaven, earth, and underworld. This lower world is in bondage to the "powers" and needs redemption.

(d) The Redeemer, who descends to the lower world to accomplish this, passes through five stages of existence: (1) preexistence, (2) becoming incarnate, (3) incarnate life, (4) ascension, (5) exalted state.

(e) The preexistence of the Redeemer (*en morphe theou*—in the form of God) is to be interpreted not on the basis of image (*demuth*) and likeness (*selem*) in Genesis 1:26 but in the light of the parallel phrase in the context—to be equal with God. The term *morphe* means a mode of existence.

(f) The preexistent Redeemer dwelt in an existence equal to that of God before becoming man as Jesus of Nazareth. This is more than the claim made for the wisdom of God (*sophia*) in Hellenistic Judaism, for the preexistent Redeemer is not merely a hypostatization of the being of God but an actual divine being.

(g) *Morphe* cannot mean "something to be snatched at" but is closer to meaning "something to be held on to."

(h) The process of becoming incarnate is here a voluntary act of the preexistent Redeemer who surrenders the *morphe theou,* i.e., equality with God as a mode of existence, in order to become poor, i.e., to be born as a man and submit to the death of the Cross. He takes on the *morphe doulou,* the slave's mode of existence. The word *doulos* is probably not the ebed Yahweh but signifies his coming into bondage to the evil powers which hold this present world in thrall, particularly the power of death.

(i) By using the word "likeness" the way is kept open for asserting the distinctiveness of this particular man, Jesus, from all other men.

(j) More is affirmed than the revelatory presence of the Heavenly Wisdom to man. That the preexistent Redeemer actually becomes incarnate is without precedent. "Accordingly, it [i.e., Philippians 2:1–11] must be pronounced a Christian adaptation of the myth to the concrete history of Jesus."[3]

Now here we have a myth, i.e., the story of a divine being, adapted by Paul to explain the significance and meaning of what had been accomplished through the life and death of Jesus of Nazareth in enabling man to escape from the bondage to evil, and particularly death. The ambiguity of the word

---

[3]*Ibid.,* p. 210.

"myth" has been noted earlier. Here again we have what Ian Ramsey calls a "model," an image which suggests its meaning through the use of temporal and spatial categories. The question we are concerned with here is whether this is an illuminating way of expressing the significance of Jesus Christ. Does this myth imply divinity and in what sense? Did Paul intend it to suggest a declaration of divinity? Has the myth been "broken," to adopt the language of Mircea Eliade? That is, has it been interpreted already in symbolic rather than literal terms? But does "symbolic" mean that it is only a useful story and no more? Or is a kind of truth being conveyed through the myth, and if so, what kind of truth? Furthermore, is the use of this myth an indispensable way of expressing Christian convictions about the divinity of Jesus or is it only a cultural and historical accident that it came to be bodied forth in this particular kind of tale? These questions will demand an answer before we are through with our study. Similar problems have arisen in regard to the use of preexistence and the language of descent and ascent. Philippians 2:1–11 is another variation on the same theme.

Before we try to answer these questions, however, we shall outline the characteristic features of what has come to be called kenotic Christology. This appeared in the middle of the nineteenth century in response to special difficulties caused by the application of the principles of scientific historical criticism to the origins of the Christian faith, and more specifically to the New Testament documents. This raised issues in regard to both the nature of historical truth and the continuing validity for Christians of the classical doctrinal formulations about the humanity and divinity of Jesus Christ. The development of kenotic Christology produced a notable line of Christian scholars and thinkers which includes, among others, Thomasius, Charles Gore, A.B. Bruce, H.R. Mackintosh, Oliver Quick, and more recently Vincent Taylor. Many others who would not have called themselves kenoticists in this sense nevertheless accepted the real limitations of knowledge and power in the historic Jesus and were very cautious about the literal acceptance of this model of a preexistent divine Redeemer who became man.

It is worth pointing out that the validity of this kenosis Christology does not depend upon any specific exegesis of the Philippian passage, even though the basic idea was suggested to these men by it. Even if Paul had never adopted the "hymn" and put it to Christian use, these scholars could quite consistently maintain that some doctrine of kenosis would have to be advanced in order to reconcile the historical facts with the Christian claim of divinity for Jesus of Nazareth. It is not a sufficient refutation of kenotic Christology, therefore, to argue that all this was not in the mind of Paul, or even that it is not plainly implied by the Philippian passage. Its plausibility will depend upon the degree to which the employment of such a model can be shown to be either necessary or helpful or both in spelling out what Jesus means to men of faith.

Oliver Quick roundly declared some years ago now that the central principle of the kenotic Christology, namely that "the Eternal Son or Word in his incarnation by a voluntary act limited himself to a historical human consciousness and human faculties of knowledge and action, has, I believe, proved itself to be the most important fresh contribution to Christology which has been made since the time of Irenaeus."[4] A bold claim indeed! The first point to be observed concerns the "picture" of Jesus of Nazareth which emerged as the result of the modern critical approach to the New Testament. It hardly seemed open to doubt to these early pioneers of criticism that whatever Jesus was, He was not immune from limitation and weakness. He grew in wisdom and stature with all that that implies. He was not omnipotent in the absolute sense since He could do no mighty works there because of their unbelief. He was not omniscient in the sense in which this might be attributed to the infinite and transcendent Creator. He confessed His own ignorance of the date of the final consummation at the end of the world. More serious perhaps, He may have held views about the authorship of some Old Testament writings which modern scholarship has been inclined to think mistaken. He may even have employed the language and images of a Jewish apocalyptic whose worldview can no longer claim authority over the minds of men. It was assumed without question that His human body was real in the fullest sense—subject to hunger, thirst, weakness, and finally death. However remarkable Jesus was, He was a Jew of the first century.

Now if only half of this was true, serious issues clearly arose for the Christian faith as expressed in the ancient creeds. Several responses to this situation were possible. The whole intention and result of modern historical scholarship could be impugned. So much the worse for scholarship if it leads to such blasphemous conclusions. Another response was the sceptical one, to say, So much the worse for the historic Christian faith. It has made claims for Jesus which can no longer be substantiated. This is the end of the Christian faith as we have known it. Some in the nineteenth century took this option—David Strauss, Karl Marx (under the influence of the very radical biblical criticism of the Tübingen school), Nietzsche (though many other factors were operative in his case), writers such as George Eliot in England, to name only a few. A third option was the one taken by the kenotic theologians, and it is upon them that we shall concentrate here. They were Christians who wanted to retain the basic Christian affirmations about the divinity of Jesus while at the same time preserving their intellectual

---

[4]Quick, *Doctrines of the Creed,* pp. 132ff.

integrity in the matter of biblical scholarship. Their development of the kenosis idea seemed to them a viable way of doing this. We have already touched upon several of these issues in our discussion of some of the problems connected with the doctrine of the Trinity. At the risk of some repetition, the same questions must be raised again but this time in the specific context of the kenosis Christology.

If Christ was a divine, preexistent being before becoming man in Jesus of Nazareth, what does this do to our doctrine of God? Does it destroy the Christian claim to be worshipping one God? We have already contended for a richer concept of divine unity than that involved in the notion of an undifferentiated One. Somehow the Father-Son relationship must be a reflection of a reality in the Godhead. This would seem to commit us at least to two divine beings in the Godhead which are yet mysteriously one personal Being. This, however, appears to run counter to the results of recent study and analysis of the patristic language and in particular that of the Trinity. The more it is insisted that *persona* and *hypostasis* do not mean personality in the modern sense, the more difficult it is to talk of two (or three!) separate persons in the modern sense as constitutive of the being of God. Father, Son, and Spirit are modes of the real activity of the one living and personal God in creation, redemption, and sanctification. They are not three separate personalities or divine beings conceived after the analogy of the human personality. Can there, therefore, be more than one preexistent divine being, namely God, even if He can be properly known only through the threefold activity we have just described? This raises difficult questions for the interpretation of the Philippian passage, as well as for some forms of the kenotic Christology.

It is well known that Thomasius in the nineteenth century made the distinction between on the one hand the divine attributes of omnipotence, omniscience, and omnipresence (which he rather misleadingly called the physical attributes) and on the other hand the moral qualities of holiness, righteousness, love, etc. which give moral and spiritual content and meaning to the rather abstract concept of absolute and unqualified knowledge and power. When God became man in Jesus of Nazareth, He surrendered in that activity what would now be called the metaphysical attributes and chose to express His purpose in terms of the moral attributes within the limits of a genuine human existence. Thus Jesus was divine only in the sense that He embodied and expressed in action the holy love which constitutes the essential nature of the Godhead. It is important to note that for the kenosis theologian, this is not equivalent to saying that Jesus was only a good man. He is, to use Pittenger's more recent language, the self-expression of God in His nature as holy and redeeming love. But as the historical Jesus He is not omnipotent, omniscient, and omnipresent. It is worth remembering that most modern theologians would agree, though some radical conservatives would call this into question too. Notable critics of kenotic Christology such as William Temple, Donald Baillie, Eugene Fairweather, and F.W. Beare, to mention only a few, would agree that the historical Jesus was not omnipotent, etc. in any absolute sense. They have drunk too deeply of the wells of modern biblical scholarship to adopt this stance. The issue between the kenoticists and their opponents is not, therefore, concerned with the problem of "limitations" in the historical Jesus. Both accept this fact. The critics of the kenotic Christology concentrate rather upon what they consider to be the "mythical" form in which the kenotic idea is expressed. Their contentions are roughly as follows:

(a) If the distinctions in the Godhead (*personae, hypostases*) are pressed to the point where God is really divided into three separate beings on the analogy of personality in the modern sense, then to say that the second person of the Trinity became man would be equivalent to leaving two-thirds of the Godhead out of the Incarnation.

(b) On the other hand, the more we emphasize the unity of God and vigorously repudiate, as Barth does, the idea of God as three separate personalities, then we have the problem of explaining how God can become man while still exercising His creative functions as the maker and sustainer of the universe. We cannot identify God so completely with the incarnate life as to imply that God emptied Himself wholly into the man Jesus of Nazareth. Or perhaps one should say that one could, as Altizer does in *The Gospel of Christian Atheism*. In this case, however, we have become Christian atheists. God has ceased to be except within the limits of the human existence of Jesus. We would then have to speak of God literally dying in the death of Jesus. This has certainly not been the faith of any major branch of the Christian church, not to mention the further difficulty that it is impossible to make sense of a concept of the Creator-God in the biblical sense who voluntarily chooses to liquidate Himself. William Temple made a similar criticism of some earlier forms of kenotic Christology. If the Eternal Son, the second persona of the Trinity, is identified with the creative and cosmic functions of the Logos or Word, and then it is asserted that the Word emptied Himself of His metaphysical attributes in becoming man, this would be equivalent to saying that while the baby Jesus was in the manger, the universe was for the time being divorced from any effective divine control and conservation.[5] Similar criticisms, and others, have been repeated by

---

[5]Temple, *Christus Veritas* (London: Macmillan, 1939), p. 140.

Baillie, Grensted, Fairweather, and others.[6] Baillie contends that this gives us only a temporary theophany. Jesus was God, then man, then God again after the Resurrection, but at no time truly the God-Man. Grensted comments that the kenotic theory safeguards the humanity but gives us no security in regard to God becoming man.

It has to be admitted that if this really was the inevitable consequence of a kenotic Christology, then indeed it would have to be rejected as untrue both to Scripture and to Christian experience as well as involving an essentially incoherent notion of God. Can a doctrine of kenosis be formulated which is not open to these objections? Let us first of all state a number of convictions which almost all Christians have felt compelled to make. God as Infinite Spirit is the creator and sustainer of the universe. On Him all things depend for their existence and continuance in existence. This implies that God must not be limited in power and knowledge in the way any finite creature is. If God in this sense "is," then at no time could He cease to "be" without the universe itself collapsing into disorder and chaos, nor could He ever cease to perform this creative and sustaining function. In this sense, there can be no kenosis of God, which would be equivalent to the death of God. An atheism which denies that there ever was such a God would be a more consistent position.

Granted the validity of this first point, how could God become man while continuing to be the creative source and sustainer of all things? Could He not add to His creative and cosmic functions the fact that He became man? If becoming truly man means that Jesus of Nazareth was in fact limited in power, etc. (and this both sides to the dispute seem to admit), then the question becomes, How could God infinite in power, knowledge, and wisdom become a man who was limited in power and knowledge and whose wisdom was the result of a real process of growth and development? Since we cannot solve the problem by making God cease to be God, then how can these facts be conceived as truly integrated in the Person of Jesus of Nazareth, the Christ?

As we have already seen in earlier chapters, this raises the question of the biblical doctrine of creation. How could God bring into existence a created order having a relative independence and autonomy over against Him? Assuming this possibility, how can God be related to or be present to a created being without destroying the creature as such? It is well to note that this problem arises not only in regard to the Incarnation but in relation to all

---

[6]Baillie, *God was in Christ;* Laurence W. Grensted, *The Person of Christ* (London: Nisbet, 1933); and Eugene R. Fairweather, "The 'Kenotic' Christology," appended note to F.W. Beare's *Commentary on Philippians* (New York: Harper, 1959).

talk about God's presence. How can God indwell any human being without annihilating the freedom and responsibility of the creature at the level of both thought and action? H. Wheeler Robinson wrote perceptively on this theme some years ago:

> We can see also that the indwelling of the divine Spirit in humanity, whether by the Incarnation of our Lord Jesus Christ or by the continuance of His presence through the Holy Spirit in the hearts of believers, must always involve a kenosis, a humiliation and an acceptance of the lower as the medium of the higher, though this principle of limitation need not imply the duality of mind and matter.[7]

In the case of the Incarnation, therefore, the issue at stake is how God accepts the lower as the medium of the higher.

We have already seen that John Knox is troubled by the problem of the identity between the Eternal Son and the man Jesus. He seems to feel that such identity cannot be maintained without destroying the authentic humanity of Jesus. Professor Vincent Taylor, however, has rallied to the defence of a form of kenotic Christology, asserting that such is essential to any "worthy doctrine of the Incarnation."[8] He insists on the need to admit limitations in power and knowledge in Jesus. This is based, not on any speculative theory, but according to Taylor on a plain reading of the New Testament evidence itself. On the other hand, he contends, "If His Ego were only human, He would be a man, a prophet and a teacher but not the Son of God."[9] Thus, "all the relevant facts compel us to affirm that the subject of the human life of Christ is the Logos, the Eternal Son, but in the form and under the conditions of human existence."[10] Taylor then has recourse to the concept of "latency" to explain how this could be. Jesus may not have been conscious of the attributes of omnipotence etc. which belonged to Him as the Eternal Son. Yet these attributes may well have remained latent or potential, really existent, but no longer consciously exercised by the Son. This leaves open the possibility that they might be exercised in appropriate circumstances (intermittently, as H.R. Mackintosh suggests). To the criticism that this is frankly inconceivable, Taylor replies that such criticism is tantamount to saying that the Incarnation in any form is impossible. Yet if the Christian conception of God and His relation to the created order is well founded, who are we to say that such a form of kenosis is impossible? We do not need to assume, says Taylor, that the divine consciousness of Jesus was always at

---

[7]H.W. Robinson, *The Christian Experience of the Holy Spirit*, p. 83.

[8]Vincent Taylor, *The Person of Christ in New Testament Teaching* (London: Macmillan, 1958), p. 270.

[9]*Ibid.*, p. 289.

[10]*Ibid.*

the same pitch of intensity. "In Jesus, the flash is followed by a permanent glow."[11]

Oliver Quick offers somewhat similar views. To Temple's criticism that the self-emptying of the Word leaves the world without divine control, Quick argues that the supporters of the kenotic view do not have to affirm that the creative Word had "no being except in the infant Jesus."[12] What the theory demands is a "limitation of consciousness" rather than of actual being. On any view of the Incarnation which is faithful to the New Testament, such a limitation must be affirmed. Nor, says Quick, can the implication of this be denied by appealing to the doctrine of the Trinity. Since the latter doctrine was formulated in the first place to express the Christian conviction that Jesus Christ must be both distinguished from and identified with God, "the truth and significance of the Trinity must be tested by an apprehension of the truth and significance of the Incarnation and not vice-versa."[13] In our discussion of preexistence, we have already pleaded for courage in following the logic of faith and carrying back into the heart of the Godhead the eternal reality of the Father-Son relationship. This certainly leaves us with a tension between a concept of God thought of as "bare unity" and a social analogy for God which seems always to be hovering on the brink of tritheism. Here we seem to have no option but to use both models, believing that they both point to the nature of God, even though we cannot see precisely how unity and diversity are reconciled in the fullness of the divine being.

Assuming for the moment that the Father-Son relationship points to an eternal reality in the Godhead, what significance would this have for a doctrine of kenosis? If the Eternal Son, like the Eternal Father, is free from the temporal and spatial limitations of human personality as known by us in this present world, then it would seem as if the same difficulties would arise in regard to the divine Son becoming man as when we say that God the Father becomes man. In both cases, the eternal becomes finite and limited in a way which seems to baffle our understanding. This is true. Christian faith must acknowledge that at this point of supreme mystery the human intellect has to admit that it sees "through a glass, darkly." No theological formula will ever be invented which enables the mystery of the Incarnation to become completely transparent to human understanding. While it is bad theology to invoke mystery as an excuse for intellectual laziness, it is equally foolish and arrogant to refuse to recognize genuine mystery when we meet it. This is as true for the scientist and the secular philosopher as it is for the Christian

---

[11]*Ibid.*, p. 302.
[12]Quick, *Doctrines of the Creed*, p. 136.
[13]*Ibid.*, p. 139.

thinker. If the Christian dares to use the language of self-limitation about God, this is not the result of a speculative hypothesis but because faith knows that it has truly encountered God in this Jesus in the unique manner we have been discussing throughout this book. If we carry the fullness of this divine revelation, including the Father-Son relationship, back into the nature of the Eternal Godhead, it is again not because of a purely philosophical urge but because we have known the Father-Son relationship in Jesus with a power to save and renew found nowhere else. God in His very being cannot be less than we have found Him to be in that life, death, and resurrection. God is neither a mathematical unit nor a society of human personalities in the strictly literal sense. Nevertheless, the models are not simply imaginative inventions of misguided human minds. They point, inadequately enough, to the structure of the reality made known. Jesus is man, yet the living and saving God present for our redemption. For this to be so, some divine self-limitation must be fact, even though we cannot understand the mechanics of the divine operation. But we cannot remain utterly silent if we are to praise and adore. Since we must speak, the language of preexistence, descent and ascent, and indeed of kenosis in this sense of divine self-limitation, will always seem meaningful to Christians, however puzzling to outsiders. Perhaps in the ongoing life and experience of the Christian community, new models will emerge which will have the same power to express the profoundest Christian convictions and evoke the same sense of wonder, awe, and gratitude.

The conclusions which seem to follow from our discussion are as follows. Whether we use the word *kenosis* or not—and in view of the many theories which the term covers, it may be wise not to do so—the fact remains that Jesus of Nazareth does not exercise all the functions of deity, nor was He in His historical actuality in the full possession and exercise of what we have called the metaphysical attributes. This view does not spring from any modernizing attempt to play down the significance of Jesus or to deny the Christian claim. It is a fair deduction from the testimony of Scripture itself.

Again, if Jesus is truly man, since by God's intention He too is a finite creature, then if God is to become man, God must adapt Himself to the limitations of the finite creature, limitations which are of God's ordaining as far as the finite creature is concerned. Any doctrine of the Incarnation must take full account of these facts. This means that Christian theology must work with the concept of divine self-limitation.

This implies that when we speak of the divine fullness in a human being, this cannot mean that the finite becomes infinite. This would be a contradiction in terms. It can only mean that the finite, while remaining finite, becomes the vehicle of the divine presence and activity as far as finite reality can embody this.

> The point to be emphasized here is that, on the purely historical plane, no distinction could be drawn in the result, between human personality perfectly achieving the potentialities of its kinship with the divine, in a given environment, and divine personality manifesting itself in the same environment.[14]

It is again important to be clear about what H.W. Robinson is here saying and is not saying. He is not saying that this interpretation is reducing Jesus to perfect man where perfect man is an achievement in the strength of resources present universally in human nature as we know it. Nor is he denying the classical description of "truly God." This would imply that Jesus realized in His relationship to God that fullness of moral and spiritual perfection by virtue of human strength alone and human resources alone. This indeed would be a denial of the doctrine of the Incarnation. It would be to evade the problem of how the finite historical figure did in fact become the vehicle of the divine presence and the divine saving love in the manner it did. It is, therefore, of the greatest theological importance whether the fact of Jesus is interpreted as the work of man only or the result of the divine initiative.

The classical models we have considered thus far—preexistence, descent and ascent, kenosis—are all intended, however imperfectly, to stress the fact that the divine initiative and intention are present both in eternity and in time as the necessary presuppositions of Jesus being the sort of finite creature He was, namely one in and through whom God was reconciling the world unto Himself. It is not enough to leave the uniqueness of Jesus as if it were a perfectly reasonable and normal thing to happen, indeed as something which might have happened by a lucky historical accident. This is to throw up our hands in despair and leave Jesus as a bare, unexplained fact. Of course, it is possible to do this. Christian faith, however, as long as it remains Christian, must seek to articulate in language the meaning of the fact of Jesus and seek to explain why Christian faith has found it necessary to talk of God becoming man and not simply of a remarkable man finding God.

---

[14]H.W. Robinson, *Revelation and Redemption*, p. 212.

11.
Miracle as Confirmation of Spiritual Fact

Our argument to this point now compels us to consider the relation of miracle to the unique historical fact which is Jesus. Many would feel that our thesis so far, whatever our disclaimers, is in fact a humanistic reduction of the Incarnation and the surrender of the supernatural. The fact that God's holy love fully indwelt the man Jesus, as far as the finite limitations of human personality permit, does not, it is asserted, make Him God. It is worth observing that holy love is not a detachable set of divine attributes operating in the abstract. It is the holy love of God acting within and through the finite, acting not by proxy, but in reality. This could be denied in principle only if we said that under no circumstances could God work and act through His creatures but must always be at a distance. This, however, would be to attack the whole biblical concept of God and not merely the doctrine of Incarnation. It would effectively eliminate the very notion of divine presence in and to the human. If such a radical stance is taken, then it must be admitted that there is no basis for any doctrine of Incarnation, including the one we have advanced.

This, however, is not the usual criticism advanced against our position as so far described. It usually takes the form of arguing that the direct presence of holy love in Jesus requires further buttressing by unusual facts in the natural order. The Virgin Birth, the healing and nature miracles, the "bodily" resurrection, are invoked as necessary confirmation of the claims made by Jesus as the unique bearer of the Kingdom and as Himself the direct manifestation in action of the holy love of God. Without such signs, regarded as confirmatory evidence, it would be impossible to go the further step and speak about Jesus as Christians have done. We shall therefore attempt to deal with this issue confessing at once that the extreme liberal and conservative positions often harden into assertions which defend one truth while denying another. Our position is that it would be tragic if men are to be confronted with a simple either-or.

It is not necessary at this stage to decide the vexed question of what is fact and what is symbol in the miracles mentioned above, nor to offer a precise definition of "miracle" which would satisfy the theologian, the philosopher, the scientist, and the man in the street. The issue we wish to tackle now concerns the question whether the miracles, if factual in any sense, would add to what has already been said about the uniqueness of Jesus. What light do they throw upon the mystery of the Incarnation that has not already been seen in our treatment of the special Father-Son relationship which is at the heart of the Christian affirmation of His divinity? Even at this point, however, it needs to be said that if the miracles are only interpretations of the life and ministry of Jesus expressed in symbolic form, then naturally they do not add anything theologically vital. For example, if Jesus was not born of a virgin in a manner which involves clear biological implications, then one cannot appeal to this fact as further evidence for the view as to what or who Jesus was. One has already decided His uniqueness on other grounds, namely the facts of His life and ministry. The Virgin Birth then becomes an appropriate way of symbolizing this, though why one should choose this particular symbol is by no means clear. In any case, it would be unreasonable on this basis to make the use of this symbol a necessary element in any affirmation of the fact that God had become man. It becomes a matter of personal preference whether a particular individual finds this symbol useful and illuminating. In the same way, if, as Bultmann contends, the "resurrection is really the same thing as faith in the saving efficacy of the Cross,"[1] then the Resurrection as a distinguishable factor cannot add anything to what faith has already discerned in the Cross. It is true that Bultmann says that Christ meets us in the preaching as one crucified and risen and that the "word of preaching confronts us as the Word of God. It is not for us to question its credentials."[2] This latter is a rather surprising statement coming from Bultmann since according to him we are justified in questioning the credentials of the Easter message if it includes the empty tomb and some version of bodily resurrection. It is difficult on this basis to resist the conclusion of Marxsen that though it was quite natural for the early disciples to interpret the Cross in terms of the Resurrection, we cannot affirm that this interpretation is necessarily binding upon us.[3]

Let us take the case of the Virgin Birth again. Assuming that Jesus was born without a human father, would that fact in itself guarantee the reality of

[1]Bultmann, *Kerygma and Myth*, ed. Hans Werner Bartsch (New York: Harper, 1961), p. 41.
[2]*Ibid.*
[3]C.F.D. Moule, ed., *The Significance of the Message of the Resurrection for Faith in Jesus Christ*, Studies in Biblical Theology, 2nd Series (London: S.C.M., 1968), pp. 48ff.

the Incarnation in the Christian sense? Would denying the Virgin Birth necessarily be to deny that God had become man in the sense previously discussed and affirmed? It is hardly necessary to add that nowhere in the birth narratives of Matthew and Luke is it suggested that Jesus had to be born without a human father in order for Him to be sinless. Whatever the later doctrinal developments, with their associated ideas of sin as biologically transmissible and the logical implication of this for the "immaculate" conception of the Virgin, it is clear that Scripture itself does not spell out the theological significance of the Virgin Birth in this sense. One would first of all have to make out a case that Scripture clearly and unambiguously develops a doctrine of sin as a physical or quasi-physical reality or something which could be biologically transmitted, and this would be by no means easy to do. If, however, we detach the Virgin Birth from such complex theories as to the origin and transmission of sin, would it then follow that, if a fact, the Virgin Birth would cease to have any decisive theological significance for Christians? Would it not be possible still to affirm that God became man in Jesus of Nazareth and that in this Jesus, God has drawn near to man with saving efficacy, reconciling them to Himself? The answer to this is surely Yes, for we discover the power of God in this sense in Jesus through our knowledge of the total life and ministry, and not through the fact of virginal conception at the beginning of His earthly career. If, for example, we knew that Jesus was born of a virgin but had no further knowledge of the sort of person He was and what He thought and did, then it would not make sense to talk of Incarnation. The concept would be there in a generalized sense, but it would be a concept with no definable content. It cannot, therefore, be stated as a necessary theological proposition that God could not have become man for us and our salvation unless Jesus had been born of a virgin. Who are we to say that God could have acted redemptively only in this way? This, however, does not answer whether God did in fact act in this way through a Virgin Birth. This issue still has to be faced in the light of the evidence.

One can, of course, ask many speculative questions. Did God need to become man at all in order to save man? Could He not have done it in some other way? There is no way to answer this question in the abstract. One can only say that this is how in fact God chose to manifest His saving activity. It could be argued at length in the abstract that it was highly appropriate that any divine effort on man's behalf should involve some close identification of God with man such as the doctrine of the Incarnation affirms, and this would be true. In the last resort, however, there is no way of answering categorically the theoretical question whether God could have done it in some other way. In actual fact, He has chosen to do it in this way. So in relation to the Virgin Birth, one cannot enunciate a necessary theological proposition to the effect that Jesus could not be the Lord and Savior of men, as the Word made flesh, unless He had been born of a virgin. On the other hand, there is no inconsistency in arguing that God has in fact acted in a special way of His choosing and that this includes the Virgin Birth. If this were so—and we go on to ask what theological significance this fact could have—the answer would have to be along the lines suggested by Karl Barth if we are not to tie up the significance of the birth with the problem of sinlessness, as we have argued it is unwise to do. Indeed, Barth himself, while affirming the factuality of the Virgin Birth as a divinely given sign pointing to this new creative act in His becoming man, also agrees with what has just been said: "Again and again the Christian church and its theology has insisted that we cannot postulate that the reality of the Incarnation, the mystery of Christmas, had, by absolute necessity, to take the form of this miracle."[4]

Whether a man, therefore, affirms the Virgin Birth as the way in which God has in fact acted will depend upon a number of factors: his assessment of the birth narratives in the gospels, the presence of this article of belief in most of the early confessions and creeds, the congruity and appropriateness of such a sign for the one whose whole life, ministry, death, and resurrection bear witness to the kind of uniqueness we have previously discussed. For our part, we hold that it is still possible to say "conceived of the Holy Ghost, born of the Virgin Mary" not as a burden to the faith but as a joyous recognition of the fact that God has, in becoming man, also given us this sign to point without ambiguity to the new creative and saving activity which now begins in this man Jesus. We do not think it is possible to deny categorically the name of "Christian" to the man who finds himself in intolerable perplexity in the presence of this sign. One cannot say that repentance, faith, acceptance by God, reconciliation with the Father through the saving death and resurrection, the new life in Christ, are all meaningless if this sign is not a biological and historical fact. "No attempt is made in the New Testament to show any connection between belief in the Virgin Birth and saving faith in Christ."[5] Nevertheless, such a man should ask himself whether this same perplexity is not experienced in relation to the empty tomb and the fact that Jesus truly lives after death. The total denial of the Resurrection would be much more serious than the denial of the Virgin Birth. Whereas this latter receives very limited attention in the New Testament, the Resurrection affects all the documents and seems to be a basic presupposition of the New Testament message in the various forms in which it is there presented. The divinely attesting sign at the end of Jesus' life seems quite indispensable and

---

[4]Karl Barth, *Dogmatics in Outline*, trans. G.T. Thomson (London: S.C.M., 1949), p. 100.
[5]Quick, *Doctrines of the Creed*, p. 159.

is more difficult to bracket as optional than the Virgin Birth. It would appear that the Resurrection does add something vital to the position that in the days of His flesh Jesus experienced a Father-Son relationship of such a kind as to warrant the later Christian language about His divinity.

This is not the same as saying that the divinity of Jesus becomes fact only after the Resurrection, as Pannenberg seems to suggest. Christian faith has always had great difficulty accepting the thesis that in the earthly Jesus we know only a man, however remarkable, and that any proper ascription of divinity must wait until after the Resurrection. There are really two different questions involved here. One is whether the earthly life and ministry was more than a proxy pointing to God, whether the man Jesus is Himself the real presence of God among men, a presence all divine, as Newman said. The other question concerns the idea of vindication by God, i.e., God giving a sign whereby what Jesus was in His earthly life becomes clearly attested and confirmed in the fact of the Resurrection. But the special Father-Son relationship we have emphasized as central to any doctrine of the Incarnation cannot be separated from the ethical fruits of that relationship in the goodness which shines through Jesus' human life and action. We agree with what Oliver Quick said some years ago when he discussed the issue of the moral perfection of Jesus.[6] As he insisted, the perfect holiness and goodness of Jesus seems axiomatic for the New Testament writers, even though the New Testament does not spell it out in a formal doctrine of sinlessness, though it does tell us that He "was in all points tempted like as we are, yet without sin" (Hebrews 4:15). It is true that Jesus said, "Why do you call me good? There is none good but God" (Luke 18:19). Is this a denial of His own goodness by Jesus or is it rather a denial of an independent, humanly achieved goodness detached from dependence on the Father? We incline to the latter view. Jesus was not good if by that one means that He achieved a human perfection in the strength of His human willing and resolution alone. His goodness, if it was a reality, was the fruit of His utter dependence upon the Father and His conformity to the divine will. Nevertheless, He was in this derivative sense good, and this goodness is in fact a significant element in what is called divinity. For some people, this linking of divinity with Jesus' human goodness seems only another version of the old liberalism, but this is not so. After all, as we have contended earlier, the full indwelling of God in a human being would take the form of a reflection of God's holy love in Jesus' actual judgment, love, and compassion toward men. Since Jesus' goodness is the result of God's activity in and through Him and not the fruit of human action working independently of God, it is therefore quite proper to see the

---

[6]*Ibid.*, pp. 171ff.

goodness as true evidence of the divine in Him, and not simply as evidence of His humanity as an isolated factor. While, therefore, the Virgin Birth and the Resurrection are factual signs given by God to point to His activity in Jesus, Jesus' divinity is not to be simply equated with these manifestations of divine power through natural process and historical actuality. The "human goodness" is also a sign of divinity, since it discloses to us through the humanity the source of all goodness, namely the loving and redeeming activity of God Himself.

A brief digression may perhaps be permitted here to comment upon some recent criticisms which impugn the goodness of Jesus. Obviously no appeal can be made to the moral goodness of Jesus if He did not possess it, or if it were only intermittently evident in His life and conduct. If there were serious moral flaws in His character, this would undercut any moral claim based on ethical values. Bertrand Russell is one of many who have been puzzled by the cursing of the fig tree, the story of the Gadarene swine, and the fierce denunciations of the Pharisees in Matthew's gospel.[7]

It is well known that in the case of the cursing of the fig tree, we have one account in Mark 11:12–25, repeated in substance in Matthew 21:12–22, except that in the latter account the tree withers instantaneously whereas in Mark the withering is only noticed to have happened on the following day. In Luke 13:6–9, however, the story of the barren fig tree is frankly given as a parable, and there seems to be in the total context of this section in Luke the implication that the tree is a symbol of a barren Israel, not bringing forth the fruits of repentance now that the Kingdom has drawn near in the Person of Jesus. It would solve some problems if it could be assumed that the parable is basic, and the Markan and Matthean accounts elaboration of what was originally a teaching of Jesus about judgment upon unrepentant Israel. Nor is this explanation simply to be ruled out as an evasion.

However, some scholars point out that the Markan account does not lend itself to this solution. Nor, it should be observed, does Mark specifically mention the episode of the fig tree as a miracle. The cursing takes place on one day and the withering is observed the following day. There could have been obvious natural reasons for this, especially if the tree was defective in the first place. In the case of Matthew, no such hypothesis is possible. The tree withers immediately at the words of Jesus and the implication is that the divine judgment is not only proclaimed but executed then and there on the spot.

In the denunciation of the Pharisees in Matthew 23, the issue is not complicated by the question of miracle. The problem is basically an ethical

---

[7]Bertrand Russell, *Why I am not a Christian* (New York: Simon & Schuster, 1957).

one. If Jesus was perfect goodness, as Christians maintain, then could He possibly have spoken of His enemies in the light of what He has to say elsewhere about love and forgiveness? Thus the ethical problem seems to center on two points: Is Jesus' attitude toward nonhuman objects or things, e.g., the fig tree and the swine in the Gadarene incident, compatible with a claim to perfect moral goodness? Secondly, is anger always a sign of moral defect? The first issue depends on whether it is believed that Jesus possessed the power directly to change natural processes in a manner which goes beyond any reasonable scientific or historical account of the matter. Second, if He had such power, did He use it in a manner which is open to ethical objection?

We have already argued that it is difficult to dispute that the Synoptics do believe that Jesus did in fact have such extraordinary power, though as we shall try to maintain later the possession of such power does not necessarily mean that Jesus was literally omniscient and omnipotent in the days of His flesh. Even if Jesus accommodated Himself to the contemporary idea of demonic possession, it does not follow that He accepted it quite naively and uncritically, as in the case of the Gadarene incident. Nor could it be ruled out that if Jesus did exercise extraordinary power on some occasions, the impression of such events was such as to lead his followers to interpret other quite natural events as the result of such power, to heighten the miraculous for its own sake.

The familiar description of the fig tree incident as a cursing has led to a lot of needless misunderstanding. To modern ears it sounds as if Jesus was simply piqued and lost his temper and swore at the tree. There is simply no indication in the text that Jesus swore at it in the sense which modern people give to the words "curse" and "swear." He pronounced judgment against it, which is not exactly the same thing. Whatever one does with these different Synoptic accounts which are not all reconcilable with each other, it hardly seems legitimate to see it as pointless and selfish anger against an innocent tree. It is clearly a symbol of momentous events in the life of contemporary Judaism vis-à-vis the ministry of Jesus. It is Jewish spiritual barrenness and the failure of the Jews to produce fruits worthy of repentance which take us to the heart of the matter. It is incredible that the man who had fasted for such a long time in the wilderness, wrestling with the problem of His spiritual vocation, should have vented His spleen upon a tree just because the satisfaction of His immediate physical hunger was thwarted.

In our view, therefore, the real ethical issue concerns Jesus' showing of anger at certain important moments in His ministry. If all anger is a sign of moral imperfection, then Bertrand Russell's charge can be sustained. But Russell himself has expressed passionate anger or indignation against particular individuals for the sake of the good causes to which he was committed. This, for us, is not a criticism of Russell. It expresses the depth of his own moral commitment to such values as compassion and justice, and he would have been a lesser man, not a nobler man, if he had been incapable of such indignation.

We would, therefore, contend that Jesus' anger was never just personal pique and pointless emotion. It sprang from a profound compassion and concern for those who are the victims of wickedness, oppression, and sheer spiritual stupidity in men who did know better and were responsible for what they said and did. That Jesus spoke out strongly against the Scribes and Pharisees seems to be attested by all the sources of the Synoptic tradition (Mark. 12:38–40, Matthew 23:1–36, Luke 11:37–52). Even if Matthew 23 is assigned to M (the exclusively Matthean material) and its force weakened by the prejudice of the writer, there is still enough material elsewhere, and also in such events as the cleansing of the Temple, to support the view that Jesus was capable of intense righteous anger. It is worth observing, however, that the attack is generally not against Pharisaism as a system nor against its interpretation of the Law, though Jesus had irreconcilable differences with that. It is against the Pharisees' *practice* that the attack is directed.[8] This supports the view that Jesus is not launching a sweeping and indiscriminate attack upon all Pharisees as such, irrespective of the way in which any particular Pharisee might have acted. He is evidently pointing out special moral and spiritual dangers in what could be called the Pharisaic outlook, and certainly denouncing those who make fine professions but live a life of moral hypocrisy. We can hardly use this as evidence of moral defect, unless all indignation prompted by hatred of wrong is to be so described. The fact that for men in general righteous indignation is rarely, if ever, purely righteous is not conclusive as far as Jesus is concerned. Certainly for us imperfect men and women moral anger is always mixed with pride and selfish motives which make our anger judgmental in the bad sense. Some modern psychologists have said so much about the damage done to human relationships by this kind of negative, judgmental attitude that they seem to exclude even the possibility that a judgment of evil can be compatible with love for the person judged. In any case, one ought not to read the woes against the Scribes and Pharisees without reading also the compassionate outburst of Jesus about Jerusalem: "How often would I have gathered your children together as a hen gathers her brood under her wings, and you would not" (Matthew 23:27ff.). Judgment and love combined may be well-nigh

---

[8]H.D. Major, T.W. Manson, and C.J. Wright, *The Mission and Message of Jesus* (New York: Dutton, 1938), pp. 143–144.

impossible for sinful men. It may not have been impossible for Jesus, if He is what the gospels imply and what Christian faith has always found Him to be.

As far as the Bible as a whole is concerned, it is not to be denied that sometimes in the Old Testament all too human anger is sometimes ascribed to Yahweh. Yet even here we can see a refinement of the idea of anger developing along with a profounder and truer conception of God. Yahweh's anger is not now simply prompted by ritual mistakes or transgressions of external commands. It is moral wrongdoing, injustice between man and man, oppression of the weak, which prompts His anger. Anger in this sense was never denied either by Jesus or the later church. "The idea of the divine anger," observes Edwyn Bevan, "was not something which penetrated into Christianity from its pagan environment; it was something which the church maintained in the face of adverse pagan criticism."[9] As Bevan goes on to say, there are some kinds of anger which we should not expect a good man to show. On the other hand, "In the presence of such things as cruelty to the helpless, to a child or an animal, or acts of disgusting meanness, we should not like a man who felt no stirring of anger."[10] And it is clear that Bevan does not intend us to take "like" here as a mere feeling of a rather sentimental kind. We would feel that such a man was lacking in that moral sensitivity which makes a man truly human. The same spontaneous moral intuition must also apply at the level of the divine. A divine being incapable of reacting against such moral evils would be far less worthy of our respect and adoration than the best human beings we know.

We conclude, therefore, that the charges against Jesus' moral goodness on this score cannot be sustained. Until more convincing evidence can be found of the moral defectiveness of Jesus, we must take the verdict of the early witnesses and Christian experience as justified. Jesus was a good man, and His goodness is one important aspect of His divinity if we are going to speak of a unique and divine disclosure not only in His death and resurrection but also in His earthly life and ministry.

All this is a warning against a simple identification of divinity with power, in the sense of control over natural processes, and of humanity with weakness and suffering. After all, was there nothing divine even in the obedience which led to the humiliation and suffering of the Cross? Does the suffering testify only to the weakness of the humanity and not to the condescension of the holy love of God seeking men in the far country of human sin? This kind of dichotomy would seem to be impossible. Those events which show Jesus' extraordinary power over nature and the divinely

---

[9]Edwyn Bevan, *Symbolism and Belief* (London: Allen & Unwin, 1938), p. 210.
[10]*Ibid.*, p. 215.

given signs of the Virgin Birth and Resurrection do indeed point to the power of God. But as we have maintained in our previous discussion, ''power'' is not a simple word. Power is of different kinds. There is a power of compassionate love which accepts weakness and suffering for love's sake, and this surely is divine in the profoundest sense which Christians can give to that word, since by it the very heart of the Godhead is revealed.

The healing and the nature miracles do not raise such fundamental theological questions as the Virgin Birth and the Resurrection. The reason for this is that while Jesus sees in them the signs of the coming of the Kingdom, He neither gives them nor sought for them the kind of publicity which would be required if they were to be regarded as public attestations of His claims. He never uses them nor appeals to them to buttress or prove the claims He is making about the nature of the Kingdom and about Himself as the bearer and bringer of that Kingdom. This does not mean that these miracles or signs have no significance at all. They do throw a good deal of light upon the way in which the divine compassion operates when it is present among men in the Person of Jesus. In this sense they point to the divinity if we acknowledge that the manifestation of God's love in Jesus is in fact a showing forth of the nature and activity of God. They are not proofs of divinity only in as far as they involve a control of natural processes which defy any possible explanation by man in terms of his current scientific understanding of the world. If we agree, as we very well might on the basis of the New Testament evidence, that Jesus exercised extraordinary powers in the days of His flesh, this is not to ascribe to Him omnipotence in the absolute and unqualified sense in which this is applied to God as creator and sustainer of the world. While this position has been and still is held by some, it runs, as we have seen, into intolerable difficulties on the basis of the New Testament evidence itself. Do we really want to say that Jesus, by sheer fiat, could as man have controlled and altered the paths of the planets and the functioning of the whole cosmos? Could He have built a nuclear reactor in first-century Palestine if He had been so minded? Could He have given the disciples a detailed description of all the historical events which were to unfold after His death and resurrection? Once one begins to think in these terms, it is clear that we are moving into a realm of speculation and into concepts of divinity for which the New Testament itself affords no evidence. Thus we do not have to deny all significance to the miracles, as some would do. On the other hand, in claiming more for them than Jesus Himself did, we put stumbling-blocks in the way of belief which it is difficult to think would have had the approval of Jesus.

Let us now try to sum up. There are some who would contest very strongly any attempt to tie up spiritual realities with physical facts of any kind. If the holy love of God is present in Jesus with a fullness without parallel, what could possibly be added of major significance? What conceivable difference could unusual physical events make to the spiritual judgment already made in our meeting with God, in this unique sense, in Jesus? That many today, even in the Christian fold, think in this way can hardly be denied. Yet it will not stand up to critical examination. The sharp dichotomy between physical fact and spiritual reality cannot be asserted in this way if we wish to be truly biblical.

The case of Jesus, however, raises many issues. We have agreed that the spiritual content of the term "divinity" must be defined in terms of the holy love which seeks us and redeems us through the Person of Jesus. This is obviously a value judgment interpreted by faith as a spiritual discernment of the true character of God. It is still possible to ask, however, whether the God so discerned in Jesus is in fact in effective control of His world, including the world of physical fact. It is not true, therefore, to say that physical fact is irrelevant to this question. A demonstration of divine power in events which involve physical processes and realities does not prove the validity of a spiritual judgment as spiritual. Agape love is discerned to be the highest possible concept of God in terms of value by what can only be called a spiritual judgment. But whether such love is really in effective control in the long run of all physical process, including death, demands something more than a value judgment taken in isolation. We want to know whether our value judgments truly refer to a God who is effectively sovereign in and over His world. Whatever our views, it can hardly be denied that the Virgin Birth and the Resurrection might be relevant, if they were factual, to this issue.

It is strange how many modern Christian thinkers are unwilling to see any connection at this point. While it is true that some reject the Virgin Birth on the grounds that the historical evidence is too slight to justify a confident assertion of its factuality, others, probably the majority, refuse to affirm it on the grounds that even if it were fact, it could have no religious or spiritual significance. It might be added that if unusual physical facts are spiritually irrelevant, then what we call normal physical processes would likewise have no spiritual significance. Professor John Smith has some very pertinent comments in his essay on "The Status of Natural Theology."[11] He is discussing two different ways of approaching questions concerning the reality of God—the ontological and the cosmological. For the former, the idea of God cannot be derived from the nature of the cosmos but is given in the religious consciousness directly as the awareness of the unconditional or of the absolute claims of truth. Such "experienced" truth is God immanent

---

[11]John E. Smith, *Reason and God* (New Haven: Yale Univ. Press, 1961), p. 171.

in the soul and known there "directly." The cosmological approach starts with the world of limited things and processes as known through ordinary experience and proceeds by inference to attain some kind of certainty "through the cumulative force of mediate argument."[12] Smith's thesis is that both approaches are needed and complement each other. "If the cosmological way runs the risk of losing the contribution of man's religious dimension, the ontological way runs an even greater risk of losing nature and its processes."[13] An adequate idea of God requires the insights of both.

This is not irrelevant to the issue we are now discussing. The totality of physical process is relevant to the value judgments we make on the basis of the awareness of absolute truth given in the religious consciousness. This raises a number of questions as to what is included in the term "physical process." Assuming for the moment that the Virgin Birth and the "bodily" resurrection of Jesus could be established as involving physical facts as well as spiritual value judgments, then these physical facts would be part of the total physical process of which we are a part. This raises the further question whether some physical processes are more significant than others in view of the context in which they take place. One could argue, of course, that no physical process, whether usual or unusual, could have any relationship to spiritual judgments of value. In this case, the Virgin Birth and the Resurrection would remain unusual elements in the total physical process, at present inexplicable by natural science of the "orthodox" kind. In principle they would remain scientific problems waiting to be solved, completely irrelevant to any judgments we might make about the nature and reality of God. This, however, is to separate the God of spiritual experience and the God of nature in a radical way which neither Scripture, philosophy, nor even science can really countenance. Our conclusion, then, is that we are not justified in starting off with the a priori assumption that physical fact and process are always irrelevant to spiritual affirmation and value judgments. Both belong to the same world, and they complement each other. Professor Ninian Smart in his discussion of Hume and miracles has rightly conceded to Hume that there is "no absolute necessity why things should continue to operate in the way in which they have in the past."[14] Thus we cannot rule out in advance that the miraculous (in the sense of inexplicable by science) might occur. Yet if it does occur, it is often argued that it is not causeless but has a supernatural cause. The latter, however, cannot be appealed to unless we have other grounds than the miracle itself for asserting the reality of a supernatural being who could do things beyond the power of man's science to explain.

---

[12]*Ibid.*, p. 169.
[13]*Ibid.*, p. 171.
[14]Ninian Smart, *Philosophers and Religious Truth* (London: S.C.M., 1964), p. 54.

Thus we agree that miracles could not be a conclusive demonstration of the validity of a divine revelation; they presuppose the truth of such a revelation to invoke the God who could or might do the miracle. On the other hand, if it could be shown on general grounds that belief in God is reasonable and rests on strong evidence mediated in a nonmiraculous way, then the appearance of miracle in the context of significant divine activity could be both significant and meaningful, even when not used as proof of the reality of the God disclosed in revelation.

For this reason, other arguments are often adduced for the dismissal of the Virgin Birth and the Resurrection as "religiously" or "spiritually" irrelevant. The Virgin Birth, it is asserted, really destroys the meaningfulness of the Christian claim that Jesus was truly man. We may cite the following examples: "The majestic wonder of the Incarnation of the Son of God is not made greater but smaller by the biological theory of procreation through one sex alone."[15] "There can be little doubt that the stories [about the Virgin Birth] that have come down to us are legendary rather than historical."[16] A similar opinion is expressed by Paul Tillich in his *Systematic Theology* (Vol. II). Bultmann agrees and comments that both Christ's preexistence and the "legend" of the Virgin Birth are clearly "attempts to explain the meaning of the Person of Jesus for faith."[17] "The story of the Virgin Birth bears all the marks of a legend that has been constructed out of an etiological interest, namely in order to illustrate the title Son of God. It is, therefore, highly probable that the story is to be judged as non-historical."[18]

It might seem foolhardy to question the judgments of such a formidable array of scholars, but it is possible that they have not said the last word on this question. Austin Farrer, by way of contrast, comments that Bultmann

> writes as though he knew that God never bends physical fact into special conformity with divine intention; the Word never becomes flesh by making physical fact as immediately pliable to his expression as spoken symbols are. Bultmann seems to be convinced that he knows this, but I am not convinced that I know it, and I cannot be made to agree by the authority of the truism that symbolism ought not to be mistaken for physical fact. For it still ought to be taken for physical fact, if and where God has made it into physical fact.[19]

Donald Mackinnon also writes:

> But (to speak very crudely) the emptying of the tomb is in some sense such an event, or group of events, as . . . [the burial of Jesus or the visit of the mourners

---

[15]Emil Brunner, *The Mediator* (London: Lutterworth, 1934), p. 325.

[16]Macquarrie, *Principles of Christian Theology,* p. 257.

[17]Bartsch, *Kerygma and Myth,* p. 35.

[18]Pannenberg, *Jesus: God and Man,* p. 149.

[19]Bartsch, p. 216.

to the tomb]. That is to say, if the tomb was empty, there must have been a moment in time when the body of Jesus was in the tomb, and a moment afterwards when the body of Jesus was not in the tomb. And if we say this [and it is the present writer's view that we must] we are in some sense putting ourselves in bondage to the settlement of questions which are questions of historical fact.[20]

The point Mackinnon is making applies equally to the question of the Virgin Birth. He goes on to make the valid claim that faith is not just another name for historical certainty and that faith remains a problem and a mystery. Nevertheless, the mystery of faith does not mean that all historical fact is irrelevant to faith. E.L. Mascall criticizes severely those who want to retain the symbolism of the Virgin Birth without the fact and asks about the meaning and appropriateness of this symbolism if we are dealing with a legend: "I can only say that in the absence of the Catholic doctrine of the Word made flesh of a virgin, this seems to me to lead at best to an unhealthy sentimentality and at worst to downright superstition."[21]

This raises in turn some interesting questions. The implication is that there can be no "real" man who is not born of the normal act of sexual intercourse between a man and a woman. Such a "man" would be so abnormal as not really to be a member of the human race at all. God could produce a genuine human being only in the way in which modern biological science conceives the process. God can never depart from normality in anything pertaining to the truly human. But this view hardly seems to be borne out by experience. The appearance of extraordinary genius may be just as striking a departure from the normal as a Virgin Birth would be, yet somehow this is supposed to be perfectly natural and to present no problems. Nor does all our learned talk about genes and chromosomes really affect the issue. In both cases, we have unexpected deviations from the normal which are not explicable in terms of the factors operating and scientifically understood at the moment when the deviation took place. Similar problems arise in regard to the attempts of modern science to produce a test tube baby or to create a human life by bio-chemical methods. Would such a product really be a "man"? The only test could be the practical one. If a scientifically produced "baby" grew up with all the characteristics of the true manhood we have earlier considered, on what grounds would one deny the product to be a human being? The implication would clearly appear to be that it is not the method by which a human being comes to be such which is decisive but the end product itself, namely a human being. Maybe there is more than one

[20]Donald C. Mackinnon, *Borderlands of Theology and Other Essays* (London: Lutterworth, 1968), p. 79.

[21]E.L. Mascall, *The Secularization of Christianity* (London: Darton, Longman & Todd, 1965), p. 268.

way of bringing creatures like ourselves into existence. There seems little reason, then, theological or scientific, for denying categorically that this is possible. The question again becomes not one of possibility, but of the evidence for the possibility having in fact been realized.

But what is meant when it is asserted that no truly human being could emerge apart from the sexual relationship as at present known? Of course, if it is claimed that the mere fact of an unusual birth makes it "not human," then so be it, but this is a playing with words. The real question concerns the criteria we use to decide what constitutes true humanity. In an earlier chapter, we attempted to draw up such a list. If those criteria are provisionally accepted, then the basic question is, Could a man arise who would fulfil these criteria unless he was born in exactly the same way as the rest of us? It is difficult to see on what basis such an opinion could be dogmatically affirmed! It might be argued that it was overwhelmingly improbable that it would happen or that the evidence is too slight to permit us to affirm that such an "improbability" has in fact taken place. It can hardly be categorically stated that it could not in any circumstances have taken place. Needless to say, this line of argument can also be used in defence of the Resurrection where the Resurrection is believed to involve some exception to the normal disintegration of the physical body.

Having said this, it must further be said that apart from a certain understanding of God and His relationship to the world, the proper attitude toward such unusual occurrences would be agnosticism, a waiting upon further light on facts at present obscure. It is often said, of course, that at this point Christians appear at their worst in their willingness to make a *sacrificium intellectus* in the interests of faith. Faith, it is argued with some heat, is not entitled to settle matters of historical and biological fact in a way which is congenial to faith, irrespective of the evidence. This is to turn faith into mere wishful thinking. Yet the question is far more subtle than this positivist dogmatism would suggest. If there were no evidence at all which pointed in the direction of the unusual facts, then the above contention would be valid. Yet, as everyone knows, what constitutes evidence and what makes a "fact" is one of the most difficult of the questions to be decided.

Our conclusion, then, is that we cannot start with this absolute dichotomy between physical process and spiritual reality. Both are aspects of the one real world which we inhabit. If we do start with such a dichotomy, we are in difficulties, not only in regard to unusual occurrences such as the Virgin Birth and the Resurrection, but also in regard to the Incarnation itself. The Word of God comes to us as a person, which means in and through a physical body, which is not to suggest that Jesus was no more than His body, any more than we are no more than our physical bodies. Denis Nineham cites

Bultmann's contention that if anyone finds support for the gospel in the historicity of the story itself, he has not fully appreciated the true nature of the gospel.[22] He concludes that Bultmann is mistaken: "I cannot see why it must be wrong to draw assurance from the fact that the Gospel was brought out in the life of an historic figure." But he goes on to say, ". . . equally I cannot see why it must be wrong to be gripped and saved by the Gospel *without such assurance.*"[23] He further comments that his justification for speaking like this rests on the assumption that Bultmann is as thoroughly gripped by the gospel in the full and true sense as anybody else. This is unfortunately expressed because it puts the critic in the embarrassing situation of seeming to throw doubt upon the moral and spiritual sincerity and integrity of Bultmann. It cannot be questioned that Bultmann sincerely believes that a saving "word" and "act" of God is mediated to us through the church's proclamation of the kerygma. He has spoken powerfully and movingly of the significance of this for him. However, it may quite properly be asked whether Bultmann's understanding of the relationship of the preached message to the historical realities out of which the preaching came is adequate, particularly in relation to the Resurrection, to name only one vital element. It may also be asked whether Bultmann's faith would be adequate to sustain the life and mission of the Christian church in the long run. The past history of the church certainly leaves open to doubt Nineham's contention that men can be gripped and saved by the gospel apart from any assurance about the life of the historic figure. The gospel is not a message which can be detached from the Person of Christ and presented as if it were an independent reality no longer anchored in the history. The fact that Nineham is not personally of the opinion that we are forced into such a radical scepticism about the history, does not invalidate the above point. The very suggestion that we can conceive the gospel at all without some assurance about the historical reality is misplaced. The dynamic of the Christian faith has derived from the conviction not simply that I encounter the living Christ now in the church's preaching but that the Christ thus experienced is in more than a metaphorical and symbolic sense in direct continuity with the life, death, and resurrection of Jesus of Nazareth. It is difficult to see how this conviction could remain without some assurance about the history. We are not saved by a Christ-idea or a Christ-principle but by the actual presence and reality of God Himself in the historical actuality of Jesus. The fact that we know Christ now "in the Spirit" does not mean that we can dispense with the Christ "in the flesh." Tempting as it is to escape from the problem of

[22]Denis Nineham *et al.*, *Historicity and Chronology in the New Testament* (London: S.P.C.K., 1965), p. 12.
[23]*Ibid.*

history into an ahistorical Christ-mysticism, this is the path which the church has resolutely refused to tread in the past. It is very difficult to imagine how the gospel could survive if the church takes this dubious route in the future.

The relation between physical fact and spiritual value would seem to be a great deal more subtle than is often suggested. Van A. Harvey is correct in saying that we can no longer appeal to "The Christian Faith" as though this were a self-evident norm,[24] because it obviously is not to many contemporary men. Yet it is equally not self-evident that "contemporary man," however this ambiguous term is defined, is the final judge as to whether there is a norm at all and whether it is grounded in such sufficient reason as to enable us to declare it to be true. Certainly it would not be justifiable to start with the premise that the Christian faith is true without giving any reasons at all for such an assertion and then go on to affirm that certain historical facts must inevitably be the case, apart from any consideration of the range and reliability of the historical evidence to which an appeal is being made. Van Harvey is also right in saying that the criteria for believing that belief in God is a morally responsible act are not exactly the same as the criteria for deciding whether an historical event took place in such and such a manner.[25] The conclusion to be drawn from these considerations is that a judgment about historical fact is a result of employing a complex set of criteria which involve God, nature, man, history, and all the other sciences and disciplines. While no man with intellectual integrity and moral honesty can simply invent history to suit his own personal caprices, it is also true that what is historical fact will in the last analysis depend upon a man's interpretation of the totality of experience, including God if he honestly believes that all the evidence points in that direction. It is not necessarily dishonesty or cowardice, therefore, if a Christian finds certain historical evidence convincing from the standpoint of Christian faith which it would be unreasonable to accept if that faith was sheer illusion. What may be fact is determined by what is possible and what is possible may be arbitrarily limited by a one-sided perspective which claims to be able to imprison reality within its own straitjacket.

---

[24]Harvey, *The Historian and the Believer,* p. xvi.
[25]*Ibid.,* p. xvii.

12.
Jesus or Gotama?*

Our discussion so far has concentrated exclusively upon the figure of Jesus and the Christian claim made on His behalf. Whatever the situation in the past, it would be parochial in the extreme to deal with the divinity of Jesus today as if there are no other claimants to the religious leadership of the race. Today we cannot avoid asking whether there are any serious rivals to Jesus, and if so, on what level this rivalry is to be considered. Some no doubt will claim that the word "rival" is badly chosen, and that it is simply a matter of acknowledging many men of great spiritual genius without attempting to make invidious comparisons. Nevertheless, if Jesus was truly God in the way urged in our previous discussion, then the Christian has no option but to claim uniqueness for Jesus. Unless, of course, we are open to the suggestion that the history of the race has seen several incarnations, and that it is proper to use the word "divinity" of all of them. In this case, if the term "uniqueness" is to be used at all in a meaningful sense, it would have to refer to a group rather than to a single individual. This is a difficult idea for most Christians, but not for Hindus and Buddhists. We have contended earlier that the word "divinity" takes on a precise meaning only in the context of a specific belief about the reality and nature of God.

Where the meaning of the word "God," or the absence of it in the Judaeo-Christian sense, is involved, then obviously "divinity" will also change its meaning. It has then to be decided what is precisely the basis of comparison, if indeed meaningful comparison can be made at all between religious figures who appear in the context of sharply contrasting or differing worldviews. Even if the Christian insists that "divinity" is applied to Jesus in a sense totally different from the way in which it could be applied to any other religious personality, he is still faced with important questions concerning his assessment of these other figures. If they are not divine in the

---

*Special Note: In view of the difficulty of achieving consistency in diacritical marks for the Sanskrit and Pali terms, they have been deliberately omitted.

same sense as Jesus, must the Christian simply dismiss them as impostors or inferior? Can he ever talk of God speaking to him, a Christian, through Confucius or Buddha or Mahomet? And if he does talk in this way, is he in fact denying or rendering void the heart of his own faith?

Professor Parrinder[1] has referred to the unusual question raised by Cantwell Smith of Harvard: "Is the Qur'an the Word of God?"[2] To realize the revolutionary import of this question, it has to be remembered that it is addressed not to Muslims, who would obviously say Yes, but to Christians, who in the past would almost unanimously have said No. Is there any sense at all in which a Christian could admit that God, as Christianity understands the term, might also speak to him through the Qur'an and thus through Mahomet? It might not seem impossible to give a guarded Yes to this question since the three great Semitic faiths have some beliefs in common. The same question might appear to be impossibly difficult if it were asked of Gotama or the Buddhist sacred writings, where our concept of God seems to be totally lacking.

In order to avoid getting lost in vague and unverifiable generalizations, we shall choose the more difficult option and seek to make some kind of comparison between Jesus and Gotama. Looking at Gotama from a frankly Christian perspective, could the adjective "divine" be applied to him in a sense not completely different from the use of similar language about Jesus? Could a Christian possibly talk of God in the Christian sense as speaking to him through Gotama? In the case of the Buddha, we do have a genuinely universal figure who has exercised a powerful fascination and influence upon men and women completely outside the Hindu tradition from which he came. There is evidence that this influence may become ever more powerful in the Western world as we come to know more about Buddhism at first hand. Both because of his large following and because of his intrinsic nobility, Christians can hardly ignore the Buddha. Any claim for Jesus' divinity must surely include some estimate of the role of the Buddha and how he fits into the Christian interpretation of the gracious purpose of God for the whole of mankind, past, present, and to come.

In our previous discussion of Jesus' divinity, we defended a Christology "from below" as a legitimate starting-point for Christian reflection. We have also urged that Christianity cannot simply evade the vexed questions of historicity and how much we may know about the man Jesus as distinct from the faith interpretations of His significance given by His early followers and developed in the doctrinal traditions of the church. In our view a similar

---

[1]Geoffrey Parrinder, "And is it True?" *Religious Studies,* VIII, No. 1 (March 1972).
[2]W. Cantwell Smith, *Questions of Religious Truth* (New York: Scribners, 1967), pp. 39ff.

approach could be and should be applied to Buddhism, though the difficulties here are even greater than in the case of Jesus. For example, could one talk of the "Quest of the Historical Gotama" in the same way in which Christian scholars have spoken of the "Quest of the Historical Jesus"? Is it possible to make any distinction between the life and teaching of the historical Gotama and the later developments of Buddhology, as some have described them? To this question some would reply with a definite No, just as some Christian scholars deny that it is possible to separate the Jesus of history from the Christ of faith. Even if there is such a distinction, it is now impossible, as some would urge, to disentangle the different elements from the written records and the oral tradition. In this true of Gotama also?

In the case of Gotama, we are dependent on the sacred texts of the Pali canon, which were not committed to writing till late in the first century B.C. As E. J. Thomas has pointed out, the tendency to regard the Pali canon as the final court of appeal is by no means to be taken as a definitive judgment. Since Gotama's utterances were not recorded in writing but were preserved in oral tradition for a considerable time after his death, it is not surprising that differences should arise among the different schools which preserved the oral tradition. By the third Buddhist council of 247 B.C. we have evidence of the existence of a body of Scriptures approximating the present Pali canon.[3] But this was only the collection of one school, the Theravada. The Sanskrit versions, for example, can no longer be dismissed as historically useless. Sometimes they may preserve material as ancient as anything in the Pali canon. The same problem emerges, of course, in the assessment of the Christian documents, though as Thomas points out, the problems in regard to the Buddhist canon are much more complicated because of the long period between the oral and the written tradition. The problem raised by the Sanskrit works is similar to the Christian one concerning versions of the Greek text. For example, a Latin version of the third century A.D. may give us a more reliable knowledge of the original text in Greek, when translated back, than a very late Greek manuscript which has been subject to a long process of editorial redaction and copying. The textual problem in both Buddhism and Christianity raises many difficult issues. This does not mean that no results can be obtained, but only that the elements of the developing tradition need to be disentangled by a very careful textual, literary, and historical analysis. One simple illustration of the problems involved is the question of the date of the birth of Jesus and Gotama. It is well known that Christian scholars differ over the date of Jesus' birth, but only a very few

---

[3]E.J. Thomas, *The Life of Buddha as Legend and History* (London: Routledge & Kegan Paul, 1969), p. xix.

years' difference is involved. On the other hand, ''the various calculations for the date of Buddha's death in Pali and Sanskrit works vary by centuries.''[4] This does not mean, however, that no reliable historical information is to be gained from them. As we have already seen, there is every reason to believe that the material of the Pali canon was assembled long before its being committed to writing and that this was passed on by a very skillful method of oral transmission. The modern popular prejudice against oral transmission, especially in our educational system, where learning by memory is at a discount, is not shared by modern scholars. In cultures where few people could read or write and written material was not available, a remarkable accuracy of memory and transmission was often obtained. Thus, the existence of a long oral tradition from the time of Gotama's life to the closing of the canon in the reign of King Asoka and its eventual committal to writing does not mean that we do not have historically authentic material. As we have seen, however, the disentangling process is much more complex than in the case of the Christian scriptures. While the Christian gospels and the New Testament itself also presuppose an oral tradition, the time span between the oral tradition and the written record is very much shorter (in the case of Paul probably only a generation after the crucifixion and in the case of the gospels a period of about two generations in the case of Mark, Matthew, and Luke and possibly a little longer in the case of the Fourth Gospel). This, of course, is putting it in very crude terms. Students of the New Testament will know the discussion that has gone on in regard to the dating of the gospels and the change of opinion that has taken place about the earlier dating of the Fourth Gospel. For the moment, our concern is only with a rough comparison of the time spans between the oral and written traditions in Christianity and Buddhism.

The situation is complicated by the fact that the historicity of Gotama is not as vital to Buddhism as the historicity of Jesus is to Christianity. Thus, for example, we find Dr. Conze writing that ''the existence of Gautama, or Shakyamuni [the sage from the tribe of Shakyas] is . . . a matter of little importance to Buddhist faith.''[5] It is the doctrine of Gotama that counts. The historical figure is only an archetype, as it were, manifest in different personalities at many different periods in the history of the present world-order or age.[6] Thus Conze would maintain that Buddhism must be taken in its entirety as an organic development and that its claims do not depend upon

---

[4]*Ibid.*, p. xxi.
[5]Edward Conze, ed., *Buddhism: Its Essence and Development* (New York: Harper, 1959), p. 34.
[6]*Ibid.*, p. 35.

our ability to reconstruct a modern historical account of the personality of Gotama. Even if this view is accepted, and perhaps it is by no means universal even among Buddhists, it is still possible to reach some conclusions with reasonable certainty about the historical figure of Gotama.

There seems no reasonable doubt that Gotama emerged from the context of Hinduism in the middle of the sixth century B.C., being born about 563 B.C. We do know some important facts about his career and the main outlines of his teaching. Although the historical Gotama pointed away from himself to the doctrine, the respect and love of Buddhists for this particular historical figure has given Gotama a position in Buddhist devotion and worship which the teaching of the Buddha himself perhaps does not warrant. Before a Christian can define his attitude to the Buddha, however, it is inevitable that he should ask certain questions about Gotama's beliefs as far as they can be reasonably ascertained.

It is often said that Buddhism is atheistic, with the implication, of course, that Gotama was himself atheistic. Needless to say, the meaning of the term ''atheistic'' in this context is usually defined in relation to the concept of God in the Judaeo-Christian tradition. Gotama, of course, was not nurtured in the Hebrew and Jewish faith and therefore cannot be expected to share these presuppositions. This, however, does not decide the question unless we dogmatically affirm that Hinduism in all its forms is atheistic. It would be difficult to defend such a thesis, especially in view of the strong emphasis on the transcendent in the Hindu tradition and sacred writings. Brahman, Atman, the various interpretations of the Upanishads, the theology of the Gita may not be exactly what a Jew or a Christian would mean by ''God,'' but it is clear that we have in these writings an emphasis upon a reality transcendent to the world. The dating of the Gita seems to be a matter of dispute. It has generally been put at about 400 B.C., but Professor Das Gupta is inclined to regard it as pre-Buddhist. In the case of Buddhism, we are not dealing with the humanism of a naturalistic or a secular kind in the Western sense. In asking whether Gotama was atheistic, we are asking in the first place not whether he had a Jewish or a Christian concept of God, which would be highly unlikely under the circumstances, but how far he completely dissociated himself from the emphasis upon transcendence in the Hindu tradition. This is an exceedingly difficult question to answer. As H.D. Lewis has contended, if we ask whether Gotama made any pronouncements about the ''beyond'' or about any other reality than the world we normally experience, the answer appears to be No.[7] He dismissed ''all speculation

---

[7]H.D. Lewis and R.L. Slater, *World Religions* (London: Watts, 1966), p. 159.

about other ultimate questions as a useless and even misleading diversion of energy."[8] He advised silence in the face of certain ultimate metaphysical questions. According to Lewis, however, the question cannot satisfactorily be left there. We can still ask whether the Buddha's silence indicates a complete agnosticism about the transcendent or whether it is the silence of the mystic who feels that the transcendent cannot be adequately described in human symbol and image or in terms of the discursive thought of the philosopher. Lewis's conclusion is that it is highly improbable that the goal of the Buddhist quest, and of Buddha himself, was a purely negative one.

Dr. Conze reaches a somewhat different conclusion. He first distinguishes among different meanings of the word "God": a personal God who created the universe; the Godhead, conceived either as impersonal or superpersonal; or a number of gods or of angels not clearly distinguishable from gods.[9] The first is the most crucial for the question we are asking. Conze admits that Buddhist tradition does not exactly deny the existence of a Creator but that it has never been really interested in the origin of the world as such. It has also asserted the superiority of the Buddha, at least in the later developments, over Brahma, the God who created the universe. Thus he concludes: "If indifference to a personal Creator of the universe is atheism, then Buddhism is indeed atheistic."[10] If this is the case, and if this represents the view of the historical Gotama himself, then it follows that the question of divinity in the precise Christian sense could hardly arise. One could not speak of Gotama as *homoousios* with God as defined by a Christian, since God in this sense is not affirmed. If, on the other hand, one held that Gotama was not totally agnostic but assumed a transcendent reality, though affirmed to be impersonal or superpersonal, then one might talk of some kind of disclosure of this transcendent reality in the "enlightenment" experience of Gotama. One might adopt Paul Tillich's language and speak of a disclosure of a transcendent Ground of Being in the experience of Gotama, or even of the "God above God" which transcends the theistic idea of God.[11] In this case, the word "divinity" might be meaningfully used. If the word "God" is applied to the transcendent and impersonal One and if the word "divine" was also considered an appropriate word, Gotama could be considered in this sense to be divine, i.e., the manifestation of the reality and character of the transcendent. The question, however, could still be raised whether this understanding of the transcendent is exactly what a Christian

---

[8]*Ibid.*

[9]Conze, *Buddhism,* p. 39.

[10]*Ibid.*

[11]Paul Tillich, *The Courage to Be* (New Haven and London: Yale Univ. Press, 1959), p. 186.

means when he speaks of God. There are obviously great difficulties in affirming such an identification of the One with the living and personal God of biblical and Christian faith and devotion. Only if such an identification is made could it be asserted that Gotama and Jesus were divine in exactly the same sense. I realize that in speaking above of the transcendent "Ground" I am mixing the images of height and depth, but the point remains that both spatial images point to a reality beyond the world as normally experienced. It is, then, the character of the transcendent which becomes the real issue.

On Dr. Conze's view, however, one could not use the word "divine" in the same sense of Gotama and Jesus since a personal Creator is eliminated from Gotama's own thinking. If, therefore, one wanted to affirm that God in the Christian sense had disclosed Himself in the experience of Gotama, one would have to say that this was in spite of and not because of the views which Gotama held about the nature of the transcendent, if indeed he held such views at all. Even if we could not speak of Gotama's experience of God in the precise Christian sense, it could still be urged that he experienced an ultimate transcendent of some kind. We have already noted H.D. Lewis's partiality to this interpretation. He points out that although we do not know how familiar, if at all, Gotama was with the Upanishads, he was at least nurtured in a community imbued with their spirit. The probability is, he argues, that if Gotama was atheistic, it was a very special kind of atheism. "All these considerations seem to combine with Buddha's silence and negativism as mutually supporting strands of cumulative evidence showing that the silence was in fact the caution of one who sensed how difficult, and even dangerous, it was to characterize directly the supreme religious reality."[12]

Since there are significant strands in the Christian tradition which emphasize the inadequacy of human language for a literal description of the Godhead, this is a genuine issue. One need only cite the Christian mystic's emphasis upon silence in the presence of God, the mediaeval doctrine of analogy, and a modern Christian philosopher's use of models, as in the case of Ian Ramsey. All these agree that God as transcendent can only be spoken about "indirectly," as it were, and not by literal description. Before we take up this question again, we must try to delineate in more detail what we know of the teaching of Gotama and the nature of his enlightenment. We must also consider the concept of incarnation (*avatar*) in Hinduism and in later Buddhism's doctrine of successive incarnations of the Buddha to see what common features, if any, can be discovered between these views and the Christian view of incarnation as previously expounded.

---

[12]H.D. Lewis, "Buddha and God," *The Monist*, Vol. 47, No. 3 (Spring 1963).

What, then, are the historical facts about Gotama? In our discussion of Christology, we have noted the way in which various models are used to express the significance of Jesus—preexistence, descent and ascent, kenosis or divine self-emptying. We also raised the question whether these models could be said to have any roots or intimations in the thinking of Jesus Himself about the significance of His Person. Similar tendencies can be discerned in the development of later Buddhist tradition, though it is even more difficult than in the case of Jesus to distinguish between the mind of the historical Gotama and the Buddhist models employed to express his significance. As already noted,the presuppositions from which Gotama started were completely different from those which governed the Judaism in which Jesus was nurtured. The most notable differences are in regard to the Hindu and Buddhist doctrine of reincarnation and the anatta doctrine of the nature of man. Says Dr. Conze: "It is obvious to Buddhists who believe in reincarnation, that Gotama did not come into the world for the first time at 563 B.C."[13] Whether one should use the word "reincarnation" is itself a matter of dispute. The word suggests a permanent and enduring self which can occupy different kinds of physical body ranging through all nonhuman living creatures and finally to man. If, as seems generally accepted, Buddhism rejects the notion of an eternal and permanent self or ego, then in contrast to Judaism it might be more accurate to talk of "rebirth" rather than of reincarnation.[14]

The problem we are now raising concerns the relation of the historical Gotama to the previous existences of the Buddha and the possibility of later rebirths. Dr. Conze has objected that for the Christian and the agnostic historian only "the human Buddha is real, and the spiritual and magical Buddha are to him nothing but fictions."[15] He rightly points out that for the Buddhist believer this is not so and that the Buddha-nature and the Buddha's glorious body are as important as Gotama's human body and historical existence, if not more important. "Both Theravada and Mahayana Buddhism believe there are numerous Buddhas past and to come."[16] There are, however, parallel situations to this in the development of the Christian faith. In as far as Christians put the emphasis upon the preexistent, eternal Son of God and the post-resurrection Christ seated at the right hand of the Father, it is clear that the meaning of the historical Jesus is being extended into a cosmic and nonhistorical realm. It is true that Christianity has never asserted

---

[13]*Buddhism*, p. 35.

[14]Ninian Smart, *The Religious Experience of Mankind* (New York: Scribners, 1969), p. 81.

[15]*Buddhism*, p. 38.

[16]Geoffrey Parrinder, *Avatar and Incarnation* (London: Faber & Faber, 1970), p. 149.

a plurality of eternal Sons or Christs, but it has certainly given to Jesus a cosmic significance. To this extent there is a real parallel, though not an exact resemblance. It ought not, therefore, to be impossible for the Christian to enter sympathetically into the Buddhist developments. If the Christian has to reject the Buddhist claims in the end, it will not be because of these larger claims for the glorified Buddha but because of a fundamentally different worldview involving quite dissimilar concepts of both God and man.

There seems no good reason to doubt that Gotama was an historical figure and that he had an "enlightenment" experience from which derives the basic Dharma or doctrine of Buddhism. The legends about his family and his unusual birth it would seem impossible to substantiate by the historical methods used by a modern Western historian. Was Gotama of royal descent, or the son of a prince? Do we know the names of his father, his wife, and his son? Do we know precisely his itinerary after his enlightenment? All these questions are difficult to answer with confidence, as Professor E. J. Thomas' careful analysis of the sources indicates. Nevertheless, Gotama was a real human being, and it would seem excessive scepticism to doubt that we know anything about his fundamental cast of mind and the basic thrust of his teaching.

The statement that Gotama was a real human being encountered the same sort of difficulties that we have already met in the case of Jesus. The fact that the church formally defined and defended the true humanity of Jesus did not prevent popular piety and some theological reflection from expressing views which seemed to discount or even cancel out any claim that Jesus was fully human. The same tendencies toward docetism can be discovered in the later Buddhism. The accounts of the birth of Gotama illustrate this point. As Parrinder points out, it is not presented strictly as a virgin birth, but the birth is due to a celestial influence which renders the role of the human father irrelevant: "When the child was born, he had none of the offensive matter which smears other children."[17] The future Buddha left his mother's womb erect, "like a preacher descending from a pulpit."[18] His excreta excelled all other fine perfumes. Parrinder is of the opinion that whereas docetism was regarded as heretical and gradually weakened in the development of Christianity, in Buddhism it tended to increase and remained acceptable to a large body of Buddhists.[19] Despite the fact that the Pali canon retains some of the real human traits of the historical Gotama, this attitude rapidly changed. Later it was asserted that even before his enlightenment, the body of the Buddha was made of diamonds and had no passions, no birth, and no

---

[17]*Ibid.*, p. 135.
[18]*Ibid.*
[19]*Ibid.*, p. 245.

death.[20] The Lotus Sutra declares that the Buddha did not die, "it was a device of mime."[21]

Some Buddhist thought affirms that Gotama was both compassionate and omniscient, though the exact meaning of these terms is not easy to determine. If, as we have noted, Buddhism has no place for a personal Creator-God, then it cannot mean exactly the same as when a Christian asks if Jesus was omniscient, a point already discussed. On the other hand, if the Buddha is superior to the gods (i.e., of Hinduism) and is omniscient, then it would seem as if there is being ascribed to the glorified Buddha the omniscience which belongs to God in Christian theism. But does omniscience apply to the human Gotama or only to the glorified Buddha, and are we justified in distinguishing the two? Against this kind of question can be set the emphasis upon Gotama's bodily ailments and weaknesses. The Vinaya says he was troubled with wind in the stomach. He appears to have died of dysentery at an advanced age. If he was married and had a son, as the tradition says, he was obviously not without sexual power and experience, in sharp contrast to the renunciation of marriage by Jesus. There is evidence of some discussion as to why the Buddha died at all. The reality of Gotama's death does not appear to have been disputed, at least at the beginning. His last words were a reminder of the decay inherent in all compounded things and an exhortation to his followers to work out their salvation with diligence.[22]

Despite all the miracles and legends, there does emerge through the texts a portrait of a genuinely human figure who was born, lived, and died like other men. The modern Christian, influenced by historical methods of investigation, is apt to concentrate upon this human reality, to try and peer through the mists of legend, miracle, and later interpretations to see the human Gotama as he really was. Since the historical reality of Jesus is basic to the Christian doctrine of the Incarnation, he is apt to assume that the same must be true for Buddhism. Yet here we appear to come to the parting of the ways. Dr. Conze remarks that it is possible to consider the Buddha as a human being, as a spiritual principle, as something in between.[23] It has already been noted that despite the strong insistence on certain human traits of Gotama, the spiritual principle of "Buddhahood" plays a decisive role in the way in which this human person is viewed. The Abhidhamma, the third section of the Pali canon, which gives us the later, more scholastic developments of Buddhism, affirms the uniqueness of the Buddha's powers. He alone is Conqueror, Buddha, Supreme, All-Knowing, All-Seeing, Lord of

---

[20]*Ibid.*

[21]*Ibid.*

[22]*Ibid.*, pp. 137–141.

[23]Conze, *Buddhism,* p. 34.

Dhamma, Fountainhead of Dhamma. He abounds in wisdom and goodness. He is omniscient and superior to the gods. Parrinder goes so far as to say, "He is closely similar to the Krishna of the Bhagavad-Gita, and has many of the attributes of the God of the monotheistic religions."[24] Divine qualities are ascribed to him in the Pali texts. The Lord Buddha is the super-god (atideva) and the god beyond the gods (devatideva). He bears the thirty-two marks of the Superman (Maha-Purusha) and also a halo that spread around him for a fathom's length.

All these developments are set in the context of the belief that the spiritual enlightenment of Gotama the Buddha cannot be the result of only one life. It could be the result only of a spiritual maturing through a succession of existences. The historical Gotama thus emanates from a spiritual principle, a Buddha-nature which exists in some sort of transcendent glory prior to its manifestation in a series of incarnations or rebirths. This spiritual principle is referred to as the Tathagata or the Dhamma body. One must penetrate through the human body of Buddha to the real being of the Buddha, the glorified body, the enjoyment body, the unadulterated body, the body which expresses the Buddha's true nature.[25] It is clear that devotion has moved far from an interest in an historical personality as such to the reverence and worship of the Buddha as a god. It is worth noting in passing that there is a significant difference here between the Christian view of the post-resurrection reality of the glorified and risen Christ and this view of the Buddha's glorified body. If one asks whether the Buddha still exists after death, an answer cannot be given without taking into account the Buddhist view of the nonreality of the self. When Buddha was asked whether a Tathagata exists after death, he apparently dismissed it as one of those speculative questions which it is not profitable to ask. It is a question to which neither a plain Yes nor a plain No can be given. To ask such a question is not conducive to true religion, peace, or nirvana.

Yet if there are to be further incarnations of the Buddha-nature after the death of Gotama, must there not be an eternal Buddha-nature somewhere in a transcendent realm, a kind of Platonic Buddha-nature archetype after which the particular incarnations or rebirths are modelled? The model of preexistence, already considered in the case of Jesus, appears in relation to the Buddha also. We have already noted that most Buddhists hold that the historical Buddha became such only after more than five hundred previous lives on earth. "From his bliss in the Tushita heaven, he looked down to the earth and decided to be born for the last time."[26] Yet again, as Parrinder

---

[24]Parrinder, Avatar, p. 143.
[25]Conze, Buddhism, p. 36.
[26]Parrinder, Avatar, p. 247.

maintains, even if one uses words like "incarnation" of the historical Buddha, there is no God manifest in him, especially if God is thought of as a personal Creator, as in Judaism and Christianity, or even in some forms of Hinduism (Brahma). One might perhaps talk of Buddha as incarnating the Dharma, but "there is a wide difference between this and the Christian faith in God who so loved the world that he comes in person to seek and to save the lost."[27]

It seems fair to say, however, that despite the docetic tendency which appears in both Buddhism and Christianity, there is no reason to doubt that in each case we have at the origin of both religions genuine human persons, real historical figures. In both cases, we can raise the proper question of whether later developments were legitimate interpretations of the significance of these figures or whether they were simply faith-interpretations far removed from the way in which either Gotama or Jesus actually thought about themselves. When that difficult question has been resolved, the assessment of the truth of either religion or both can still be raised.

We must, however, defer this issue until the end of the study, because any assessment of the truth of these religions demands a more careful study of what it is that is being compared and assessed. This in itself is a very difficult question to answer, as we have already discovered. What, for example, are the resemblances and differences between the doctrine of avatars in Hinduism and Buddhism and the Christian doctrine of the Incarnation? What exactly is at the heart of the Buddha's message of salvation, as far as we can discover it? What is the meaning of nirvana, both as a state of the enlightened man here and now, while still in the body, and as a state to be realized after the empirical personality has ceased to be? Until some of these questions have received at least a provisional answer, we are in no position to raise the question of truth or decide in what sense, if at all, the category of divinity can be applied to either Gotama or Jesus.

It is obvious in what follows that the writer has leaned heavily upon the work of Parrinder, Das Gupta, and others. This is inevitable. If the Christian is to wait until he has mastered every great religion with the thoroughness which he devotes to his own, then he is reduced to complete silence. Perhaps this would be the path of wisdom. Yet at this moment in time the questions press upon him in a manner which makes it impossible for him conscientiously to avoid them. The only way open, therefore, is for him to strive after as much objectivity as is humanly possible and to seek not to distort the nature of the religion he is trying to compare with his own. This is a risky undertaking. He can only leave it to the experts in the other religions and,

---

[27]*Ibid.*

perhaps more important, to those who are sincere believers in those religions to correct his one-sidedness and put right his serious distortions.

Avatara means, then, a descent, a down-coming (from a verb *tri*—to cross over, attain, save, with the prefix *ana*—down), and so *ava-tri*—descend into, appear, become incarnate.[28] The contemporary debate in the West about religious language will find further material here for its analysis of spatial symbolism in the articulation of religious experience. "The Avatar is an appearance of any deity on earth, or descent from heaven, but it is applied especially to the descents or appearances of Vishnu."[29] The word *avatar* apparently does not occur in the classical Upanishads, where the early word is "manifestation" (*pradurhhava*). There are early avatars of Krishna in animal form, but the most notable is the avatar of Vishnu in Krishna in the Gita. Already it is evident that, in contrast to Christianity, we are dealing with a plurality of possible avatars and not simply with one. Various avatars are mentioned in the Mahabharata, including ten of Vishnu. Krishna is the greatest human avatar of Vishnu and is both man and "God." Whether the figure ultimately derives from an actual historical person is perhaps impossible to determine at this late stage of the tradition. Certainly, he is spoken of as having a human body and some human limitations. He admits ignorance, eats, drinks, plays, sleeps, and finally dies.[30] In the Gita, he appears as the charioteer of Arjuna and speaks as the Avatar-God, though it is interesting to note that the word *avatara* does not appear in the Gita.

In asking whether there is any real resemblance between the "coming down" of Vishnu in Krishna and the divine Word becoming man in Jesus, it is obviously necessary to clarify some basic meanings. In the case of Krishna, there appear to be scholarly differences of opinion as to whether he is an avatar of Vishnu or of Brahman. Then we would have to decide the respective meanings of Vishnu, Brahman, and God in the specific Christian sense, and ask about the resemblances. Then we would have to study the nature of the incarnation in each case. Here again we are faced with critical and hermeneutical problems. Does the Gita present a consistent point of view? Zaehner agrees with Otto that the Gita is a heterogeneous collection of treatises adapted to the Krishna theology.[31] Otto had suggested that the God of the Gita vision is not Vishnu but the "wholly other" identified with Rudra.[32] Parrinder dismisses this as too Hebrew, even too Barthian! Gonda

---

[28]*Ibid.*, p. 19.

[29]*Ibid.*

[30]*Ibid.*, p. 29.

[31]R.C. Zaehner, *At Sundry Times* (London: Faber & Faber, 1958), p. 118.

[32]Rudolf Otto, *The Original Gita*, trans. and ed. J.E. Turner (London: Allen & Unwin, 1939).

and Hill say that Krishna is the avatar of Brahman and that the Gita teaches not devotion to a personal deity but pure nondualistic monism after the manner of Sankara. Zaehner, on the other hand, affirms that Sankara's commentary is a complete perversion of the Gita[33] and accuses Radha-krishnan of a gratuitous translation of Brahma as God, which can only be misleading. To his way of thinking, Ramanuja's commentary is much nearer the mark. Apparently, in chapter ten of the Gita, Krishna is directly called Brahman by Arjuna.

It would be folly for an outsider to step into this intricate debate with any confident pronouncement. Parrinder sums it up by saying that whatever the deity who reveals himself in the Gita, he does reveal himself to man and shows grace and compassion. These latter qualities certainly point beyond the neuter, impersonal Brahman to a "God" about whom one can speak seriously in personal symbols. Arjuna calls Krishna the supreme Brahman (only once), the eternal divine person (Purusha), unborn Lord (compare patristic descriptions of the Christian God as *agennetos*), primal deity (*adi-deva*), God of gods (*deva-deva*). Arjuna asks mercy, grace, and human kindness from the "father of the world":

> As father to his son, as friend to friend,
> As lover to beloved, have mercy, O God.

(Gita II. 41–6)

Das Gupta says the God of the Gita is one who "could be a man and be capable of all personal relations."[34] Certainly, if all this is true, we have a real resemblance between the Christian and the Gita's teaching about grace. If we do not play down the personal relationship between man and deity, as Sankara did, the resemblance is even closer. It can, however, still be asked whether the Gita's vision of a God of grace involves a real incarnation, God's actually becoming man. Certainly, as Parrinder says, the avatar doctrine requires some degree of transcendence, so we are not dealing here with a mere humanism. The avatar is a heavenly being who comes to earth to show grace, restore right, and destroy wrong. But how close an identifica-tion of God and man is involved in this way of speaking in the Gita? This is a difficult question to answer until we have decided how far Krishna takes on a real human existence or whether he is only the object of Arjuna's vision. In any case "in a logically monistic system there is no room for either Isvara or avatar, any more than for worship or prayer."[35]

---

[33]Zaehner, *At Sundry Times*, p. 119.
[34]Surendra Das Gupta, *A History of Indian Philosophy* (Cambridge: Cambridge Univ. Press, 1932), II, 525.
[35]Parrinder, *Avatar*, p. 61.

It is clear from this very cursory study of the avatar concept in Hinduism and Buddhism that there is at least a resemblance between it and the Christian understanding of the Incarnation. The ambiguities consist in the different concepts of God (Brahman, Atman, Yahweh, the God and Father of the Lord Jesus Christ, Nirvana, if conceived of as pointing to some transcendent reality) and of man and how far the transcendent is truly manifest in a real man. Parrinder notes, in his discussion of modern Indian thought and Christianity, certain reactions against the avatar doctrine because of the fear of emotionalism and idolatry.[36]

As is well known, Mahatma Gandhi had the highest regard for Jesus as martyr, embodiment of sacrifice, and divine teacher but could not consider Him as the most perfect man ever known.[37] Even in Hinduism itself, some were anxious to distinguish the divine Krishna from any specific historical person. Radhakrishnan does not appear to make any doctrine of avatars central to this position and in any case insists that ''these have no servitude to historic fact.''[38] The same seems to be true of Sri Aurobindo Ghose (1872–1950). While he dissociates himself from the extreme nondualism of Sankara and insists that the power of Brahman to enter into the finite is fundamental, he does not really give a central position to the idea of the avatar. Despite this, there is a tendency to insist that the avatar is a true incarnation, even to the point of undergoing sorrow and suffering as a necessary prelude to joy. It is difficult to be sure how far Aurobindo has been affected by the Christian idea of God in Christ entering into human suffering and transforming it in a redemptive manner. Here again, however, he refuses to regard any avatar as unique and continues to speak of many avatars.[39] For this reason H.H. Farmer accepts the view that an avatar may be a real incarnation, but his conclusion is not to assimilate the Christian doctrine of Incarnation into the avatar concept. Rather, he dislikes the emphasis on incarnation, which puts the stress primarily upon taking ''bodily'' form only, and prefers, in the case of Jesus, to speak of ''inhistorization'' of God.[40] For him the word ''incarnation'' can too easily be taken to mean merely ''taking a bodily form.'' Equally unsatisfactory is the avatar notion, which suggests a divine being ''who merely drops into the human scene in an embodied form from the realm of eternity, unheralded, unprepared for, without roots in anything that

[36]Ibid., p. 100.
[37]Ibid., p. 103.
[38]Sarvepalli Radhakrishnan and Charles A. Moore, A Source Book of Indian Philosophy (Bombay: Oxford Univ. Press, 1957; Princeton: Princeton University Press, 1957).
[39]Sri Aurobindo, Essays on the Gita (Calcutta: Arya, College St. Market, 1928).
[40]H.H. Farmer, Revelation and Religion (London: Nisbet, 1954), p. 193.

has gone before in history and without any creative relationship to the unfolding of events in what comes after."[41]

It is not our intention to discuss the Christian doctrine of the Incarnation in relation to Hinduism as such or to the other major religions, but rather to concentrate specifically upon the figures of Jesus and Gotama. Nevertheless, it may be useful here to summarize the basic issues which would be involved if the wider application were made.

(a) The affirmation of a transcendent sacred reality is not peculiar to Christianity. The basic question concerns the nature and character of that transcendence and the symbols men have employed to point to that reality.

(b) How fundamental are personal analogies in religious symbols? Grace, love, mercy, forgiveness, etc. depend for their meaning upon the personal character of God.

(c) What personal symbols and analogies are used outside Christianity, and what understanding of divine grace emerges?

(d) Even where a personal God is lacking, or even where it is present in some form (e.g., Krishna), can one talk of grace in the same sense as in Christianity?

(5) Can one talk of the grace of God in the Christian sense in non-Christian religions, even though there is no understanding of God in the Christian sense?

(6) Can one talk meaningfully of "unconscious Christianity" as some modern theologians are doing?

Must one say with W. Cantwell Smith that one cannot speak in a general way of the truth of Christianity or Buddhism or any other religion but only of the truth for an individual? The question of truth is crucial, but the basic issue is, Where does it lie and does it lie in the religions? "I am suggesting," says Smith, "that it does not, that it lies elsewhere, namely in persons. It becomes true as we take it off the shelf and personalize it in dynamic actual existence."[42] The question still arises, however, Does one person possess the truth more than another and what would be the criteria for determining this?

Applying the ideas of Smith to our consideration of the Buddha and the Christ, few would dispute that in the case of both Jesus and Gotama, religion, whatever it is, was realized in dynamic actual existence. Though both of these men were nurtured in ancient and impressive religious traditions, neither of them is simply a passive reflection of the tradition. Both select from and interpret the tradition on the basis of a highly individual

---

[41]*Ibid.*, p. 196.
[42]Smith, *Questions of Religious Truth,* pp. 67–68.

experience and put the stamp of their personal experience upon all later developments. Thus, according to Smith, the question we are grappling with is not, is Christianity or Buddhism the truest religion, but what kind of truth was it which both men grasped? What sort of truth was it, and truth about what or whom, and can one say that one was nearer to the truth than the other? Smith's assertion that truth is for persons does not really deliver him from the urgency of this question. The word "truth" is again assumed to be more than the assertion that both men held certain views about man, the world, and maybe God. Rather truth is here assumed to have this personal existential meaning. Both men experienced what they conceived to be reality in the deepest sense. Though this experience included intellectual elements and formulated ideas, it was more than an intellectual position; it was a spiritual discernment and experience involving the commitment of the whole man. We agree.

An interesting linguistic point is the intellectualizing process which took place in the transition from the Hebrew '*emeth* to the Greek *aletheia*. The Hebrew term is more closely allied to the notions of veracious, sincere, trustworthy than to the intellectual apprehension of truth as such. Thus by a subtle change, the Hebrew "faithfulness" of God and man's corresponding trust tends to be transformed into the pursuit of truth understood in a more intellectual way.[43] The Hebrew view is, therefore, nearer to Cantwell Smith's existential interpretation of the nature of religion. Nevertheless, one must be on guard against a too simple assumption that the Hebrew and Greek conceptions of truth are a simple either-or. Trust can never be in a bare X without any intellectual affirmations about the reality or nature of that which is trusted.

Before we can speak about Jesus and Gotama in any intelligible sense, we must try to uncover as accurately as possible what was the nature of the enlightenment of Gotama, what was the nature of his message to his followers, and what kind of human being results from trying to follow in his way. Gotama worked with ideas that were already current in the Hindu tradition—reincarnation, karma, and the possibility of release from the round of rebirth. He gave a subtle and original interpretation of these ideas as a result of his enlightenment. He does not appear to have believed in a Good Creator nor assumed the validity of the Brahman-Atman understanding of the Transcendent in traditional Hinduism. "Thus the Buddha's enlightenment did not occur in the context of prior belief in God."[44] He did not interpret his enlightenment as a kind of contact or union with God, as Jews,

---

[43]C.H. Dodd, *The Bible and the Greeks* (London: Hodder & Stoughton, 1935), pp. 70ff.
[44]Smart, *The Religious Experience of Mankind*, p. 79.

Christians, and Muslims might do. "In Buddhist thought the universe itself is the given fact. No explanation for its existence is offered or sought. . . . Buddhism is more accurately described, therefore, as a system of thought which, so far as the notion of a Creator is concerned, is agnostic; it is uncommitted one way or the other."[45]

What, then, was the nature of the enlightenment? Let us start with the teaching. The four noble truths enunciate the following:

(a) Life is permeated with suffering and dissatisfaction (*dukkha*), ill-fare as opposed to welfare.

(b) The origin of suffering lies in craving or grasping—i.e., tanha, a burning thirst for the things of this world.

(c) Suffering can be stopped by the removal of craving.

(d) The way to end suffering is the noble eightfold path.[46]

To quote from what has been called the first Sermon of Gotama, as translated by E.J. Thomas: "Now this, O monks, is the noble truth of pain: birth is painful, old age is painful, sickness is painful, death is painful, sorrow, lamentation, dejection, and despair are painful. Contact with unpleasant things is painful, not getting what one wishes is painful. In short the five khandhas are painful"—the khandhas (groups or aggregates) are form, feeling (or sensation), perception (volitional disposition), predispositions (or impressions), and consciousness. "Now this, O monks, is the noble truth of the cessation of pain: the cessation without a remainder of that craving, abandonment, forsaking, release, non-attachment."[47]

In this first sermon, Gotama first warns the monks against the extremes of indulging the passions on the one hand and ascetic torture of the body on the other and points them to the Middle Way. This is then defined as the noble eightfold path, namely right views, right intention, right speech, right action, right livelihood, right effort, right mindfulness, right concentration. The Westerner must be careful not to read into this word "right" all the ethical content which he is apt to give the word when used in Jewish and Christian context. The meaning of right must be seen here in direct relationship to the diagnosis given by Gotama in his analysis of suffering. From this analysis of the human condition follows the doctrine of dependent origination, showing the links between birth, existence, attachment, desire, contact, sensation, the six organs of sense, consciousness, name and form, karma, ignorance.[48] The aggregation of misery, previously described, can

[45]Trevor Ling, *History of Religion East and West*, p. 91.

[46]Radhakrishnan and Moore, *Source Book*, pp. 272ff.

[47]From the Samyatta-nikaya V. 420, translated by E.J. Thomas in *The Life of Buddha as Legend and History* (New York: Knopf, 1927), pp. 87–88.

[48]Radhakrishnan and Moore, *Source Book*, p. 278.

be overcome only when the causal link which binds all the above (karma) is effectively broken. "On the cessation of birth ceases old age and death, sorrow, lamentation, misery, grief and despair."[49]

Then follows later Gotama's theory of the No-Soul (or Self). The body is soulless. The body here includes feeling, perception, the aggregates, and consciousness, and thus the impermanence of the body means that there is no enduring self.

> Thus perceiving, monks, the learned noble disciple feels loathing for the body, for feeling, for perception, for the aggregates, for consciousness. Feeling disgust he becomes free from passion, through freedom from passion he is emancipated, and in the emancipated one arises to the knowledge of his emancipation. He understands that destroyed is rebirth, the religious life has been led, done is what was to be done, there is nought [for him] beyond this world.[50]

This quotation is from the Samyatta-Nikaya III. 66.

If this is a reasonably accurate account of Gotama's analysis of the basic problem of human existence, what, then, was the nature of his experience of enlightenment that formed the basis of his doctrine of deliverance from suffering into the bliss of nirvana? There are two problems here. One is to get back to reliable accounts rooted in Gotama's own interpretation of his experience.[51] In particular, we must define nirvana as Gotama understood it, as distinct from later elaboration of the doctrine. The other problem for the Westerner is to free himself from Christian ideas and to try to see what nirvana means in a Buddhist context.

In offering men release from craving, Gotama changed the inherited doctrine of rebirth. He appears to have dissociated himself from the idea of a plurality of eternal souls or selves. The three characteristics of things and persons are dukkha (suffering), anatta (absence of self), and anicca (impermanence). "Rebirth is not pictured as the transmigration of a soul from one body to another."[52] This would imply a notion of the self which the Buddha has rejected. Thus the goal of the cessation of craving cannot be thought of as an individual nirvana, i.e., a state of a permanent self or personality conceived in Western terms, because this idea has been abandoned. What, then, is nirvana?

Professor Ling, taking Dr. Conze's advice about not seeking to define nirvana by a series of disconnected quotations, attempts to clarify this

---

[49]*Ibid.*, p. 279.
[50]*Ibid.*, p. 281 (quoted from E.J. Thomas).
[51]Thomas, *Life of Buddha,* chapter VI.
[52]Smart, *Religious Experience,* p. 82.

subject by concentrating upon the Sutta Nipata, which is agreed to contain some of the most ancient material in the Pali canon.

> The Pali word nibbana is formed of ni and vana. Ni is a negative particle and vana means craving or selfish desire. Nibbana, therefore, literally means the absence of craving. The Sanskrit word Nirvana comes from the root va which means to blow and the prefix nir which means off or out. Hence, Nirvana in its Sanskrit form means the blowing out.[53]

Trevor Ling follows E.M. Hare in rendering nibbana as "the cool."[54] It is the noun, he says, which is important as meaning the extinction of craving. Since it is customary in the West to associate the idea of nirvana with a state realized at or after death, it is important to give full weight to Ling's emphasis upon its realization in this life. A man can become nibbuta, one who has become cool or who has experienced the cessation of craving, in this life. The nibbuta man can live and move about in this world, as Gotama did. Only later, perhaps, was the distinction made between the entry into nibbana now through the dying way of moral defilements (the *kilesa nibbana*) and the dying away of all the constituents of empirical existence when the chain of karma is finally broken (*khanda nibbana*). Most of the references in the Sutta Nipata are to nibbana in this life as a realizable goal here and now. Professor U Thittila, already quoted, makes the same point in his insistence that nibbana is not a negative concept implying annihilation at death. It is a positive, realizable goal now. It is the freedom from personal desire now. "That man is free here on earth. He has reached nibbana in this world."[55] In terms of later doctrine, a man can reach nibbana with substrate, i.e., he will go on living in this world and his mind and body remain.

Despite this emphasis upon nibbana here and now, the logic of Gotama's teaching would seem to point to a state when our present empirical existence wholly ceases. This is sometimes referred to as the transcendent state of nibbana, or nibbana without substrate.[56] What can this mean? It cannot mean transcendent as referring to the reality of God in the Christian sense, since for Buddhism there is no God in this sense: "In Buddhism there is no such thing as belief in a body of dogmas which have to be taken on faith, such as belief in a supreme Being, a creator of the universe, the reality of the immortal soul etc."[57] It cannot, therefore, mean personal immortality or union with God. "The substrate will simply cease. But, then, since indi-

[53]U Thittila, Maha Thera, *The Fundamental Principles of Theravada Buddhism,* cf. Kenneth W. Morgan, *The Path of the Buddha* (New York: Ronald, 1956), p. 111.
[54]Ling, *History of Religion,* p. 92.
[55]Morgan, *Path of Buddha,* p. 112.
[56]Smart, *Religious Experience,* p. 82.
[57]Morgan, *Path of Buddha,* p. 71.

viduality is made up merely of the succession of mental and physical states, we can no longer speak of the individual as existing after death in a state of final nirvana.''[58] Thus, whatever is meant by nibbana in this life, it is difficult, if not impossible, for the Christian to regard nirvana without substrate as other than the equivalent of annihilation. It can only be positive in the sense of the absence of certain evils, but this is a very negative kind of positiveness, since no self is conscious now of the absence of these evils.

Another penetrating discussion of the nirvana concept by a Westerner with much experience of the East is to be found in the works of Ninian Smart already quoted.[59] He warns the Christian against the reading in of ideas and passing these off as the real meaning of the Buddhist tradition. He is clear in his own mind that nirvana is not the Absolute underlying all empirical phenomena, nor does it involve personal survival in the Christian sense, nor is it a personal entity comparable to the God of theists.[60] Nevertheless, despite the denial of the soul or self, he says "there remains in the Buddha's teachings a strong flavour of the pluralistic and individualistic views of the self and salvation.''[61] It is true that Gotama denied annihilationism, but this may have been the denial of a materialistic view which saw death as the final end. This would involve a denial of karma and the principle of rebirth, a position which Gotama does not seem to have adopted. Whether the Buddha himself or a Buddhist saint continues to exist after death was put by Gotama in the category of undetermined questions. The survival of death, therefore, cannot be said to have been central to Gotama's teaching, whatever the later developments of Buddhism. Until nirvana without substrate is reached, one could speak of the continuance of the soul through its many experiences of rebirth, provided it is remembered that the word "soul" does not connote personal identity. The vital question which the Christian is disposed to ask is whether nirvana, when the law of karma is finally broken, involves the survival or the immortality of the nibbuta man. The answer to this, as far as Gotama and the Hinayana is concerned, would appear to be No. Even if the answer were Yes, it would still have to be said that it would be nirvana without God, since God as personal Creator is not a basic idea for early Buddhism. "But unlike the Semitic faiths [Judaism, Christianity, and Islam], it [Buddhism] starts from an interior mystical quest rather than from the prophetic experience of a dynamic personal God. It is mysticism without God.''[62]

---

[58]Smart, *Religious Experience*, p. 82.
[59]See also Smart's *Doctrine and Argument in Indian Philosophy* (London: Allen & Unwin, 1964).
[60]*Ibid.*, p. 36.
[61]*Ibid.*, p. 37.
[62]*Ibid.*, p. 39.

Now if our summary is a reasonably accurate account of the basic thinking of Gotama as far as we can recover it from a careful analysis of the sources, then how does it compare with the teaching of Jesus of Nazareth?

1. Human Existence as Suffering (dukkha)

How far is Gotama's analysis of the human situation accurate? That suffering in one form or another is a universal and continuing feature of all human existence can hardly be doubted. It must have had a special poignancy in the India of the sixth century B.C., before modern scientific medicine had developed its many ways of relieving the impact of disease and physical weakness. The Bible too recognizes the inescapable fact of suffering. One need only mention the Psalms, the Book of Job, and Ecclesiastes. In the New Testament Jesus is presented as devoting a considerable amount of His time and energy to healing men's physical and mental disorders. Jesus Himself, the pioneer and perfecter of our faith, was made perfect through suffering (Hebrews 5:7–10). The centrality of the cross for all the New Testament documents hardly needs to be emphasized. St. Paul speaks of the groaning of the whole creation in travail until the final redemption of our bodies (Romans 8:22–25). The Book of Revelation gives us the vision of the holy city, the new Jerusalem, in which mourning, crying, and pain will have passed away (Revelation 21:1–4). Both Gotama and Jesus, Buddhism and Christianity, recognize the widespread and pervasive reality of suffering of all kinds.

Yet there are profound differences in the way Christianity and Buddhism handle the reality of suffering. There is nothing in Buddhism comparable to the joyful declaration of Psalm 24 that the earth is the Lord's and the fullness thereof. The attitude of the Song of Songs toward sexual love and the very positive attitude toward marriage in the Jewish tradition is in sharp contrast to Gotama's renunciation of the flesh, even if he does put aside the more extreme forms of asceticism. The contrast is still present in the New Testament. Superficially, it might seem that Jesus' renunciation of marriage brings him nearer to Gotama, but this is not really so. The reasons which led Jesus to remain single were of a quite different order. They sprang from an undivided loyalty to the will of the Father in the light of the coming of the Kingdom and the final consummation. That Jesus was not ascetic in Gotama's sense is demonstrated by His presence at the wedding feast in Cana, an incident for which there is no parallel in regard to Gotama. The fact that Jesus came eating and drinking and that He did not found an order of monks or even of celibate clergy distinguishes him sharply from Gotama. Needless to say, Jesus' attitude toward all these questions was determined by His understanding of His relation to God and His view of man as a dependent but free person within that divine-human relationship. The doctrines of karma, rebirth, and the impermanence of the self are not the presuppositions which govern His thinking. The result is that though Jesus in no way underestimates the tragedy and suffering of human existence, He does not on the other hand take this to be the final word about human life, even here and now. The Father cares for the fallen sparrow and for sinful man, and even now men can come under the blessed rule of God and enjoy a joyful and abundant existence, though its complete consummation is still to come. The eschatological perspective of Jesus' teaching does not lead, as Albert Schweitzer once suggested, to an ironic detachment from life in this world. There is, after all, a profound difference between a detachment which springs from the deep conviction that human life derives its meaning from the reality of the Eternal and the Gracious God and the detachment which springs from the view that human existence is basically an evil from which deliverance is to be sought. There is no hint in the Buddhist tradition that Gotama positively valued his marriage as the vehicle for legitimate joys or as the context for the creative experience of parenthood or of family life. We do not need to suggest that he actually despised his family. The point is that it had no positive valuation in the context of his total view of life. The contrast here is very sharp, as is shown by Jeremias' study of Jesus' attitude toward women.[63] Jesus' strong pronouncements about the indissoluble nature of marriage as ordained by God (e.g., Mark 10:9) certainly put Him at a far remove from Gotama. This does not mean that Jesus would never have shown compassion when a marriage breaks down. It does, however, involve a very positive evaluation of marriage in the context of the divine will of which there is no trace in any of the recorded sayings of Gotama. No one can deny the tragic and mysterious interweaving of suffering and joy in human existence, but Gotama never refers to the latter and thereby gives a one-sided view of human life.

2. The Origin of Suffering

For Gotama the origin of suffering lies in craving or grasping (*tanha*), the burning thirst for the things of this world. Again, at first sight, there seem to be significant resemblances between Jesus and Gotama. Jesus had much to say about the need for freedom from unworthy desires and the need to escape from bondage to such. "What comes out of a man defiles a man," and these are debased and perverted desires (Mark 7:20–23). A man must be

---

[63]Jeremias, *New Testament Theology*, I, 223ff.

willing to give up his life, i.e., a false clinging to a self ruled by selfishness, in order to enter the Kingdom.

In both men, therefore, we find this distinction between the false self in bondage to evil desire and the state of release from this bondage to a new bliss of true freedom. But again we must not be deceived by similarity of language. Jesus nowhere suggests that desire as such is evil or that the rooting out of evil desire means the destruction of the self. All He has to say about love of God and love of neighbor would be meaningless if this were the case. A man loses his life to gain it again on the higher level of unselfish devotion to God and his fellow man, but he does not lose his self. He remains a child or a redeemed son in the Father's house.

What was really new in the teaching of Jesus was not its strictness but the emphasis on motive. He clearly broke with the notion of merit in the practice of Pharisaic Judaism.[64] But does Jesus' language about reward simply reintroduce the idea of merit? This again would not be consistent with Jesus' insistence that the disciples must free themselves from the hope of reward in any simple earthly sense, and that when we have done all that we can do, we are still unprofitable servants. Merit looks to human achievement, the disciple of Jesus looks to the faithfulness of God.[65] "The divine forgiveness means God's claim on the life of the one who is forgiven."[66] This is incompatible with the idea of the complete destruction of the self as such, for no person would be left to whom the divine claim could be directed. Gratitude for God's grace, which is the mainspring of Christian action, implies a relationship between God and man, not the disappearance of the second factor in the relationship.

This discussion shows how difficult it is to compare Jesus and Gotama, for their presuppositions are so radically different. Christian discipleship has never aimed at resolving the problem of suffering by the total extinction of desire but by the cleansing and purification of the whole man who remains a man. This seems to be very different from anything the Buddha suggested or intended. We have already noted Trevor Ling's emphasis on the present experience of the man who can become nibbuta in this life, one who here and now has become "cool," who experiences now the quenching of desire. It is true that the man who is nibbuta here and now is still a man in the world. He lives and moves about in the body. Even if his desire for food has been much reduced, he must still eat a minimum if he is to live in this world. Insofar, however, as he is concerned to bring other men to the nibbuta state, his concern is still a kind of desire, indeed a nobly compassionate desire. It

---

[64]*Ibid.*, p. 215.
[65]*Ibid.*, p. 217.
[66]*Ibid.*

could be argued that this introduces an inconsistent element of love for the neighbor into the Buddhist scheme of thought. One could admire Buddha and other nibbuta men for not immediately seeking the final nirvana, the dying away of all the constituents of selfhood. Yet there seems to be a profound difference between the positive outgoing love to the neighbor enjoined upon the Christian on the basis of God's love for all His children and the Buddhist pity for the intolerable lot of men in bondage to the law of karma. Canon Streeter once said, "Where the Buddha was most himself, there he was most like Christ."[67] This must seem intolerably patronizing to the Buddhist, but it is important to see the point that Streeter was concerned to make. The modern Western intellectual who is attracted by the realism and pessimism of Gotama often conveniently forgets the law of karma, which is a basic presupposition of his thought. It is the greatness of Gotama that in spite of this fundamental article of belief "he chose a life of sacrifice and labour to bring suffering humanity his message of salvation."[68] This implies a positive love of neighbor which breaks with the strict logic of the Buddhist worldview, and the Christian should gladly acknowledge this fact. It is Streeter's contention that the deepest divide between Jesus and Gotama lies in the worldviews they inherited, and that when we penetrate behind these to the original moral insights of both men, they become surprisingly close to each other. Both were deeply and passionately concerned for the true welfare of men as they conceived it.

When this has been said, it is still a fact that the difference between the two remains in relation to the nature and reality of God and the importance of the person as a potentially redeemable child of God. There is no way in which the basic presuppositions of their respective worldviews can be reconciled or harmonized. Gotama's agnosticism about a personal Creator, even if interpreted as the mystic's caution about using human language to point to the transcendent, his acceptance of karma and the anatta doctrine of the nonpermanence of the self—all these simply cannot be reconciled with a Christian theism rooted in the Hebraic and Christian view of a living, personal Creator-God who fashioned man for an eternal fellowship of love with Himself. The joy in heaven over one sinner who repents simply does not make sense in the context of the ideas in which Gotama taught and developed his doctrine of nirvana. At this point each man must make his own crucial spiritual choice. In the light of this, it is impossible for the Christian to speak of the divinity of the Buddha where the word "divinity" would make sense.

It is quite true that Christian faith does not give a philosophical explana-

---

[67]B.H. Streeter, *The Buddha and the Christ* (London: Macmillan, 1932), p. 71.
[68]*Ibid.*

tion of the problem of suffering, though Jesus links some suffering with sin. The problem of innocent suffering can hardly emerge at all from a strict Buddhist view. The difficulty with the Christian view is that if all suffering does not stem from human failure and desire, then at least some suffering belongs to the nature of the cosmic process as such. If God is wholly responsible for this, then He seems to be responsible for much undeserved suffering. The Christian faith leaves this an intellectual mystery but offers a practical resolution of the problem in its eschatological hope of the ultimate reign of God which banishes sin and conquers death.[69]

The question, however, can now be raised from the Christian perspective, Why did God allow the rise and flourishing of Buddhism? What will be the fate of millions of Buddhists if the Christian view of God and Christ is valid and true? A number of answers to this problem have been suggested in the course of Christian history. All who have lived and died without a knowledge and confession of the Incarnate Christ as the divine Savior have perished in the sense of being permanently estranged from God. This estrangement has often been interpreted in the context of a doctrine of hell as eternal or everlasting punishment. On this view, all Buddhists past and present will go to hell and there is no more to be said. Such a rigorous view has been and still is held by some Christians.

But many Christians have naturally found it difficult to reconcile this view with the assertion that "God is love." In the early Christian centuries a way out of this difficulty was found in the assertion that the unincarnate Logos was present and active among men before the Word was made flesh. This made it possible for philosophers and virtuous men of the pre-Christian classical civilization to be reckoned as Christians before Christ. We find this in one form in Justin Martyr in the second century:

> And those who lived rationally are Christians even if thought to be atheists, as among the Greeks Socrates and Heraclitus and others like them and among the barbarians Abraham and Ananias and Misael and Elias and many others—but they lived and are living in accordance with reason as Christians and fearless and undisturbed.[70]

Justin was not perhaps as broad-minded as he sounds, since he was concerned primarily to assert Christ's universal influence and authority. Hence Moses was more ancient than the Greeks who got their truth from him. However, the Greeks received their truth from the Logos from which Moses and the prophets also obtained whatever truth they had. In the sixteenth century, Zwingli's broad-mindedness toward pre-Christian men was deter-

---

[69]John Hick, *Evil and the God of Love* (London: Collins, 1968).
[70]Justin, Apology I, 46.

mined by a doctrine of election and predestination which makes election precede conscious faith. Hence God's election could include not only Old Testament saints but such ancient worthies as Hercules, Theseus, Socrates, Aristides, Antigonous, Numa, Camillus, Cato, and the Scipios.[71]

These views are certainly preferable to the first one in their honest attempt to do justice to the mercy and compassion of God who would not reject men merely because of the historical accident that they had not lived to know the Word made flesh in Jesus of Nazareth. Though Justin did not apply his view to Hinduism and Buddhism, of which he knew practically nothing, the logic of his position could have included them, since the unincarnate Logos was active among them as well as among the ancient Greeks and Romans. The theological weakness of this point of view, from the perspective of Christian orthodoxy, which made the divinity of Christ central, was that it suggested the possibility of salvation apart from a conscious relationship to Jesus Christ.

Another way to resolve this problem was suggested by Origen with his vision of a cosmos totally redeemed from evil when the final Kingdom of God is established as the present cosmic order reaches its fulfilment in God. Origen does not assume a series of rebirths governed by karma in the Hindu and Buddhist sense, but he does allow room for the purification and redemption of all souls after death. Though again Origen does not apply this explicitly to our problem, the logic of his vision implies an answer to it. Buddhists would continue to pass through this redemptive and purifying process until they too arrive at the true vision of God in the Christian sense and acknowledge Christ as the saving Mediator of that vision. The theological attractiveness of this view is that it does relate the total historical process to the final fulfilment of the divine purpose through Christ. At the same time, it leaves open the possibility that those who have died without a knowledge of the incarnate Word will have the chance to know the glorified divine-human Savior and be reconciled to God through Him when it pleases God to bring the present order of the world to an end.

On what basis, then, can we select among these three options? If what we have already said about the divinity of Christ is a valid deduction from what Christian faith is constrained to say about Jesus of Nazareth, then it follows that salvation from a Christian perspective, however defined, cannot be realized apart from a relationship to the God-man. In other words, Christianity must reject a God-mysticism which regards Christ as a useful ladder of spiritual ascent which can be kicked away when the goal is reached. Both in time and in eternity Christ remains the indispensable Mediator of our

---

[71]Zwingli, *Works* IV, 55 (8 vols., ed. by Schuler & Schulthess, Zurich, 1828ff.).

reconciliation with God. In the light of this, however, what of all those both in B.C. and A.D. who have not known the incarnate Christ? What of the Buddhist who has been nurtured in Buddhism and lived his whole life in that religious and cultural context? What of Gotama himself? It seems incredible that the God whom Jesus revealed, the God of the shepherd heart who seeks the one lost sheep, the God who in Jesus submitted to the Cross to bring about the deliverance of men, would condemn millions of Buddhists to eternal separation from Himself simply because in their earthly life they were Buddhists. Even less believable is the idea that He would condemn them to eternal punishment, however crude or refined are the symbols in which this doctrine is expressed. I have argued elsewhere that the doctrine of eternal punishment is not as firmly rooted in the teaching of Jesus as many have maintained.

If this is the case, then in discussing the destiny of Buddhists, we shall have to choose Justin's version of the unincarnate Logos or Origen's version of an eschatological redemption of the whole cosmos. This is not to say that we can accept the total cosmological scheme as outlined by Origen in the *De Principiis* and his other writings. Christian theology cannot be bound to Origen's conception of salvation as a return of the soul to a preexistent sinless state. There is indeed in Origen an unresolved tension between this idea of a predetermined cyclic process and his strong emphasis upon the reality of human freedom. "For if man is predetermined to a pre-existent state, then indeed God does not take man's freedom very seriously, nor need man take it too seriously."[72] What is valid in Origen's vision is his defence of human freedom, coupled with his view that the final fulfilment of the divine purpose must somehow be related to the whole of mankind, past, present, and future and not simply to a select number of people in a *Heilsgeschichte* which would exclude all Buddhists, for example, from even the possibility of sitting down in the Kingdom with God's redeemed people.

What are the implications of all this for such theological concepts as universalism (i.e., the ultimate universal salvation of all men), the notion of unconscious Christianity, the idea of conversion, and the missionary enterprise of the Christian church? Arnold Toynbee has argued powerfully and persuasively for a symphonic harmony of the higher religions—Hinduism, Buddhism, Islam, and Christianity—rather than the exclusive claim to truth of any one of them. He sees Christianity as tainted with an intolerance and an arrogance inherited from its Jewish past. He quotes with approval the saying of the pagan Symmachus, contemporary with Ambrose, that "the heart of so

---

[72]William Thompson, "The Doctrine of Hell," *The Ecumenist,* Vol. 10, No. 3 (March/April 1972).

great a mystery can never be reached by following one road only."[73] Christianity must, therefore, surrender its exclusiveness, and this implies the surrender of any Christology which would imply any exclusive claim for the uniqueness of Christ as the one and only way to salvation. To make this outrageous claim, as Toynbee sees it, would be to assert that the spiritual goal of all mankind can be attained only by "one arbitrarily favoured portion of mankind that happened to be psychologically equipped for following this particular spiritual path."[74]

Toynbee is obviously attacking more than a doctrine of hell as applied to non-Christians. He is rejecting outright the claim that men can find their way to God in the fullest and truest sense only through Christ. It is to be assumed, therefore, that Toynbee would reject a universalist view which makes it possible for all men, including Buddhists, eventually to come to God through Christ. Even this would for him seem to be intolerable arrogance. He seems to be saying that the true goal for mankind can be reached as effectively and truly through the Buddha as through Christ. Our comparative study of Gotama and Jesus has shown the difficulty of accepting this view. The true goal of mankind is not the same for these two religious figures, as we have seen. They differ fundamentally in their understanding of both God and man. The Christian does not have to denigrate Gotama in order to make his point. He does not have to despise the Buddha's nobility or his compassion. He does have to question the ultimate truth of the Buddha's vision of a nirvana divorced from the reality of a loving, personal, and gracious God.

It is still possible for a Christian to see in the other higher religions a foreshadowing of the truth as it is in Christ, even to see in Buddha up to a point a preparation for the gospel. Nor does he have to say with Barth that the non-Christian religions are always a human seeking but never a finding of even partial truth about the real God. The doctrine of the divinity of Christ, as we have expounded it, does leave open the door for an activity of the God and Father of our Lord Jesus Christ, even prior to the Word becoming flesh. But it is the activity of the God who became man in Jesus. It is not the activity of a God other than the One whom Christ fully disclosed.

This raises some crucial points about conversion. Much discussion has taken place in recent years in W.C.C. gatherings about proselytism, the attempt to win Christians from one church allegiance to another. This has been condemned by some as a sin against the true ecumenical spirit, as a refusal to accept members of other churches as Christians. Others defend proselytism on the grounds that a Christian must commend the truth as he

---

[73]Arnold Toynbee, *A Study of History,* Vol. 7B: *Universal Churches* (New York: Oxford Univ. Press, 1963), p. 442.
[74]*Ibid.,* p. 443.

sees it, and since it is not possible to reconcile all statements made by all churches, there may come a point when he has to deny some version of Christian truth held by others and to seek to win others to what he considers to be a more adequate version of Christian truth. It is difficult to deny that this stance can make out a strong case for itself. Nonetheless, we are working our way, painfully at times, toward accepting the view that it is possible to differ theologically without denying the name Christian or the reality of Christian experience to those from whom we differ. If this more gracious and tolerant understanding is possible between Christians of differing ecclesiastical allegiance, why not the same between Christians and those who are members of the non-Christian religions? This is the crux.

This brings us back to conversion and what this means for a follower of Jesus. If the conversion of a Buddhist meant that he must accept Western culture, habits, clothes, thought-forms, language, etc., then it goes without saying that this would be Christian Western imperialism of the worst kind. If it meant that the Buddhist must regard his whole Buddhist tradition and culture as sheer error and superstition in the light of his Christian conversion, this too would be a demand difficult to justify. Here again, however, we do well to remember H. Kraemer's point that a living religion is an integral organic whole and not merely a detached set of ideas offered for intellectual acceptance.[75]

What, then, would be involved in the conversion of a Buddhist to Christianity? Certainly, on any definition of the meaning of conversion, it is more than the substitution of one set of ideas for another. Conversion is the turning of the whole man away from self to God. Nevertheless, though this is not merely an intellectual process, it does involve some change of ideas. It is not necessary at this stage to emphasize the variety of conversion experiences when examined from the psychological point of view after the manner of William James and his successors. Whether conversion is sudden and dramatic or more gradual is not the crucial question. Nor is the question which elements of the psyche happen to be predominant in any particular case. There may be, and undoubtedly are, many different psychological paths by which a man may turn from self to God. The fundamental theological question concerns the nature of the "God" to whom he is turning.

The assumption behind Arnold Toynbee's hope for a harmonious symphony of the living higher religions seems to be the essential oneness of the reality to which they are tending. Since all human language is inadequate to express the nature of that ultimate goal, it must be recognized that the vast

---

[75]See Hendrik Kraemer, *The Christian Message in a non-Christian World* (London: Edinburgh House, 1938) and *World Cultures and World Religions* (London: Lutterworth, 1960).

variety of symbols and analogies employed are only veils through which men can penetrate, if only partially, to the mysterious reality on which we all depend. Any exclusive claim made by any of the higher religions for their symbols or the finality of their language must be rejected. When this is acknowledged, the way is then open for each of these religions to have a tolerant understanding of the goal of the others. Furthermore, they must recognize that the reality of which their experience is a partial apprehension can never be exhaustively expressed in human language and its various symbols, analogies, or models. This means that there can be no "theology," i.e., no definitive intellectual articulation of the knowledge given in and through the religious experience. This is Toynbee's way of overcoming the conflict between heart and head which he sees as the supreme issue confronting modern men. Only when this reconciliation has been achieved can the human race look forward with confidence to peace both political and religious and continue the path of creative spiritual advance already exemplified in the higher religions.

Attractive as this solution sounds, its fundamental weakness is that it still leaves us with a conflict between heart and head. By opting for an essential mystical experience behind the intuitions of all the higher religions and by denying any theological or intellectual articulation of that experience in norms which the intellect can recognize as true, we are put in the position of having no criteria for discriminating between various kinds of religious experience. The more we insist on the ineffable, mystical experience underlying the symbols and analogies of language, the more impossible it would seem to know what we are talking about. In fact, we ought not to talk about it at all.

As this bears upon our special problem, namely the comparison of Jesus and Gotama and the experience which they presumably had of the nature of reality, all we could say, on Toynbee's premises, would be that both men experienced the same reality, however diverse and mutually contradictory is the linguistic symbolism in which they tried to articulate it. How we can know that the basic experience is identical or even similar when all linguistic interpretation has been eliminated or relegated to very secondary importance is hard to tell. It would hardly be possible without writing another book even to begin to explore all the problems connected with experience and its linguistic interpretation in symbol and analogy. In our earlier discussion of Jesus and dogma we rejected the idea that a "pure" experience can somehow be completely disentangled from all intellectual articulation in human language. On the other hand, we have conceded that all human symbolism is inadequate to the reality of the God to whom the symbols point. We can only use qualified "models," to adopt Ian Ramsey's terminology. Nevertheless, we can never dispense with the models nor can we evade the difficult questions concerning the degree of truth and adequacy of the respective models we employ. Nor is it possible to employ an endless variety of models, some of which appear directly in conflict or contradiction with others. This is to reintroduce the conflict between head and heart about which Toynbee has had so much to say. Of course, we can say with Professor W.T. Stace, in his brilliant book *Mysticism and Philosophy,* that the logical principle of noncontradiction can no longer be applied in our evaluation of the mystical experience: "What the paradoxes show is that, although the laws of logic are the laws of our everyday consciousness and experience, they have no application to mystical experience."[76] The best we can do is to say that mysticism is nonlogical or superlogical or transcends logic. As applied to our problem, this means that although Gotama rejected the idea of the living Creator-God while Jesus affirmed it on the basis of His Jewish experience, both men were in fact experiencing the same reality. Their models and linguistic symbols were radically different, but the experience implies a reality which transcends both sets of symbols.

The difficulties with this view are enormous, and it is doubtful whether either Buddhist or Christian can be finally content with it. The Christian at least cannot rest in the position as long as he wants to affirm the reality of God as made known in Christ. He is not free to use any kind of linguistic symbols or none at all. If he does so, the reality itself seems to evaporate and leave him with the ineffable and the intangible. Certainly, to affirm the divinity of Christ is by that very act to opt for certain models rather than others. It is to introduce a selection of certain symbols as more appropriate than others to point to the God experienced. However sympathetic or tolerant he may be, the Christian has no option but to say at this point that these other symbols will not do. Not to say this would be to make nonsense of our understanding of God who became man in Jesus of Nazareth.

This means that experience and interpretation cannot in the last analysis be separated, even if one recognizes that in some instances the interpretation may be a misinterpretation or a misreading of the experience. The interpretation in language, symbol, analogy, and model is not a mere additional factor which can be eliminated without loss. It is an integral part of any understanding of the experience itself. Our problem is easy to solve if we are content to talk of "bliks" (Hare) or purely personal perspectives. It becomes acute the moment we want to speak about the truth of a particular vision of reality, and therefore to make metaphysical assertions. The writer is well aware of the bad associations of the word "metaphysics" in some

---

[76]Stace, *Mysticism and Philosophy,* p. 270.

philosophical and religious circles today. The Christian will readily admit that there has been and still is bad metaphysics, just as there has been bad religion. It is quite another thing to dismiss altogether either religion or metaphysics because of the possibility for perversion. Professor H.H. Price has put the matter forcibly from the theistic point of view. The theist, he maintains, is not simply commending a certain way of "seeing" the facts of human life.

> He is doing more, whether he likes it or not. He is making assertions. He does not merely propose that we make use of the concept of a creative and loving Supreme Being. He asserts that this concept has an instance, that there actually is a Supreme Being who created the world, that He actually is infinite in power, wisdom and goodness, and moreover that he actually does love every single person whom he has created.[77]

A Christian theism can hardly say less without reducing both the concept and the reality of God to the vanishing point. If this is so, then it is difficult to maintain that Jesus and Gotama were mediating the same truth to men.

It is, of course, possible to argue that Gotama was neither an agnostic nor an atheist, but that in fact he did approximate to the Christian view of the transcendent reality on which man depends. One can also try to show that in some forms of Hinduism or of Mahayana Buddhism there are very close approximations to the Christian idea of a gracious and caring God. We need to be clear, however, that when we do this, we are assuming that we already have a concept of God which is more than a concept but has an instance, to use Price's language. It is in the light of this concept that we are able to talk about approximations. Furthermore, this concept has not come to us through the distillation of certain common elements taken from all the higher religions. We have received it from the Christian experience mediated through Jesus of Nazareth as "truly man and truly God." We confess God to be such because we confess Jesus to be the truest embodiment of the presence and activity of the One creative and loving God. If this is intolerance, then the Christian will have to bear the charge as best he can. On the other hand, the more the Christian embodies the spirit of the One he declares to be divine, the less will the non-Christian feel that the God revealed is the instrument of a merely transient imperialism of whatever kind. The non-Christian can bring all the treasures of his religion and culture and lay them at the feet of the Christ, knowing that nothing that is of true worth in them will be rejected by Him.

An interesting approach to this same issue is found in *The Structure of*

---

[77]H.H. Price, *Belief* (London: Allen & Unwin, 1969), p. 460.

Christian Existence, by Professor John Cobb, Jr.[78] Cobb does not wish to take his stand at precisely the same point as Toynbee, for he wants to claim some kind of finality or normativeness for Christian existence. His use of the word "existence" is meant, among other things, to emphasize the fact that the differences between the great world religions are not simply a matter of ideas. For those who are active participants in the life of the great religions, a new mode of existence and a new way of life for the whole man are involved. "The major religions and cultures of mankind embody different structures of existence, and that is the deepest and the most illuminating way to view their differences."[79] Cobb contends further that just as with the rise of man "a major threshold was crossed, not only biologically but also existentially or psychically,"[80] so with the great religions a threshold was crossed which resulted in a new mode of existence. Given his adopted terminology, therefore, Cobb is able to select several historical periods at which a threshold was passed and a new structure of existence emerged. His list includes civilized existence, Axial existence, Buddhist existence, Homeric existence, Socratic existence, Christian existence. In chapter twelve, however, Cobb considers the "Question of Finality." After his interesting and always illuminating phenomenology or description of the different structures of existence, he now raises the question of norms. He obviously is not content simply to list them as live options always available for different sorts of men, even in the contemporary world. He wants to evaluate the structures from a "Christian perspective." This has been our concern too in our attempted comparison of Jesus and Gotama.

If, says Cobb, some kind of finality is to be claimed for Jesus Christ, then the structure of existence brought into being by Him "must be shown to be final in some humanly decisive way."[81] If Christian agape love is taken as normative, then we cannot say that it is higher than Buddhist love since the Christian can think of no higher kind of love than that of the Boddhisattva "who renounces his own final blessedness for the sake of the world."[82] We have already noted the paradox involved in the contrast between Gotama's doctrine in the strict sense and the way in which he consents to continue to live out of deep concern for men.

The real issue between Christianity and Buddhism, however, cannot be summed up simply in the one question of whether Christian love is higher than Buddhist love. We may still ask whether love means the same thing in

---

[78]J.B. Cobb, Jr., *The Structure of Christian Existence* (London: Lutterworth, 1968).
[79]*Ibid.,* p. 19.
[80]*Ibid.,* p. 21.
[81]*Ibid.,* p. 139.
[82]*Ibid.,* p. 138.

these two different religious contexts. Cobb himself admits "that Buddhist love differs from Christian love in that the Buddhist lover is not a self and consequently makes no distinction between lover and beloved, whereas Christian love is that of a self for other selves.''[83] Yet this is a distinction of enormous importance, as we have already contended, and produçes two different structures of existence, to use Cobb's language. Furthermore, the distinction between Christian and Buddhist love is not simply between two ideals of love, neither of which has been effectively realized between man and man in this life. For the Christian, agape love is not simply an ideal waiting to be realized in human lives. It is already the deepest present reality because God is this kind of love. Josiah Royce's remark, quoted by John E. Smith, has an application here: "The man who has only morality is like the man who serves the ideal master who is forever in a far country.''[84] The man who knows agape love only as a distant and as yet unrealized ideal is in a very different situation from the man who believes that he can have even now, and in spite of his sin, fellowship with a God who *is* love.

Cobb is concerned, and rightly, to emphasize that such love has never been actualized fully in a human existence with the possible exception of Jesus. When he says, "The claim for the finality of Christian existence is not a claim that any mode of its embodiment now or in the past is final," Cobb is presumably referring to imperfect Christians and not to Jesus Himself, though this is not always made clear. Yet any claim to the normative and final quality of the structure of existence derived from Jesus would seem to depend upon some doctrine of the reality of the divine love and its complete embodiment in Jesus. Can we go this far, however, without being involved again in some kind of Christology or divinity? Cobb evidently fears that all such doctrines of the deity of Jesus only put unwarranted obstacles in the way of the acceptance of Jesus by His fellow Jews. He says that if the acceptance of the finality of Jesus can be dissociated from the acceptance of particular dogmas about Him, "the obstacles to a full appropriation of Jesus and of spiritual existence would be still further diminished.''[85] Thus, we should not expect a mass conversion of Jews but an inner transformation of Judaism.

Yet what is the finality of Jesus but a dogma and a startling and far-reaching one at that? If the Jew seriously came to accept the finality of Jesus in this sense, would this not compel him to a drastic reevaluation of Judaism itself—not necessarily a total repudiation of his Jewish heritage, which there is no evidence that Jesus would have demanded, but certainly a rethinking and reassessment of Judaism about a new center. Have we any

---

[83]*Ibid.*, p. 139.

[84]Smith, *Reason and God*, p. 202.

[85]Cobb, *Christian Existence*, p. 142.

reason to think that the Jew would find it easier to accept the finality of Jesus in this sense than the dogma of His divinity as developed by Christians? It would hardly seem so.

The laudable desire to purge Christian attitudes of unworthy elements in regard to the Jewish people should not blind us to the fact that Jesus demands of both Jew and Gentile a radical reinterpretation of the way God deals with men. There is no place for arrogant claims of personal or ecclesiastical superiority over the Jew. It is another question whether both Jew and Gentile should confess that all have fallen short of the glory of God and that we are all saved, if at all, not by our religious achievements but by the gracious and justifying love of God.

The basic weakness in Cobb's handling of his theme in terms of existence is that it easily tends to push the God question into the background. The advantage of his method is that it anchors religious doctrines of all kinds in the transformation of actual human existence. It cannot, however, bear the whole weight which Cobb seems to want to put upon it. If he wants us to take with utter seriousness, as he does, the "finality of Jesus," then it seems impossible to avoid the long and agonizing attempt of the Christian church to articulate this in some satisfactory doctrine. Certainly, human language never exhausts the mystery, but it must at least point as unambiguously as possible to the Jesus whom faith discovers to be final in all that vitally pertains to man's reconciliation with God and the new human existence which derives from it.

13.
What Difference Does It Make?

For some people the kind of investigation we have undertaken in this book seems remote and irrelevant to their personal lives and actions. Naturally, the nonbeliever will feel this to be the case. What is more important for our immediate purpose is that many Christians themselves feel like this. This final chapter, therefore, will be devoted to the relationship between theological confession on the one side and Christian devotion and action on the other.

Karl Marx once said that the business of the philosopher is not to understand the world but to change it. One might, of course, ask whether a true understanding of the world can ever leave a man's attitude and action unchanged. Can theory and practice in fact be as completely divorced as Marx's remark would suggest? It is difficult to imagine a really convinced Platonist not being influenced in his life and practice by the view he takes as to the nature of things, as to where "reality" is to be found. For such a man as Spinoza, philosophy was evidently a way of life as well as a way of understanding the world. One could argue ad infinitum whether a philosophy shapes a man's attitude and action or whether a temperamental inclination to take a certain attitude determines his understanding. The answer would seem to be: both. Professor Hodges has rightly insisted that "one thing which emerges clearly from all this discussion is that the determinants of belief lie at least as much in the region of character as in that of intelligence."[1] Marx, however, and many of the existentialists since, were attacking a kind of intellectual detachment which seemed to encourage a certain toying with ideas without any serious attempt to relate such ideas to the way in which men actually live and the decisions they have to make. Against this background it would have to be said that Christianity is not only a way of understanding but a way of action involving radical transformation

---

[1]H.A. Hodges, *Languages, Standpoints and Attitudes,* Riddell Memorial Lectures (London: Oxford Univ. Press, 1953), p. 65.

of the individual personality, and, as a consequence, of the way in which men seek to live together. Perhaps it would be more accurate to say that the Christian is concerned with action because God is acting to bring about change in the world. Whitehead once said that Christianity is first and foremost a religion in search of a metaphysic, not a metaphysic generating a religion.[2] Nevertheless, this distinction between theory and practice cannot be pushed too far. Just as Marxist action is determined by a certain understanding of the nature of the universe and man's history within it, so Christian action is determined by the way Christians understand God's nature and action and what He is seeking to do in the world.

Let us, then, turn to the bearing of this issue upon the Christological problem with which we have been concerned. What difference does it make whether men confess Jesus as "truly divine" or not? If it made no practical discernible difference in life and action, then it is unlikely that anyone would continue to be much interested in it as a merely academic question. Christians on the whole have always believed that it did make a difference, and the passion generated by the early Christological debates shows that more than a speculative question was involved. The vigorous discussion as to whether Jesus was only like God (*homoiousios*) or of the very "essence" of God might appear to a sceptic like Gibbon to be a futile debate about a diphthong. Certainly Christians did not view it this way and the reason was surely that more was involved than one intellectual theory as against another. Rightly or wrongly, it was felt to involve profound issues which not only shaped men's thinking in the abstract but determined whether a man could be rescued in practice from the power of sin, guilt, and death, and therefore actually live his life in a manner radically different from the way in which he would have lived it otherwise. The problem we raise, therefore, is whether there is a relation between theological confession and the sort of human beings we are and the way we act. This is more than the question discussed in Chapter One as to whether a sharp dichotomy can be justified between religion and theology, or between nondogmatic religion and religion involving dogma. We saw that it is impossible to accept such a sharp distinction. There is no religion, however simple, which does not involve some ideas, however unsophisticated and undeveloped these ideas may be. The question we raise now involves this issue but goes a step further. It asks how the theological dogmas actually determine the total existence of the man who holds them, with all that this involves for the quality of personal existence and the kind of action which flows from a transformed personality.

To answer this kind of question demands an analysis of faith or belief

---

[2]Whitehead, *Religion in the Making*, pp. 39–40.

and an attempt to see what role is actively played by theological ideas in the act of faith. A certain semantic confusion needs to be clarified at the start. Are "faith" and "belief" interchangeable terms or do these words suggest significantly different nuances or shades of meaning? As popularly used, faith is probably understood as a certain kind of trust in a person, whereas belief for many connotes the mental assent to certain theological propositions. One has faith in Jesus Christ but one believes in the Nicene or the Athanasian creed. The prejudice against dogma often springs from the assumption, often unexamined, that it is feasible to give some kind of intellectual assent to a theological statement without that act of personal trust and commitment which makes a real difference to life and action.

It is no doubt possible to give a kind of assent to the Nicene creed which makes absolutely no difference to the way in which a man lives. Obviously such an assent could not be called a "conviction," for the latter implies that a man is conquered by the truth and feels a strong urge to submit to its sway. A man might assent to the Nicene creed for psychological and sociological reasons. He is, for example, a member of the Church of England. He is perhaps only a nominal member, an infrequent worshipper, an irregular communicant. Nevertheless, since his church stands for Christianity in a way which to this man may be rather vague but yet real, he still wishes to consider himself as a Christian and a churchman. He himself would find it difficult to say how far social class, culture, and religious conviction combine in this attitude. Since the Nicene creed belongs to his church's confession, he would not think of questioning its truth, although he might be completely puzzled and inarticulate if challenged to say exactly what it meant and whether he believed it. As a loyal but not very active member of the church, he gives his assent to it. In such a case, we might say that his assent is more or less formal only, though even here it is not easy to determine the indirect influence of his assent upon his conduct. To the extent that as an Anglican he inherits a certain scale of values which are rooted in the Christian past, his present conduct is in part determined by his assent, even if it is limited to the belief that he ought to act like a Christian gentleman. What believing the Nicene creed has to do with acting like a gentleman might be obscure to him, though he might feel fairly sure that if he cut himself off completely from the church, his scale of values would in some real sense be altered and for the worse.

This example from an English context depends very much for its point upon the local English situation, where church and state, culture and religion, religious and social values, have been subtly mingled for generations. Something similar, however, might be true of many men and women nurtured in countries where the Roman or the Orthodox churches have dominated for centuries and shaped the life and culture of whole peoples. In North America, where the state church is not known and where this fusion between religion and culture is not nearly as complete, the situation is very different. Certainly, in many Protestant churches and sects the individual may have been brought up so strictly that he gives his mental assent to certain dogmas because he is afraid to do otherwise. This would seem, however, to be less and less true in a religiously pluralist society, even in those churches with strong theological and liturgical traditions. It becomes more and more difficult to answer with confidence our question concerning the relation of dogma to conduct. Inasmuch as North American Christianity has become more and more assimilated to what has been loosely called "the American way of life," the difficulty is compounded. When the life styles of Christian and non-Christian often seem indistinguishable, it is a natural deduction that whatever people say they believe theologically, such belief has a minimal effect upon conduct. Even so, it is dangerous to generalize. Perhaps there are still areas of conduct and practice where Christians act differently from non-Christians because they are Christians and hold certain views about the nature of reality and the goal or purpose of human life. One obvious difference is the attendance at public worship, however conventional the critic considers this to be. In sensitiveness to moral demands and the claims of compassion and justice, it is more difficult to decide. Obviously Christians do not have a monopoly of these moral values. More to the point at the moment is the question whether Christians are influenced by their beliefs about God and Christ in regard to their concern for justice and compassion, or whether they draw their inspiration, when it exists at all, from some undefined humanitarian impulse which owes little or nothing to distinctively Christian convictions. To return, however, to our particular concern: while it is no doubt true that some people still assent to theological doctrines on the basis of authority and tradition, their number must be far less than in some previous ages and is probably diminishing at least in Western society. Our problem here is to discover the relationship of belief to practice where the assent is a significant and meaningful acceptance of certain theological truths, namely that God exists and that Jesus Christ is divine or truly God.

We are greatly indebted to Professor H.H. Price's analysis of all the varied facets of belief in his Gifford Lectures, published as *Belief*. No one can read this perceptive book without a much clearer understanding of the complexity of a subject which seems at first sight so simple. The reader is urged to consider carefully the many examples given by Price of the way in which the words "belief" and "believing" are used in both secular and religious contexts. For our purposes, we shall use certain terms in certain ways and try to be consistent in our use. Faith for us includes both the total commitment of a person in trust and assent to certain theological truths. It would seem impossible to have trust in something or someone about which or whom one "knows" absolutely nothing at all. One might have faith in God while admitting that the mystery of the Godhead in its fullness is beyond the complete comprehension of any finite mind. On the other hand, one could hardly put one's trust in a God about whose character and purpose nothing was known at all. All faith, therefore, in our sense presupposes some knowledge and thus some assent to theological truths, however implicit or intellectually undeveloped these truths may be. In Price's language, faith is both a "believing in" and a "believing that."[3] Price also shows that given our customary use of language, it is not possible to confine "believe in" to a person, whether human or divine, and "believe that" to a proposition. In ordinary language we "believe in" institutions and causes as well as in persons. Sometimes "believe in" turns out on analysis to be a form of "believing that," where the element of trust in the sense above is nonexistent. On the other hand, a person may believe in a theory, even when the theory is not conclusively proved and when it is acknowledged to possess unresolved paradoxes.[4] There does seem to be a merely formal or factual belief in, an existentialist belief in, as when we say "I believe in British Railways" or "I believe in the American Constitution" or "I believe in the Canadian form of Federal Government." These statements are not simply reducible to "believing that" in the sense of declaring that there exist such realities as British trains or an American or Canadian Constitution. "Something like esteeming or trusting is an essential part of 'belief' in this sense,"[5] even though a person is not in these cases the object of trust.

Applying this to faith in the religious sense, all these elements seem to be combined. Faith does involve "believing that" in the sense that something or someone is real or "exists" in the sense intended. God is real and Jesus is real and the fact that Jesus is divine is a statement about what He is, not merely about what I think He is. Yet more than affirmations about existence is involved. Esteeming or trusting is also an essential element, and where the existential statements are about a "personal" fact, whether God or man, trust then comes into play. We prefer, therefore, to use the word "faith" in the comprehensive sense to indicate the assent to statements about the reality or existence of the object of faith as well as the trust which the object of faith evokes when that object is considered to be personal. This definition of faith can be defended on the grounds that this is how men of faith interpret their attitude and state of mind. Whatever the sceptic says, and

[3]Price, *Belief,* Lecture 9, pp. 426ff.
[4]*Ibid.,* p. 431.
[5]*Ibid.,* p. 436.

even if faith is wishful thinking from the external standpoint of the critic who lacks faith in this sense, the fact remains that for the man of faith, he is asserting both the reality of God and his own personal trust in Him. Our definition does not imply that the religious man's faith is validated simply by the assertion that this is how he understands faith. On the other hand, if we are to consider whether faith is valid in the sense of trust in an extra-mental reality, God, then there is obvious merit in defining faith as it is understood by men of faith and not faith as arbitrarily defined by the detached scholar.

Having defined faith in this sense, we shall use the word "belief" primarily to denote those propositions which purport to make true statements about the object of faith, in this case God and Jesus Christ. "Belief," therefore, will for us always indicate assent to dogma, interpreted as theological and doctrinal statements which make affirmations, claimed as true, about such realities as God or about Jesus as "truly God." In the light of this definition of terms, it makes sense to ask whether one can have belief without faith, or faith without belief. We have already contended that it is not possible to have faith without belief of some kind. But can one have belief, in the sense of assent to theological doctrines, without faith? To a limited extent our answer to this has been Yes. It is possible to assent to doctrines for cultural, psychological, sociological, and traditional reasons without such assent resulting in faith in the comprehensive sense above defined.

The issue can be stated in other terms. How do we pass from a merely "notional" assent to a "real" assent, where real means that in addition to accepting the true propositions about the nature and reality of God, one at the same time experiences with the whole being a vivid sense of the present reality of the God about whom such statements are being made? It is well known that this distinction between "notional" and "real" assent was first made by Cardinal Newman in his *Grammar of Assent*.[6] Again we are indebted to H.H. Price for his careful analysis of what Newman meant by this distinction.[7]

To deal with this difficult question of faith and practice, it is imperative to free ourselves from the temporal parochialism which concentrates exclusively on the contemporary world. We need to look at the history of Christianity as a whole. Can we see certain distinctive qualities of life and action which emerge again and again in Christian history and which appear to be rooted in Christian faith as above defined? That Christian history has been marred by all too human failures and sins is not at issue here. This is true of all religions. The question is, Can we discern amid the confusion of

---

[6]J.H. Newman, *Grammar of Assent* (New York: Doubleday, 1955).
[7]Price, *Belief,* Series II, Lecture 6; Series II, Lecture 5.

human self-will and pride the emergence of Christian character such that it would be inconceivable apart from the basic belief which Christians hold?

Our thesis has been that Jesus of Nazareth has so impressed men as to compel them to talk "divinity" language about Him, even if they have used many models to do this—Messiah, Logos, Son of God, preexistence, descent and ascent, *homoousios,* "very God of very God," etc. Was the instinct of Christian men sound at this point? In using these models, they were not merely entertaining propositions about Him. They were not merely holding certain notions or concepts. They were giving real assent in the sense that they believed they were talking about realities, namely God and Jesus Christ as the Word of God who became man. They had faith in the sense in which we have defined it, i.e., belief as the affirmation of truths and trust as the proper response to God in Christ about whom these affirmations were being made. The problem with which we are grappling in this chapter is what difference does it make to have "faith" in this sense? Are behavior, action, attitude, etc. vitally affected by such faith? If the answer to this is Yes, then it is no longer possible to treat dogma or doctrine as an abstraction which can be eliminated while leaving Christian character and action intact. Faith without belief is then itself an abstraction. One cannot, as Dean Inge once said, have the Christian fruits (Galatians 5:22–25) without the roots, where roots are the realities of God and Jesus Christ in which the Christian life is anchored. To treat Jesus as only man will in practice produce a different attitude toward life and death, toward God and man than if one confesses Him to be divine in the sense of Christian faith. To see Jesus only as man, even extraordinary man, leaves men without the confidence that God is real and in control of His world. Jesus remains as the revealer of the potentialities of human nature, but not of the reality of the grace and power of God. This is not to say that to accept such a humanist view of Jesus makes no difference at all to the way in which a man lives and acts. A man may deny the divinity of Jesus in the sense intended by the creeds and confessions of the church and still regard Him as the most noble expression to date of what man might be. If a man is serious in so regarding Him, it is obviously going to affect his values and the way in which he acts towards other men. There have been notable examples of men who have dedicated themselves to live in the spirit of Jesus but who would not confess His divinity. One thinks of Albert Schweitzer, perhaps some of the so-called radical theologians such as Van Buren, Hamilton, and Altizer, the strange figure of Simone Weil, or even Mahatma Gandhi reading his New Testament every day but certainly not confessing the divinity. All these have been profoundly influenced by the spirit of Jesus, though all would repudiate the classical dogmas. For some this will only reinforce the argument that if such admirable people can be in one sense disciples of Jesus without confessing His divinity, then does it really matter? In fact, let us have more humanist disciples of this kind rather than orthodox believers who often seem less sensitive and compassionate and less admirable people in general. Such a reaction is natural, but it cannot be taken at face-value. More needs to be said.

Others, however, would contest our earlier statement that to see Jesus only as man is to leave us without confidence in God. Surely, it will be urged, it is possible to accept what Jesus taught about God and trust in such a God without affirming that He was "truly God" in the sense of the Christian creeds. The modern Unitarian could reason in this way. So in fact could the orthodox Jew. One does not have to reject all that Jesus says about God when one rejects the Christian claim as to His divinity.

To be scrupulously fair, it must be conceded that this is so, as the lives of both Jews and Unitarians show. One can repudiate divinity and still exalt Jesus as a revealer of God. Nevertheless, it is still a real question why one should trust Jesus as revealer of God in this absolute and unique sense if He is only one man among many, even if a particularly noble one. To justify the central position still given to Jesus, one would have to maintain at the very least that He had a unique and unparalleled insight into the nature of God. Yet to go this far is already to have qualified to a significant degree the claim that Jesus can be accounted for as only a very eminent human representative of the potentialities of men for some awareness of the reality and nature of God. The revealer and what is revealed cannot be so easily separated. Donald Baillie has pointed out that if the God we know in Jesus is essentially a seeking and redeeming God and if Jesus is a trustworthy revealer of such a God, then His total life and ministry is in fact the showing forth of the essential nature and reality of God in active redeeming love. Jesus is not only a symbol which points to the divine love. He *is* the divine love in action. "If Jesus is right in what He reported, if God is really such as Jesus said, then we are involved in saying more about Jesus Himself and His relation to God, and we must pass beyond words like 'discovery' and even 'revelation' to words like 'incarnation.' "[8] In other words, we are on the threshold of confessing His divinity.

Let us return for a moment, however, to the humanist view. By "humanist" is here meant a view of Jesus which excludes from consideration the idea of God as well as the divinity of Jesus. Examples of those holding such a position would be Julian Huxley,[9] Albert Schweitzer,[10] and

[8]Donald Baillie, *God was in Christ,* p. 64.

[9]Julian Huxley, *Religion Without Revelation* (London: Watts, 1967).

[10]Albert Schweitzer, *Civilization and Ethics,* trans. John Naish (London: A. & C. Black, 1923) and *My Life and Thought,* trans. C.T. Campion (London: Allen & Unwin, 1933).

the "God-is-dead" theologians, where this slogan is intended to describe not only a mood or a sense of the absence of God, but a denial that God "is."[11] Some forms of mysticism could be added to this list.[12] Such a humanist view of Jesus cannot talk consistently of God as Creator and Redeemer. If there is such a reality as holy love (agape), it is only the love of man for man, even in the special case of Jesus. In the same way, the rest of the Christian language must be translated into terms which exclude God if the humanist is to be really consistent. A particularly interesting attempt has been made by Father Gregory Baum to show that all language about God can be translated into language about man.[13] It is obviously not the intention of Baum to embrace the kind of humanism described above, though he has some difficulty in carrying through his basic thesis without giving this impression. However, our point, we believe, remains valid. The consistent humanist cannot talk about God. For this reason, he cannot talk about forgiveness and reconciliation except between man and man. He cannot use language about God's sharing or entering into the human experience of sin, guilt, and estrangement. He cannot talk of victory over death except in the existentialist sense of courage to face death as not destructive of life's meaning. Unless, of course, he wants to argue for a life after death without God. One could find this idea in Hinduism and Buddhism. In the Western tradition, immortality without God is something of an oddity, though it is represented by such men as McTaggart. Generally speaking, if the humanist wants to use the language of victory over evil and sin, he must do so strictly within a this-worldly context. The victory must be achieved in historical situations by men and not by God. He cannot talk of an eternal kingdom beyond time and space.

The question we are asking is whether the presence of the transcendent dimension makes any significant difference in practice to the nature and quality of the life lived. Does the presence of faith, in the sense we have defined, make any difference to the kind of human being which results? The difficulty in answering this question springs very often from the assumption that to suggest such a difference involves an unlovely kind of Pharisaism. It assumes that a purely negative judgment is being passed about the humanist, and that the Christian is adopting an undesirable posture of moral and spiritual superiority. We shall concentrate first of all, therefore, upon the difference between the humanist and the Christian in terms of attitude, action, and personal experience without attaching any value judgment to the

[11]Thomas J.J. Altizer and William Hamilton, *Radical Theology* (Indianapolis: Bobbs-Merrill, 1966).

[12]Aldous Huxley, *The Perennial Philosophy* (London: Chatto & Windus, 1946).

[13]Gregory Baum, *Man Becoming* (New York: Herder & Herder, 1970).

difference. It is realized that this is difficult, some would say impossible. However, it may prove to be worthwhile to attempt such a phenomenology of the humanist and Christian ways of life, even if it is well-nigh impossible to exclude altogether value judgments.

The difference between the Christian and the humanist will tend to be located in the areas where faith in God results in worship, prayer, the sense of divine presence, the assurance of divine grace and help, and the experience of forgiveness by God and not simply by one's fellow men. It also has important implications for the quality of Christian hope—for the way in which a man faces the future, whether his own personal future or that of the human race as a whole. The difference emerges, therefore, at those points where the Christian is affected by his conviction that religion includes more than morality. The problem is to clarify what this more is, and how it affects practice precisely at the point where the Christian understanding of God is integrally bound up with his confession that Jesus is "truly man and truly God."

The basic difference, then, would appear to be that whereas the humanist believes that he must struggle towards the realization of his ideals in the strength of his own human resources alone, the Christian believes that he is in vital touch now with a present reality, namely God, infinite in power, holiness, and love. The Christian is not only struggling towards an ideal, He believes that all that he aspires after and longs for is already actual in the reality of God, and that God's power and grace is available to him now in his struggle, despite his weakness, imperfection, and sin. The humanist cannot pray in the sense of seeking a present communion with God, even though such men as Julian Huxley would defend the psychological and therapeutic value of prayer, meditation, and contemplation, notwithstanding the fact that there is no God to whom such activities could be directed.

The Christian faith, however, goes one step further. Not only may the Christian be in present touch with God as with a reality beyond space and time, but he also believes that God's holy love and presence are perfectly embodied in the man Jesus of Nazareth. The reality of perfect holiness and love is not simply a remote, transcendent realm. It has become historical actuality in Jesus. This is where the confession of His divinity becomes relevant and important. The Christian believes that he is related to God through the mediation of this historical actuality which is Jesus Christ and that Jesus is still alive and His presence knowable through the present activity of the Spirit of God.

It follows that the quality of Christian faith and devotion will be profoundly influenced by these convictions. The humanist does not have this resource open to him. There is a difference between devotion to moral and spiritual ideals, envisaged as the proper goals of human striving and effort, and the sense of warm devotion to a living Person in whom these ideals are already actualized realities in the world we know. Agape-love is not simply an ideal concept to guide future human action. It is this, but for the Christian it has already been perfectly expressed amid the brute realities and sins of actual historical existence. It is this conviction which makes a subtle difference to Christian faith and action as contrasted with humanist idealism. It is not that the Christian necessarily disagrees with all the humanist's moral and spiritual values and ideals, though "humanist" is a broad term which might conceivably take the form of a certain understanding of human existence which clashes head on with the Christian vision of what human life ought to be and might become. Nietzsche is a case in point,[14] even if some humanists would want to argue that he was not a true humanist. The fact remains that the Christian confession of the divinity of Christ does give a significantly distinctive quality to his activity in the sense that he is able here and now to draw upon the resources of God in Christ for his grappling with his present experience of the human predicament. "It is not the case that the Christian takes the same view of morality as non-Christians, differing only in that they add 'duties to God' to their list of moral principles. Rather, the whole framework of the practice of the moral life will be different for a Christian and for a secular thinker."[15]

This question has assumed a very contemporary aspect in the appearance of the Jesus people and in the role played by Jesus in popular musicals, such as *Jesus Christ Superstar*. Christians are not simply Jesus people but people who confess Him as Lord and as truly man and truly God for the reasons previously given. Is the use of the Jesus figure a sign of a renewed faith in the specifically Christian sense? The answer to this can hardly be an unambiguous Yes or No until we know more about the particular individual's attitude and what he understands by loyalty to Jesus. The epithet "Superstar" is taken from show business. A star is one who belongs to the top ratings and is usually very interested in drawing attention to himself. Yet to apply it to Jesus is to move from one area of discourse to another with entirely different associations. In Jesus we have one who did not wish to draw attention to Himself in this modern sense but to the Father whose agent He is. Yet, paradoxically, this profound humility of Jesus has in fact drawn the eyes of the whole world to Him. Certainly the writer and composer of *Jesus Christ Superstar,* on their own admission, are not orthodox Christians and were concerned to present the man Jesus rather than the divine Lord of

---

[14]See Walter Kaufmann, *Nietzsche: Philosopher, Psychologist, Anti-Christ* (New York: Meridian Books, 1956).

[15]Keith Ward, *Ethics and Christianity* (London: Allen & Unwin, 1970), p. 273.

Christian faith. It remains to be seen whether *Jesus Christ Superstar* and its interpretation of Jesus will produce such human witnesses to Him as the world has hitherto regarded as the noblest products of the Christian faith.

The conclusion we wish to draw from this lengthy discussion is that it does make a difference whether a man confesses the divinity of Jesus, assuming that the confession is a sincere expression of a commitment of the whole man and not simply the formal assent to a dogma. That such sincere commitment is often to be found mingled with human error, imperfection, and sin is not to be denied. To affirm the divinity of Jesus is not to affirm my own personal perfection as a fully mature Christian, conformed to the Son who is the express image of the Father. It is, however, to affirm the reality of God in the Christian sense and the divine resources which are available to me even now in my attempt to live my life in conformity with the will of the Holy and loving God.

The affirmation of the divinity is, therefore, first and foremost a Christian conviction. One can hardly expect the nonbeliever to affirm it as true for him apart from the response of faith and the consequent experience of God's grace which would make the affirmation meaningful. Furthermore, we can never hope to win the unbeliever to such an affirmation by the most rigorous of intellectual arguments alone. This does not mean that the Christian is unable to offer any reasons at all for the faith that is in him. It does mean that the Christian knowledge of God is not simply the conclusion of an intellectual argument, though this latter may play an important part, sometimes a necessary part, in the individual Christian's total experience which leads him to the Christian affirmations. In the last analysis, the proof of the divinity of Jesus must be found in the evidence afforded by the transformed lives of His followers. "If the Christian church wants to convince the world of the supreme value of its ideal of love, it can only do so by steadily confronting it with the actual thing."[16]

Let it be stated again. This does not mean that Jesus is divine only because we think Him to be so. The Christian can never be content to affirm that the divinity is the product simply of his own psychology. Jesus is what He is. The point we are making is a rather different one. We cannot expect the unbeliever to come to a knowledge of Jesus as He truly is unless some evidence is afforded in life and experience of the difference which Jesus makes in men and women when He is accepted as Lord and Savior and confessed by His followers as truly man and truly God. If no such link can be found between theological confession and actual human experience, the confession must appear to be no more than formal assent to abstract con-

---

[16]Edwyn Bevan, *Hellenism and Christianity* (New York: George Doran, 1922), p. 273.

cepts. That such has been true and often is today can hardly be denied. It has been the contention of this book that such divorce between faith and practice need not necessarily be the case and that in the long history of the church there have been enough cases in which this dichotomy has been gloriously overcome to justify the Christian hope and faith that He will draw all men unto Himself, except where the stubborn and unrepentant will of man makes it impossible. Whether any person will finally and permanently reject the divine love and say, "Evil, be thou my good," is a matter about which we cannot dogmatize. If human freedom is real, such a possibility is there, and we must remind men of the serious consequences of their moral and spiritual choices, both here and hereafter. Meanwhile, our positive task is to help men to see the divinity of Jesus, not as a mere dogma but as the glorious expression of our conviction that God is really as we have known Him to be in Christ.

Appendices

Appendices

Appendix A

Professor Maurice Wiles and the Remaking of Christian Doctrine

Since the section in the text of the book devoted to the views of Professor Wiles was written, Professor Wiles has taken up again the theme of his article in the above book. In his newer and equally stimulating volume, *The Remaking of Christian Doctrine*, Wiles develops some of the ideas previously put forward and replies to some of the criticisms which were levelled against them. He does not depart from the basic thesis of his earlier article and consequently our previous comments upon it remain in order. Nevertheless, the further development of his ideas deserves our attention, both for their intrinsic interest and because of their bearing upon our chosen theme of Christology.

Professor Wiles has difficulty with the whole question of doctrinal development, whether the model used is one of identity through change or the analogy of growth taken from biology. Both models imply that we have a clear knowledge of what is in process of development, so that we discern identity in the process or judge between legitimate and illegitimate ways of making explicit what is implicit in whatever was given at the beginning. It is this kind of knowledge which Wiles doubts, as is evident from his comment upon Barth: "It seems unmistakably clear to me that we simply do not have this kind of explicit self-revelation [i.e., of God] that such a scheme requires."[1] This is obviously the crux of the matter. If we are not sure of the original revelation of God, we cannot be sure what is a legitimate development from it, whatever model we use.

The reason for Wiles' confident statement apparently springs from the nature of modern historical study. Fact and interpretation are so interwoven that absolute certainty about the so-called facts behind the interpretation can never be attained. Thus Barthian confidence in the unsurpassable and definitive self-revelation of God in Christ rests on an authoritative view of

---

[1]Maurice Wiles, *The Remaking of Christian Doctrine* (London: S.C.M., 1973), p. 24.

Scripture which can no longer be held as an unquestioned premise from which either the historian or the theologian can start. Even if we grant that the Word of God is disclosed to man through the biblical history and supremely in and through the Person of Christ, "the medium through which it comes to us is so much a part of our ordinary world that we have to assess it, to judge it, to evaluate it."[2] From this, it follows that "we have no other starting-point than our ordinary experience of the world."[3] Here again the crucial point is what are the limits of such ordinary experience. It can hardly mean ordinary in the sense of average, otherwise most of the great religious figures of the race, not to mention mystics and outstanding converts, would simply have to be eliminated on the grounds that their experience does not fit within the confines of the average. Or does ordinary experience mean what appears to be such to twentieth-century so-called secular man? But then we would have to give some reason why that experience should be regarded as normative. We are back with the question as to whether it is legitimate to select certain types of experience as more significant and valid disclosures of the reality of God than others. In trying to answer this, however, ordinary experience does not supply any kind of satisfactory or easily applied criterion of judgment.

It is clear also that, for Wiles, affirmations about God as truly transcendent have become entirely problematic in the contemporary intellectual climate of opinion. Theology cannot simply start with our experience of the world and move by deduction to a God "beyond the world." This move cannot be demonstrated, says Wiles, by any of the classical forms of natural theology or by any sophisticated revisions of the so-called proofs. Nor can we start from an authoritative Bible or church. Where, then, can we start? We have seen that Wiles stresses ordinary experience. At the same time, he admits that the Bible is a record of some kind of experience and therefore deserves our attention and study. To what degree this comes within the scope of his "ordinary experience" is not made clear.

Against this background, Wiles would urge us not to try to talk about God in Himself but only "of the effects of God as experienced." Here he invokes the Lutheran principle that salvation is to know Christ and His benefits, i.e., to experience the saving and transforming work of God in Christ on the existential and not on the metaphysical level. To speak of a knowledge of God "in Himself," abstracted from a relationship of faith and adoration,[4] is to offer a God who is merely the object of detached intellectual contemplation, not the living God of actual religious experience. This,

---

[2]*Ibid.*
[3]*Ibid.*, p. 25.
[4]*Ibid.*, p. 26.

however, is surely to oversimplify a very complex situation. When Christians in the past have spoken of God in Himself, they have done so not simply on the basis of metaphysical speculation. They believed, rightly or wrongly, that they were drawing the necessary implications of an experience of God rooted in faith and adoration. To limit the knowledge of God to His effects as experienced, says Wiles, is not an abdication of any vital religious concern.[5] Yet, as Austin Farrer once remarked, how do we know that these effects are indeed effects of God in Christian experience? For Wiles also, it is not possible to speak of God's relation to nature in the traditional theological way.[6] Yet "it is still the Creator God of Christian theism with whom we have to do here."[7] Again, later in the same chapter, when discussing the problem of evil, "there is no possibility of going back on the Christian conviction of creation ex nihilo."[8] But why? How do we know that this view of God as Creator is valid? Do we derive it from ordinary experience? Hardly, if we have declared it illegitimate, as Wiles has done, to argue from the finite to the infinite according to some metaphysical principle of causation and sufficient reason. Do we, then, derive it from an authoritative revelation in the Bible? The Bible, however, for reasons already mentioned, cannot be regarded as authoritative and therefore as settling this kind of question merely from the fact that certain statements about God as Creator appear in the Bible. How, then, do we know that the experienced effects, in the Lutheran dictum, are in fact the effects of God's activity in and on the human personality?

Do we, then, ignore metaphysical argument and deduce God directly from the Christian experience of redemption itself? On this point, Professor Wiles is obviously conscious of a tension in his own thought. He even seems to backtrack upon some of his previous statements. Personal knowledge of another person does involve an element of objectifying knowledge of him.[9] Why not, therefore, in the case of God? May there not be an objectified knowledge of Him as well as an I-Thou existential one, even if all knowledge and talk of God must be indirect and analogical? We are nearly back to talking about God "in Himself," despite Professor Wiles distrust of this kind of language. Indeed, he claims that "it is doubtful whether one can properly claim to know the effects of something and yet be able to say nothing whatever about the thing itself."[10] Here Wiles seems to leave open

---

[5]*Ibid.*
[6]*Ibid.*, p. 27.
[7]*Ibid.*
[8]*Ibid.*, p. 33.
[9]*Ibid.*, p. 29.
[10]*Ibid.*

again the possibility of knowing God in the cosmological relationship (Farrer) as well as in the redemptive effects of divine love in the human heart (the Lutheran benefits). In theory, perhaps, yes, but in practice, according to Wiles, extreme caution is in order. Wiles appears to conclude that it is not possible to develop a clearly structured and coherent set of beliefs about God.[11] This is a misplaced confidence and its inevitable failure is seen, according to Wiles, in contemporary efforts of this kind, whether it be H.P. Owen's defence of classical theism[12] or Schubert Ogden's advocacy of a process theology.[13]

All this does indeed leave the concept of God very problematic, and it is difficult to see why Wiles should seem so anxious to retain the notion of God as Creator in the more or less traditional biblical and doctrinal sense. It cannot be taken to include an emphasis upon creation at a moment of time. Nor can we rely on insecure distinctions between God's creative and sustaining activity. The doctrine of creation for Wiles seems, therefore, to be reduced to the following elements: the wonder that there should be anything at all (the basic insight of the cosmological argument) and our awareness of our ultimate dependence and all that is upon this mystery which evokes our wonder.[14] Whatever elements of truth there may be in this, it is a far cry from the classical ex nihilo doctrine and still further removed from creation as the act of a transcendent and loving will of a personal God, even if personal must be interpreted analogically. This being so, Wiles has obvious difficulty in admitting specific activities of God within the context of His general activity. "What is indicated by speaking of God as Creator is something that is uniformly true of his relation to the world all the time."[15] This does not mean only that God is related through His uniform action to all of creation. It seems also to mean the refusal to entertain either special providences or distinctive acts. We have already cited William Temple's comments on this way of looking at it. It certainly seems more deistic than theistic in the usual sense of theism. Yet Wiles seems again to balance precariously between two different positions. He tells us that we ought not to rule out a priori the idea of a special relationship of God to particular events within the world.[16] He admits that the Christian tradition does speak of special occurrences which embody the divine purpose in a manner significantly different from His general activity in creation. Thus the idea of special occurrences is not

---

[11]*Ibid.*, p. 30.
[12]H.P. Owen, *The Christian Knowledge of God.*
[13]Schubert M. Ogden, *The Reality of God* (New York: Harper & Row, 1966).
[14]Wiles, *Remaking of Doctrine*, p. 34.
[15]*Ibid.*
[16]*Ibid.*, p. 36.

logically absurd, but ''a logical possibility is not by itself sufficient to justify positive affirmation. Nor do I think such a positive affirmation can in fact be justified ''[17] This seems clear enough. No special divine activities are to be claimed in specific occurrences. Wiles admits that in Christian experience the idea of divine guidance and providence plays such an important part that it would mean so many special divine causative activities that it would make havoc of our normal understanding of the world in terms of causal regularities. God would be specially intervening at almost every moment. What, then, becomes of the regular order of the world?

How, according to Wiles, are we to resolve the problem? Certainly there are ''occasions which arouse in us at the time or in retrospect a sense of divine purpose.''[18] But, he says, this ''does not necessarily entail any special divine activity in those particular events.''[19] Here we have it. Wiles admits that this view is deistic in the sense of refusing to claim any ''effective causation on the part of God in relation to particular occurrences.''[20] We have had to spend so much time in expounding Professor Wiles' discussion of God since this is obviously crucial to his later consideration of Christology and the doctrines of the saving work of Christ. Obviously on his assumptions no doctrine of Incarnation or Atonement can be developed which implies a specific divine causal activity. The language of uniqueness in any strong sense must obviously be out of place.

We have already noted more than once Temple's reply to this conception that ''personal wisdom is not shown in rigid uniformity of behaviour but in constancy of purpose expressed through infinitely varied response to different conditions.''[21] This involves a view of God as transcendent personal will in a much stronger sense than Wiles seems willing to countenance. Temple also replies to his other point by maintaining that what holds the world together as an ordered sequence of events is not mechanical or uniform causality but the constancy of the divine will and God's intention that there shall be a universe and not a chaos. Therefore, special occurrences, whether the Incarnation or a miracle, would not necessarily throw the world into sheer and utter confusion. It does not follow, according to Temple, that a divine act transcending ''normal'' causality would necessarily mean the collapse of all regularities which would make science impossible. This would be true only if God were performing ''miracles'' all the time, so that

---

[17]*Ibid.*, p. 37.
[18]*Ibid.*, p. 38.
[19]*Ibid.*
[20]*Ibid.*
[21]Temple, *Nature, Man and God*, p. 307.

no regularities could be discerned in the natural order. No form of the Christian faith has ever maintained this to be the case.

It has become clear that given the presuppositions from which he starts, Wiles must drastically reinterpret some familiar language about the uniqueness of Christ and of a special activity of God in Jesus which is distinguishable from His general activity. We cannot treat the traditional Christological formulation, truly man and truly God, as an unquestionable axiom.[22] The very concept of Incarnation demands that one start from above, namely from a certain understanding of God become man.[23] This, however, is to make an assumption that is widely questioned today. If we are going to affirm such language as "God became man," it must stand at the end of the process of enquiry. It cannot be the starting-point.

In one sense, this is true since the historical development of dogma took time, and the credal formulations followed at a later date than the New Testament writings. Furthermore, their final form took several centuries to complete. It seems as if Wiles is asking us to reverse this process and go back behind the dogma to the events and experiences out of which the dogmatic scheme came. This sounds very much like Harnack, though in Wiles the attempt has become much more sophisticated. The crux of the matter for him lies in the development of the modern historical consciousness which "has, in some degree or another, made historical relativists of us all."[24] Our basic problem, says Wiles, is the difficulty of ascribing "absolute authority to any particular occasion or to any particular set of experiences within the world."[25]

This again is reminiscent of similar discussions of this theme by Lessing and Troeltsch, not to mention Kierkegaard's reaction in the *Concluding Unscientific Postscript* to Lessing's famous dictum that "accidental historical truths can never serve as proofs for eternal truths of reason."[26] This, however, says Wiles, does not mean that we cannot ascribe any authority to special events, only that we cannot ascribe "absolute" authority. To do this, we would have to have sufficient reliable knowledge of the life of Jesus. This we do not have. Neither the old nor the new quest of the historical Jesus has given or can give us this kind of knowledge. "The framer of a doctrine of the Person of Christ has to recognize that the kind of

---

[22]Wiles, *Remaking of Doctrine*, p. 43.

[23]*Ibid.*, p. 44.

[24]*Ibid.*, p. 45.

[25]*Ibid.*

[26]Soren Kierkegaard, *Concluding Unscientific Postscript,* trans. D.F. Swenson and W. Lowrie (Princeton: Princeton Univ. Press, 1941).

information about Jesus which we have so often looked to the New Testament to provide is not available."[27] The conclusion appears to be that although it is not impossible in principle to ascribe absolute authority to an historical figure, it is the tentativeness of our historical knowledge which in fact renders it impossible.[28] Because this is so, we must be equally tentative in our talk about the relationship of Jesus to God, and this must undercut, therefore, any confident and dogmatic statement about Incarnation after the manner of the traditional Christology. We may still be able to adduce impressive historical evidence from the impact of Jesus upon the men of His generation, and upon the apostles and disciples in particular. This, however, must fall short of the special evaluation of Jesus which lies at the heart of traditional Christian orthodoxy. The problem is also accentuated today, says Wiles, by the fuller knowledge of the great non-Christian religions. To tie the special activity of God to this man Jesus seems less and less plausible the more we know of the religious life and aspirations of other men in other climes and of other races. The problem for us, according to Wiles, is whether a convincing case can be made for a nonincarnational theism in which Jesus may certainly have great authority, at least for Christians, but not that absolute authority which the historic Christian faith has claimed for Him in the doctrine of the once-for-all, unique act of God becoming man.

If the objections raised by Professor Wiles against the classical Incarnation language are valid, it follows that similar qualifications would have to be made about the Christian claim for a unique "saving" activity through the death and resurrection of Jesus Christ as well as attempts to make the Christian experience of the Holy Spirit distinctive in some absolute way when compared with the universal activity of the Spirit in the non-Christian religions. Since most of this book is devoted to dealing with the fundamental challenge made by Wiles and others to the Incarnation as a special and unique activity of God, these other questions will not be considered here. The further development of our main thesis has, it is hoped, thrown some light upon what our conclusions might be in regard to the redemptive implications of the Incarnation doctrine. It is evident that the points already raised by Wiles are the fundamental ones. Unless they can be answered, the other problems too must remain unanswered and perhaps unanswerable.

---

[27]Wiles, *Remaking of Doctrine,* p. 48.
[28]*Ibid.,* p. 49.

Appendix B

Recent Process Theology

Several references have been made in the text of this book to process theology. Since our concern has been to develop a Christology from a particular point of view rather than to criticize those who take a different approach, critical references have not been expanded in detail. It seems desirable, however, in view of the wide and growing influence of what is called process theology, to indicate in more detail the grounds for the present author's dissatisfaction with it. Even this brief treatment must be inadequate, but I hope it will show that my comments about the process theology have some reason and not merely prejudice behind them. Like most labels, of course, the term needs to be applied with caution. It would obviously be unfair to apply it without discrimination to a variety of theologians each of whom has his own distinctive perspective. While the philosophical conceptuality involved is usually associated with Alfred North Whitehead and Charles Hartshorne, this in itself involves a number of problems. What is the correct interpretation of Whitehead? Is Hartshorne to be regarded simply as a disciple of Whitehead, or does he represent a distinctive and independent view, utilizing some of the insights of Whitehead but in no way to be described simply as a Whiteheadian? That these questions are very difficult to answer is evident from the essays to be found in the publications listed in the notes below.[1]

All we can do here is to describe some of the basic features of this thought and indicate their adequacy or inadequacy in relation to our own thinking about God. Note should be taken especially of the recent work of David Griffin, who is concerned with the question of Christology and

---

[1]James W. McClendon, Jr., ed., *Philosophy of Religion and Theology 1974,* American Academy of Religion Annual Meeting, 1974; and W.L. Sessions, *et al., Two Process Philosophers: Hartshorne's Encounter with Whitehead,* American Academy of Religion Studies in Religion, No. 5, 1973.

believes he can find in process thought adequate categories for restating the traditional Christology in a manner more acceptable to modern thought.[2] We are entirely sympathetic with Professor Griffin's contention that the experiential appeal to Jesus and His benefits requires some elucidation in terms of God's objective presence in Jesus. "This is why Jesus' significance for the volitional and affective side of our being finally depends upon his significance for the cognitive side."[3] We also agree that though the term "revelation" is not heavily used in the New Testament, it is still a necessary category to express Jesus' significance for our vision of reality.[4] Nor is it necessary to repeat in detail his penetrating critique of Tillich, Bultmann, H. Richard Niebuhr, and Schleiermacher, with most of which we are also in agreement. None of these thinkers does full justice in his view to the objective presence of God in Jesus and Jesus' own unique and decisive revelatory significance for our vision of reality or our knowledge of God. The problem, then, is, How do we do justice to those factors in any developed Christology, and what kind of conceptuality can we employ in order to express their significance?

Griffin is quite clear that this cannot be done by forcing the Christian revelation into a conceptual pattern derived from a supposedly neutral philosophical stance. If there is a prior understanding of God, whether called natural theology or not, "it must be radically reformed under the impact of the Christian revelation."[5] Again we agree. At this point, however, we simply cannot fall back upon an appeal to the practical fruits of Jesus' impact upon the believer. The whole point of a Christology is to try to express in language which is reasonably intelligible what Jesus was "in Himself," i.e., Jesus as the objective presence of God among men. This, of course, does not exclude the believer's experience of the saving power of Jesus in his own life. It is simply going a step further to try to indicate how God is really present in Jesus in the manner required to account for what He has in fact done for men in a saving way.

What are the advantages, according to Griffin, of employing the conceptuality of the process philosophers to express this truth about the decisive revelation of God in and through Jesus? They appear to be as follows:

(a) It is assumed that any doctrine of Jesus' Person must be judged in "terms of its adequacy to the Scriptures as currently understood."[6] This presumably does not mean that the theologian must be in bondage to the

---

[2]David Griffin, *A Process Christology* (Philadelphia: Westminster, 1973).
[3]*Ibid.*, p. 17.
[4]*Ibid.*
[5]*Ibid.*, p. 140.
[6]*Ibid.*, p. 143.

latest fashion but that he must give full weight to responsible biblical scholarship and exegesis.

(b) Process philosophy, as its name indicates, seeks to do justice to the dynamic and "becoming" quality of all existence. This makes it more serviceable for thinking of a God whose essential nature is to be living, dynamic, and active.

(c) It also permits us to speak of special events or acts or occasions without denying God's relationship and presence to all events and occasions. Thus the dichotomy between God's general and uniform activity and His miraculous or exceptional activity is overcome in a manner which does not require the breach of natural law.

(d) Since the classical doctrine of divine impassibility (i.e., God's inability to suffer or to react in any way akin to feeling) makes it impossible to do justice to Jesus' vision of a God who cares and loves and enters into human suffering through the Cross, this doctrine must be abandoned. God not only causally acts upon creatures through the lure of ideal aims, but He is reacted to and affected by events, affected in the strong sense of moved in feeling. This, however, is impossible, so it is claimed, if God is the transcendent, infinite, incorporeal, and impassible Spirit who controls all things through His omnipotent causality.

(e) There must, therefore, be a place for genuine freedom and spontaneity in events and occasions, not only at the level of human decision and self-determination but even at the organic and inorganic level, where the interaction of entities reveals an element of spontaneity and of self-determination. Not only is God not in absolute control of human freedom, He is not in absolute control of the natural order as a whole, the total process of occasions. "God's action," we are told, "is always persuasive, never coercive."[7] This, let it be remembered, is true of all the energies operative in the process, not only at the human level where this claim might seem to have its proper validity. It is important to note in passing that such a God would have no power to give a person existence after death in view of his lack of complete control over the process. It is also contended that this view of God's relation to nature, including man, greatly alleviates the problem of evil. God may supply the initial aim for each occasion, but He is in no way responsible for its detailed working out, whether by man himself or by the sequence of occasions we call nature. Certainly this view frees God of responsibility, but we have yet to count the cost of this solution.

We cannot attempt here a detailed critique of the positions of either Whitehead or Hartshorne. The basic issues, as far as the concept of God is

---

[7]*Ibid.*, p. 214.

concerned, are these: Is the doctrine of a finite and limited God adequate either religiously or metaphysically? And how useful is the body-self or body-soul analogy in giving conceptual expression to the way in which God is related to the order of nature, including man?

Whitehead, who once said that all European philosophy is a series of footnotes to Plato, remains faithful to his famous predecessor on this important point. Just as Plato's God is doubly limited by the Forms on the one hand and matter (or necessity) on the other, so Whitehead's God is limited by the existence of the world and the incorporation of its experiences within his being.[8] This involves the rejection of classical theism's view of God as omnipotent.[9] Plato's God and Whitehead's God cannot be self-existent Being, since they are limited by existing matter, which originates in some mysterious way or exists eternally, independent of God's activity. But as Owen rightly asks, Can we be content with a divine Orderer who is not also a Creator?[10] Certainly Whitehead wishes to retain anthropomorphic concepts of God as the ideal companion, "the fellow sufferer who understands,"[11] as well as the poet who beckons men into the future with the vision of beauty, truth, and goodness. God is love, but only in the sense that He persuades real finite entities into some kind of order and mutual harmony. This is very difficult to understand on the basis of Whitehead's dipolar theism with its distinction between God's primordial and consequent natures.[12] Since God in His primordial nature is not conscious and is deficiently actual and far from "eminent reality," it is not easy to know in what sense words like "will," "purpose," "orderer," and "love" could be applied, even analogically, to God in His primordial nature. He acquires consciousness and presumably love only in His consequent nature as "He" (?) responds to the world-process of becoming through the interaction of finite entities. He provides the inner subjective aim to such entities but must then allow them freedom, spontaneity, and the possibility of refusing to try to realize this aim. Whitehead also seems to be leaving not only man, but the whole natural process outside the scope of divine control, except through persuasion. How God persuades the basic energies operative in the atomic and subatomic is not made plain.

On this view, it is obviously impossible for God's persuasive agency to secure the survival of death of any such finite entity. Any doctrine of

---

[8]H.P. Owen, *Concepts of Deity*, p. 50.

[9]Whitehead, *Religion in the Making*.

[10]Owen, *Concepts*, p. 51.

[11]Whitehead, *Process and Reality* (New York: Macmillan; Cambridge: Cambridge Univ. Press, 1929), p. 497.

[12]*Ibid.*, p. 486.

immortality must take the form of the preservation of values in God or the divine memory. It is equally difficult to see, if we follow Whitehead, how words like "memory" can be intelligibly applied to a God who is primordially not conscious and becomes conscious only in finite entities through the process of becoming. We find Professor John B. Cobb, Jr., talking in a similar way: "The best analogy in human experience for reflection on the divine is to be found in memory."[13] This is based on the claim that memory, even in human beings, is a nonsensory kind of apprehension and, therefore, cannot be unconscious in God, who also experiences in a nonsensory way. How this is applied to God, whether literally or analogically, is not easy to make out. Cobb insists that "the world does not exist outside God, or apart from God, but the world is not God or simply part of God."[14] Yet how can this distinction between God and the world be maintained without His genuine transcendence of the whole spatio-temporal process? But then we are back with the mutual externality of God and the world of which Cobb disapproves. Again, how can Cobb say that the "primordial nature of God is here pictured [i.e., in *Adventures of Ideas*] as the love which lures men to adventure"?[15] How can we apply the notion of love in any meaningful sense to the primordial God of Whitehead who is unconscious and deficiently actual?

Hartshorne also talks in this way: "In such a perfect memory or perception the past might be literally immortal, adequately preserved in all its quality, all its beauty, forever."[16] But what does God remember of Buchenwald or Hiroshima? This is not just an illegitimate appeal to emotion. Presumably God takes up what was of value in all the individuals thus killed, but what are these abstract values detached from the suffering individuals concerned? Would it have comforted them at the time? In any case, Hartshorne's limited God couldn't do anything about it. Such a God may have no responsibility at all for the conditions which brought about such disasters. But equally He cannot be strong tower or fortress in time of need and the guarantor of an eternal hope expressed in real personal existence.

Or can we speak of God's consciousness in His consequent nature as transcending all finite centers of consciousness? These finite centers are constantly perishing, which is an added difficulty. But what kind of consciousness can God have above and beyond the process if He Himself is limited and finite, even if preeminent and very much greater than the finite

---

[13]Ewert H. Cousins, ed., *Process Theology* (New York: Newman; Toronto: Paramus, 1971), p. 161.

[14]*Ibid.*, p. 165.

[15]*Ibid.*, p. 169.

[16]*Ibid.*, p. 59.

entities which appear in the process? He is only one entity among others, however preeminent. And, as Owen asks, ''how could we be sure that God Himself might not perish, like the perishable occasions He is supposed to be informing and persuading?''[17] It need not be denied that Whitehead's God satisfies some religious needs, but the question remains whether He satisfies the fundamental needs which spring from our sense of absolute dependence and the numinous experience. No doubt this sense of absolute dependence might be questioned by some, nor do we intend it in the precise sense of Schleiermacher or as an endorsement of Schleiermacher's theology. Classical theism has always allowed, as it must, that if God is infinite and omnipotent, He could have limited Himself to permit the creature to have a limited freedom. Yet this freedom is exercised in the context of pattern and order established by God and under His control. Cobb, on the contrary, thinks that God has given us full responsibility for ourselves and the world.[18] This is a bold claim and a terrifying one at that if ''full'' means literally what it suggests. Whitehead's view frees God from direct responsibility for natural disasters and some forms of moral evil, but by making God a limited being, it deprives Him of the power to deal with these problems either by action in the world or by assuring the individual of a life after death in blessed communion with Him and other finite creatures. It is little comfort to the inmates of concentration camps or victims of other natural disasters that somehow all these evil elements will be transformed and harmonized in a divine experience when they themselves have perished forever. Even the assurance that all of value, however interpreted, is preserved in the divine experience lacks solid foundation when God Himself lacks ''necessary being'' and may just be perishable like other transient occasions. The emphasis on God's persuasive power also involves some kind of personal influence on men, but does this not require a more full-blooded use of personal analogies in relation to God than the Whiteheadian or the Hartshornian systems would seem to allow?

Those who follow Whitehead in believing that God is ''not before all creation but with all creation''[19] are faced with the problem of how this ''with all creation'' is to be construed. Though Whitehead constantly affirms that God's being is distinct from the being of the world, it is obviously difficult to conceive this since God is not a distinct or transcendent Spirit or self-existing Creator. He is a nontemporal actual entity who ''includes'' the world in Himself. The only way to make this at all intelligible is to adopt the body-soul or body-self analogy and see if it can be applied on this cosmic scale. This analogy also implies that God is like a human person in that He

---

[17]Owen, *Concepts,* p. 56.
[18]Cousins, *Process Theology,* p. 154.
[19]Whitehead, *Process and Reality,* p. 486.

develops and enriches His experience through His response to His environment, which can only on this view be the world process. If this is so, can we go all the way with the analogy? Is God developing from imperfection to a greater degree of perfection, like the human individual? Whitehead and, still more clearly, Hartshorne do not want to say precisely this. There is an unchanging perfection in God which they then try to reconcile with His thoroughgoing involvement in the process. Can this be done without getting into intolerable contradictions? Can we intelligibly apply to God at the same time such contrasting concepts as absolute and relative, perfect and imperfect, eternal and temporal? Nor does it seem to solve the problem by asserting that God's unchanging perfection is His abstract essence, whatever that could mean.

Let us concentrate for the moment upon what Farrer called *anima mundi* theology,[20] i.e., the attempt to view God as the soul of the universe. Griffin also favors this approach, arguing that if we think of God's relation to the world as analogous to that of mind to body, this frees us from the intolerable difficulties connected with the classical theistic view as it struggles to reconcile God's omnipotent causality with genuine freedom, at least on the human level, and the problem of evil as presented by natural disasters. It also, he claims, frees us from the problem of divine intervention considered as the breaking through the ordinary process of creation. These are bold claims indeed. Can they really be sustained?

Ian Barbour lists four models which have been used by Christian thinkers: the monarchical, deistic, dialogic, and agent models.[21] The analogies respectively derive from a king and his kingdom, a clockmaker and a clock, one person and another person, an agent and his actions (in one version, a self and his body). It is worth observing in passing that these models were probably not understood in an absolutely literal sense, even in the Bible. Furthermore, a great variety of biblical models qualify the dominant model. In any case, the Old Testament Hebrew was quite aware of the difference between an earthly king and the Heavenly King. He could not have been as naive as some modern commentators seem to think. Nor does Whitehead seem to allow for the possibility that the monarchy model was considerably modified in the Jewish as well as in the Christian theological tradition. It does not do justice to this development simply to say that ''the Church gave unto God the attributes which belonged exclusively to Caesar.''[22] Nor does Whitehead consider that the Bible does not think of God's omnipotence as sheer unqualified power. Furthermore, God's om-

---

[20]Farrer, *Faith and Speculation,* pp. 142ff.
[21]Ian G. Barbour, *Myths, Models and Paradigms* (New York: Harper & Row, 1974), pp. 155ff.
[22]Whitehead, *Process and Reality,* p. 485.

nipotent causality is not that of mechanistic determination but of a sovereign will which can limit itself to allow real spontaneity without surrendering ultimate control of the process. "The divine purpose is to achieve our individual good through social action and mutual concern."[23] To these four models, Barbour adds a fifth, which is taken from recent process philosophy and theology, namely "that of a society of which one member is pre-eminent but not absolute."[24] Whitehead's philosophy is given as an illustration of this fifth model: "The universe is pictured as a community of interacting beings, rather than as a monarchy, a machine, an interpersonal dialogue, or a cosmic organism."[25]

All of these models, for Barbour, will obviously have to be qualified, to use Ramsey's language, to make them applicable to God. None of them can be used in a strictly literal sense, though all may be suggestive and illuminating. All have limitations which have to be acknowledged. The monarchical model tends in the direction of sheer omnipotence, predestination, and authoritarianism, with their threat to a genuine human freedom and responsibility. It also involves a kind of supernaturalism that creates difficulties in regard to the "lawfulness" of nature, which is a basic assumption of the scientific outlook. It also accentuates the problem of suffering and evil, for which God is made wholly responsible. But again does this do justice to the complexity and subtlety of the way in which these problems are dealt with in the Bible? The model of the divine clockmaker, though widely accepted in the eighteenth century under the influence of Newtonian physics and the deists, no longer has any defenders in that form. The idea of the universe as an autonomous and self-regulating mechanism no longer commends itself, especially since Darwin and the later influence of evolutionary theory. The dialogic or person-to-person model has obvious advantages for a theology which wants to stress human freedom and such words as "forgiveness," "love," and "reconciliation" as characteristic of the divine-human relation. Its inadequacy today consists in its tendency to separate man and nature too strictly and to relegate the reality of God almost exclusively to man's inner states. In any case, God is not simply another human person. The agent model, on which we shall concentrate here, does allow us to speak of divine intentions and actions, while admitting the adequacy of scientific explanations for specific purposes, without claiming total adequacy. Unity of action can be thought of in terms of intentionality rather than of omnipotent causality after the manner of the monarchical model.

This at first sight is a much more promising line of approach and seems to fit better the kind of language the Bible uses about God and His purposes

---

[23]Farrer, *Faith and Speculation*, p. 153.
[24]Barbour, *Myths*, p. 161.
[25]*Ibid.*

and actions. Yet the agent model runs into some difficulties. Barbour seems to reject any form of dualism which thinks of the human person as a mind-body dualism of two distinct substances.[26] He defines an agent as "a living body in action, not an invisible mind interacting with a visible body."[27] We simply "talk" of a single set of events by using the language of intention and purpose and the scientific language appropriate to physical and bodily movements. This, however, will not do. It is doubtful whether we can make full sense of the language of intention and purpose unless the agent transcends his bodily activity in fact and not merely as a matter of different languages. If the agent transcends any single action, not to mention his body, then we are back with some kind of dualism. The latter may have taken unacceptable forms in the past, but it can still be ably defended, as it is very effectively by Austin Farrer, H.D. Lewis, H.P. Owen, and others. One advantage of the intention model, according to Barbour, is that we can talk about divine intentions without clashing with scientific accounts. One can give a physiological account of a bodily movement without bringing in the divine intention. We can further maintain that "God is not fully expressed in historical action even as a human agent is not fully expressed in any sequence of actions." Thus, we are able to substitute divine intentionality for causality as the dominant category in the theological account of the world.

Yet, as Barbour realizes, the objections to this view are serious. After all, we can identify human intention only through bodily action. This objection is all the stronger if we accept the view that the distinction between mind and body is primarily a matter of language and does not indicate any real ontological difference between mind and body. The only alternative is to view the world as God's body through which we are able to discern His intention. Can we do this convincingly, however, except on the basis of a body-soul model which accepts a real ontological dualism of mind and body and their interaction, however mysterious this is? Yet Barbour, and it seems also the process thinkers, do not like this kind of dualism except as a matter of using two different kinds of language. Thus we must ask, Can this body-mind model or body-self model be worked out in a way which is philosophically convincing as well as religiously adequate? In any case, since the universe is not a human body in the strict sense, then we would have to substitute a more sophisticated concept, such as that of organism, and regard the world-process as the organism through which the divine intention is being realized.

Yet this model too has obvious difficulties. If the analogy is developed

---

[26]*Ibid.*, p. 159.
[27]*Ibid.*

in too literal a way, then the world becomes passive to the directing intention of the world-soul or the world-self, and we are back with some of the problems of the monarchical model. If the world, including human beings, are only cells in a vast cosmic organism, then what again becomes of human freedom? The difficulty tends to make more attractive the fifth model, which sees reality as a society of which one member is preeminent but not absolute. The universe is not strictly a cosmic organism but a community of interacting beings in which there is one preeminent actual being which provides each entity with its subjective aim and works through the ingression of the eternal objects to produce order in the universe and uses the persuasiveness of aesthetic harmony and love to bring these entities into higher patterns of mutual harmony. It is important to remember that this preeminent, nontemporal actual entity is not the God of biblical and Christian theological tradition who creates the world ex nihilo. He is not in absolute control of the process, nor can He (?) control it on any level otherwise than by persuasion. Yet how does God go about "persuading" electrons and molecules, even if with Cobb we insist on calling them "subjects"?[28]

Let us return for a moment to the first question as to whether the universe bears any resemblance to a body directed by a mind in the manner of the human physical organism. Obviously, the word "organism" is a model which requires modification like all the others. Human organisms develop and grow in interaction with an environment, both physical and human. Since God's body or organism on this view includes all that is, there can be no interaction between Him and His environment in this simple sense, since all interactions would be internal to the organism. This, then, requires at least one major qualification of the organism model. Even allowing for this, how in this model do we leave room for real creativity, novelty, and freedom in any of the actual entities which interact within the body of God? It does not help very much to argue that even in the case of the human being, the body has a certain independence and is not the mere passive instrument of the will. This is not much comfort religiously, whatever can be said for it philosophically. The trouble is, of course, that the human individual bears little resemblance, if any, to a cell in a biological organism. It is no answer to talk about the wisdom of the body to indicate the way in which it goes on acting whether we are consciously controlling it or not. Still less does it help to insist that each cell has a measure of independence. The fact remains that the human person is not a cell but a body-mind integrated whole. Whitehead's custom of using such terms as "subjective," "feeling," and "experience" of subhuman organisms may have its merits when properly used, but it may obscure the real and not the fancied distinction between the human and

---

[28]Cousins, *Process Theology*, p. 164.

nonhuman. Dorothy Emmet justifiably asks whether this language is another glaring example of the pathetic fallacy, i.e., the interpretation of the whole of nature in terms applicable only to highly developed stages of existence.[29] Such language may still be defended, but it remains true that the human being is organism *plus,* and it is the plus which is important at this point. Griffin contends that for process thought it is the human mind which is technically the person and that "a person's acts in the primary sense are the psyche's acts of self-constitution in each moment."[30] Despite his concern for real freedom and creativity, he does not hesitate to apply the monarchical model to the total human organism.[31] However, the mind is not a dictator but a benevolent monarch. When a part of the body suffers, it is felt as pain by the mind. "The mind literally shares the experiences of the cells in its body; it sympathizes with their suffering and rejoices with their positive experiences."[32] This is going very far indeed. In fact, the mind is not aware of many bodily processes. A cell may become cancerous without pain being immediately felt and the mind may be blissfully unconscious of the disintegrating process going on in the flesh. Even more curious is Griffin's attempt to argue that the actual entities in the body are partially self-creating subjects. They are nor merely objects to be pushed or coerced. They can be influenced only by persuasion. Yet this seems absurd and is a very peculiar use of language. In no ordinary sense does the mind consciously persuade the bodily cells to do their necessary business. The self-organism model is being pressed to a point where it simply breaks down. The plain fact is that my relationship to God is not at all like the relationship of a cell to an organism—not if our sense of freedom and moral responsibility is genuine, whether vis à vis God or my neighbor. Farrer roundly declares, and in our view correctly: "My body is an organism to all evidence, the universe is no such thing."[33] Again, "the action of a cosmic superorganism is a very violent hypothesis, which fits none of our scientific or other natural knowledge."[34] One of the curious features of the process theology is its idea that natural entities have a freedom of their own over which God has only a very limited control. Barbour cites Compton's remark that on this view, God "is, as we are, in fact incomplete, incomplete in knowledge and control over natural bodily history."[35] Just as I do not have total control of my body, even by persuasion, so God does not and cannot on this analogy have full control

---

[29]Dorothy Emmet, *Whitehead's Philosophy of Organism* (London: Macmillan, 1932), p. 143.

[30]Griffin, *Process Christology,* p. 209.

[31]*Ibid.*

[32]*Ibid.*

[33]Farrer, *Faith and Speculation,* p. 148.

[34]*Ibid.,* p. 152.

[35]Barbour, *Myths,* p. 160.

over the cosmic superorganism which is His body. Farrer's conclusion seems to be irresistible. "To be the mind not merely of you or of me but of all creatures, God must be a free Spirit, whose action is prior to the actions of them all."[36] Again it may be observed that classical theism does not rule out the possibility of a divine self-limitation which would allow real spontaneity to the subhuman as well as the human. What it refuses to accept is that God has relinquished ultimate control of physical process.

If this conclusion is sound, then the fifth model, which sees the universe as a society of interacting entities, with God as the preeminent entity without complete control, is open to the same criticism as made against the self-body or self-organism model. Both Whitehead and Hartshorne reject monism, the idea that the ultimate reality is one and all multiplicity is only appearance, though we shall have occasion to quote later a rather remarkable comment of Whitehead upon F.H. Bradley. However, monism would seem to run counter to their view of the process as a becoming which takes place through the interaction of actual entities. They also insist that God and the world process are substantially distinct. God's being is distinct from the being of the world. However much they insist on this, it may be questioned whether they make good their claim in the terms of their process philosophy. The difficulties arise from their assertion that God "includes" the world in His consequent nature, and that God too grows and changes. Just as the human individual becomes the person he is through interaction with his environment, so God grows by His responsiveness to His environment, which is the process of becoming. God not only affects this process by His persuasion but is in turn affected by the way in which the actual entities of the process respond to His persuasion. God may be enriched in the process, though because His control is limited to persuasion, there is the possibility that the spontaneous and free action of the entities, including human freedom, will not respond universally to His persuasive agency. This has in fact happened, as we see illustrated by disorder at the physical level and by the waywardness of the human will. Evil, whether natural or moral, cannot, however, be attributed to God because He can only persuade. He is not fully responsible for what happens otherwise. This alleviates the problem of evil only to a limited degree since there is not a God who can be counted on eventually to transform natural and moral evil into the fulfilment of His purpose beyond the decay and perishing which are the universal features of all process.

The attractiveness of this view to many lies in its claim that it does full justice to God's direct involvement in the world-process and that it escapes from a doctrine of divine impassibility which makes nonsense of the Chris-

---

[36]Farrer, *Faith and Speculation,* p. 154.

tian view of God as participating and suffering love. Yet even the process philosophers admit the difficulty in conceiving God as sheer becoming. Further, to say that God is a better God at the end of the process than at the beginning certainly sounds odd. In any case, there is no end to the process of divine development. "God as consequent is fluent, reaches no final completion, contains succession, and is ever in process of further creation."[37] What, however, of the claim that the God of process philosophy is no longer distorted by an alien philosophical concept of impassibility? For God to have sympathy, empathy, or compassionate love for His creatures, does He have to be as closely tied to the process of becoming as these philosophers insist? It may be that the doctrine of impassibility has been developed under Greek influence in a way which makes it difficult to speak of God's love. On the other hand, how can the divine love help the sufferer if it is subject to all the limitations and sufferings which result from its entanglement with temporal process? Yet how can God become man, as Christian faith asserts, without His sharing in some way the pain and suffering which belong to real manhood? Owen's suggestion is that while God cannot directly experience pain, suffering, sadness, etc., because He is without a body, He can by His imaginative response enter vicariously into such painful experiences. Yet we must also say that such vicarious suffering is immediately transfigured by joy, God being God.[38]

Such a view is likely to prompt the most vigorous, indeed passionate, dissent. If there is a God, so it is contended, and if He is to deserve our worship and adoration, He must know pain and suffering directly and in a way which closely resembles our own. Such a suffering God can win from man the response of love which can give meaning to life, since only a love which suffers deserves to be called love. One recalls Bonhoeffer's remarks about God's being "weak and powerless in the world" and that "only a suffering God can help."[39] Whether Bonhoeffer would have been satisfied with the God of Whitehead or Hartshorne, it is impossible to say. As we have seen, it is one of Hartshorne's contentions that the idea of a loving God cannot be reconciled with the impassible God of classical theism. "Cosmic beauty as a value must be actualized in cosmic experience and this, as we have shown, can only be cosmic love."[40] He goes on, "for who knows what love could be combined with immutability?"[41] But what is cosmic love? On

---

[37]Charles Hartshorne and William L. Reese, *Philosophers Speak of God* (Chicago: Univ. of Chicago, 1953), pp. 282–283.
[38]Owen, *Concepts*, p. 24.
[39]Bonhoeffer, *Letters and Papers from Prison*, p. 122.
[40]Cousins, *Process Theology*, p. 110.
[41]*Ibid*.

Hartshorne's premises, it cannot be the love of a truly transcendent personal spirit for His creation. It is, on the other hand, absurd to think of the galaxies, the stars, the whole spatio-temporal process as in some way conscious except on a literal view of the body-soul model in relation to God and the world, and the defects of this view have already been exposed. Further, the love of Hartshorne's God is a powerless love. He can lure us towards some kind of ideal, but He cannot rescue us from decay and corruption.

It seems obvious to many, however, that if God is Infinite Spirit and incorporeal, He cannot experience pain in the same sense that we can. But then can He love? The psychological impetus behind one aspect of process philosophy and panentheism is to resolve this difficulty by giving God a body, namely the cosmic superorganism we call the world. The inadequacies of this view we have already indicated. What else, if anything, can be said in defence of Owen's suggestion? His claim that God's loving is vicarious imaginative sympathy leaves many cold on the grounds that such sympathy is not in fact the same as actual suffering. Unless there is actual suffering, the sympathy is bound to be incomplete. This, of course, might be so, if God's imagination were as limited as ours is. Our imaginative sympathy or empathy is often so restricted that sometimes we appear to be almost indifferent to the sufferings of others. But we are not God nor do we nor can we love with the kind of love, based on complete knowledge, which is possible to God if God is as Christians believe Him to be, complete in wisdom, love, and power. The argument against Owen would seem to accept the view that in an almost literal sense God must experience our toothache. His imaginative and vicarious sympathy is not a sufficient proof of His love and concern.

This whole issue is obscured by Hartshorne's ambiguous use of such spatial language as "inside" and "outside." He agrees that God must have some sympathetic participation or love and that if His knowledge of them includes the actual concrete feelings of creatures,[42] then this must mean that He "includes" them in His being: "Strange that men should think to exalt God by putting everything outside him as knower."[43] The ambiguity of this language is intolerable. To know does not mean that the object known is in some mysterious way assimilated into the subjective reality of the knower. The most profound sympathy and love between human persons does not involve the literal merging of their selves. Their distinctive identity and individuality is indeed the basic presupposition of such loving communion. For classical theism this is also true of God. God loves me but He does not

---

[42]*Ibid.*, p. 108.
[43]*Ibid.*

literally absorb me into Himself. Hartshorne seems to be influenced by non-Christian ideas of the Absolute, plus a quasi-Buddhistic view of personal identity. Yet if these ideas are carried through rigorously to their logical conclusion, the whole idea of cosmic love evaporates into a vague abstraction, more abstract indeed than any statements made by traditional theism.

Quite a few years ago, Baron Von Hügel asked the question: "Is God, then, to be so different from man as to be less than man? God is love, is He not? Is His love, then, to be but nominal?"[44] Surely a suffering God who bears His suffering nobly and heroically for us is a greater God, more deserving of our adoration and love, than a God who merely enters into our suffering vicariously through imaginative sympathy. As everyone knows, for Von Hügel the otherness of God is as important religiously as His likeness to man. Without it, what confidence can we have that our suffering may one day be transformed into permanent and enduring joy? The real answer to the problem of human suffering is whether we can have confidence that God is able to deliver us in the end from death and corruption as well as from sin and selfishness by loving us into the true freedom of His children. It is not enough that God suffers as we suffer. The question is, Can He finally deliver us from it? A God who is as deeply entangled in "becoming" as process philosophy suggests can hardly fulfil this role. Our earthly suffering will end in death, but this should not worry us, says Professor Hartshorne, because God has an excellent memory. To quote Farrer again: "He [God] will get just as much satisfaction out of thinking what splendid souls we were in our lifetime as He would out of divinizing us eternally by association with his god-head."[45] Some will regard it as irrelevant, if not downright reactionary, to drag in the issue of personal immortality. But this is the crucial issue. It must be remembered that for the process philosophy and theology there is no personal immortality, only the retention of values in the divine experience. This is true of Whitehead and Hartshorne and process theologians such as Norman Pittenger, John B. Cobb, Jr., Schubert Ogden, and David Griffin. They have given us a God who in their view really suffers with us. They have not given us a God who can deliver us from the last enemy, death. Yet what kind of answer is this to the problem of suffering? Even if the God of process philosophy suffers with us by direct involvement

---

[44]Friedrich Von Hügel, *Readings from Friedrich Von Hügel* (London: Dent; New York: Dutton, 1929), pp. 351ff.

[45]Farrer, *Reflective Faith,* p. 190. Note that the word divinize in this context does not mean to make us God, which would be nonsense, but to transform us into the divine likeness as far as our finite nature permits the reflection of the divine through the image of God in man.

in the process of becoming, there is no suggestion in these writers that He will or can actually deliver us from suffering, except to a limited degree, in this mortal life. Our consolation must rest exclusively in the belief that, while we are not delivered now and cannot hope to survive death in eternal fellowship with Him, at least some "value," partially realized in us in our present existence, will somehow be preserved in God's memory.

It was no doubt such considerations as these which led Von Hügel to emphasize the otherness of God and to deny to Him suffering: "Sympathy, Yes, indeed overflowing Sympathy . . . but no suffering in God."[46] He also goes on to defend the traditional position that God suffers only in the manhood of Christ, not in His divinity. This too has its problems, to which we shall return in a moment. Meanwhile, we shall take note of a biblical scholar and theologian who is too much neglected these days. In 1940 Dr. H. Wheeler Robinson published his book *Suffering Human and Divine*. Despite all that has been written on this subject since then, few better books have been written. Dr. Robinson undertakes in one of his chapters to make that reexamination of the doctrine of divine impassibility for which we too have asked. Further, he wishes to defend such language as the "Suffering of God," which is the title of his chapter: "We may welcome the return to the doctrine of a suffering God as one inspired by a genuine religious interest."[47] He cautions us, however, against accepting such a view lightly and unthinkingly because of the real difficulties involved. He then proceeds to point out these difficulties to see if they can be met. In so doing, it is clear that Robinson is also seeking to safeguard some of the truths implied by the historic doctrine of impassibility.

Suffering usually means on the human level frustration of human desires and purposes, together with the limitations which belong to finite creatures as such. God's suffering cannot be due to these limitations. Otherwise, He is not the Creator-God of biblical faith and Christian experience. Robinson would evidently not have looked with favor upon the drastic limitations set by the process thinkers upon the power of God, nor apparently would he have been sympathetic to the model of the universe as God's body, despite the profound influence upon him of the philosophy of Pringle-Pattison. Even if we regard the suffering of God as transient, later to be transformed into joy, "we seem to have entangled Him in the time-process, and to have conceived a changing God, moving like ourselves to something better."[48] Obviously, Robinson was no Hartshornian born out of due time. He even quotes Whitehead's remarks about pathos and the lapse of time and

---

[46]Von Hügel, *Readings*, p. 351.
[47]H.W. Robinson, *Suffering Human and Divine*, p. 165.
[48]*Ibid.*, p. 167.

asks: "How can a God exposed to such pathos be adequate to our religious needs, to say nothing of our philosophical speculation?"[49] How can a suffering God be reconciled with the all-comprehensive and self-existent Being which is a demand both of the religious consciousness and of rational thought?

Is there, then, a form of suffering which can be attributed to God without entangling God in frustration, change, and limitation? Robinson thinks there is, and that it is a suffering which does not arise from bodily frustration but is "voluntarily accepted for the highest ends."[50] This too is a model taken from heroic and costly suffering love found from time to time even in imperfect men and women. If, he asks, the will to suffer vicariously ennobles and enriches human personality, then how much more must this be true of God? The more sensitive we are to the sufferings of others, a sensitiveness lacking in the hardened and the brutal, the more anguish we shall experience. Such moral suffering is more than the imagination of the suffering of others. It is a deep participation in it with all the anguish this entails. Furthermore, such suffering by God must be freely chosen. It is not merely imposed on Him, as would appear to be the case with the God of process theology, who is limited, as we have seen, by a process of becoming over which He has no assurance of mastery in the end.

Nor can God's suffering mean His complete entanglement in the time-process. The same point is made later by Farrer: "It is folly no less extreme to think that we bring God and His creatures together by attaching our temporal conditions to his existence."[51] The problem, then, becomes, How can we preserve the truth that if our lives in time mean something to us, they must mean something to God? If the blood, toil, tears, and sweat of human existence issue in the value of transformed human personalities (e.g., new creations in Christ), then must not these persons become a part of God, belong to His very being? Our use of language here must be subject to the most cautious appraisal. We have noticed the tendency of process thinkers to talk of God as "including" the world, but the spatial and physical implications of this word call for careful analysis. The difficulty of preserving the distinction of selves when using the cosmic organism model has already been noted. Furthermore, if God is in any meaningful sense a "self," He cannot literally include other selves in His being, no more than on the human level it is possible for one self to include another self in its being. The same ambiguity attaches to applying the word "enrich" to God. We have already noted that thinkers as different as Wheeler Robinson and Charles Hartshorne

---

[49]*Ibid.*
[50]*Ibid.*, p. 168.
[51]Farrer, *Faith and Speculation*, p. 165.

both use the word. God cannot be enriched in His being in the sense of a development from the imperfect to the more perfect unless He is growing and developing in exactly the same way as a human being, but no one wants to speak literally of God in this way. Even the process thinkers want to say, inconsistently no doubt, that God's perfect essence is eternal and unchanging through all the process of change. It has to be remembered, however, that God is not conscious in His primordial nature but only in His consequent nature, i.e., through His involvement in the temporal process in which self-conscious persons arise. God's memory, therefore, which preserves the values but not the persons, actualized in the process, can hardly be ascribed to God in His primordial nature. Yet how can a "memory," developed only in the process, preserve values which are transcendent to the process? This whole way of speaking involves intolerable difficulties and contradictions.

The conclusion to be drawn from this discussion is that there is more to be said for the classical view of God as infinite and incorporeal Spirit than for the God of panentheism, whether conceived as the soul or self of the world thought of as His body or His organism, or as a society of interacting entities of which He is only a preeminent entity limited to persuasion and in no way able to shape the process to final victory for His purpose. Such a God may persuade some entities, e.g., human beings, to pursue and realize certain values. He cannot rescue them from the ultimate threat of death.

It must be admitted that the God of classical theism is more mysterious than the all-too-human God of Hartshorne, despite Hartshorne's emphasis upon the cosmic aspects of deity. However, since God is also described by Whitehead as the "ultimate irrationality," this can hardly count as a decisive point in the debate between classical theism and process thought. There is no human analogy which throws much significant light upon the way in which the Infinite Spirit creates ex nihilo a created order distinct from Himself and possessing limited spontaneity and freedom of initiative. It does, however, leave God in final control of nature and it frees us from using such ambiguous and questionable language as that of God enriching Himself by including the world in His being. Such a God can leave enough freedom to men and women to ensure both their moral responsibility and their openness to the persuasive grace of God and to make the language of love and reconciliation meaningful. Nevertheless, the creativeness and openness evidenced at certain levels in the process of becoming is not for the God of theism ultimate. Since He is the author of and the final controller of the process, He can guarantee not only the preservation of values in His memory, but the real existence of redeemed personalities on the other side of death. These are not included in His being in the strict sense, since one self cannot include another. There is no reason for classical theism why God should not will the continuance of a society of redeemed persons when the present process of becoming has ceased. We say the "present process," for again classical theism is able to allow for the possibility of a continuous exercise of divine creativeness without becoming panentheistic in the sense of the process thinkers.

Also classical theism can do justice to Hartshorne's claim that if God is to be personal and loving, He must be a society in some significant sense. Christians find a "social" element in the triune God, based not merely upon philosophical speculation but upon the Christian experience of Father, Son, and Holy Spirit. They do not accept the claim that without the world process of becoming, God would exist only as a solitary and lonely monad. God's creation is the result of His overflowing goodness, not of His need for love. Hartshorne asks why God should "clutter up existence with beings which can add nothing to the value that would exist without them."[52] One writer once expressed the view that one reason for the rejection of classical theism is that modern man finds it intolerable that God could possibly get along without him. But a God so dependent upon us cannot in the end be the God who has power to save us from sin and death. There is no reason intrinsic to classical theism why God should not be infinitely concerned with beings to whom He has given actuality through His sheer self-diffusing goodness, even though He does not "need" them in the strict sense to know what love is. For Christian theism does in fact maintain that God has involved Himself in the lives of His creatures through the incarnation of His presence and love in the Person of Jesus Christ. Though He did not need them, once they existed, He went to the uttermost limits of costly self-sacrifice to persuade them or love them into faith, trust, and new life and to open the way for them to enter into a full and blessed eternal life and existence with Him.

It must be emphasized again that what has been called classical or Christian theism in this discussion is not irrevocably bound up with Aristotle, Plotinus, or any other such pagan thinkers. The attack of the process thinkers upon their kind of God may be justified, though it has to be admitted that Aristotle and the others look very different when Aquinas and Augustine have finished with them. In any case, the triune God of Christian faith and experience is not the God of Aristotle, and the latter would hardly have recognized his views in the later Christian developments. Hartshorne assumes that the only alternative to the Greek view is panentheism as he expounds it. Our view is that there is a Christian theism which is neither of these positions and which does fuller justice to the power as well as the love

---

[52]Charles Hartshorne, *Reality as a Social Process* (London: Collier-Macmillan, 1963), p. 40.

of God while preserving the real distinction between God and human selves as well as between one human self and another.

Let us return for a moment to the Christological issue, which is the crucial one. Can the Incarnation even be conceived as a possibility if God is thought of as classical theism does? In our discussion of impassibility, we have noted the way in which some theologians in the past and recently have advanced the view that God suffers only in the humanity and not in the divinity.[53] Does it make sense to speak as if in the historical Jesus pain is swallowed up in joy in a manner analogous to the way in which we believe this to be the case in the divine experience? Certainly there are suggestive texts such as "He endured the Cross, despising the shame, for the joy that was set before Him."[54] However keen we are to insist that God enters into the physical and spiritual suffering of Jesus in more than a metaphorical or symbolic way, it can hardly be satisfactory to see the suffering of Jesus as sheer unmitigated suffering. Even before the Resurrection, there was a kind of transformation of the suffering through Jesus' attitude toward it and His acceptance of it as the Father's will. It is true, as Wheeler Robinson says, that there is no evidence in the gospels of the idea of a suffering humanity and an impassible divinity. Yet there is the implication of victory in and through the suffering, even if the language of victory is yet another metaphor. Some might argue that suffering is not real if one is certain of victory over it and final deliverance from it, but this plainly is not so. That this is not true on the level of human experience has been nobly demonstrated by Christian saints. In any case, for Christian faith, with all due respect to Bonhoeffer, the last word about Jesus Christ cannot be suffering but triumph, victory, and peace: "Yet I am not alone, because the Father is with me. I have told you all this so that in me you may find peace. In the world you will have trouble. But courage! The victory is mine; I have conquered the world."[55] Whether these are the *ipsissima verba* of Jesus or not, they express an element vital to Christian faith and implied by Jesus' own attitude toward the Cross. Christians must not be put off by the suggestion that this is a turning of the gospel into a romantic story with the traditional happy ending. As the Puritans used to say, "No Cross, No Crown." The problem today is that Christians are afraid to accept the crown. But this is to deny both the power and the love of God. It is to cut God down to our own size and think of Him as a persuasive agency only who cannot in the last analysis save His people, not only from their sins but from the decay and transiency of all finite creatures (or occasions, if the reader is a Whiteheadian).

---

[53] Von Hügel, *Essays and Addresses*, 2nd Series (London: Dent, 1928–1930), p. 209.
[54] Heb. 12:2.
[55] John 16:32–33.

There are many technical points about process philosophy and theology which there has been no time to consider in this brief survey. The basic points, however, have been emphasized. In short, the Christian is not tied forever to the God of Aristotle or of Greek speculation, nor is he left as the only option the "limited" God of process thought. Rather he worships the eternal God whose infinity and omnipotence do not preclude a self-limitation in the interests of the spontaneity and freedom of agents in the created order. Nor if God is all powerful does it preclude an act of self-giving which shows the persuasive power of His love for us men and our salvation. Yet neither nature nor man can remake the world entirely according to their plans or "subjective aims." God is ceaselessly working toward a goal in which all created things will be subject unto Him. Even death will finally give up its dominion, for God is God, and this is the destiny He wills for His children. Obviously, we can learn much from process theology, particularly in its impressive attempts to integrate scientific knowledge of nature and its processes with a concept of God which both satisfies religious aspirations and needs and makes philosophical sense. Unfortunately in pursuing this laudable aim, the process thinkers have in our view developed ideas of God which are not reconcilable either with the biblical witness or, we still believe, with the deepest religious longings of mankind. The "limited" God of process thought cannot in the end rescue man from sin and death and inspire him with the hope and certainty of a transformed community of persons who will survive not only as preserved values in the divine memory but in full and blessed existence and fellowship with the God and Father of our Lord Jesus Christ.

It is clear from the foregoing discussion that the crucial issue is the sovereignty and omnipotence of God. Certainly the problem of evil cannot be resolved by attributing its origin and occurrence exclusively to human free will. This does not do justice either to the immense pressures of natural forces upon human freedom, or natural disasters, which are obviously not the result of human action. If one wishes to hold to divine omnipotence, one must conclude that God deliberately took the risk of creating such a world as this in the confidence that He could bring permanent good out of it,[56] not only for Himself but for the suffering individuals involved in the process. Classical theism does not have to affirm that every moment, whether on the physical level or on the level of will, is rigidly and mechanically determined. It does have to affirm, however, that such freedom is "permitted" and can in fact be abrogated if God so wills. Nature, and the spontaneities of entities in interaction, will continue as long as God wills it to continue for the fulfilment

---

[56]Cf. John Hick, *Evil and the God of Love.*

of His purpose. Nor does classical theism have to refuse the idea that God chooses to work through persuasion rather than sheer coercion in His dealings with human beings. Even in this area, however, classical theism refuses to accept the view that God will never bring the process of persuasion to an end. Certainly He is infinitely patient, and we have no means of measuring chronologically the point at which He will withdraw freedom, and therefore, the option of responding freely to His persuasive agency. Yet again, however, classical or Christian theism believes that God's power will at some point come into play. He will not tolerate massive accumulations of evil forever.

The problem with process theology is that God's persuasion of any finite entity is limited to this mortal life. We must not be fooled by the ambiguous language of Whitehead about the perishing occasions passing into "objective immortality." There is no room in this philosophy for any continuance of persuasion after the moment of physical death. It is true that some developments of Christian eschatology have also attached supreme importance for heaven or hell to the moment of physical death. I have argued elsewhere, however, that the final judgment in this sense is set by the New Testament at the Parousia.[57] Further, we have also maintained that the temporal language of the New Testament must be taken seriously in regard to the course of history and its future consummation. This means that as far as the individual is concerned, the future both in history and after death is open until God chooses to pronounce final judgment upon it.

Certainly for process theology the individual who dies, conscious of his spiritual imperfection and the poverty of his spiritual life, cannot look forward to any further spiritual growth until he is transformed into a more complete conformity to the Christ he acknowledges as his Lord and Savior. The only consolation he has is that though he may die before the work of divine persuasion has been fulfilled in him, somehow the divine experience will take up into itself and preserve in the harmony of God what was of value in that limited and imperfect human existence while on earth. Lewis Ford, in his persuasive essay on "Divine Persuasion and the Triumph of Good,"[58] hardly meets the challenge to his point of view expressed in his quotation from George F. Thomas. The latter makes the very telling point that on the Whiteheadian view God does not appear to save the world but only harmonizes its evils and discords in His own experience.[59] A very similar

---

[57]Aldwinckle, *Death in the Secular City.*
[58]Delwin Brown, *et al., Process Philosophy and Christian Thought* (Indianapolis: Bobbs-Merrill, 1971), pp. 287ff.
[59]G.F. Thomas, *Religious Philosophies of the West* (New York: Scribners, 1929), p. 368.

criticism was made some years earlier by Stephen Lee Ely in *The Religious Availability of Whitehead's God.* [60] The same basic point was made that God in this view is the ultimate enjoyer of value and that God is not concerned with persons as persons.

Such a view is obviously not the same thing as the redemption of the world envisaged by Christian faith in its historic form. The conceptual harmonization of the divine experience is a poor substitute for the redemption of individuals through the divine love into a mode of existence which continues after death. One ends up not with an eternal community of the redeemed as the fulfilment of the divine purpose but with a divine experience in which all the discords have been resolved in the intensity of a harmonization conceived in aesthetic terms. To argue that evil can be made to serve an ultimate beauty expressed in the divine experience is not the same thing as to affirm that suffering and sinful persons may hope by the grace of God to enter into an eternal community of men and women perfected in Christ.

The Whiteheadian view is much nearer to certain forms of idealism than it is to anything advocated by classical Christian theism. It is odd that more attention has not been given by exponents of Whitehead to his own admission that although he is in sharp disagreement with F.H. Bradley, "the final outcome is after all not so greatly different." [61] This is a most revealing admission. Whatever may be said in defence of Bradley's Absolute and its "experience," it is not theism in any sense which Christian faith and experience would recognize as doing justice not only to the Christian concept of God but to the importance of persons both in this earthly life and after death.

To return to Lewis Ford, he asks, "Yet is it God's task to transform the world?" [62] The assumption seems to be that the Christian hope is that God will transform the present world in and during its historical existence. He tells us that if God ushered in a perfect world tomorrow, not only would it destroy the openness required for real moral aspiration and endeavor, but it would still have to cope with present evil. Nor would it compensate for the suffering of one innocent baby in the present world. [63] Yet it has not been part of Christian faith to believe that the problem of innocent suffering can be resolved in this world by a perfect society realized on earth at whatever point of time. The trouble is that the process thinkers have succumbed so completely to the modern antipathy to bringing in a future life to redress the evils of this one that they have left us only two options—either a perfect society

[60]Stephen L. Ely, *The Religious Availability of Whitehead's God.*
[61]Whitehead, *Process and Reality,* p. vii.
[62]Brown *et al., Process Philosophy,* p. 302.
[63]*Ibid.,* p. 303.

now or the knowledge that the divine experience will enjoy the harmonious resolution of all discords, even though historical individuals have perished forever as distinct selves or persons. It is true that the notion of divine omnipotence is beset with many vexing problems. Some views of it may justly be criticized on various grounds. Yet, finally, for Christian theism, it cannot be replaced by the "limited" God of process philosophy and theology. Despite the protests, their God is limited and in the end must be found wanting, both philosophically and religiously.

This discussion has obviously not been intended as a complete treatment of all phases and facets of process thought. If it had been, such interesting figures as Teilhard de Chardin would have been included, not to mention many others who have contributed to the debate about process thought. Our purpose has been simply to try and show how unwise it would be to try to make our Christology depend upon the process conceptuality for its expression. Nor have we attempted to disentangle the elements which belong to specific thinkers. What would be valid comment upon Whitehead might not be so for Hartshorne and vice versa. Other thinkers borrow from both of these men without being necessarily committed to everything each of them has said. This is relatively unimportant as far as the present discussion is concerned. What we have tried to show is the basic difference between Christian theism and the various concepts of God developed by a wide variety of process thinkers. That the difference is wide and deep is, in our view, clear from the previous limited analyses. There are other contemporary thinkers, such as the Death of God theologians, who cling to Jesus without God. The process thinkers, let it be said to their credit, rightly see this as a dead end, but trim their concept of God to meet what they consider to be the implications of a particular philosophical system of thought. Yet what shall it profit a man if he gain Jesus and lose God? It is this fundamental question which is going to be with us, apparently, for some time to come.

Bibliography

Adam, Karl. *The Christ of Faith.* Burns & Oates, London, 1957.

Aldwinckle, Russell F. *Death in the Secular City.* Allen & Unwin, London, 1973; Eerdmans, Grand Rapids, 1974.

————. *Did Jesus Believe in God? Some Reflections on Christian Atheism* (New Theology No. 5; ed. by Martin E. Marty and Dean G. Peerman). Macmillan, New York, 1968.

Altizer, Thomas J.J. *The Gospel of Christian Atheism.* Westminster, Philadelphia, 1966.

Altizer, Thomas J.J. and Hamilton, William. *Radical Theology and the Death of God.* Bobbs-Merrill, Indianapolis, 1966.

Athanasius. *The Incarnation* (trans. by A. Robertson). David Nutt, London, 1911.

Aurobindo, Sri. *Essays on the Gita.* Arya, College St. Market, Calcutta, 1928.

Baillie, Donald M. *God was in Christ.* Faber and Faber, London, 1956.

Baillie, John. *The Idea of Revelation in Recent Thought.* Columbia Univ. Press, New York, 1956.

Baker, John A. *The Foolishness of God.* Darton, Longman & Todd, London, 1970.

Barbour, Ian G. *Issues in Science and Religion.* Prentice-Hall, Englewood Cliffs, New Jersey, 1966.

————. *Myths, Models and Paradigms.* Harper & Row, New York, 1974.

Barth, Karl. *Christ and Adam* (Scottish Journal of Theology Occasional Papers #5). Oliver & Boyd, Edinburgh, 1956.

————. *Church Dogmatics I, 1 and 2* (ed. by Geoffrey W. Bromiley and Thomas F. Torrance; trans. by G.T. Thomson and H. Knight). T. & T. Clark, Edinburgh, 1935 and 1956.

————. *Dogmatics in Outline* (trans. by G.T. Thomson). S.C.M., London, 1949.

Bartsch, Hans W. *Kerygma and Myth* (trans. by Reginald H. Fuller). S.P.C.K., London, 1953.

Baum, Gregory. *Man Becoming.* Herder & Herder, New York, 1970.

Beare, Francis W. *Commentary on the Epistle to the Philippians.* Harper & Row, New York, 1959.

Berkouwer, G.C. *The Person of Christ.* Eerdmans, Grand Rapids, 1954.

————. *The Triumph of Grace in the Theology of Karl Barth.* Eerdmans, Grand Rapids, 1956.

Betz, Otto. *What do we know about Jesus?* S.C.M., London, 1967.

Bevan, Edwyn R. *Christianity.* Home University Library, London, 1932.

Bindley, Thomas H. *The Oecumenical Documents of the Faith* (rev. by F.W. Green). Methuen, London, 1950.

Bonhoeffer, Dietrich. *Christology* (trans. by John Bowden). Collins, London, 1966.

Bornkamm, Günther. *Jesus of Nazareth* (trans. by Irene and Fraser McLuskey with James M. Robinson). Hodder & Stoughton, London, 1960.

Borsch, Frederick H. *The Son of Man in Myth and History.* S.C.M., London, 1967.

Bouquet, Alan C. *The Christian Faith and the non-Christian Religions.* Nisbet, London, 1958.

Bousset, Wilhelm. *Kyrios Christos.* Vandenhoeck & Ruprecht, Göttingen, 1926.

Bowker, J. *The Sense of God.* Clarendon Press, Oxford, 1973.

Bowman, A.A. *Studies in the Philosophy of Religion* (Vols. 1 and 2). Macmillan, London, 1938.

Brown, Delwin *et al. Process Philosophy and Christian Thought.* Bobbs-Merrill, Indianapolis, 1971.

Brown, Raymond E. *Jesus: God and Man.* Bruce, Milwaukee, 1967.

————. *The Virginal Conception and Bodily Resurrection of Jesus.* Paulist, New York; Paramus, Toronto, 1973.

Brunner, Emil. *Dogmatics Vol. II: The Christian Doctrine of Creation and Redemption.* Lutterworth, London, 1962.

————. *Dogmatics Vol. III: The Christian Doctrine of the Church, Faith and the Consummation* (trans. by David Cairns and T.H.L. Parker). Lutterworth, London, 1962.

————. *The Mediator* (trans. by Olive Wyon). Lutterworth, London, 1934.

Bultmann, Rudolf. *Essays Philosophical and Theological.* S.C.M., London, 1955.

————. *Kerygma and Myth* (ed. by Hans Werner Bartsch). Harper, New York, 1961).

Cadoux, Cecil J. *The Historic Mission of Jesus.* Lutterworth, London, 1941.

Campbell, Charles A. *On Selfhood and Godhood.* Allen & Unwin, London, 1957.

Christian, William A. *An Interpretation of Whitehead's Metaphysics.* Yale Univ. Press, New Haven, Connecticut, 1959.

————. *Meaning and Truth in Religion.* Princeton Univ. Press, Princeton, New Jersey, 1964.

Cobb, John B., Jr. *God and the World.* Westminster, Philadelphia, 1969.

————. *Living Options in Protestant Theology: A Survey of Methods.* Westminster, Philadelphia, 1962.

————. *The Structure of Christian Experience.* Westminster, Philadelphia, 1967.

Conze, Edward (ed.). *Buddhism: Its Essence and Development.* Bruno Cassirer, Oxford, 1954; Harper & Row (Torch), New York, 1959.

————. *Buddhist Texts Through the Ages.* Bruno Cassirer, Oxford, 1954.

Conzelmann, Hans. *Jesus* (trans. by John Bowden). Welch, Toronto, 1973.

————. *Outline of the Theology of the New Testament* (Study Edition; trans. by John Bowden). S.C.M., London, 1969.

Cousins, Ewert H. (ed.). *Process Theology*. Newman, New York; Paramus, Toronto, 1971.

Craddock, Fred B. *The Pre-Existence of Christ*. Abingdon, Nashville, 1968.

Cullmann, Oscar. *Christology of the New Testament* (trans. by Shirley G. Guthrie and Charles A.M. Hall). S.C.M., London, 1959.

————. *Salvation in History* (trans. by Sidney G. Towers and the editorial staff of S.C.M. Press). S.C.M., London, 1967.

Daniélou, Jean. *Christ and Us* (trans. by Walter Roberts). Blackwell, Oxford, 1961.

Das Gupta, Surendra Nath. *History of Indian Philosophy* (Vol. II). Cambridge Univ. Press, Cambridge, 1932.

Davies, John Gordon. *He Ascended into Heaven*. Blackwell, Oxford, 1958.

Davies, W.D. *The Setting of the Sermon on the Mount*. Cambridge Univ. Press, London, 1964.

Dillistone, F.W. *The Christian Understanding of the Atonement*. Nisbet, London, 1968.

Dodd, C.H. *The Bible and the Greeks*. Hodder & Stoughton, London, 1935.

————. *The Founder of Christianity*. Collins, London, 1971; Macmillan, New York, 1970.

————. *The Interpretation of the Fourth Gospel*. Cambridge Univ. Press, London, 1953.

Downing, Francis G. *The Church and Jesus* (Studies in Biblical Theology, Second Series, No. 10). S.C.M., London, 1968.

————. *Doing Theology Thoughtfully is Really Like Thoughtfully Doing All Sorts of Other Things*. Unsworth Vicarage, Bury BL9 8JJ U.K., 1974.

————. *Has Christianity a Revelation?* Westminster, Philadelphia, 1964.

————. *A Man for Us and a God for Us*. Epworth, London, 1968.

Eberling, Gerhard. *Introduction to a Theological Theory of Language*. Collins, London, 1973.

Emmet, Dorothy M. *The Nature of Metaphysical Thinking*. Macmillan, London, 1935.

————. *Whitehead's Philosophy of Organism*. Macmillan, London, 1932.

Farmer, Herbert H. *Revelation and Religion*. Nisbet, London, 1954.

Farmer, William R., Moule, C.F.D., and Niebuhr, R.R. (eds.). *Christian History and Interpretation* (Studies presented to John Knox). Cambridge Univ. Press, London, 1967.

Farrer, Austin. *Faith and Speculation*. A. & C. Black, London, 1967.

————. *Finite and Infinite*. Dacre Press, Westminster, 1943.

————. *The Glass of Vision*. Dacre Press, Westminster, 1948.

————. *Lord, I Believe*. S.P.C.K., London, 1962.

————. *Reflective Theology* (ed. by Charles C. Conti). S.P.C.K., London, 1972.

Ferré, Frederick. *Basic Modern Philosophy of Religion*. Scribners, New York, 1967.

Ford, Lewis S. (ed.). *Two Process Philosophers: Hartshorne's Encounter with Whitehead* (A.A.R. Studies in Religion, No. 5, 1973). American Academy of Religion, Tallahassee, Florida, 1973.

Forsyth, P.T. *The Person and Place of Christ*. Independent Press, London, 1930.

Fuchs, Ernst. *Studies of the Historical Jesus* (Studies in Biblical Theology No. 42; trans. by Andrew Scobie). S.C.M., London, 1964.

Fuller, Reginald H. *The Foundation of New Testament Christology*. Lutterworth, London, 1965; Collins (Fontana), London, 1964; Scribners, New York, 1965.

George, Raymond. *Communion with God*. Epworth, London, 1953.

Gilkey, Langdon. *Maker of Heaven and Earth*. Doubleday, New York, 1959.

––––––. *Naming the Whirlwind: The Renewal of God-Language*. Bobbs-Merrill, Indianapolis, 1969.

Gollwitzer, Helmut. *The Existence of God as Confessed by Faith* (trans. by James W. Leitch). S.C.M., London, 1965.

Grant, Frederick C. *New Testament Thought*. Abingdon, Nashville, 1950.

Grensted, Laurence W. *The Person of Christ*. Nisbet, London, 1933.

Griffin, David R. *A Process Christology*. Westminster, Philadelphia, 1973.

Grillmeier, Aloys. *Christ in Christian Tradition, from the Apostolic Age to Chalcedon* (trans. by J.S. Bowden). Mowbray, London, 1965.

Gustafson, James M. *Christ and the Moral Life*. Harper & Row, New York, 1968.

Hamerton-Kelly, R.G. *Pre-Existence, Wisdom and the Son of Man: A Study of the Idea of Pre-Existence in the New Testament*. Cambridge Univ. Press, London, 1973.

Hanson, Anthony T. (ed.) and others. *Vindications*. S.C.M., London, 1966.

Harnack, Adolf. *History of Dogma* (Vols. 1–7; trans. by Neil Buchanan). Dover, New York, 1961.

Harvey, Van A. *The Historian and the Believer*. Macmillan, New York, 1966; Collier-Macmillan, Toronto, 1969; S.C.M., London.

Hendry, George S. *The Gospel of the Incarnation*. Westminster, Philadelphia, 1958.

Henry, Carl F.H. *The Protestant Dilemma*. Eerdmans, Grand Rapids, 1949.

Hick, John. *Christianity at the Centre*. S.C.M. (Centrebooks), London, 1968.

––––––. *Evil and the God of Love*. Macmillan, London, 1966; Collins (Fontana), London, 1968.

––––––. *Faith and Knowledge*. Macmillan, London, 1967.

Hick, John (ed.). *The Existence of God*. Macmillan, New York, 1964.

––––––. *Truth and Dialogue* (Studies in Philosophy and Religion). Sheldon, London, 1974.

Hodges, Herbert A. *Languages, Standpoints and Attitudes* (Riddell Memorial Lectures). Oxford Univ. Press, London, 1953.

Hodgson, Leonard. *And was made Man*. Longmans Green, London, 1928.

––––––. *Christian Faith and Practice*. Blackwell, Oxford, 1952.

––––––. *The Doctrine of the Trinity*. Nisbet, London, 1943.

––––––. *For Faith and Freedom* (Gifford Lectures Vols. I and II). Blackwell, Oxford, 1956.

––––––. *Towards a Christian Philosophy*. Nisbet, London, 1942.

Hodgson, Peter C. *Jesus: Word and Presence*. Fortress, Philadelphia, 1973.

Huxley, Aldous. *The Perennial Philosophy*. Chatto & Windus, London, 1946.
Huxley, Julian. *Religion without Revelation*. Watts, London, 1967.

Jacob, Edmond. *Theology of the Old Testament* (trans. by Arthur W. Heathcote and Philip J. Allcock). Hodder & Stoughton, London, 1958.
James, E.O. *The Saviour God*. Manchester Univ. Press, Manchester, 1963.
Jensen, Robert. *God after God*. Bobbs-Merrill, Indianapolis, 1969.
Jeremias, Joachim. *New Testament Theology: Part 1, The Proclamation of Jesus* (trans. by John Bowden). S.C.M., London, 1971.
Johnson, H. *The Humanity of the Saviour*. Epworth, London, 1962.

Kähler, Martin. *The So-Called Historical Jesus and the Historic Biblical Christ* (trans. by Carl E. Braaten). Fortress, Philadelphia, 1964.
Käsemann, Ernst. *Essays in New Testament Themes* (Studies in Biblical Theology No. 41; trans. by W.J. Montague). S.C.M., London, 1964.
———. *Jesus Means Freedom* (trans. by Frank Clarke). S.C.M., London, 1969.
Kaufman, Gordon D. *God the Problem*. Harvard Univ. Press, Cambridge, Massachusetts, 1972.
———. *Systematic Theology: a Historicist Perspective*. Scribners, New York, 1968.
Kaufmann, Walter. *Nietzsche: Philosopher, Psychologist, Anti-Christ*. Meridian Books, New York, 1956.
Kelly, John N.D. *Early Christian Doctrines*. A. & C. Black, London, 1958.
Knight, G.A.F. *A Christian Theology of the Old Testament*. S.C.M., London, 1964.
Knox, John. *The Church and the Reality of Christ*. Harper & Row, New York, 1962.
———. *The Death of Christ*. Abingdon, Nashville, 1958.
———. *The Humanity and Divinity of Christ*. Cambridge Univ. Press, London, 1967.
———. *Jesus: Lord and Christ*. Harper & Row, New York, 1958.
Kraemer, Hendrik. *The Christian Message in a non-Christian World*. Edinburgh House, London, 1938.
———. *World Cultures and World Religions*. Lutterworth, London, 1960.

Lawton, John S. *Conflict in Christology* (1889–1914). S.P.C.K., London, 1947.
Lee, Jung Young. *God Suffers for Us*. Martinus Nijhoff, The Hague, 1974.
Lewis, H.D. *The Elusive Mind*. Allen & Unwin, London, 1969.
———. *Our Experience of God*. Allen & Unwin, London, 1959.
Lewis, H.D. and Slater, R.L. *World Religions*. Watts, London, 1966.
Ling, Trevor. *Buddha, Marx and God*. Macmillan, London and Toronto, 1966; St. Martin's, New York, 1966.
———. *A History of Religion East and West*. Macmillan, London, 1968.
Lonergan, Bernard. *De Deo Trino*. Apud aedes Universitatis Gregorianae, Rome, 1964.
———. *Insight*. Philosophical Library, New York, 1958.
———. *Method in Theology*. Darton, Longman & Todd, London, 1972.

Lubac, Henri de. *Aspects du Bouddhisme* (trans. by George Lamb). Editions du Seuil, Paris, 1951.
————. *La Rencontre du Bouddhisme et de l'Occident*. Aubier, Paris, 1952.

McArthur, Harvey K. *In Search of the Historical Jesus*. Scribners, New York, 1968.
McClendon, James W., Jr. *Philosophy of Religion and Theology 1974*. American Academy of Religion, Tallahassee, Florida, 1974.
McIntyre, John. *The Shape of Christology*. S.C.M., London, 1966.
Mackinnon, Donald. *Borderlands of Theology and Other Essays*. Lutterworth, London, 1968.
Mackintosh, Hugh R. *The Person of Christ*. T. & T. Clark, Edinburgh, 1937.
Macquarrie, John. *Principles of Christian Theology*. Scribners, New York, 1966.
Malet, André. *The Thought of Rudolf Bultmann* (trans. by Richard Strachan). Irish Univ. Press, Shannon, Ireland, 1969.
Manson, T.W. *Studies in the Gospels and Epistles* (ed. by Matthew Black). Manchester Univ. Press, Manchester, 1962.
Marxsen, Willi. *Beginnings of Christology: A Study in its Problems*. Fortress, Toronto, 1969.
Mascall, E.L. *Christ, the Christian and the Church*. Longmans Green, London, 1946.
————. *Christian Theology and Natural Science*. Longmans Green, London, 1956.
————. *The Secularization of Christianity*. Darton, Longman & Todd, London, 1965.
Matthews, Walter R. *The Problem of Christ in the Twentieth Century*. Oxford Univ. Press, London, 1950.
Mitchell, Basil (ed.). *Faith and Logic*. Allen & Unwin, London, 1957.
Mooney, Christopher F. *Teilhard de Chardin and the Mystery of Christ*. Collins, London, 1966.
Morgan, Kenneth W. *The Path of the Buddha*. Ronald, New York, 1956.
Moule, C.F.D. *The Phenomenon of the New Testament* (Studies in Biblical Theology, Second Series, No. 1). S.C.M., London, 1967.
————. *The Significance of the Message of the Resurrection for Faith in Jesus Christ* (Studies in Biblical Theology, Second Series, No. 8). S.C.M., London, 1968.

Newman, John H. *Grammar of Assent*. Doubleday (Image Books), New York, 1955.
Niebuhr, Reinhold. *The Nature and Destiny of Man* (Vols. 1 and 2). Nisbet, London, 1941 and 1943.
Niebuhr, Richard R. *Schleiermacher on Christ and Religion*. Scribners, New York, 1964.
Nineham, Denis. *Saint Mark* (Penguin Gospel Commentaries). Penguin, Harmondsworth, 1963.
Nineham, Denis *et al. Historicity and Chronology in the New Testament*. S.P.C.K., London, 1965.

Ogden, Schubert M. *Christ without Myth*. Collins, London, 1962.

Otto, Rudolf. *The Idea of the Holy* (trans. by J.W. Harvey). Oxford Univ. Press, London, 1957.

————. *The Kingdom of God and the Son of Man: A Study in the History of Religion* (trans. by Floyd V. Filson and Bertram Lee Woolf). Lutterworth, London, 1938.

————. *The Original Gītā* (trans. and ed. by J.E. Turner). Allen & Unwin, London, 1939.

Owen, H.P. *The Christian Knowledge of God*. Athlone, Univ. of London, London, 1969.

————. *Concepts of Deity*. Macmillan, London, 1971.

Panikkar, R. *The Trinity and Religious Experience of Man*. Darton, Longman & Todd, London, 1974.

Pannenberg, Wolfhart. *Jesus: God and Man* (trans. by Lewis L. Wilkins and Duane A. Priebe). S.C.M., London, 1968.

Parker, T.H.L. *Essays in Christology for Karl Barth*. Lutterworth, London, 1956.

Parrinder, Geoffrey. *Avatar and Incarnation*. Faber & Faber, London, 1970.

Pelican, Jaroslav. *Historical Theology: Continuity and Change in Christian Doctrine*. Hutchinson, London, 1971; Corpus, New York, 1971.

Perrin, Norman, *A Modern Pilgrimage in New Testament Christology*. Fortress, Philadelphia, 1974.

Peter, James. *Finding the Historical Jesus*. Collins, London, 1965.

Pittenger, W. Norman. *Christology Reconsidered*. S.C.M., London, 1970.

————. *Proclaiming Christ Today*. Oxford Univ. Press, London, 1962.

————. *The Word Incarnate*. Nisbet, London, 1959.

Preiss, Théo. *La Vie en Christ*. Delachoux et Nestlé, Paris, 1951.

Prestige, George L. *God in Patristic Thought*. S.P.C.K., London, 1952.

Price, H.H. *Belief*. Allen & Unwin, London, 1969.

Price, Lucien. *Dialogues of Alfred North Whitehead*. New American Library (Mentor Books), New York, 1956.

Quick, Oliver. *Doctrines of the Creed*. Nisbet, London, 1938; Collins (Fontana), London, 1963.

Radhakrishnan, Sarvepalli and Moore, Charles A. *A Source Book of Indian Philosophy*. Oxford Univ. Press, Bombay, 1957; Princeton Univ. Press, Princeton, New Jersey, 1957.

Rahner, Karl. *Theological Investigations* (Vol. I). Helicon, Baltimore, 1961.

————. *Theological Investigations* (Vol. V). Helicon, Baltimore, 1965.

————. *The Trinity*. Herder & Herder, New York, 1969.

Ramsey, Ian T. *Christian Discourse*. Oxford Univ. Press, London, 1965.

————. *Christian Empiricism* (ed. by Jerry H. Gill). Sheldon, London, 1974.

————. *Models and Mystery*. Oxford Univ. Press, London, 1964.

————. *Religious Language*. S.C.M., London, 1957.

Ramsey, Ian T. (ed.). *Prospect for Metaphysics*. Allen & Unwin, London, 1961.

————. *Words About God*. S.C.M., London, 1971.

Ramsey, Ian T. *et al. The Miracles and the Resurrection* (Theological Collections No. 3). S.P.C.K., London, 1964.

Raven, Charles E. *Apollinarianism*. Cambridge Univ. Press, Cambridge, 1923.

Relton, Herbert M. *A Study of Christology*. S.P.C.K., London, 1917.

Richardson, Alan. *History Sacred and Profane*. S.C.M., London, 1964.

————. *An Introduction to the Theology of the New Testament*. S.C.M., London, 1958.

Richardson, Cyril C. *The Doctrine of the Trinity*. Abingdon, Nashville, 1958.

————. *Early Christian Fathers* (Library of Christian Classics, Vol. 1). S.C.M., London, 1953.

Robinson, H. Wheeler. *The Christian Experience of the Holy Spirit*. Nisbet, London, 1928; Harper & Row, New York, 1928.

————. *Inspiration and Revelation in the Old Testament*. Clarendon Press, Oxford, 1946.

————. *Revelation and Redemption*. Nisbet, London, 1942; Harper & Row, New York, 1942.

————. *Suffering Human and Divine*. S.C.M., London, 1940.

Robinson, J.A.T. *The Human Face of God*. S.C.M., London, 1973; Westminster, Philadelphia, 1973.

Robinson, James M. *A New Quest of the Historical Jesus*. S.C.M., London, 1959.

Robinson, James M. and Cobb, John B., Jr. (eds.). *The New Hermeneutic* (Vol. II). Harper & Row, New York, 1964.

————. *Theology as History* (New Frontiers in Theology, Vol. III). Harper & Row, New York, 1967.

Rowlingson, Donald T. *The Gospel Perspective in Jesus Christ*. Westminster, Philadelphia, 1968.

Rust, Eric C. *Evolutionary Philosophies and Contemporary Theology*. Westminster, Philadelphia, 1968.

Schleiermacher, Friedrich. *The Christian Faith* (trans. by H.R. Mackintosh and J.S. Stewart). T. & T. Clark, Edinburgh, 1928.

————. *Life of Jesus* (trans. by A. Maclean Gilmour). Fortress, Philadelphia, 1974.

Schmaus, Michael. *Dogma 3: God and His Christ* (trans. by Ann Laeuchli and William McKenna). Sheed & Ward, New York, 1972.

Schweitzer, Albert. *Civilization and Ethics* (trans. by John Naish). A. & C. Black, London, 1923.

————. *My Life and Thought* (trans. by C.T. Campion). Allen & Unwin, London, 1933.

Sellers, Robert V. *The Council of Chalcedon*. S.P.C.K., London, 1961.

Singh, Surgit. *Christology and Personality*. Westminster, Philadelphia, 1961.

Smart, Ninian. *Doctrine and Argument in Indian Philosophy*. Allen & Unwin, London, 1964.

————. *Philosophers and Religious Truth*. S.C.M., London, 1964.

————. *The Religious Experience of Mankind*. Scribners, New York, 1969.

Smith, John E. *Reason and God*. Yale Univ. Press, New Haven, Connecticut, 1961.

Smith, W. Cantwell. *Questions of Religious Truth*. Scribners, New York, 1967.

Stace, W.T. *Mysticism and Philosophy*. Lippincott, New York, 1960.

Streeter, B.H. *The Buddha and the Christ*. Macmillan, London, 1932.

————. *Foundations*. Macmillan, London, 1929.

Sykes, S.W. and Clayton, J.P. (eds.). *Christ, Faith and History* (Cambridge Studies in Christology). Cambridge Univ. Press, London, 1972.

Taylor, A.E. *The Faith of a Moralist* (Vols. I and II). Macmillan, London, 1937.

Taylor, John V. *The Go-Between God*. S.C.M., London, 1972.

Taylor, Vincent. *The Names of Jesus*. Macmillan, London, 1953.

————. *The Person of Christ in New Testament Teaching*. Macmillan, London, 1958.

Temple, William. *Christus Veritas*. Macmillan, London, 1934.

Tennant, Frederick R. *Sin and Its Propagation*. Cambridge Univ. Press, Cambridge, 1906.

Thomas, Edward J. *The Life of Buddha as Legend and History*. Routledge & Kegan Paul, London, 1969.

Thomas, George F. *Religious Philosophies of the West*. Scribners, New York, 1929.

Thornton, Lionel S. *The Dominion of Christ*. Macmillan, London, 1952.

————. *The Incarnate Lord*. Longmans Green, London and New York, 1928.

Tillich, Paul. *Christianity and the Encounter of World Religions*. Columbia Univ. Press, New York and London, 1964.

————. *The Courage to Be*. Yale Univ. Press, New Haven, Connecticut, and London, 1959.

————. *Dynamics of Faith*. Harper & Row (Torch), New York, 1957.

————. *A History of Christian Thought* (Vol. 1). S.C.M., London, 1968.

————. *Systematic Theology* (Vol. 1). Nisbet, London, 1953.

————. *Systematic Theology* (Vol. 2). Univ. of Chicago Press, Chicago, 1957.

————. *Systematic Theology* (Vol. 3). Univ. of Chicago Press, Chicago, 1963.

Torrance, Thomas F. *God and Rationality*. Oxford Univ. Press, London, 1971.

————. *Space, Time and Incarnation*. Oxford Univ. Press, London, 1969.

Toynbee, Arnold. *A Study of History, Vol. 7B: Universal Churches*. Oxford Univ. Press (Galaxy), New York, 1963.

Trocmé, E. *Jesus As Seen by His Contemporaries*. Westminster, Philadelphia, 1973.

Turner, Henry E.W. *The Pattern of Christian Truth*. Mowbray, London, 1954.

Van Buren, Paul. *The Secular Meaning of the Gospel*. Collier-Macmillan, London, 1963; Macmillan, New York, 1963.

Vawter, Bruce. *This Man Jesus*. Doubleday, New York, 1973.

Vine, A.R. *An Approach to Christology*. Independent Press, London, 1948.

Vogel, Arthur A. *Body Theology: God's Presence in Man's World*. Harper & Row, New York, 1973.

Vögel, Heinrich. *Gott in Christ*. Lettner, Berlin, 1951.

Wainwright, Arthur W. *The Trinity in the New Testament* (ed. by Samuel G. Craig). S.P.C.K., London, 1962.

Ward, J. *Psychological Principles* (2nd ed.). Cambridge Univ. Press, Cambridge, 1920.

Ward, Keith. *Ethics and Christianity*. Allen & Unwin, London, 1970.

Warfield, B.B. *The Person and Work of Christ*. Presbyterian Publishing, Philadelphia, 1950.

Watts, Alan. *The Supreme Identity: An Essay on Oriental Metaphysics and the Christian Religion*. Pantheon, New York, 1972.

Welch, Claude. *In this Name; The Doctrine of the Trinity in Contemporary Theology*. Scribners, New York, 1952.

Whitehead, Alfred North. *Religion in the Making*. Cambridge, Univ. Press, Cambridge, 1930.

Whiteley, D.E.H. *The Theology of St. Paul*. Blackwell, Oxford, 1964.

Wiles, Maurice. "Does Christology Rest on a Mistake?" *Religious Studies,* ed. by H.D. Lewis, Vol. 6, No. 1 (March 1970). Cambridge Univ. Press, London, 1970.

_____. *The Making of Christian Doctrine*. Cambridge Univ. Press, London, 1967.

_____. *The Remaking of Christian Doctrine*. S.C.M., London, 1973.

Wolfson, H.A. *The Philosophy of the Church Fathers* (Vol. 1). Harvard Univ. Press, Cambridge, Massachusetts, 1956.

Zaehner, R.C. *At Sundry Times*. Faber & Faber, London, 1958.

_____. *Concordant Discord: The Interdependence of Faiths* (Gifford Lectures 1967–1969). Clarendon Press, Oxford, 1970.

_____. *Evolution in Religion: A Study in Sri Aurobindo and Pierre Teilhard de Chardin*. Clarendon Press, Oxford, 1971.

_____. *Hindu and Muslim Mysticism*. Athlone, Univ. of London, London, 1960.

_____. *Mysticism Sacred and Profane*. Oxford Univ. Press, London, 1961.

Zahrnt, Heinz. *The Historical Jesus* (trans. by J.S. Bowden). Collins, London, 1963.

Zimmer, Heinrich R. *Philosophies of India* (ed. by Joseph Campbell). Meridian Books, New York, 1956.

Zwingli, H. *Works* (ed. by Schuler & Schulthess; 8 vols.). Zurich, 1828.

Index of Subjects

Index of Authors